# The Guide to Frame Relay Networking

By Christine A. Heckart
Edited by Daniel D. Briere

# THE GUIDE TO FRAME RELAY NETWORKING

Published by Flatiron Publishing, Inc.



ISBN 0-936648-63-5
Manufactured in the United States of America
First Edition, December 1994

Cover design by Saul Roldan
Printed at Bookcrafters, Chelsea, MI.

## Other Books We Publish

Flatiron Publishing publishes books and magazines and organizes trade conferences, computer telephony, telecommunications, networking and voice processing. It also distributes books of other publishers, making it the "central source" for all the above material. Call or write for your FREE catalog.

ATM Users' Guide
Complete Traffic Engineering Handbook
Customer Service Over the Phone
Frames, Packets and Cells in Broadband Networking
The Guide to Frame Relay
The Guide to SONET
The Guide to T-1 Networking
Local & Long Distance Telephone Billing Practices
Moore's Imaging Dictionary
Newton's Telecom Dictionary
PC-Based Voice Processing
SCSA
Speech Recognition
Telephony for Computer Professionals
VideoConferencing: The Whole Picture

## Quantity Purchases

If you wish to purchase this book, or any others, in quantity, please contact:

Christine Kern, Manager
Flatiron Publishing, Inc.
12 West 21 Street
New York, NY 10010
212-691-8215
1-800-LIBRARY
facsimile orders: 212-691-1191

# Table of Contents

## CHAPTER 7:
## ALTERNATIVE APPROACHES AND TRADE-OFFS



## CHAPTER 8:
## SNA, FRAME RELAY, AND IBM



## CHAPTER 9:
## LAN AND SNA CONSOLIDATION



## CHAPTER 10:
## MATTERS OF PROTOCOL

# COMMENTS?

We tried hard to catch any errors or mistatement prior to publication, but we're really techies and not editors. So, if you see anything we should reconsider, please fax this form to 201-239-4443, or send an E-mail to Christine Heckart at CHECKART (696-6902) @ MCI Mail Com.

Chapter: ____________________

Page: ____________________

Comments: ____________________________________________________________

____________________________________________________________

____________________________________________________________

____________________________________________________________

____________________________________________________________

____________________________________________________________

____________________________________________________________

____________________________________________________________

____________________________________________________________

Name: ______________________________

Address: ______________________________

______________________________

______________________________

Telephone: ______________________________

Fax: ______________________________

Email: ______________________________

## AUTHOR'S NOTE:

Albert Einstein is reported to have said that everything should be a simple as possible, but no simpler.

This book attempts to make technical topics as simple as possible, while still providing a practical insight into frame relay networking. In some cases, very technical topics will be explained at a high level; in other cases, it will be necessary to dive into the muck. We have tried to make everything as simple to understand as possible, but no simpler than is required to give the reader a comprehensive view of implementing a frame relay network.

I would like to sincerely thank the people that have contributed greatly to this book, including:

Danny Briere, President of TeleChoice, Inc. and the editor in chief.

Chris Finn, TeleChoice Senior Analyst, for his assistance in developing the chapter on RFP design.

All of the consultants and analysts at TeleChoice who assisted in the development and assembly of the many graphs and charts.

The reviewers of the book and the people who provided technical guidance and information, as listed below.

***THANKS:***

*Nicholas J. Lippis III - President, Strategic Network Consulting*

*Morgan Littlewood - Product Manager/WAN, Cisco Systems*

*Michael A. Viren - VP Product Development, Intermedia Communications of Florida*

*Tom Desjardins - Senior Software Engineer, FORE Systems*

*Coyne Gibson - System Architect, Research & Development, Convex Computer*

*Robert Gourley - Technical Program Manager, WilTel*

*Joe Zell - Executive Director, Application/Service Development, US West Communications !nterprise Networking Services*

*Tom Pickren - Director, Professional Services, Cascade Communications*

*Jim Cavanagh - Applications Engineer, Carrier Group, StrataCom*

*David Yates - Director, Product Management, Wellfleet*

*Sally Bament - Senior Product Manager, Wellfleet*

*Richard Klapman - Product Development, AT&T*

*Joe Murphy - Director of Managed Services, MCI*

*Bill Branch - Director, Customer Network Management Services, Sprint Communications*

*Karen Nichols - Product Manager, Frame Relay Services, Sprint Communications*

*Colin McCann - Frame Relay Product Manager, Sprint Communications*

*Pratt Parish - Senior Programmer, WAN Strategy, IBM*

*Gordon MacKinney - OpenView Program Manager, Hewlett-Packard*

*Philippe Byrnes - Product Manager, SNA-Internetworking, 3COM*

*Rajiv Kapoor - Distinguished Member of Technical Staff, AT&T Bell Laboratories*

*Alan Taffel - VP Marketing, UUNET Technologies, and President and Chairman, Frame Relay Forum*

FOREWORD:

# FRAME RELAY: A LOGICAL STEP IN THE MIGRATION FROM PRIVATE LINES TO ATM

Today's communications managers find themselves at a difficult crossroads: Yesterday's networking solutions are no longer effective and tomorrow's won't arrive in time to help. Enter Frame Relay, a logical and efficient step in the migration from low-speed private-line networks to high-speed multi-application public ATM (Asynchronous Transfer Mode) networks.

Traditional networks, constructed primarily around IBM's Systems Network Architecture (SNA), with low-speed analog and digital multidrop private lines, are quickly being eclipsed by the interconnection of LANs to support increasingly important client-server applications. These current networks, and the people who manage them, are being challenged with an increasing number of PCs and high-speed workstation users connected to LANs, and an increasing number of remote LAN sites that require WAN connectivity and support. Along with these challenges comes the stark realization that LAN-originated traffic is much more diverse, of much higher volume, and almost impossible to model compared to the relatively deterministic applications and traffic patterns of an SNA network.

As the core business becomes increasingly reliant on client-server based applications and thus on the LAN internet to supplement the traditional mainframe applications, the level of network complexity also increases. It is commonplace today to find multiple physical networks each supporting separate protocols and applications, with a core network for SNA supporting traditional host-terminal traffic, a separate network for the interconnection of NetWare-based PC LANs, and often again a separate IP network interconnecting high-speed UNIX workstations and UNIX minicomputers.

All of this diversity is driving an immediate economic need to migrate to a single physical "utility" network that supports all of the core business applications, protocols and computing platforms.

The creation of a single data utility network requires the use of sophisticated network consolidation equipment that is capable of creating multiple logical networks over a single network service infrastructure and the use of a flexible, scalable network service that can easily meet the quickly changing networking traffic requirements. Today's network solutions must:

- Support higher and wider-ranging speeds;
- Lower both transmission and administrative support costs;
- Provide high-quality, low-error rate throughput;
- Respond effectively to a mix of both deterministic host-terminal traffic and bursty LAN traffic.

Additionally, as traffic patterns mutate to support an increasing level of peer-to-peer applications, such as electronic mail and groupware (e.g., Lotus Notes), the traditional hierarchical network will flatten and require a greater level of connectivity between peer network locations.

The combination of Frame Relay services with multiprotocol routers or FRADs (Frame Relay Assemblers/Disassemblers) is an effective solution to this set of networking requirements. Routers enable the creation of multiprotocol LAN internets, supporting the consolidation of IP, IPX, AppleTalk and SNA/SDLC protocols onto a single network. Both routers and FRADs support the consolidation of traditional legacy networking protocols onto a single frame relay network, such as SNA/SDLC, Bisync, Async as well as the primary LAN protocols. With frame relay, multiple logical networks can be supported over a single physical network, reducing not only core network transmission costs, but lowering the cost for network equipment required at each site. Utilizing virtual circuit connections across a public data network, frame relay can support high levels of network connectivity at a much lower cost in most configurations than traditional private lines and can effectively provide bandwidth-on-demand for bursty LAN traffic.

Frame relay service has been widely adopted by communications managers who recognized the opportunity to reduce network costs through network consolidation, improve network quality through the use of a managed data network service, increase flexibility by relying on virtual versus dedicated connectivity, and lower their investment risk through a migration away from private networks to scalable public network facilities.

With an installed base of over 15,000 domestic business sites, frame relay has become a fundamental networking service in the US. This service has been utilized to effectively build multiprotocol networks spanning every industry and government sector, demonstrating tremendous application flexibility. The service has been embraced by every major interexchange, local exchange and VAN service provider, making its availability nearly ubiquitous across the country.

Frame relay service is today's solution to WAN internetworking and can be expected to effectively coexist in a hybrid environment in three to five years when ATM (Asynchronous Transfer Mode) public services emerge as effective solutions for higher volume network locations.

This book deals with today's problems and can effectively guide you in your design and selection of an appropriate frame relay service infrastructure.

*By:*

*Joseph R. Zell*
*Executive Director - Applications & Service Development*
*!NTERPRISE Networking Services*
*U S WEST Communications, Inc.*

## CHAPTER 1:

# WHAT FRAME RELAY DOES FOR A NETWORK

Frame relay is one of the hottest topics in telecommunications today, with due cause. Data communications managers are finding that frame relay can relieve many headaches caused by bandwidth-hungry applications that have been swallowing resources over recent years as companies try to maintain and expand private network environments.

Frame relay is a great answer for users because it can:

- Save you money;
- Increase your flexibility to reconfigure the network quickly;
- Simplify your network architecture;
- Improve the performance of data applications;
- Increase network reliability;
- Reduce the cost of network operations and ownership;
- Confer strategic business advantages to your company; and
- Position you for migration to broadband services later.

Users are constantly amazed that they can increase their flexibility and performance while reducing costs. That is what makes frame relay so attractive in so many situations.

## What Is Frame Relay?

While frame relay can be used in a public or private network, this book will concentrate primarily on how to effectivity utilize a public frame relay service.

Public frame relay services combine some of the best attributes of public and private network architectures. Unlike dedicated private lines, a public frame relay network uses virtual connections for connectivity. The virtual connection does not consume network capacity until information must be sent across it. These virtual connections offer the security and reliability of a private line with added flexibility and connectivity. The result is that many users and applications can share the network connectivity, gain performance and throughput equivalent to a private line solution at a lower cost, or increase throughput while maintaining current cost.

Frame relay services are designed to support data applications, although it is possible to run both voice and video over a frame relay network. An analogy can be found in the public analog voice network. While not designed for data, equipment emerged to convert a data signal into an analog signal in order to use the public voice network to transmit data.

The words "frame relay" are used in many contexts and refer to a switching technology; an interface standard; and a set of new public services. Put that all in one sentence and you get: Frame relay services require a frame relay interface, which passes data formatted as frame relay "frames." No wonder there has been some confusion.

### *TRANSMISSION, PROTOCOL, SERVICE*

*One important item of note is that public frame relay services are* SERVICES. *A frame relay service is much more than just the underlying transmission system and the underlying protocols.*

*The transmission system, or layer one component of the service, is typically a digital network using a DS-1 or E-1 (1.5M/2M bps) and/or DS-3/E-3 (45M/34M bps) backbone. SONET/SDH (Synchronous Optical Network) connections are likely to be used in the future.The protocol at layer two is frame relay. This defines how the network physically handles the data, and how congestion and network throughput is policed. It is at this layer that frame relay's logical connections exist making up each customer's virtual private frame relay network. Cell relay protocols (i.e., ATM) are often used in frame relay services as the backbone protocol (to be discussed in greater detail later). In these cases, frames are accepted from each user but converted to fixed-length cells before being placed on the logical connection for transmission across the network.*

*A frame relay service comprises many elements, including the physical transmission capability and the frame (and cell) relay protocol. But it is much more than the sum of these parts. A frame relay service includes:*

- *Network management;*
- *Support, troubleshooting and fault isolation;*
- *Network redundancy and automatic rerouting;*
- *Equipment and maintenance options;*
- *Configuration management options;*
- *Seamless interworking with other networks and other services;*
- *Other ancillary and complementary options;*
- *Managed network solutions and outsourcing alternatives;*
- *Other ancillary and complementary options.*

***Elements of a Frame Relay Service***

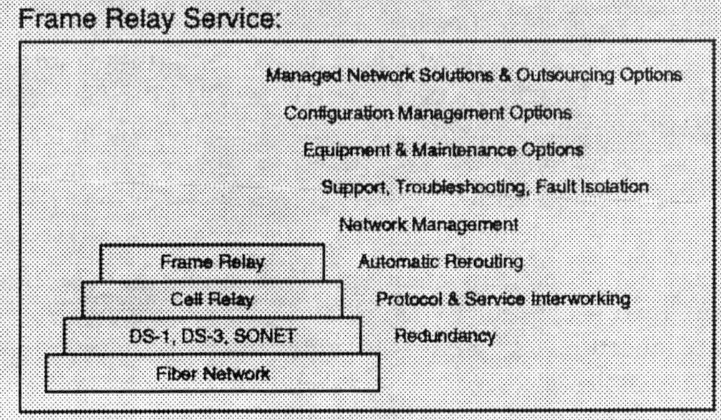


*When you choose to use a public frame relay service, you are buying a complete solution that may include all of these elements.*

Frame relay services offer an alternative to traditional private line networks and to X.25 packet switched networks. Frame relay provides the best attributes of each, combining the security, efficiency and quality of private lines with the flexibility, dynamic bandwidth allocation and many-to-many connectivity of X.25.

***Benefits of Frame Relay Compared To Private Lines and X.25***

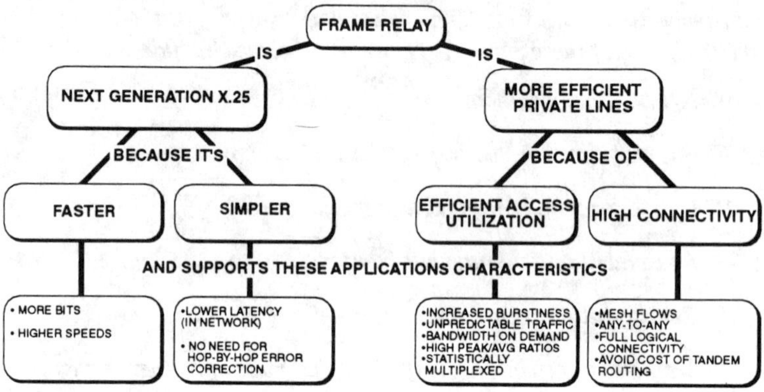


**Source:** AT&T

*Fig. 1.1: Frame relay offers the best of both X.25 and private lines, while improving upon each. It is faster and streamlined compared with X.25, while offering greater connectivity at a lower rate than private lines.*

Frame relay is a "fast-packet" data service, a term that reflects the high-speed nature of frame relay and grows out of a comparison to X.25 packet services — or "slow-packet" services, if there was such as phrase.

In the early days of the technology, the term fast-packet was more widely used than it is today. There are two main categories of these fast packet technologies: One is based on a packet length that can vary in size, and one is based on a constant packet length. The two types of technologies, frame and cell relay respectively, can be used together in a network. In fact, most frame relay services use a frame relay interface, private lines for the physical backbone, and a cell relay switching fabric (i.e., backbone protocol).

Frame relay is also "connection-oriented," meaning that you pre-define logical network paths between two locations, just like private lines. This is as opposed to "connectionless" services in which the path is not predetermined. With connectionless services, each packet will find its own way through the network; a path taken in one instance might be different from a packet taken in another instance. Switched Multimegabit Data Service (SMDS) is an example of a connectionless service.

Frame relay services use a single physical interface into the network to support multiple logical connections to remote locations. Frame relay is a full-duplex service, like private lines, in that you can simultaneously transmit and receive information.

There are three primary elements in a public frame relay network service: the frame relay access line, the port connection, and the permanent virtual circuits (PVC).

Port connection speeds in most public frame relay services range from 56/64K bps to 1.536M bps (or 2.048 in Europe). There is no reason frame relay can't operate at faster speeds. Some service providers offer frame relay up to 6M bps today. A 45M bps standard is being considered.

A PVC can be thought of as the logical connection — like a "virtual" private line — between two points. PVCs are assigned an average "guaranteed" throughput rate, called the committed information rate (CIR). CIRs are typically available in 64K bps increments from 64K bps to 1.536M bps. Many providers also offer smaller CIR options, in amounts of 0K, 4K, 16K, 32K, 48K, 56K bps, etc. More on CIR later.

*Frame Relay Network Elements*

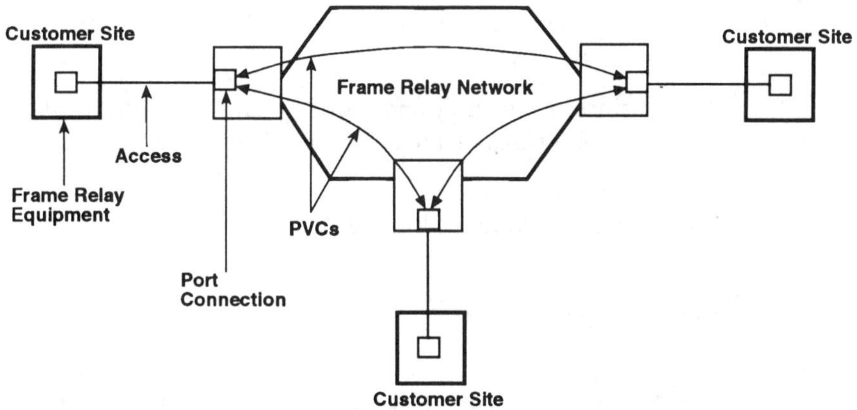


*Fig. 1.2: A frame relay service has several elements: the frame relay equipment, the access, the port connection, and the permanent virtual circuits.*

Public frame relay services can benefit small networks with minimal connectivity requirements, such as networks with as few as four remote locations at 56K bps speeds or below. Frame relay can also benefit very large networks with hundreds of locations and speed requirements ranging beyond 1.536M bps.

The most common frame relay networks today fall somewhere in the middle, providing star or partial meshed network connectivity among four to 40 locations.

You could be a candidate for using a public frame relay service if one or more of the following applies to your data environment:

- You have the need to connect many sites in a partial or full meshed environment;
- You have a star network configuration that requires more than one DS-1 local loop at the primary site;
- You operate parallel private networks for one or more data applications (such as LANs and SNA);
- You have geographically distributed LANs that need connectivity;
- You have remote front-end processors;
- You use a public X.25 network service today but need higher speeds;
- Your business is dynamic and growing, and you need the flexibility to rapidly change the network to keep pace;
- You want to implement new business applications, but can't cost-justify the additional bandwidth.

## Who Offers Frame Relay?

As with other networking services, public frame relay services are offered by a large number of different providers. Traditionally, local access providers, including regional Bell operating companies (RBOCs) and competitive access providers (CAPs) offer intraLATA frame relay for connectivity among sites within the same city or LATA. Interexchange carriers (IXCs) offer frame relay among locations in different cities or LATAs. Within the category of IXC providers, there are services national and global in scope and those that are regionally concentrated.

The regulatory climate is changing rapidly, however. These traditional breakdowns no longer hold true in all cases. Some CAPs already are providing end to end frame relay services which span intra- and inter-LATA boundaries. The IXCs offer intraLATA connectivity within the frame relay network, and the RBOCs could soon be offering services that cross LATA lines. Who knows where the cable companies will fit?

## Is Frame Relay Right For Your Network?

There is probably not a single right or wrong choice when it comes to choosing a transmission solution. There are simply degrees of optimization, which must be balanced against many other factors, such as what you have in place now. If you already have a private network installed and operational, it probably has a lot of momentum and inertia.

For many companies, a private-public hybrid network makes the most sense. For example, a virtual solution using a public data service might provide savings and flexibility. However, if you already have a sizable investment in private line equipment and training, and the network itself is performing well, it may be more economical overall to stay with the existing architecture, at least until the economics show that large savings could be achieved through a move to virtual options. Chances are that even if you decide to use a virtual networking service for your voice traffic and a frame relay service for your data applications, you may still elect to maintain some dedicated facilities within your network.

The idea of public data services is that the carrier invests in the equipment and in the network diversity, instead of the end user buying intelligent time division or statistical multiplexers and diverse dedicated lines. Many of the inherent features and advantages of these sophisticated networks are passed to users without end users having to make the investment directly.

However, this environment also means that you lose some direct control over your network. In some cases, or for some sites, this is not desirable. In other cases, this can free your resources to concentrate on core business issues.

You may find that some of your locations, or applications, exhibit characteristics indicative of private lines, while others would lead you to choose a public data solution. In these cases, users should consider having both types of services in the same network. Choose the solution that works best at each site.

## Applications Platform Profiles

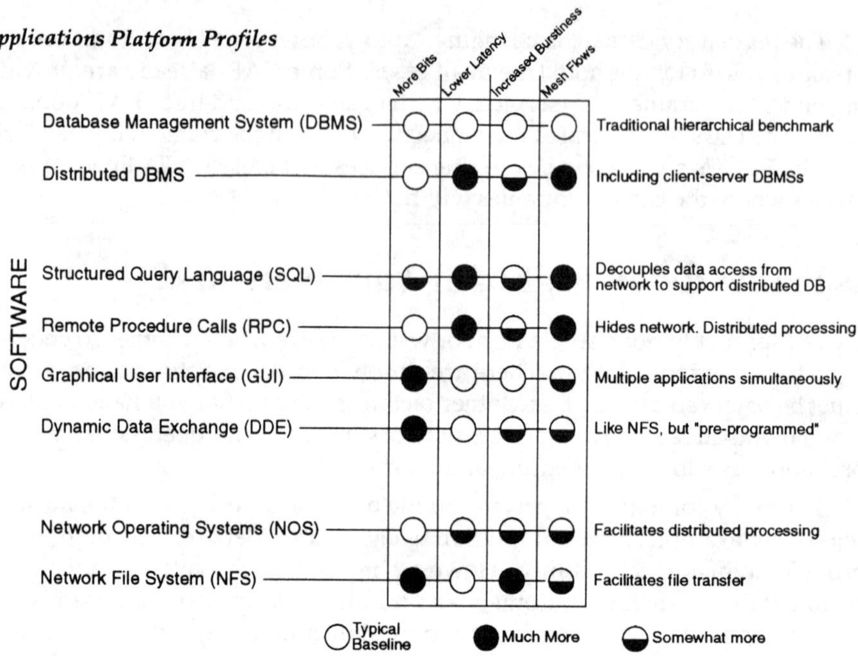


**Source:** AT&T

## Applications Profiles

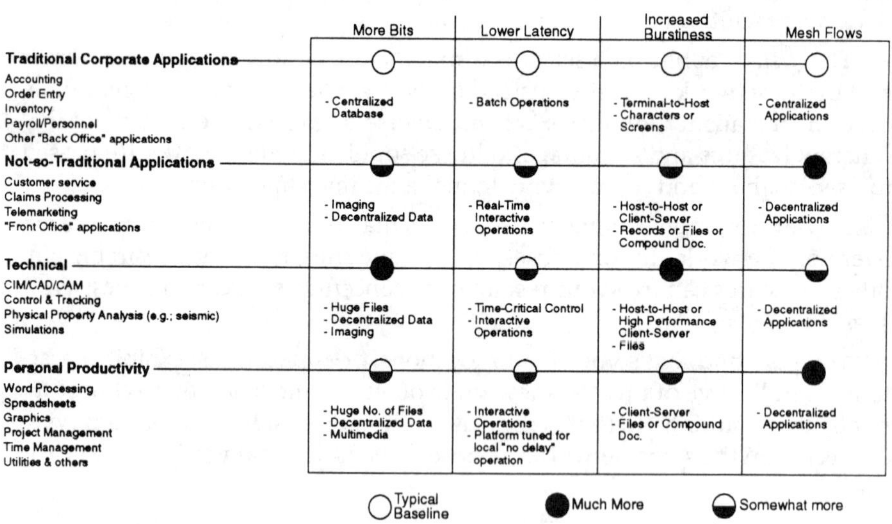


**Source:** AT&T

For example, one large computer manufacturer uses a private network between its five largest sites and then uses a public frame relay network service to gain connectivity to all other remote locations. In this example, the company happens to use a multiplexer, which itself uses a proprietary cell relay backbone protocol and can support frame relay inputs, as well as standard voice and data inputs.

However, this is not a necessary requirement for all hybrid implementations. Another company, a major multinational software developer, uses a similar hybrid network configuration and uses standard time-division multiplexers to support international leased lines and leased lines to some critical domestic sites. Frame relay services are used everywhere else. What's right for your company depends on what you have now and what you want.

The key is to choose the right tool for the job. Mixing and matching different services within the network will allow you to keep each location on the service that best meets the user and application needs at the site. Frame relay is not the Holy Grail of networking; it is instead an attractive networking alternative that when applied correctly, can save money and improve business performance.

## Frame Relay Advantages: Tactical and Strategic

When evaluating the potential advantages of a frame relay solution for your company, consider both the tactical and strategic benefits that can be gained by using frame relay. Not every network will benefit in the same manner from frame relay. However, one or more of the following advantages may be applicable to your network.

### *Benefits of Frame Relay: Tactical and Strategic*

| *Tactical* | *Strategic* |
|---|---|
| ☎ *Equipment Savings* | *Competitive Business Advantages* |
| ☎ *Access Savings* | *New Business Applications* |
| ☎ *IXC Savings* | *Improved Productivity* |
| ☎ *Decreased Operations Costs* | *Increased Profits* |
| ☎ *Improved Performance* | *A Migration Path to ATM* |
| ☎ *Increased Network Availability* | |
| ☎ *Greater Flexibility* | |
| ☎ *Simplified Network Architecture* | |

## *Tactical Benefits of Frame Relay*

Tactical benefits include those advantages that are of primary interest to the datacom manager or MIS director, such as decreased network and operating costs, improved performance, higher network availability, increased flexibility and simplification of the network architecture.

### *Savings*

Frame relay services can provide an opportunity to achieve savings in several areas, when compared with other networking alternatives such as dedicated private lines. There are at least three areas of potential savings: equipment, local access and IXC.

#### *1. Equipment Savings*

Frame relay allows many logical connections, or PVCs, to share a single network interface. With private lines, many individual physical connections and the supporting equipment interfaces are needed to connect directly to many remote sites. The frame relay solution means that fewer wide area network ports are needed on the network equipment, even when many remote locations are being directly connected. It also translates into a reduction in the number of channel service units/data service units (CSU/DSUs) needed. The reduction in ports and CSU/DSUs also reduces the number of single points of failure on the end-to-end network, thereby increasing total network reliability.

*Equipment Savings*

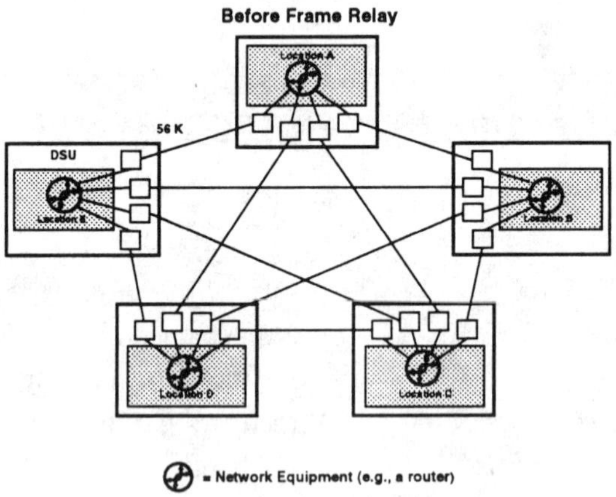


*Fig. 1.4a: Before frame relay, each direct connection to another remote location required a separate router port and CSU/DSU, which increases equipment costs.*

*Network Requirments After Frame Relay*

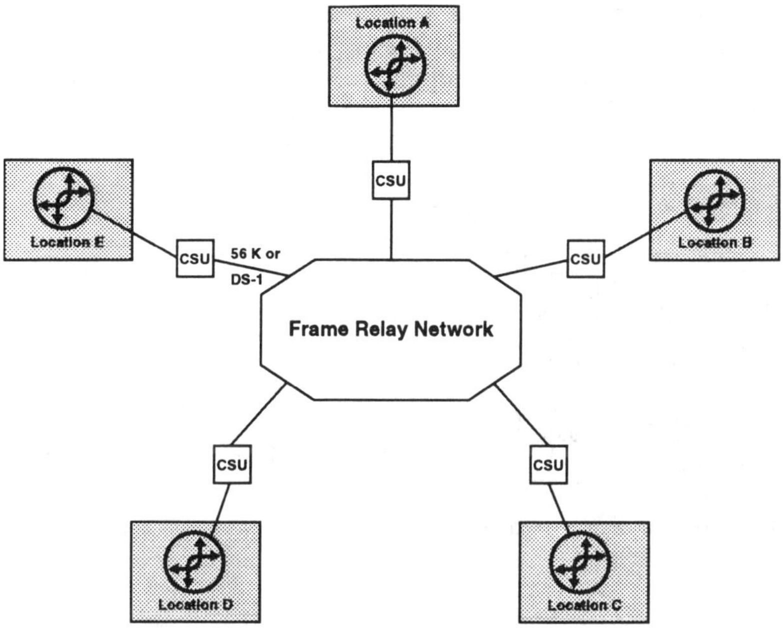


*Fig. 1.4b: After frame relay, the number of wide area network router ports and CSUs/DSUs is significantly reduced.*

### 2. Local Access Savings

Because many logical connections share the same physical interface into the frame relay network, the number of local loops needed is often reduced significantly. The impact can be seen at both remote locations and at the primary location(s).

At remote locations, separate low-speed private line networks can be consolidated into a single frame relay network connection. In fact, even different applications, such as local area networks (LAN) and IBM's System Network Architecture (SNA), can be consolidated and can share the same connection into the frame relay network. This often results in a reduction of two or more dedicated loops, down to a single loop.

At primary locations, it is often the case that a DS-1 local loop is needed for every 24 remote locations. It is not uncommon that 50 percent or less of these individual circuits are active at any one time. Frame relay allows you to take advantage of the intermittent nature of many data applications and allow a single DS-1 local loop to support more than 24 remote locations.[1] This is done through statistical multiplexing of incoming and outgoing frames and results in a more efficient allocation of access bandwidth.

*Remote Site Local Access Before Frame Relay*

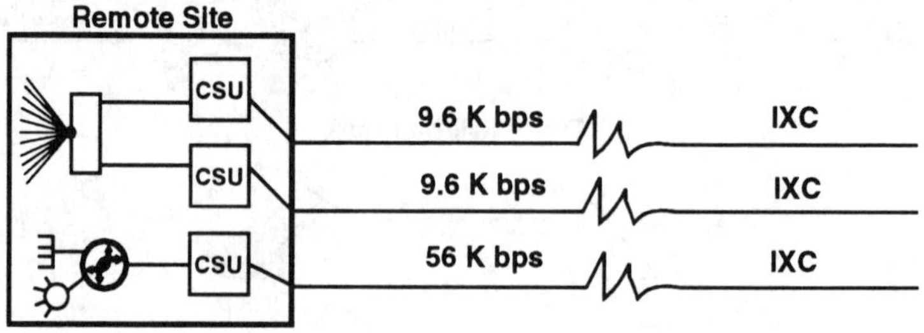


*Fig. 1.5a: Before frame relay, multiple local loops support connectivity requirements at remote sites.*

*Remote Site Local Access After Frame Relay*

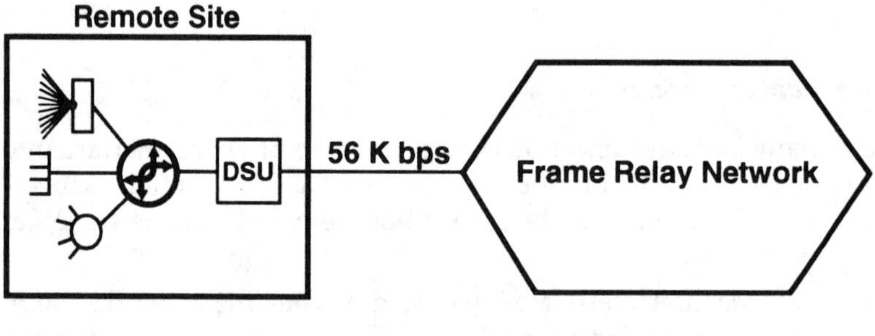


*Fig. 1.5b: The number of local loops at remote sites can be reduced with frame relay through application and network consolidation.*

*Primary Site Local Access Before Frame Relay*

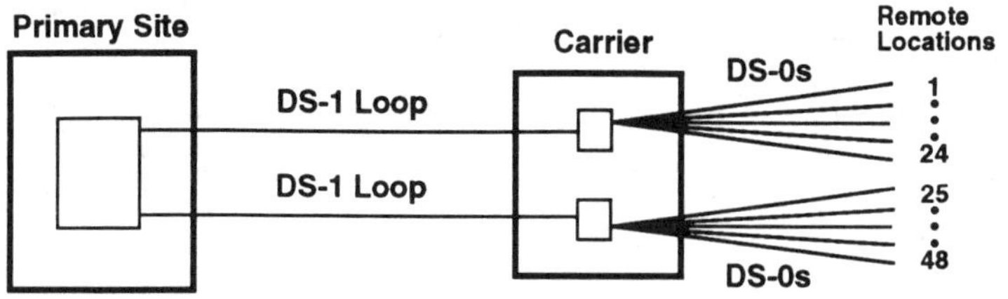


*Fig. 1.6a: Before frame relay, one DS-1 local loop is needed for each set of 24 DS-0s to remote locations.*

*Primary Site Local Access After Frame Relay*

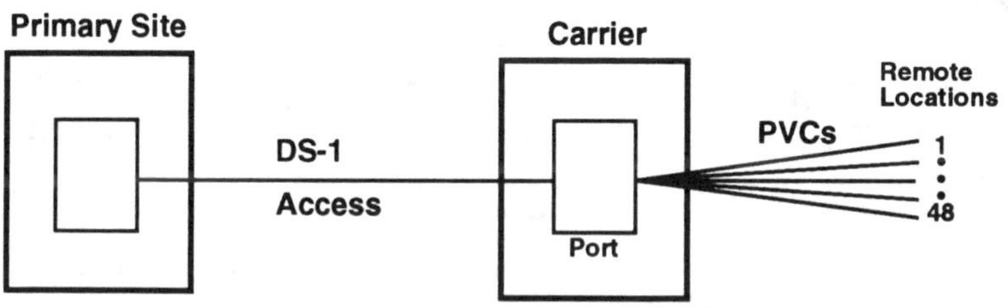


*Fig. 1.6b: After Frame Relay, a single DS-1 local loop can be used to support 48 or more remote locations.*

### 3. IXC Network Savings[2]

Frame relay can significantly reduce IXC network expenditures as well. These savings can emerge in many areas, depending upon network requirements. Frame relay rates are typically not mileage sensitive, which can mean significant savings for geographically distributed networks. Incremental connectivity is also less expensive than with private leased lines, meaning more connectivity for the dollar.

Frame relay services allow users to temporarily send data at a rate above the committed information rate, a capability called "bursting." This translates into transmission savings since you can purchase lower capacity long-haul transmission paths, even though occasionally you will actually exceed this amount to handle peak capacity transmissions. This advantage works well in conjunction with frame relay's ability to allow multiple applications to share the same PVC, reducing the number of dedicated connections required between any two sites.

*IXC Network Before Frame Relay*

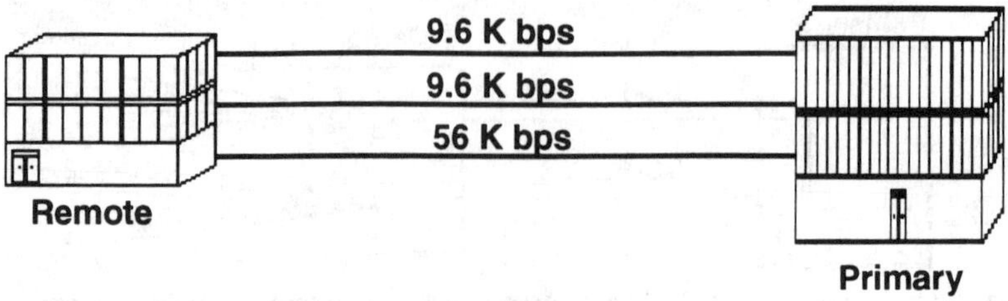


*Fig. 1.7a: Separate parallel networks, to support different application and/or peak traffic periods, increase expenses.*

*IXC Network After Frame Relay*

*Fig. 1.7b: Parallel networks can be consolidated with frame relay to save money, while busy traffic periods can benefit from frame relay's burst capability.*

Frame relay services have been built with the ability to automatically route around network failures — a characteristic of it being a public network service — and this means that you do not have to purchase excess network connections for the sole purpose of providing an alternate backup path between locations. Extra leased lines purchased solely to construct triangle and ring network configurations for survivability can be reduced, or even eliminated.

These examples represent only a few of the ways in which frame relay can help save on recurring network expenditures for long-haul circuits. Other savings, including the ability to fine tune the network so that it more closely matches traffic patterns by designing "asymmetrical PVCs," will be covered more in later chapters.

### *Reduced Operating Costs*

Network architectures are typically simplified with a frame relay network implementation. This simplification can result in reduced administration and operation costs.

As the number of leased lines and separate parallel networks is reduced, so are the ongoing administration and operating costs for managing and maintaining these facilities.

*Redundancy In Leased Line Networks*

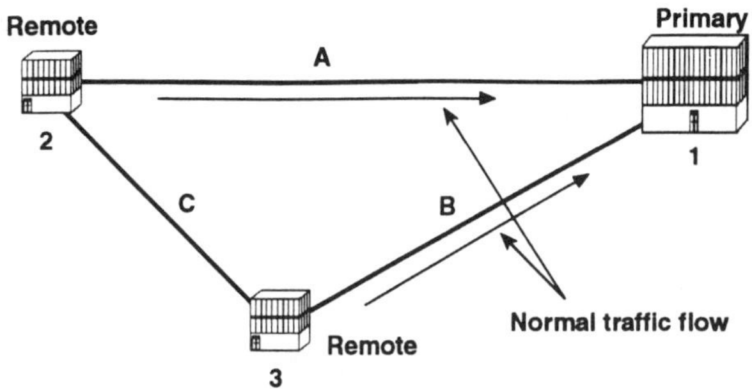


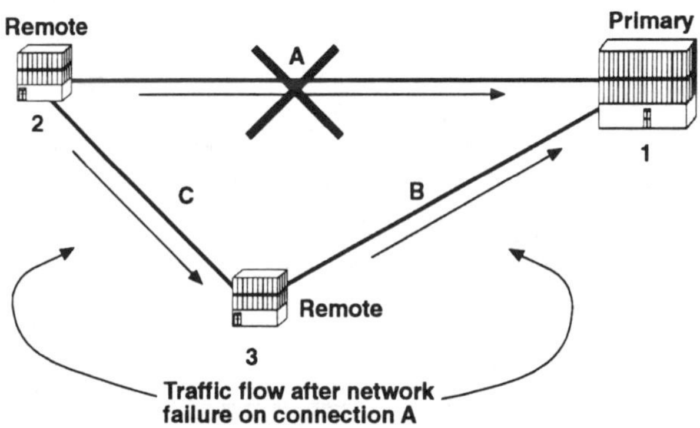


*Fig. 1.8a: Excess capacity and redundant leased lines are often designed into private networks to increase network availability.*

The amount of equipment, and equipment ports, attached to the wide area network will also be reduced, again helping to lower operation expenses. Frame relay offerings typically provide the option for bundling everything together, including equipment. Using a single vendor to provide the complete network package will reduce the number of separate vendors that you have to manage and with whom you must negotiate, which can further decrease administration expenses.

With a public frame relay network solution, the carrier will assume a larger burden for network operation and availability. For example, it becomes the carrier's responsibility to maintain diverse network paths in case of a network failure.

*Automatic Rerouting In Frame Relay Network*

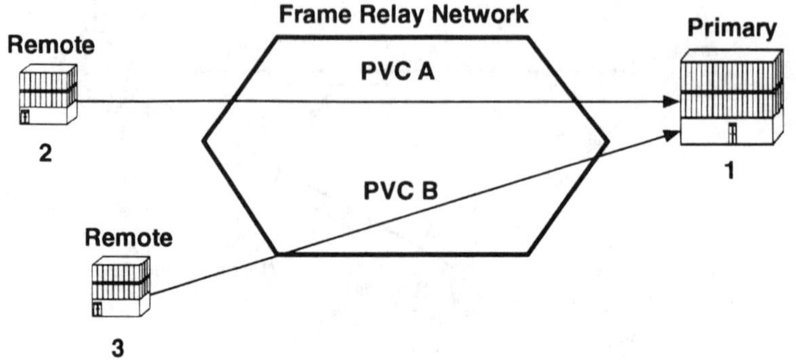


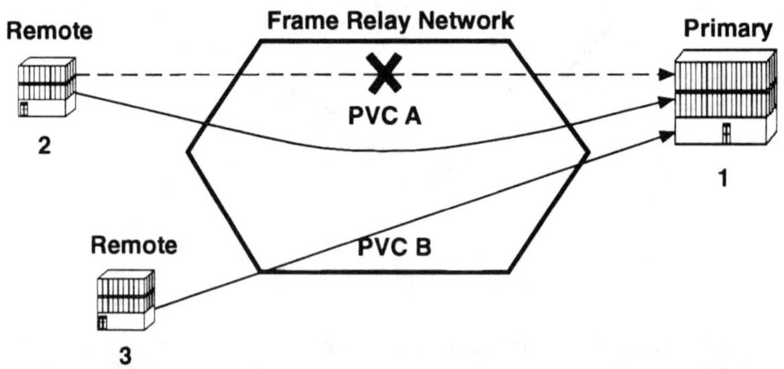


*Fig. 1.8b: The virtual connections within a frame relay network can automatically route around a network failure. A PVC would only be assigned between remote locations 2 and 3 if the traffic flow between the two locations were enough to justify a direct connection. It would not be needed simply for redundancy.*

The provisioning of new connections, or modification of existing connections, among locations already on the network is much less time consuming with frame relay than with leased lines. For example, assigning another 64K bps of capacity between two existing frame relay network locations is done in software and can typically be accomplished by the carrier in a few days or less. The carriers are working on providing tools that will allow you to directly assign and modify PVCs, reducing this interval to seconds.

### *Improved Performance*

There are many different ways in which a frame relay solution can help improve network performance.

For example, in a traditional dedicated network topology, remote sites that need to communicate directly with each other may actually do so by tandeming through a primary location. This can cause network congestion for all users with traffic going to, from or through that primary site, resulting in longer network response times and application-level delays.

*Traffic Pattern Between Remote Sites Before Frame Relay*

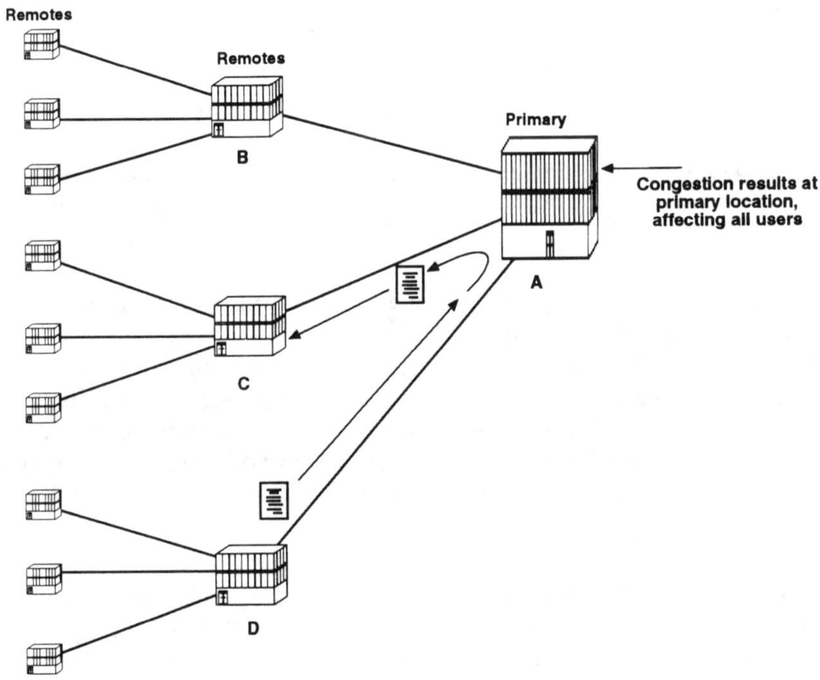


*Fig. 1.9a: Leased line configurations often force traffic between remote locations to be routed through the primary site causing delays and network congestion. In this example, a file transfer from site D to C routes through site A.*

*Improved Network Performance After Frame Relay*

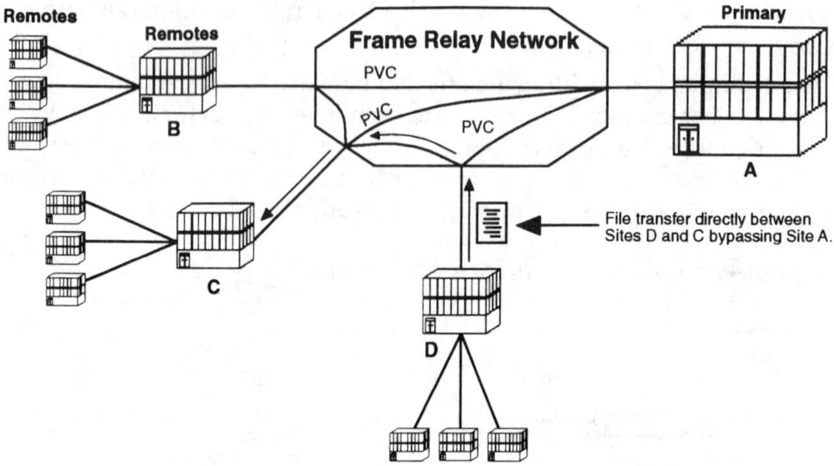


*Fig. 1.9b: Frame relay can reduce network congestion and improve performance for all users by increasing the level of direct network connectivity. In the example, the file transfer from site D to C would travel a direct path over a virtual connection.*

With frame relay, a higher level of *direct* connectivity can be cost-effectively provided between remote locations, because once a single physical connection into the network is established, additional logical connections can be added at a relatively low cost. By providing a greater level of direct connectivity between locations, nearly all network users benefit because network congestion is reduced at the primary location (and other network hubs) and because network response times are reduced.

### *Higher Network Availability*

The intelligence inherent in a frame relay network results in the ability to automatically route PVCs around a network failure. Depending upon your current network architecture and the amount of redundancy you have already built into the network, frame relay could help you increase your overall network availability. And that means keeping your users happy and the business's applications up and running.

Many network topologies today consist of multipoint circuits, tandem architectures and nodal (or hub) architectures. This topology is often implemented to save money on mileage-sensitive leased line costs. Figures 1.10a/b and 1.11 help to illustrate how frame relay can help improve network survivability and result in greater availability.

The problem with the tandem architecture shown in figure 1.10a is evident when you ask the question: What would happen to site C's and site D's ability to communicate with primary site A in the event of a network failure between sites A and B?

In the network configuration shown in 1.10b, a network failure at site B not only affects site B's ability to communicate with the primary location but also affects communications to/from site C and D. So, business at three locations is disrupted because of a single network failure.

*Leased Line Tandem Architecture*

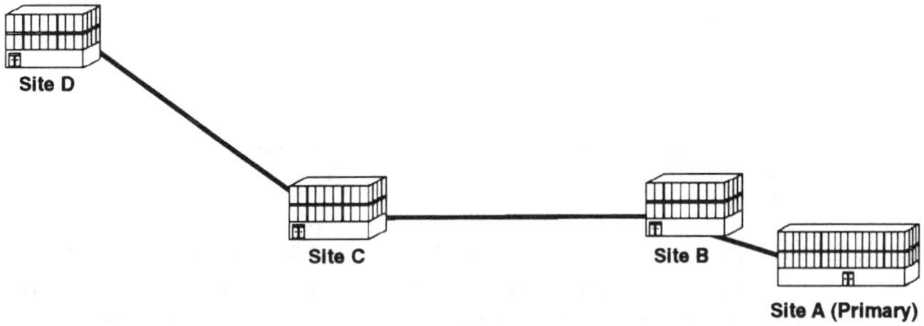


*Fig. 1.10a: Private lines often "tandem" through intermediate locations to reduce network expenditures.*

*Tandem Architectures Affect Network Availability*

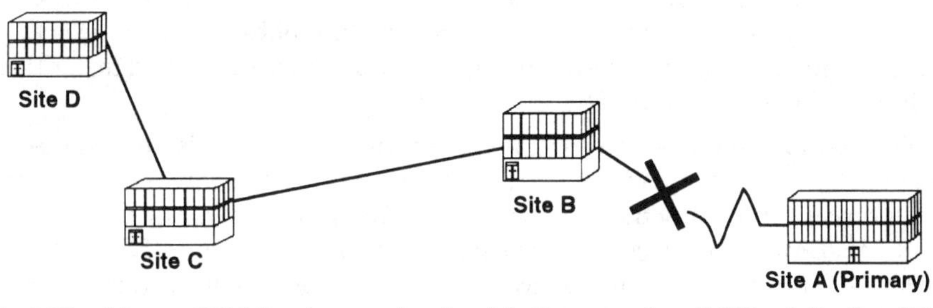


*Fig. 1.10b: A loop or IXC failure between sites A and B affect network availability at sites C and D as well.*

In a frame relay network, as shown in figure 1.11, a greater level of direct connectivity can be cost-effectively provided to remote locations. This, combined with frame relay's ability to automatically route around a network failure, can greatly improve network survivability.

*Frame Relay Network Eliminates Tandem Architecture*

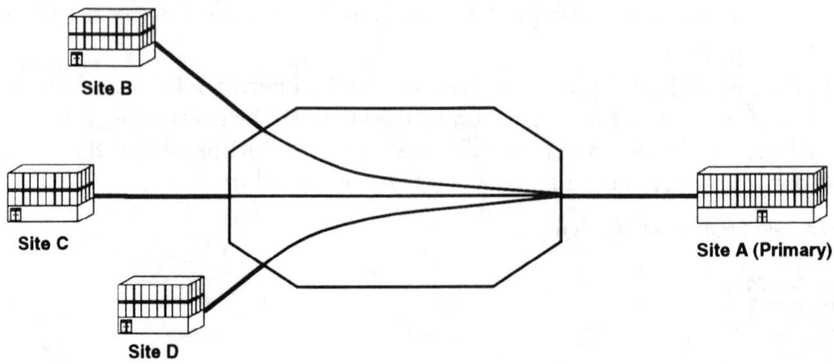


*Fig. 1.11: Each location in the frame relay network has a unique connection to primary site A.*

A network failure between location A and B would not affect the ability for locations B and C to communicate with the primary site. Site B would probably maintain its connectivity with location A as well, because the network would automatically route the connection around the failed circuit.

### *Greater Flexibility*

The logical nature of frame relay connectivity results in much greater flexibility to reconfigure the network architecture. Adding new locations is easier, and changing the capacity between existing locations is easier and faster than with traditional dedicated networks.

For example, when a new logical connection (i.e., a PVC) is needed between two locations already on the frame relay network, a three-day installation interval is probably the maximum that you can expect to wait. This would also apply to any changes to existing PVCs, such as modifying the committed information rate. Several carriers are working on realtime management tools, which will let you directly control the addition and modification of PVCs, reducing this interval to minutes or even seconds.

Adding a new site to the network is also very simple. The installation interval at the new location will be driven by the time it takes to get the local access. Therefore, you will probably not see any difference compared with leased lines in implementation intervals when installing a new site onto your frame relay network.

However, connecting the new site to existing network locations is once again very easy. New PVCs can be assigned to existing sites without adding a new access line into the existing location. It is as simple as assigning a new logical connection.

The logical nature of frame relay connectivity means that chaotic and fast-growing corporate environments are more easily supported. The connectivity within your frame relay network can be quickly modified to support changing business requirements.

This can be especially advantageous as businesses move to implement new product development and project work group concepts such as quickly assembling and disbanding cross-functional teams to work on specific research and development, marketing or business problems.

One early implementer of frame relay service accomplished a major network reconfiguration in less than a week. He estimated that the same reconfiguration in his previous dedicated network would have taken upwards of 4 to 6 months.

### *Simplification of Network Architecture*

Frame relay allows you to consolidate separate applications and separate parallel networks onto a single network infrastructure. This consolidation of applications and circuits results in a simplified network architecture. Depending upon the existing environment and the applications being supported, it is also typical to see a streamlining in the equipment infrastructure. Simplification has many benefits, including reducing costs, improving reliability and performance, and simplifying planning and re-engineering.

## *Strategic Benefits of Frame Relay*

Strategic business advantages can also be gained through a frame relay solution. These benefits are of primary interest to the president or chief information officer. These include providing your company with a competitive business advantage, getting goods to market more quickly, being able to cost-justify new business applications, improving worker productivity, and increasing profitability.

One advantage that can be gained by allowing more of the network to be self-managed and/or managed by the frame relay carrier is that more of the network manager's and MIS director's time can be allocated to looking at the strategic direction of telecommunications within your firm. The trend is for companies to get away from the day-to-day running of a telephone network and spend more time figuring out how telecommunications can better support the strategic business objectives. Frame relay significantly enables this change from an operational to a strategic perspective.

In addition, more carriers are offering complete outsourcing solutions for clients who prefer to stay focused on their core business and not the business of running the network. These outsourcing solutions include some combination of the network links, equipment, monitoring and maintenance, configuration management and on-going network optimization.

In fact, as the structure of the organization begins to change in an effort to become more fluid, dynamic and flexible, it will be critical that the network enhance and not hinder this modified business climate. Many organizations are beginning to explore faster and more flexible methods for new product development, for example. Companies are using small, quickly assembled cross-functional teams, or ad hoc work groups, with representatives from many departments and even different companies. This approach can enable new products and services to be brought to market more quickly, giving the business a strategic competitive advantage.

When the team members are geographically disbursed, this can put new and unusual strains on the corporate network. Network flexibility, scalability and connectivity become critical business requirements. Frame relay can be an enabler for this new organizational structure - helping and not hindering this movement towards greater organizational responsiveness.

### *Competitive Business Advantage*

There are many ways a frame relay network can improve a company's market position versus its competitors. As with the example above, your company may choose to design a new product collaboratively by bringing together a single team with representatives from different departments around the country or around the world. The team may even be made up of representatives from several companies. This approach can speed development time and get goods to market more quickly. The corporate network becomes the vehicle for keeping the information flowing between team members.

You may use the network to provide sales people, field engineers, and other customer support people with better and more advanced business and competitive tools. This can increase your ability to win business over competitors and better retain accounts after they are won.

A nationwide engineering consulting firm that implemented a frame relay network found that the quality of its proposals went up significantly when experts at headquarters and in other offices could contribute easily to the document. This improvement in quality was directly attributed to a 15 percent increase in the success ratio of proposals and thus a 15 percent increase in work. Network capacity and connectivity restraints had prohibited this application in the company's previous dedicated and dial-up network.

### *New Business Applications*

There are often many new business applications proposed within an organization as paths to greater productivity, better quality work, improved worker relations, etc. It is not unusual for these applications to be rejected due to high networking costs.

With frame relay, incremental additions of network capacity are typically much less expensive than in a dedicated environment, often making it cost-effective to implement these new ideas.

### *Improved Productivity*

Again, the ways in which improved worker productivity will manifest itself is a function of your business environment. By increasing the level of direct connectivity within the network and increasing capacity through dynamic bandwidth allocation, response times on the network improve. This can result in improved worker productivity.

One manufacturing company that migrated a pure SNA network using dedicated facilities to a frame relay network, found that average response times per screen dropped 12-15 seconds to 0.4 seconds. The firm estimated that this resulted in a 4 to 6 percent productivity improvement in their field offices. Since these offices were responsible for customer support functions, they also perceived that customer satisfaction increased as well.

The nationwide consulting firm mentioned above gained an unplanned-for benefit in increased worker productivity. It discovered that work loads across the country tended to be uneven. In any given week, one office might be overburdened with work and new proposals, while another office might have a much lighter work load. They used the frame relay network to more evenly distribute work to experts across the country, allowing the company to take on a greater overall level of work and improving overall productivity.

*Increased Profits*

One of the most important objectives for any executive officer is to increase corporate profits. While a president or CEO may not get very excited about local access consolidation or improved network performance, he or she can understand the bottom-line impacts of reduced expenditures, lower operating costs, and greater worker productivity. The benefits of a frame relay network often drop right to the company's bottom-line profit level.

## If Frame Relay Looks Right, What You Should Do Next?

If you decide to pursue further examination of a frame relay solution for all, or part, of your network, you will need to do some internal and external information gathering. Understand what you have in place today and what your options are, given your existing and projected applications requirements.

Once your current network environment is well understood, and the probable implications and impacts of a frame relay solution have been evaluated, you will be in a better position to help design your frame relay network and plan for its ongoing support. For the most part, you can get your vendors and carriers to do a great deal of the work for you, but there are several pieces of vital information that should be applied during this process, and chances are you will be the only one with answers. Appendix A provides a list of questions and issues to consider in evaluating a move to frame relay.

The rest of this book is dedicated to helping you understand frame relay and the design and implementation of the network.

[1] *The statement assumes that the frame relay service provider allows "oversubscription" of the port connection, as nearly all providers do. Oversubscription is covered in chapter 4.*

[2] *This section would also apply for intraLATA networks, where the access link is into the local network, and IXC connections are, instead, local carrier connections within a metropolitan area or LATA.*

CHAPTER 2:

# FRAME RELAY DEFINED HISTORICALLY

To understand the present, one must first understand the past. Since its inception, telecommunications technology has been in a continual state of evolution. One of the more recent products of this evolution is frame relay, a new networking species that represents a combination of past technologies. Its "parents" are circuit switches using time division multiplexing and X.25 packet switches using statistical multiplexing. Frame relay combines the high speed and low delay of time division multiplexing with the port sharing and packet interleaving of statistical multiplexing.

## A Short History of Frame Relay

Frame relay was originally specified in ITU-TSS (formerly known as the CCITT) Recommendation I.122. This "framework for additional packet mode bearer services" grew out of a series of ISDN specifications. ANSI (American National Standards Institute) followed with its version of I.122 called T1.617 and T1.618, which are the signaling specifications and core aspects of frame relay, respectively. The frame relay standard took some basics from the ISDN standards and created a new interface standard, which became the foundation for a new set of public network services. These standards use the ISDN

D channel signaling format, called the Link Access Protocol, or LAP-D, to carry signaling traffic over the network.

The ANSI T1S1 committee worked from these recommendations to develop a set of frame relay specifications. With cooperation from the international standards bodies, ANSI developed T1.618 for frame relay using permanent virtual connections, and the specification was adopted by ITU-TSS (formerly known as the CCITT) as Q.922. The ANSI T1.617 for switched virtual circuits equates to ITU-TSS (formerly known as the CCITT) Q.933.

Additions to the core functions were developed by the Frame Relay Forum, founded in 1991 to promote the understanding, development and adoption of frame relay products and services.

When frame relay was first introduced, it focused only on remote LAN connectivity. It did not support traditional terminal-to-host transaction applications at all. Not so today, as many companies are choosing to use public frame relay services to collapse networks that until now have been physically segregated.

Frame relay's growth has been nothing short of explosive. The first frame relay service became available in early 1991, and by the end of that year several carriers offered the service nationally. These services were limited in definition and features. In 1991, only a few router vendors supported frame relay, and non-router equipment options were not available.

***Frame Relay Growth — Public Network Services***

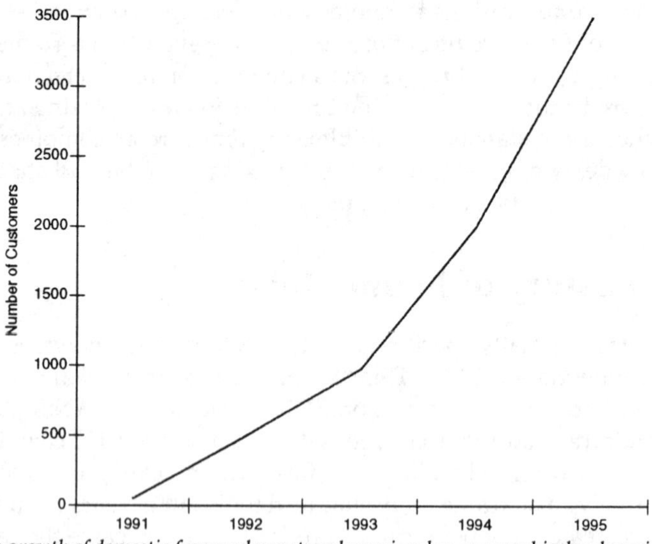


*Fig. 2.1: The growth of domestic frame relay network services has occurred in local, regional, and national markets.*

Today the story is much different. All the major carriers, most access providers and many regional carriers now offer frame relay service. Services are global in nature, robust in definition and feature-rich. Sales are escalating, with many carriers experiencing revenue and customer growth rates at 100 percent per year and greater.

Nearly all routers and bridges support frame relay. In addition, there is a variety of other equipment supporting frame relay, including cards that fit into traditional time division multiplexers and frame relay concentrators, also called frame relay assembler/disassemblers, or FRADs.

The equipment options have grown, and have opened up a new set of applications that can be supported using frame relay. For example, IBM has made frame relay an integral part of its strategic direction. Its controller family, including the front-end processor (FEP) and 3174, and most of IBM's other networking products now have a frame relay interfaces. There are even cards available from IBM that fit directly into your computer and which format the output into frame relay frames to allow direct access to a frame relay service.

Frame relay shows no sign of letting up. In early 1994, the Frame Relay Forum adopted specifications closely aligning frame relay with ATM, making sure that users have a seamless and directed growth path as their requirements grow, enabling frame relay transport across ATM infrastructures.

Frame relay came to market quickly and relatively easily, because it is so similar to existing variable-length packet protocols, and because it uses the same level two protocol at the link layer as X.25. The modifications necessary to support frame relay in Customer Premise Equipment, or CPE, were minimal and relatively inexpensive. In most CPE, support for frame relay is a simple software upgrade for which the vendor often does not charge extra. This allowed rapid adoption by end users and helped to fuel the growth.

## The Drivers of a New Network Service

Business needs drive applications. Applications drive networks. Though frame relay grew out of a need to interconnect LANs more cost-effectively, this is really not the best place to begin understanding why frame relay emerged and the problems it solves. There are two central and parallel histories to be examined. The first is a look at the changes that have occurred in processing power and the stresses these changes have placed on wide area networks. The second is a look at wide area networking solutions and the changes which have taken place in this arena to support the shift in processing power and the changing needs of the business applications.

## *The Shift in Processing Power*

The shift in processing power from a central to a distributed environment created a slow-rolling but powerful wave of change throughout the business world. It is in the wake of this movement that the need for frame relay emerged.

Frame relay services have built upon emerging requirements in both the business application and processing environments, which did not fit well with the traditional network and transmission environments. A history of frame relay necessitates an understanding of the forces in each of these areas and their interaction, which ultimately resulted in frame relay's conception.

Processing power has traditionally been centralized. Until relatively recently, desktop devices did not contain processing power or data storage capacity. Computing architectures were made up of mainframes and terminals. The business applications being served were primarily transaction-based. Only later did mini computers come along. And the personal computer was never even invited to the party, but instead snuck in through the back door.

If the corporate data network is the central nervous system of the company., then mainframes are the brains. If you look inside the mainframe, the storage facility is an adjunct to the central processing unit, or CPU. Files taken from memory travel only a very short distance before they reach the central processing unit, are processed, and then sent back to storage. The intelligence is centralized.

Network users interact with the mainframe through desktop terminals. The terminals themselves do not process or store information. Business applications are written to allow users to update information in the central data bases or to request information from them.

Remote terminals are connected to mainframes over hierarchical networks. In many terminal-to-mainframe applications, only very small requests are sent from the remote site to the mainframe, and the mainframe simply stores the new information and/or sends back a file or a very small screen update. The most common terminal-to-host architecture is IBM's System Network Architecture (SNA).

The networks built to support this traditional data processing hierarchy were themselves hierarchical The traffic flow was fairly orderly and predictable as well, at least when things were running smoothly. Speeds across the wide area network were typically 9.6K bps. There was a strict pecking order, and the flow of information went from top to bottom and bottom to top, but not side to side. The division of labor in this environment is strict. The top of the hierarchy is where all of the action occurs.

*Information Transfer and Processing In An SNA Network*

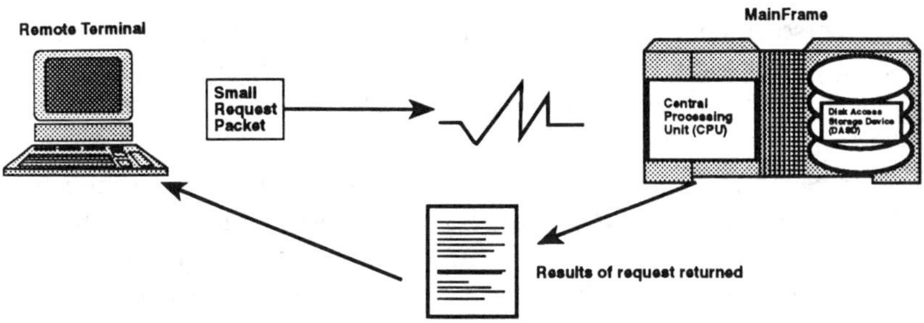


*Fig. 2.2: Small files or screen requests are sent back to the central mainframe where data is stored and processed. Only results are returned.*

*Traditional SNA Network*

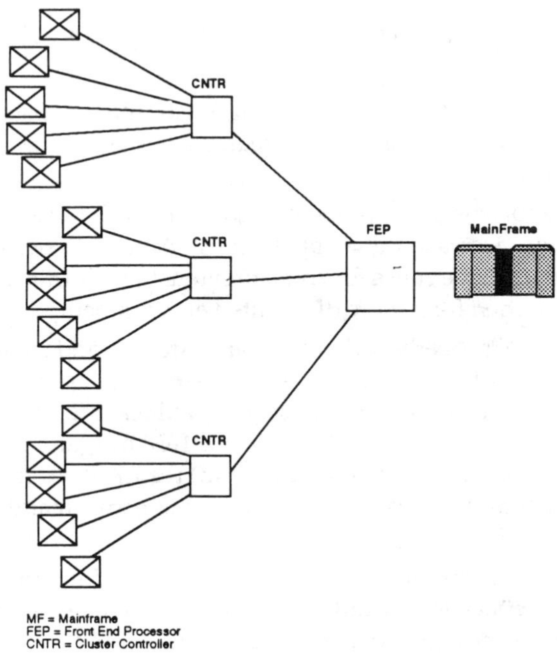


*Fig. 2.3: In SNA networks, the topology is strictly hierarchial, and the information flow is orderly.*

## Power to the Desktop

Enter the personal computer (PC) — a rebel network device that distributes processing power to the desktop. No longer is all processing and storage handled centrally. While this sounds simple and harmless, the impact on network topologies is immense.

As PCs began to proliferate in the work place, new business applications were developed that used the processing power resident in the desktop device. Files and databases were created and stored on the desktop device. And cost comparisons began to show that many applications could be developed and maintained on PCs in a dramatically less expensive fashion compared with mainframes.

In addition to the substantial cost savings possible with some applications, the time to develop new business applications can also be reduced in a PC environment. Businesses could simply not ignore the cost and speed advantages of the PC, and PC deployment exploded.

## The Advent of LANs

In overcoming the cost and development constraints of mainframe environments for some applications, the PC created its own unique and wholly new set of problems.

As applications began to be developed for the PC, it became necessary to give many users access to these applications. And since storage capacity was less expensive, it made sense for some previously mainframe-based applications to be rewritten for a more distributed environment.

Connecting PCs together to allow shared storage and shared access to printers and to information became an industry unto itself. Local area networks emerged to tie PCs within close geographical proximity together. Initially operating at speeds of 4M, 10M and 16M bps (and now going far beyond this to 100M, 155M bps, and beyond) the LAN is a fast and elegant method for turning a group of PCs into a cost-effective mainframe alternative for some applications.

The LAN solved the problem of allowing users within the same department to share applications. And groups of LANs, connected by simple bridges or gateways, allowed users on different floors or across the campus to communicate electronically and share information.

At first, linking LANs seemed fairly simple, especially since the LAN speeds were so high that congestion wasn't a big concern. The problems really began when access to remote locations became necessary.

## Comparing SNA and LAN Traffic

*Transaction-oriented networks usually utilize polling. Using IBM's System Network Architecture (SNA) as an example, the front-end processor (FEP) systematically polls each remote cluster controller to determine if any information is waiting to be transferred. The cluster controller only sends information to the FEP when it is asked to do so. The FEP acts like a traffic cop, and traffic flows in a very orderly fashion.*

*This aspect of control is very important to SNA's network operation and its traffic predictability, and is lacking in a LAN environment. In LAN environments, information can pass between any two or more sets of network devices, at any time, and in any direction. File sizes are not predictable, either. There is no polling, and no FEP, to keep all of the transactions orderly.*

*While polling works to keep the traffic orderly, one negative result of polling is a significant amount of network overhead. The continual request/acknowledgement sequences that take place between FEPs and remote cluster controllers, even when no information needs to be transferred, means that network traffic is continually being created and transmitted across the WAN. If the polling is stripped away, the traffic pattern becomes unpredictable, intermittent and bursty, just like LAN interconnect.*

# The Problems of Connecting LANs

LANs were initially intended to be local, thus the name local area network. Connecting LANs across a WAN poses some interesting challenges. To understand these challenges, and understand the elegance of frame relay as a solution, you must once again go back to the nature of the underlying applications.

When users on a terminal-to-mainframe network want to change or manipulate data in some way, the request is sent back to the place of central storage, the processing is done centrally, and only the output is sent back to the user. With LANs, the processing is not done centrally, and the processing unit does not reside adjunct to the storage unit.

If a user on one LAN wants to access and manipulate a file from a remote LAN, the entire file could potentially be sent from where it is stored on LAN A to the processor in the requesting user's desktop on LAN B. There is nothing methodical or orderly about this process. There is no predictability to the transmission, like the methodical SNA network. LAN internetworks are chaotic and reactionary. They are also more homogeneous (i.e., peer oriented), or flatter, than the hierarchical SNA environment.

*Information Transfer and Processing In A Distributed Network*

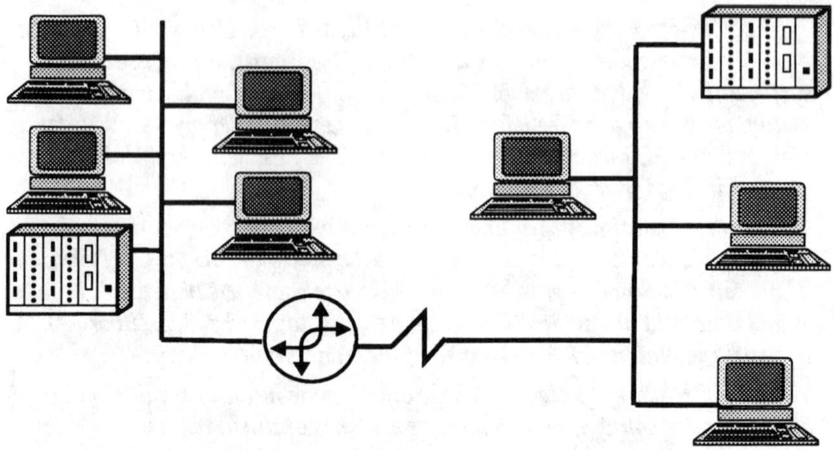

*Fig. 2.4: Storage and processing capabilities are distributed to the desktop, and information transfers can occur from anywhere to anywhere.*

Like a pig in a pipe, a large file could hit the LAN internetwork and require transmission to another desktop at any time. On a local area network where capacity is several megabits or more, the impact on network congestion of sending a 400K bps or even a 4M bps file between desktops is minimal. On a 9.6 K bps wide area network connection, on the other hand, the impact can be devastating — especially if mission-critical transaction applications get trapped behind the LAN file being transmitted.

*Information Transfer Across a LAN*

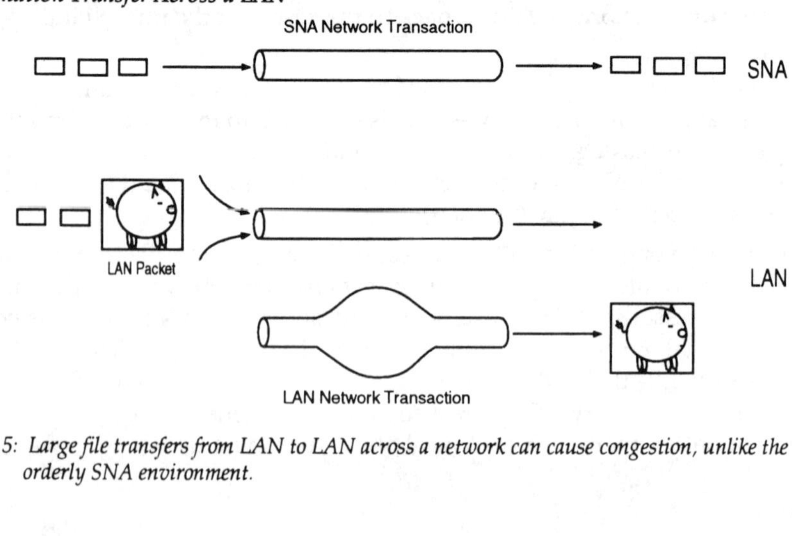


*Fig. 2.5: Large file transfers from LAN to LAN across a network can cause congestion, unlike the orderly SNA environment.*

### *LAN Internetworks*

The term internetworking emerged as a descriptor for the process of networking networks. (Internetworking should not be confused with the term "interworking," used and described later in this book.) Remote LANs connected across a WAN comprise an internetwork.

The problem of connecting LANs is that any LAN might need to get information from, or send it to, any other LAN. Especially with the emergence of electronic mail applications as a way to facilitate the exchange of documents and as an alternative to playing phone-tag, the requirement for connectivity among LANs has grown.

The problem of connecting LANs using traditional leased lines is that to maintain a full, or even a partial, physical mesh topology requires a lot of lines, router ports and CSU/DSUs. In fact, the formula for a fully meshed network is the number of LAN sites (N) times the number of sites minus 1 (N-1) divided by two.

$$\text{Number of Leased Lines Required} = N(N-1)/2$$

If you have five locations, then, to create a fully meshed physical network of private lines would take ten private lines (5(4)/2). If you have six sites, the number increases to fifteen, an increase of five circuits as a result of one new site. A few quick calculations will show that as the number of LANs to interconnect across a WAN grows in a linear fashion, the cost to maintain the mesh grows exponentially. In addition there is the high cost of WAN ports on a router (or bridge), or the cost of each CSU/DSU.

Consequently, leased line meshed networks have been costly and rarely deployed. In the best of cases, partial mesh network have been constructed and even these are costly. Router networks have included multiple tandem points, or hops, and routers have had to be sophisticated enough to continually calculate the most economical and least congested route over which to send traffic. A solution was needed that allowed interconnectivity performance to be high by maintaining a high level of direct connectivity between the LANs, but didn't present a cost structure that escalated exponentially as the number of network sites increased.

## The Politics of Networking

The problem of LAN interconnectivity has been exacerbated by many organizational incongruities within firms, too. In many companies, the central MIS department was not even consulted or involved in the process of building and connecting LANs. It was all handled by the department(s) needing the connectivity. This resulted in new sub-networks being deployed in an ad hoc fashion as requirements dictated.

The politics have gotten messy in some cases. The LAN people did not trust the MIS people to support them, because the MIS group did not really understand PCs and LANs. The MIS department preferred that all applications be put on the mainframe and did not sanction and support LANs, but they also did not want little mini-networks springing up all across the company.

Talk of consolidating these disparate applications onto a single network only raised political red flags. Getting the two sides to talk together and work towards a single, highly efficient solution was often compared to negotiating Middle East peace. And the language barrier did not help matters. For example, a 'host' in the traditional centralized environment means a mainframe, but to a LAN manager means any server-device on the LAN. To make matters more complicated, a single device could be either a client or server at different moments in time.

## *Parallel Networking*

The solution for companies needing to connect LANs across distances was often a new, parallel network just for the LAN file transfers. It was not — and is not still — unusual for a company to already support more than one 9.6K bps leased line into a remote location to meet the peak requirements of the transactional applications; the LAN connection added another leased line, usually a DS-0 operating at 56/64K bps.

The cost of running parallel networks is high. Not only are monthly recurring leased line expenditures driven up when applications cannot share a single facility, but administration and operations costs are driven up as well.

*Parallel Networks*

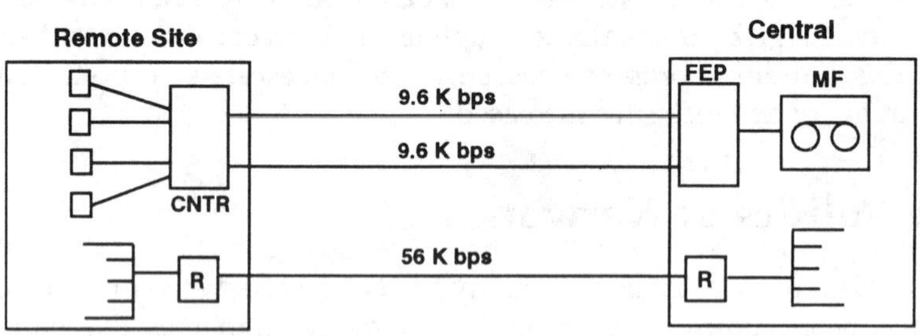


*Fig.2.6: Parallel networks prevent SNA and LAN applications from sharing a wide area network.*

This solution was necessary, however, in order to keep the LAN traffic from impacting the performance of the mission critical and delay-sensitive SNA traffic.

### *Negotiating Peace Treaties*

Fortunately, changes over the past three years have resulted in significant changes for both the centralized and the distributed application support groups.

The PC and the LAN are no longer considered rebel devices. MIS departments in most organizations now support the deployment and ongoing operation of both PCs and LANs. They will also take responsibility for connecting the LANs together, leveraging the existing high-speed backbone network where possible. Both groups have realized that there is a certain set of applications for which the PC and the LAN are very well suited, while there are plenty of other applications that work best in a centralized, mainframe environment. In order to support the LAN internetwork, many MIS departments have made staffing modifications, by adding new people who are PC and LAN experts, providing training to existing personnel, or both.

LAN users have also gained new perspective. Where LANs have sprung up to meet a specific department 's need, LAN users often find the growing complexity of these applications and the network configuration cannot be supported on an ad hoc, part-time basis by untrained personnel. Help is needed, and the MIS department is the logical place to look for that help. Budgetary pressures force all departments to consider options for keeping the cost of LAN interconnectivity in check.

The end result is that it is now more common for companies to be considering common LAN and SNA support and network consolidation. Having a single group in charge of network planning, operation and optimization makes good business sense, especially where cost containment is a corporate objective. Consolidation of LAN and SNA applications can save money, if the resulting network can insure the integrity of the mission-critical transaction applications.

## *Bridges and Routers*

*Network capacity is expensive, at least on the wide area network, and efficient use of this capacity helps to save money and increase network performance. A great deal of this increased performance can result from effective selection of equipment at the ends of the WAN.*

*Commonly, both bridges and routers can be used to connect LANs together.*

### *Bridges*

*Bridges were the first devices to hit the streets for LAN-to-LAN connectivity. Bridges operate at layer 2 of the OSI model. The only intelligence that a bridge will apply to the process of filtering traffic is to determine whether a packet stays on its LAN or goes to another (any other) LAN on the network. Other than this very simple filter, the bridge does not help to route the traffic to its specific internetwork destination.*

*Bridges operate at the lower half of the data link layer, called the MAC layer (media access control layer) in the OSI model. The technology and filtering system of the bridge is fairly simple, making bridges less expensive than their more intelligent cousin, the router. The bridge is a good internetworking solution within campus or building environments, where capacity is much less expensive compared to its cost on the wide area network. It is also a good solution where no level 3 protocols are in use, such as with many of IBM's early protocols and with DEC LAT.*

### *Routers*

*Routers operate at the network protocol layer, or layer three, in the OSI model. Routers have a more sophisticated filtering and routing system than the bridge and usually cost more. Since the filtering and routing technology is more advanced in the router, the device makes better use of expensive wide area network capacity. Routers work best with routable protocols like TCP/IP, AppleTalk and Novell IPX; however non-routable protocols can also be handled. This is done through encapsulation or by bridging these protocols via other features in the router.*

### *Networking LANs*

*The overhead and unnecessary traffic generated by a bridged network, when a file needs to be sent to a remote destination and the specific address is not known by the sending bridge, is very high. The bridge sends out explorer packets, and assumes that the first acknowledgement received represents the fastest explorer packet — or the most direct route. It then uses this same route for sending the file. These explorer packets create overhead on the network and can sometimes increase network congestion. It would be much more efficient if the bridge could preselect the route, without sending out explorer packets. This is where routers come into play.*

*Routers grew out of a need for a more intelligent bridge device. The router has a more sophisticated filtering and forwarding system than a bridge. It "routes" traffic to its correct destination by sending the packet to the correct remote LAN. Because it is more sophisticated in its filtering process and is able to select a specific route to a specific destination, the router reduces the overall level of unnecessary network overhead traffic and can improve performance on the WAN.*

*As a rule of thumb, companies use bridges to connect LANs within the same building, especially where network congestion on the LANs is not a problem. Routers work well to connect remote LANs together across a wide area network, where bandwidth is more costly.*

*However, if you have only a few sites to connect over a WAN and cost is a factor, a bridge could still be a very good solution.*

### *Boundary Routing and the Branch Office*

*The newest trend is toward developing router solutions for small branch offices. Network equipment vendors are introducing routing software that can operate on a server, small routers low in cost and designed to support a few users, and router-boards for insertion into PCs/servers. The result is lower cost routing solutions for many remote locations.*

## The Nature of Intermittent Data Applications

The second piece of the puzzle for understanding why frame relay emerged, and how it helps improve network performance and efficiency, is to understand the nature of data applications and the shortcomings of traditional solutions. You often hear the phrase, "data is bursty." What exactly does that mean, and so what?

No application, including voice and video, is really a constant stream of traffic. In fact, the whole theory of voice compression is to take a single conversation, split the speech into its natural "speech bursts" and then use the dead space between speech bursts to transport bursts from another conversation.

Data is also bursty and intermittent, meaning that sometimes data needs to be sent and sometimes it does not, like your telephone, which you are sometimes using and other times allowing to set idle. The PBX does not allow a phone not in use to take up wide area network capacity. It only allocates network space to a phone when the phone is in use.

It makes sense to do the same with data. LAN traffic patterns are intermittent, meaning that users are not all trying to send or receive information at the same time between remote locations. In fact, there could be long periods of many milliseconds, seconds or minutes, where no WAN traffic is generated at all from or to a particular remote location.

LAN applications are also bursty. Although not everyone uses the network at exactly the same time, when they do need the network, the transaction or file transfer could be very big or very small. If a large file needs to be transmitted to a remote LAN, the file transmission can take a longer time to be squeezed through a low-speed connection, or the transmission can take a shorter time and be sent more quickly through a higher speed connection.

Bursty and intermittent data traffic is not the sole property of LAN environments. Transaction-oriented applications, including SNA-based applications, are bursty and intermittent if you eliminate a great deal of the polling that takes place among network devices.[1]

### *Peak-to-Average Transmission Ratio*

The idea of bursty data is not a new science. What is "new" in the context of today's applications and high speed data services is the chasm between the average and peak traffic volumes. In the early days of data transmission over a wide area network, the average transmission requirement might have been 7.4K bps and the peak requirement 9.6K bps. Today, the average requirement for a network site, or even a single application, might be 64K with a peak of several megabits. The nature of applications is changing, from small terminal-to-host transactions to large LAN-to-LAN file transfers. The result of larger files is greater network delay. The ratio of average to peak requirements has also scaled upwards, and it is in dealing with these situations that high speed public data services can be useful.

### *Implication For The Wide Area Network*

Ideally, the wide area network that supports bursty and intermittent applications would expand or contract to meet the needs of the users at any given point in time.

A look at traditional solutions for the WAN, in light of the above discussion on data applications, will provide insight into why frame relay can be a better solution for supporting the applications in some data networks.

## The Shortcomings of Dedicated Connections

The history lesson is not complete until we also look at the history of long-distance networking and transmission solutions. In this environment the legacy is voice. The public telephone network, and most of today's wide area network services, were initially designed for voice applications. This has an enormous impact on the solutions available to us today for addressing data networking challenges.

For example, why is a single DS-0 able to transport 64K bps worth of information? Why not more? Or less? The answer lies in voice. It was found long ago that to accurately reproduce a person's speech over an electronic medium, it is necessary to sample that speech pattern 8000 times every second. The sample itself is an 8-bit byte, and 8000 x 8 = 64,000 bps!

***The Beginning Of Analog Transmission***

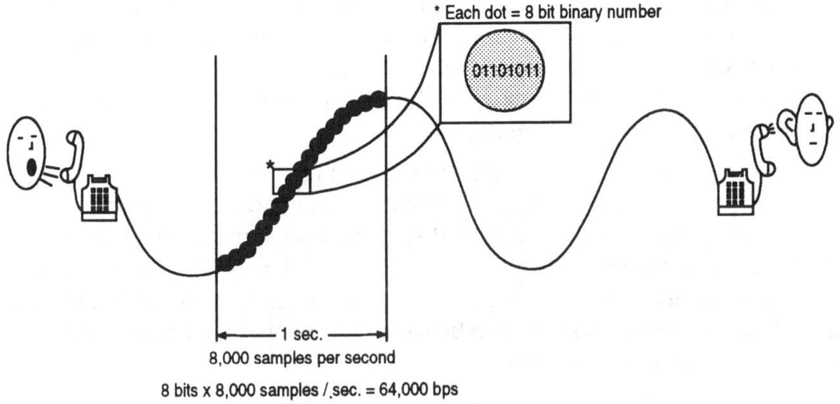


*Fig. 2.7: A single voice grade frequency connection, a DS-0, operates at 64K bps due to the original speech pattern sampling procedures which take 8000 8-bit samples every second.*

The effects of the voice legacy don't stop here. In the US digital hierarchy, for example, 24 DS-0s make up a DS-1, and 28 DS-1s (or 672 DS-0s) make up a DS-3. So you see that the wide area networking infrastructure is really designed for transporting voice applications, and today's data applications have been working in and around these definitions. If the initial application for wide area networking would have been data, the resulting infrastructure may have looked much different. It may have looked like X.25, frame relay, or cell relay.

Still, a legacy system is a legacy system, and everyone works with what they have. The digital hierarchy for the WAN is based on a process called "time division multiplexing" (TDM). With TDM, a multiplexer or channel bank divides a circuit into individual channels that are dedicated to certain user applications or communications paths. TDM resembles a Gatling gun with 24 chambers, wherein each channel has a shot at the transmission barrel on a predetermined rotation basis.

Each channel is given a certain time slot for communications. Again using the US standard as an example, TDM equipment would break a single DS-1 (i.e., T-1) link with 1.536M bps[2] worth of connectivity into 24 chunks to get 24 64K bps links (24 X 64K = 1.536M). Even if information does not need to be transmitted over a given DS-0 link, the process continues and the capacity is "wasted." Other users, or applications, cannot access this capacity, because the configuration is static. The allocation of the network capacity cannot change in real time to meet the dynamic requirements of the applications being supported. If one application doesn't really need its time division slot at a given time period, the capacity just sits idle. It can't be used by other applications in other time slots, even if those applications might need to transmit a great deal of information.

As an example, imagine a primary site that must connect with many remote locations, all for the exchange of data. A snapshot of the network usage at any point in time will probably show that some of the lines are actively transmitting data, while others are idle. For the channels transmitting data, it could very well be that more data needs to be transmitted over the dedicated connection than can be sent all at once, so some of the data using this circuit will be delayed.

***Static Bandwidth Allocation With Time Division Multiplexing***

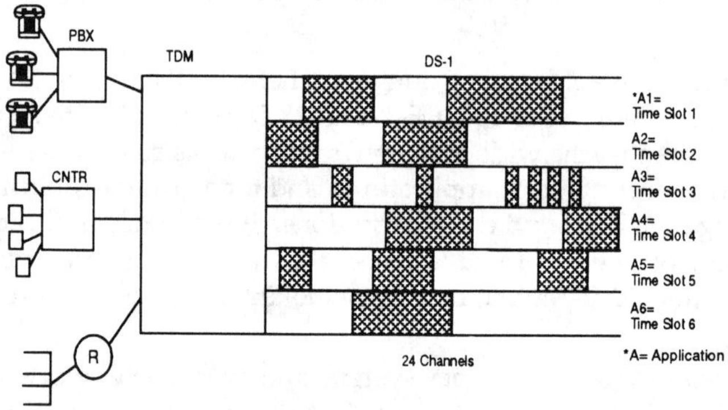


*Fig. 2.8: TDM networks use fixed time slots, which results in a static allocation of bandwidth. Unused capacity, as represented by the white spaces, cannot be reallocated to benefit active connections, so instead the capacity is "wasted."*

What a shame that the network cannot be more intelligent in its use of this capacity, allocating capacity from idle channels towards those channels needing it at the time.

## X.25

As data applications began to emerge in the early 1970s, the US government funded work on developing a protocol and networking solution for transporting data over distances. The X.25 protocol emerged. It was developed to overcome the problems inherent in transmitting data over low quality copper wires that are noisy and have a higher propensity to cause errors on the line and damage data packets. X.25 uses statistical, not time division, multiplexing. This allows capacity to be allocated dynamically to meet real-time changes in connectivity requirements.

Consider the environment in the 1970s, and you will see that X.25 was an ideal solution to solve many of that era's data communications challenges. There was basically one nationwide network — AT&T's — and it was largely copper-based. MCI was just emerging with its microwave and copper-based network, but was yet to be a major market force. Network lines were noisy, meaning there was a high degree of background sound generated by the underlying equipment and picked up from outside sources.

The transmission lines and the supporting equipment were not very reliable. Transmissions were likely to be damaged by the network. Remember that the network is transmitting information in the form of electrical signals. If an electrical positive pulse is not transmitted as a positive pulse, then a "1" might end up being interpreted by the equipment as a "0." In transmitting a voice conversation, a few of these network errors would go largely unnoticed by the parties on either end. But with data applications, changing the value of a digit is not acceptable.

Therefore, if data files were to be successfully and reliably transmitted, a solution for checking transmission accuracy and for recovering any information damaged by the network during transmission had to be developed. SNA solved this problem within the network transmission protocol, because the underlying services were not reliable enough. X.25 sought to solve this problem within the network service.

The remote desktop equipment was not intelligent. The centralized processing environment used "dumb" terminals on the desktop because at the time this the most cost-effective way to provide remote users with access to centrally stored data. This equipment could not check incoming transmissions for errors, or notify the sending device of an error and the need for retransmission.

The X.25 protocol was designed specifically to solve these problems. The protocol operates at the link layer (layer 2) as well as layer 3 and utilizes a sophisticated and thorough procedure for checking to see if the transmission facilities have damaged a file during transmission. Files are formatted into "packets" with addressing information on where the packet is going, and from where it is coming. When an X.25 network switch receives a packet, it checks to see if the packet has arrived without being damaged. It does this by running an algorithmic equation. This is called "error checking." A copy of each packet is stored by the X.25 switch before it is sent out onto the network for the next switch. The reason for making such a copy of the packet is that if the packet is damaged during transmission, another copy can be resent to that switch. This is "error correction."

The benefit with X.25 was that data communications could be reliably achieved over a WAN using the X.25 protocol. And X.25 could support high speeds of 9.6K, 19.2K, and the then-incredible speed of 56K bps. The cost of the solution was the added overhead and processing the protocol imposes on the transmission to achieve this high level of reliability. The benefits more than outweighed the costs at the time.

In fact, the Defense Department was impressed enough with the protocol that it commissioned the ARPAnet, a network based on X.25 to support the transmission of data applications. This eventually grew into what we know today as the Internet (which in today's reincarnation uses primarily TCP/IP, not X.25). In addition, the carriers moved to implement nationwide X.25 networks for commercial customers, as more businesses implemented applications requiring a highly reliable and secure underlying data transmission service.

## The Advent of Fiber and Intelligent CPE

During the 1980s, more U.S. carriers emerged, and sophisticated fiber optic networks were installed throughout the U.S. Fiber optic lines significantly increase the quality of transmission. These transmission lines are very quiet, and very little background noise intercedes the communication path. As networks became more reliable, the likelihood of the fiber network mis-transmitting a digit and thereby damaging a packet was reduced. The result is an infrastructure much better suited to the transmission of data applications.

Simultaneously, the shift in processing power discussed above resulted in intelligent desktop devices that would perform error recovery. It no longer was necessary for the wide area network to perform this function.

The problems which X.25 initially solved so elegantly are no longer problems, at least in the U.S. This is not to say that X.25 will not be around for a long time, or that it is not a very good solution for some network environments. Neither could be further from the truth. X.25 will remain a cost-effective and viable alternative for applications that require low speed connectivity among many locations, domestically and/or worldwide or where value-added services such as protocol conversion, remote polling or access control are needed.

However, for applications requiring lower delay and utilizing underlying network facilities which are highly reliable, X.25's costs — such as increased delay from higher processing overhead — may be greater than the benefits offered. A new generation of packet switching protocols has emerged to pick up where X.25 leaves off.

## The Need for Frame Relay

Frame relay was created to specifically address the changing needs of emerging data applications; dynamic, fast-paced business and computing environments; and the shift in processing power. It also emerged to take advantage of reliable fiber optic networks.

Frame relay does not impose rigid time slots on network connections like TDM does, and it can respond quickly to chaotic transmission needs. This makes it ideal for the support of intermittent and bursty data environments, like LAN and SNA.

Frame relay allows a single physical network interface to support many logical connections. It uses virtual connections that offer the security of a leased line but also allow network capacity to be dynamically allocated.

Frame relay strips out a lot of the overhead processing, such as error correction, performed at the network layer by the X.25 protocol. It instead leaves this function to the intelligent premises equipment on each end of the connection. Frame relay is a streamlined version of X.25 in that it only uses layers one and two in the OSI model, and not layer three.

The advent and deployment of fiber optic transmission, personal computers, and bridges and routers are what make frame relay possible. The reliability of the underlying transmission facilities is so high with fiber optic networks that the percentage of damaged frames is very low. This means that the error correction offered by X.25 is unnecessary; the end points rather than the network can recover from infrequent errors. By eliminating the unnecessary functionality, frame relay can operate more efficiently and more quickly.

The development of the intelligence in CPE, and the higher-layer network protocols, was a critical prerequisite. The error correction function must still exist; it just is not necessarily needed within the wide area network. By pushing this function to the edges of the network, the network is freed up to process more frames, more quickly, compared with X.25.

Similarly, private networks based on time division multiplexing require a high level of up-front investment in equipment, network and staff. In the '70s and '80s, companies had few available alternatives. The carriers simply did not offer the types and levels of service mandatory for corporate networks carrying mission-critical business applications. Therefore, corporations had to become little phone companies, creating departments specifically to build and manage the corporate network.

### *Impact on the Business*

Today's business environment is different from what it was in decades past. Companies must be nimble and quick. Global competition and competitive price pressures mean that costs must be constantly controlled. The old, hierarchical organizational structure is slowly giving way because of competitive pressures to bring goods to market more quickly, produce products and services more economically, and use resources more efficiently.

Companies are embracing the concept of highly mobile cross-functional teams — or work groups — to facilitate certain business processes such as new product development. These teams must be able to come together quickly, perform the task at hand, and then disband. Resources must be allocated quickly, without regard for distance and geography.

A single team may be made up of members from marketing, engineering, sales, management, finance, information systems, and other departments. The members may not all be located in the same city or country. The team members may even work for different companies. This is the true virtual corporation.

Communication between team members is critical. They must be able to collaborate on a variety of documents, hold brainstorming sessions and team meetings, develop presentations and product definitions, and do much more.

### *Stress in the Corporate Communications Infrastructure*

Communications throughout the whole organization is growing more critical. The ability to support sales people, customers and internal departments is more dependent upon the network than ever before. It becomes more difficult to separate the business from the network. One cannot exist without the other. Once in place, the business and the network feed one another, each causing the other to grow in a synergistic relationship.

The pressures of a slow growing economy coupled with increased global competition are driving businesses to release extraneous costs and focus resources on the core business. LAN interconnectivity, cross-functional work groups, remote database applications, the move towards computer-aided design and engineering, and the shift in processing power all place the traditional corporate network infrastructure under significant stress.

It may no longer be optimal to run a large in-house telecommunications company. In fact, what many corporations are discovering is that in-house telecommunications managers are better deployed as strategic resources. They should look forward and develop networking solutions that help the company operate and compete more effectively. The network is becoming a highly strategic resource, and someone needs to proactively manage this aspect of the business.

Some or all of the day-to-day management of the network might be left to the carrier, which is one advantage offered by frame relay services. The carrier delivers a more complete network solution and takes responsibility for delivering pre-defined levels of connectivity, availability, management, and support. You manage the carrier, freeing up more time to focus on the core business and strategic planning.

## The Business Advantages of Frame Relay

When a company is changing or growing rapidly, and the network must keep pace, a dedicated private network may not offer all of the flexibility that you need. When both traditional terminal to host transactions and LAN file transfers must be supported on the wide area network, running segregated systems may be too costly and inefficient. Frame relay may be the solution — or part of the solution.

Frame relay operates at high speeds like a dedicated private line circuit. And the logical connectivity of frame relay offers security equivalent to a dedicated circuit. However, frame relay also offers many of the advantages of the public X.25 networks. Like X.25, frame relay is specifically designed to transport data applications. It is good for many-to-many connectivity requirements, and it allows a more efficient allocation of network capacity for data applications than private circuits.

Frame relay operates optimally with LANs and other synchronous data applications. Frame relay offers:

- A data-oriented solution designed specifically to meet the chaotic transmission requirements of local area networks, while still supporting SNA (as covered in a later chapter).
- A low level of network processing to streamline transmissions and improve network throughput.
- An efficient and highly flexible wide area network.
- A solution to reduce or eliminate segregated/parallel networks.
- High-speed, highly secure, many-to-many connectivity.
- A service, not just a transmission solution, including critical elements for network operation and support.

Frame relay is specifically designed to fit the characteristics of bursty and intermittent data applications. It addresses the unique needs that emerged with the advent of the PC and the LAN.

With frame relay, the carrier invests in the equipment and sets up the public frame relay network. The public — which means you — then leverages the carrier's investment in switching equipment and network facilities by buying a share of the network.

Frame relay addresses many of the weaknesses inherent in private networking solutions based on time division multiplexing. It allows a more intelligent allocation of network capacity, because it statistically multiplexes bursts of data from one source with bursts of data from other sources. Network capacity is allocated in real time, to meet the changing requirements of the applications and users sharing the network.

Frame relay services allow the strategic resources of a corporation to be more fluidly allocated. It can free network personnel up to concentrate on the core business and future direction of the company's communications. It can also help improve overall company connectivity and competitiveness.

Frame relay addresses the many historical problems and trends discussed in the beginning of this chapter.

- **Processing Power Shift:** Frame relay is designed for distributed environments and meets the communications needs that grew out of the deployment of processing power to the desktop.

*Frame Relay Allows Dynamic Bandwidth Allocation*

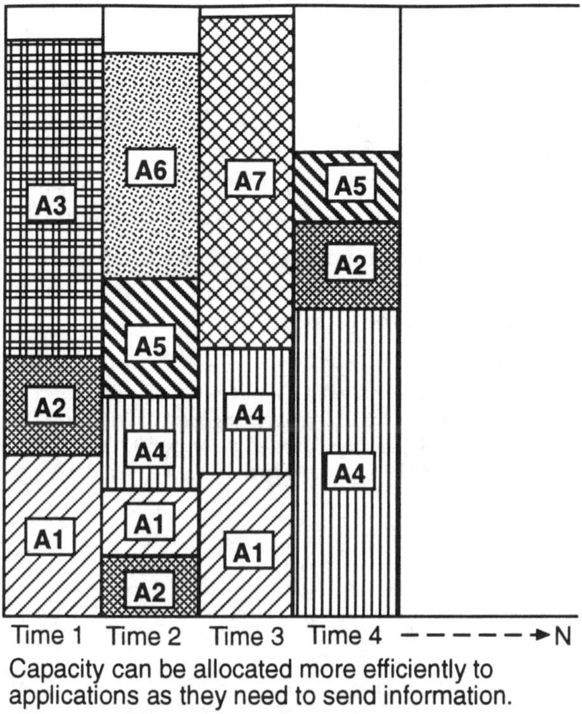


*Fig. 2.9: Frame relay does not hold applications to a static level of network capacity. Instead, it allocates bandwidth in real time to meet the changing needs of the applications being supported.*

- **LAN Interconnectivity:** Because frame relay allows a single physical interface to support multiple logical connections to many remote sites, it provides a cost-effective solution for partial and fully meshed LAN networks. The number of router ports, CSU/DSUs, and local loops needed for mesh connectivity is significantly reduced.

- **TDM:** Unlike the static bandwidth allocation of time division multiplexing, frame relay dynamically allocates network capacity to more efficiently utilize network resources and improve the performance of applications.

- **X.25:** Frame relay strips away the overhead processing for error correction included in X.25 networks, no longer necessary because of the deployment of digital facilities and fiber networks.
- **Parallel Networks:** Frame relay allows previously segregated network facilities for SNA and LAN networks to be physically consolidated. Traffic prioritization and the use of separate logical connections can still provide logical separation of the traffic, while saving money on access, IXC and operations costs.

In the following chapters, you will gain a more complete understanding of the technology of frame relay, frame relay public network services, and how to design and implement a frame relay network.

[1] *Many of the SNA over frame relay solutions available today significantly reduce the amount of polling overhead across the wide area network by terminating most of the polling locally.*
[2] *A DS-1 has a transmission rate of 1.544M bps. However, the user throughput is at best equivalent to 24 time slots times 64K bps, or 1.536M bps. The remaining 8M bps is overhead for the DS-1 line.*

CHAPTER 3:

# FRAME RELAY DEFINED FOR NON-ENGINEERS

One often hears frame relay referred to as a "fast packet" service. Frame relay is one of two main categories of fast packet services, a term coined early in the market's development but used much less today. The two fast packet categories are: frame relay, which uses variable length packet sizes; and cell relay, which uses fixed length packet sizes.

Many public frame relay network services accept a frame relay interface but utilize cell relay as the switching fabric on the network backbone, because of the added efficiencies gained at extremely high-speeds with cell relay.

## Frame Relay Functionality

The best way to understand frame relay is in terms of the OSI (Open Systems Interconnection) model. The OSI model specifies seven layers of functionality. Each layer draws from the layer above it, and provides a set of services to the layers below it. Each layer may have many protocols defined to work within it, to provide the various services specified for that layer.

Frame relay is a data link layer protocol, meaning that it operates at layer two of the OSI model. The data link layer is itself actually two different layers, the MAC (Media Access Control) layer and the data link, or just link, layer. Frame relay operates at the lower part of layer two, the link layer.

Layer two is also used by other bit-oriented synchronous protocols, such as HDLC (high-speed data link control) and SDLC (synchronous data link control). The frame formats for these protocols are nearly identical to frame relay; what is different is the purpose of the information contained in each field. The similarity of structure provides an important development advantage to frame relay, because equipment already supporting HDLC and/or SDLC can be easily and quickly modified by manufacturers to support frame relay.

***Frame Relay In The OSI Model***

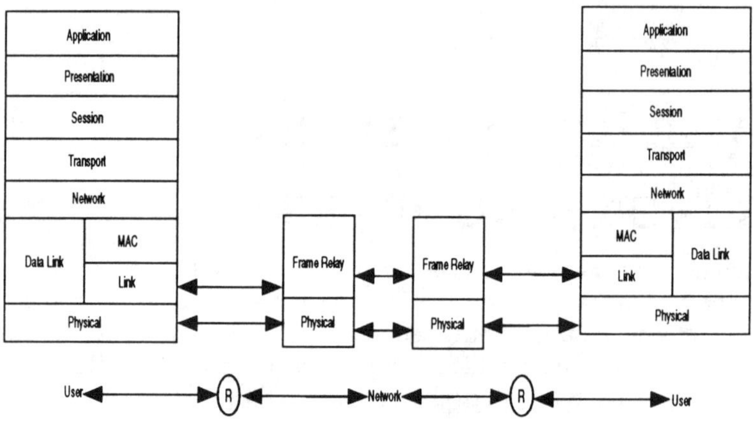


*Fig. 3.1: Frame relay operates at layer two of the OSI model.*

Frame relay uses an adaption of the Link Access Procedure-D, also called Link Access Protocol (LAP-D) as defined for layer two, called LAP-F. The LAP-F specification for frame relay is a subset of the LAP-D protocol specified in the standard's Q.921 on Digital Subscriber Signaling Systems, because it does not require the network to perform error recovery, as specified in Q.921.

The "core functions" of the frame relay specification, as performed in layer two by LAP-D, call for:

- Checking frames for validity on frame size.
- Generating and using the frame check sequence to verify accurate transmission (but not invoking corrective procedures for errored frames).
- Discarding damaged/inaccurate or invalid frames (but the intelligent end equipment is expected to handle the recovery).
- Frame delimiting, alignment and transparency.
- Frame multiplexing and demultiplexing.

Protocol functions such as sequencing, window sizing, acknowledgments and supervisory frames, are not performed by frame relay, but instead are handled at higher layers. By "stripping" these functions out of the frame relay frame handling responsibilities, transmissions can occur more rapidly, and throughput increases.

This is not to say that these important functions are ignored. They are simply not performed by the frame relay protocol or switching equipment. A combination of the higher layer protocols and the intelligent end equipment controls the end-to-end transmission and maintains responsibility for error correction, windowing, sequencing, etc.

Frame relay's LAP-F was chosen because most of the data protocols likely to utilize frame relay on a WAN also conform to this frame format under LAP-D, including TCP/IP and DECnet, in addition to HDLC and SDLC, as referenced above.

The LAP-D/F services can provide either acknowledged or unacknowledged frame transfer service to layer three, depending upon whether the layer three information on frame sequencing will be sent in the frame. The latter mode of operation is most common, with frame relay also supporting some error and flow control functions.

## Frame Relay Format

The frame relay frame format is quite simple. First, there is a flag indicating the beginning of a frame. Then there are two overhead octets[1] at the front end of the frame, and two at the tail end, for a total of 4 octets of overhead for each frame, plus the flag. For large file transfers, this low overhead ratio makes frame relay a very efficient transmission mechanism.

*Frame Relay Format*

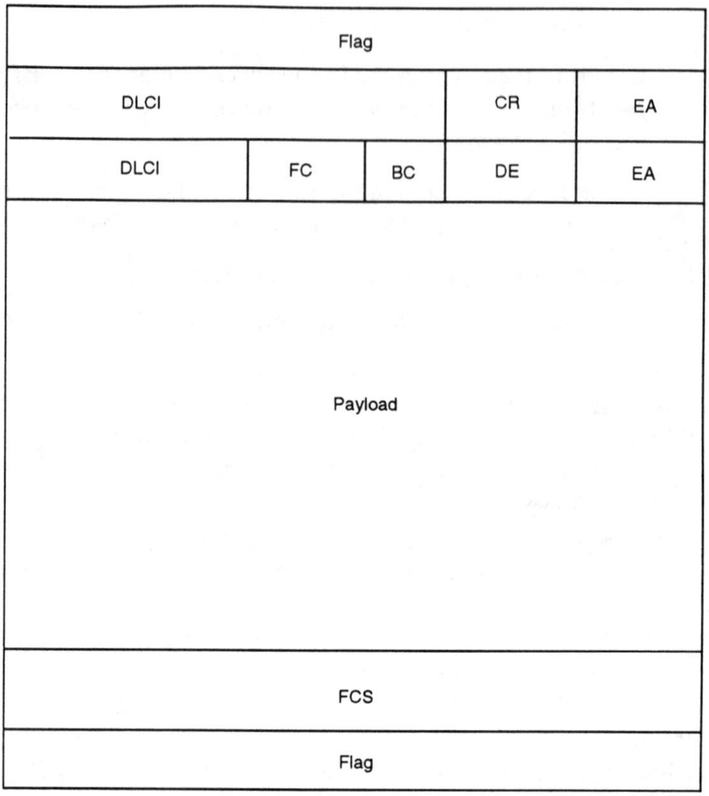


*Fig. 3.2: The frame relay format consists of overhead bytes and the payload.*

Don't let the acronyms throw you. It's really quite simple.

- The flag(s) tells the network equipment that a new frame is beginning.
- The next 6 bits are the first part of the address that the frame is destined towards. This address information is called the Data Link Connection Identifier because it specifically points to, or identifies, a PVC on the frame relay network. This is a 10-bit field spread across two octets. The DLCI will be read by the network and will be cross referenced in a routing table to the

correct logical connection providing connectivity to that port. Certain DLCI addresses are reserved for use by the network, as discussed later.

- The next bit is called the Command/Response bit, either a "zero" or a "one," and currently is not used by the protocol.
- The last bit in the octet is one of two Extended Address bits, which will allow the DLCI addressing structure to be expanded to handle more addresses. Again, this is a binary bit.
- The last octet in the header contains the last 4 bits of the DLCI.
- The next two bits are the Forward and Backward Congestion Notification bits, known as FECN and BECN (pronounced "fekin" and "bekin"). The purpose of these bits is to help with congestion control.
- The Discard Eligibility, or DE, bit is used to indicate when frames are sent in excess of the CIR and can be discarded by the network in the case of congestion.
- The last bit is the second Extended Address bit.

Then comes the actual payload. When a router or frame relay device receives an incoming packet, the MAC or LLC layer protocol overhead (i.e., the Ethernet or Token Ring packet overhead) is stripped off of the packet before being encapsulated into the payload. The overhead from the application layer and from the network layer, like the TCP/IP or SDLC overhead information, is left intact. At the destination the process is reversed. The frame relay overhead is stripped away and the packet overhead for the LAN protocol is again added so that the packet can be forwarded to the correct address.

The last two octets in the frame are again overhead.

- These two octets are called the Frame Check Sequence and provide a cell check for damage to the frame (Recall that damaged frames are discarded and not transmitted by the network).
- Following the last octet are the flags that signal the end of that frame and the beginning of the next one.

Frame relay supports variable length, as opposed to fixed length, packet sizes. In other words, the frame size (specifically, the payload) will be as large, or as small, as needed to transmit the information.

It gets a bit more complicated than this in practice, because higher layer protocols and LAN protocols will impose certain packet size restrictions. For example, the largest Ethernet packet size is 1500 bytes. Therefore, the largest frame size in an Ethernet environment will also be 1500 bytes, even if the file itself is much larger. In these cases, the file is broken down into 1500-byte or smaller units for transmission. The frame relay overhead is added to this.

## *FECN, BECN and Flow Control*

Explicit messages indicating congestion on the network have been built into the frame relay specification. Not all equipment vendors fully support FECN/BECN, and neither do all higher layer protocols. The result is that you cannot rely solely on this aspect of the frame relay standard for adequate flow control at this time.

The most effective way to establish flow control in your frame relay network will be through the level 3 and higher protocols used by your application. Nearly every off-the-shelf protocol — such as TCP/IP, IPX, DECnet, etc. — will have its own mechanism to control the flow of information over the WAN. This is done by timing the rate at which acknowledgments to transmitted frames are received, and adjusting the window size accordingly.

For example, if frames are being acknowledged at a rate during the beginning of a transmission that indicates an effective throughput rate of 128K bps, but then the acknowledgments begin to slow down, the protocol will interpret this as congestion on the network. It will react by reducing the window size.

The window size refers to the number of outstanding frames that can be sent out on to the network before an acknowledgment must be received. The larger the window, the more frames that can be sent, and the better the throughput rate. If the protocol senses congestion, it will decrease the window size, sending fewer frames out at once, and waiting for an acknowledgment before more are sent. In this way, the flow of the information is controlled.

The carriers have mechanisms to control congestion in the public network. Your best bet for complementing these capabilities and controlling the flow of your own applications in response to network congestion is through the flow control mechanisms provided in your level 3 and higher functions.

Now is when FECN and BECN come in. The FECN and BECN congestion notification bits were designed so that the network would have a mechanism for communicating the existence and direction of congestion to a customer's premises equipment (CPE). The idea was that the CPE would then notify the application of this congestion, and that the application/traffic source would restrict the rate at which it released information for transmission.

While this works great in theory, there is one big problem in practice. Even if the equipment can recognize the FECN and BECN bits, a mechanism for communicating this to the traffic source is not well established. Nor are procedures with higher layer protocols in place for interpreting the FECN and BECN bits into a change in the window size.

Some equipment vendors have established mechanisms within the router to react to FECN/BECN messages upon receiving them from the network, at least for certain protocols. If a particular network path is congested, the router can temporarily hold the packets destined for that path, lowering the effective throughput rate. This becomes a prioritization technique for traffic within the router. After being buffered in response to FECN/BECN messages, the packets that are then released are more likely to be within the CIR, and would therefore not be marked by the network as discard-eligible. It should be stressed, however, that the primary flow control management will stem from the higher layer protocols.

FECN/BECN bits can be used as an additional network management tool. The router can track the number of FECN/BECN messages received, and this can provide information on the health of the network and provide design guidance.

Just for the record, the forward notification, FECN, is sent by the switch to indicate congestion in the same direction of the received frame. The backward notification, BECN, is sent by the switch to indicate congestion in the opposite direction of the received frame.

### *User Network Interface (UNI) and Network-to-Network Interface (NNI)*

The frame relay specifications outline two types of interfaces — a user-to-network interface (UNI) and a network-to-network interface (NNI).

You will use a user-to-network interface. This is how a router[2] (or other frame relay access device) will communicate with a public frame relay network. The premises equipment can use the local management interface (LMI) protocol over the UNI in order to communicate with the network and ascertain the status of individual logical connections (see LMI below).

With a UNI connection, a frame relay access device (FRAD) is connected to a frame relay network device (FRND). An NNI connects FRNDs.

The NNI was designed as a more effective way to interconnect two public frame relay networks and allow traffic to pass between the networks. This is particularly useful in connecting RBOC frame relay networks with those of the IXCs, for example. The NNI includes some special functionality, such as the ability of each network to query the other network regarding the status of logical network connections.

Carriers do not need an NNI in order to connect two frame relay networks. However the NNI does provide some benefits to the carriers, such as bidirectional polling for network status, which can only be achieved unidirectionally with a UNI connection.

### *DLCI Addressing*

DLCIs are logical pointers, or addresses, and they identify a virtual connection. The DLCI is a label for the virtual connection, but is not the connection itself — like Route 66 is the name of the highway but not the highway itself. Often, however, you will hear these terms used interchangeably. With 10 bits available in the address, each port can recognize up to 1024 different DLCIs.

The DLCI address holds local, not global, significance. This means that the same DLCI number can be reused throughout the network at different port connections. Every port can have 1024 other remote ports it can identify and communicate with. The current 10 bit address does not pose a practical address limitation for most networks.

The number of unique addresses can be increased with the use of the extended addressing (EA) bits, if frame relay networks grow large enough to require this level of addressing. The EA bit is currently not supported by any vendors.

The DLCI tables in the router will cross reference a destination address with a DLCI. The DLCI points to a particular destination port on the network. The frame relay switch will read the destination DLCI and use its own table to cross reference the appropriate PVC to which the frame should be allocated. At the far end, the receiving frame relay switch will put the origination DLCI into the DLCI address slot, so that the receiving router will know the frame's origination point on the network.

In setting up your frame relay network, you cannot actually use all of the 1024 DLCIs at each port. Some are reserved for network-related signaling, such as the LMI, leaving 992 DLCIs for user connections. However, most of the DLCIs are available for your use. There is no secret or logic, really, to choosing DLCIs. Just start with a number, and work your way up. Some people will use area codes, cost center numbers, or a variety of other number assignments.

*Router Look Up Tables*

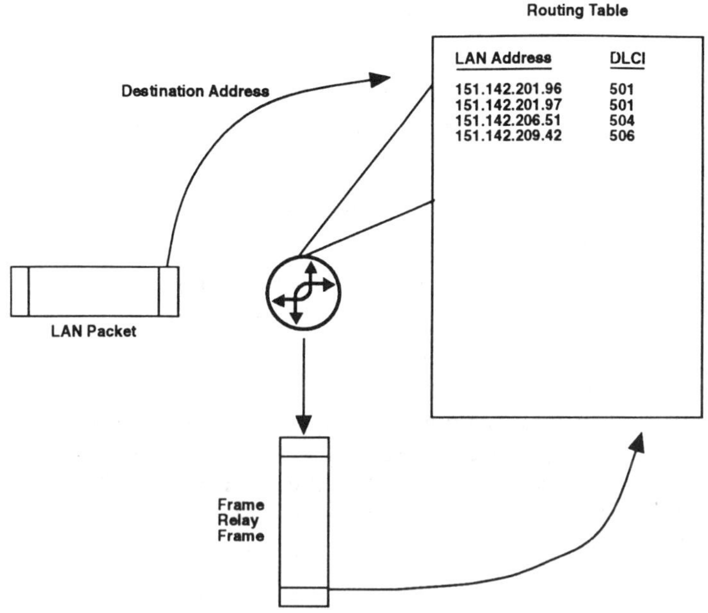


*Fig. 3.3: The router cross-references the destination address in the LAN packet with the appropriate DLCI before sending it onto the WAN.*

## The LMI

The local management interface (LMI) is a mechanism for communication between your equipment (i.e., the router or other access device) and the carrier's frame relay network.

DLCIs 0 and 1023 are reserved for the LMI, depending upon which version of the LMI is being used, as discussed below. The router can use this path to request network status information from the carrier's switch to which it is directly connected.

The initial LMI was developed as a keep-alive signal between the router and the frame relay network. A second generation of LMI called Annex D by ITU-TSS and an LMI called Annex A by ANSI, builds upon this framework by adding additional features that provide information on the health status of the network. You will implement one of the LMIs, probably the more advanced Annex A or D, in a given access device.

The router can use the LMI to:

- Request the status of active DLCIs and DLCIs that have been removed or are no longer active.
- Request the status of the local loop connection between the router and the port connection. The LMI offers a "keep-alive" signal between the router and the switch.
- Download network addresses to help simplify network configuration.

The vendors are also working to enhance the LMI to support CIR recognition for an individual PVC and to throttle the transmission rate of information to a given PVC if network congestion is occurring.

You should choose a router that supports LMI and you should enable the functionality within your network. LMI is an important part of implementation. For example, if you enable LMI, then when you add a new connection the two devices it connects will be automatically notified of its presence. When LMI is not enabled, each access device (and the network switch) must be manually updated.

## The Role of the Router

The formatting of a LAN, SDLC, X.25, TCP/IP or other data packet into a frame relay frame is done in the frame relay equipment. This is usually a router, bridge, multiplexer, concentrator or FRAD (frame relay assembler/disassembler). The packet enters the equipment, and is encapsulated into a frame relay frame by having the necessary flags, 2-byte header and 2-byte trailer added.

In order to determine where the frame should be sent, the router will read the destination address from the overhead of the incoming packet. It will then reference a lookup, table which will allow it to cross-reference this address information to a frame relay DLCI. The correct DLCI number will be placed into the DLCI address field, and the frame will be forwarded out to the carrier's network.

During this process, the router will look at the incoming packet and determine the protocol stack to which the frame must be handed off. For example, if the incoming packet is using TCP/IP, then the packet will go to the TCP/IP protocol stack for processing. AppleTalk packets will go to the AppleTalk stack, IPX to the IPX stack, etc. (Under RFC 1294, a special byte is designated for protocol ID.[3]) Any protocols that can't be routed at layer three can ordinarily be bridged by most routers, a function sometimes called brouting.

Like frame relay, LANs also operate at layer two. So, the LAN overhead must be removed and the frame relay overhead put in its place. After determining the packet protocol, the router will remove the LAN header, such as the ethernet or token ring packet header, before passing it to the protocol stack.

The protocol stack will then look at the destination address and will determine the LAN on which the address resides. It will then determine that LAN's DLCI and will apply the frame relay frame format with the appropriate DLCI for that destination on the network.

*Frame Formatting Process*

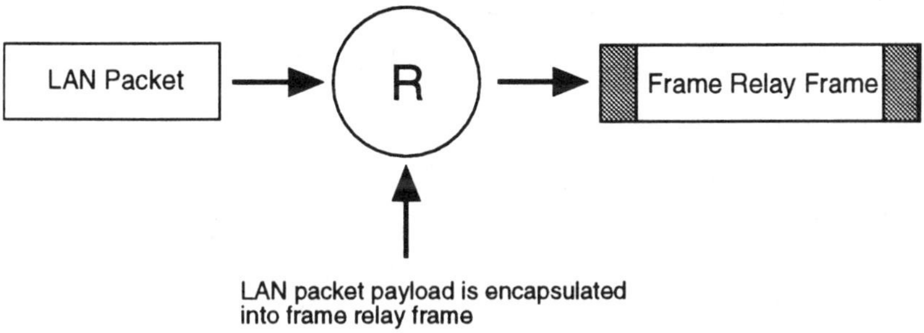


*Fig. 3.4: The LAN packet enters the wide area frame relay equipment, such as a router, and the LAN packet's payload is extracted and encapsulated into a frame relay format.*

The frame relay equipment in the carrier's network will read the DLCI and place the frame on the correct PVC. Once the frame reaches the destination, the equipment will strip off the frame relay format, read the local destination address, and forward the packet to its destination.

## The Backbone Network

Once your frame is handed to the carrier's network, it will be further processed. The address will be read, so that it can be forwarded to the correct logical connection, but that may not be all.

If your carrier is using a cell-relay switching fabric on its network backbone, and most carriers do today or soon will, the incoming frames will be divided into fixed-length cells. The DLCI address information will be translated into address information within the cell header. The cell header will also contain cell-count and sequence information, so that the complete frame can be reassembled at the destination node[4] before being sent to your premises equipment.

Each cell in a frame is placed onto your logical connection. The cells will travel in sequence. If any of the individual cells in a frame is damaged and discarded by the network, the entire frame must be discarded by the network. This means a retransmission of the frame might need to occur.

***End to End Connection***

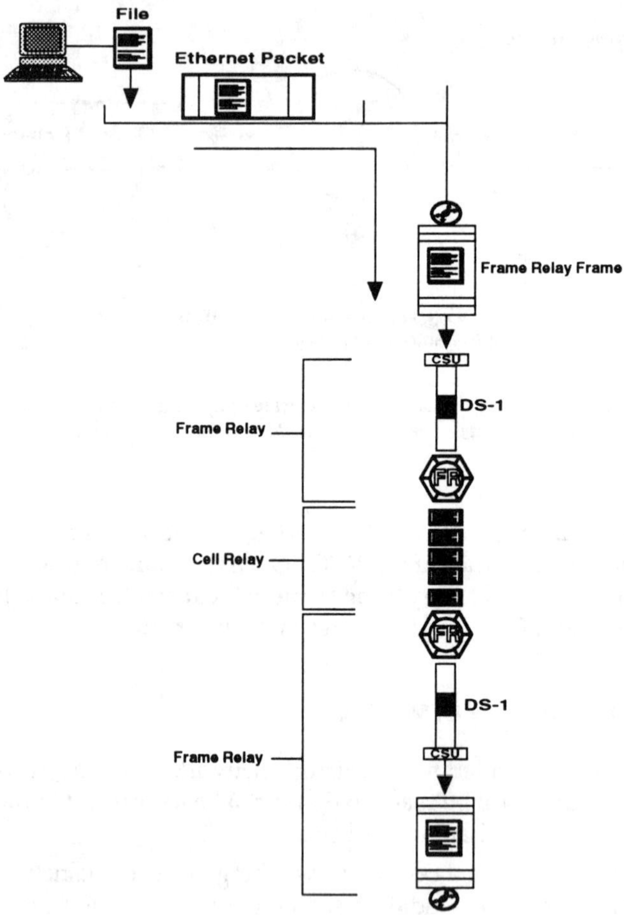


*Fig. 3.5: The router formats the packet into a frame relay format and passes it to the WAN where it may be split into cells. The reverse happens at the other end.*

The advantages of cell relay is that the initial frame relay switch does not have to wait for the entire frame to completely enter the switch before it begins transmitting the information to its remote destination. It must only wait for enough bytes to fill up one cell, and then that cell can be forwarded on to the network. This also applies for any intermediate switches your logical connection tandems through to reach its final destination. The advantage is decreased latency. If a large frame had to be stored until the entire frame was received by a switch before that switch could begin transmitting the frame, it would take longer to transmit. This is especially true for large frames.

The last switch in the network must reassemble the complete frame, and as such must wait until all of the cells making up that frame have arrived. This is the one place where the transmission will incur delay from this "store and forward" functionality. Once all the cells have been received, the switch will insure that the sequencing is correct, will strip off the cell format, and will reassemble the original frame. The frame is then placed on the local loop to be received by the CPE.

## Frame Relay Services

The next chapter will discuss frame relay services. A critical factor to keep in mind is that the frame relay specifications discussed above are *interface standards* and are not service specifications.

The frame relay standard defines how a user device will format data to send to a network device (UNI) or how two frame relay network devices will format data to send to each other (NNI).

Public frame relay transmission services support a frame relay interface conforming to the frame relay standards, and then build a complete service around this interface. Many variations between services occur, including the backbone protocol used, the methods for congestion management and flow control, the reroute capabilities of the service, and network management. Most service providers offer ancillary services to complement the frame relay transmission service, such as equipment, connectivity to other networks, protocol interworking, configuration management and outsourcing options.

[1] *The word "octet" is often used interchangeably with the word "byte." Both signify bits of information; however, there is a difference in the numbering sequence.*
[2] *Throughout this book, the term "router" will be used in most examples for the frame relay access device. However, in nearly every case where "router" is used you could substitute any one of the many available frame relay access devices, including a multiplexer, concentrator, bridge, etc.*
[3] *Request For Comment (RFC) 1294 specifies the interworking of different frame relay devices, allowing different manufacturers' equipment to interoperate over a frame relay network. Some*

*functionality may be lost.*

[4] *The term "node" is often used to describe the carrier's switching equipment ,which makes up the frame relay network. References are typically made to originating, intermediate and destination nodes, which refer to the initial carrier switch accepting the incoming frames from your premises equipment, any intermediate switches the frame passes through, and the final network switch interfacing with your premises equipment on the receiving end.*

## CHAPTER 4:

# FRAME RELAY SERVICES

To make educated evaluations about where and how frame relay might be part of a cost-effective network solution, you should have a thorough understanding of the available services. This understanding will also aid you in later chapters that deal with designing a frame relay network.

There are many companies, and network managers, using frame relay today with an incomplete and even incorrect understanding of the service they have purchased. Ultimately, this leads to inefficiency and missed opportunity.

We cannot attempt to define the individual differences among the various service providers' products — the book would be obsolete before it was printed. However, there are many attributes of public frame relay services that are consistent across most offerings while other attributes are unique to a few carriers but are likely to be duplicated by others in the future.

If you understand this chapter, you will have a much more productive time discussing service and design alternatives with carriers. The information will also help you when it is time to select a carrier.

# The Make-Up of a Frame Relay Network

A frame relay network is typically made up of three elements: the access link, the port connection, and the associated virtual connections (PVCs today).

We will cover the port connections and the virtual connections in this chapter. Access is covered in detail in Chapter Five.

While we will talk about each element separately, it is important to understand that these elements are part of an integrated whole. A port connection without its complementary virtual connections to other port connections is not useful. The elements work together to make up the complete frame relay network.

*Frame Relay Service Elements*

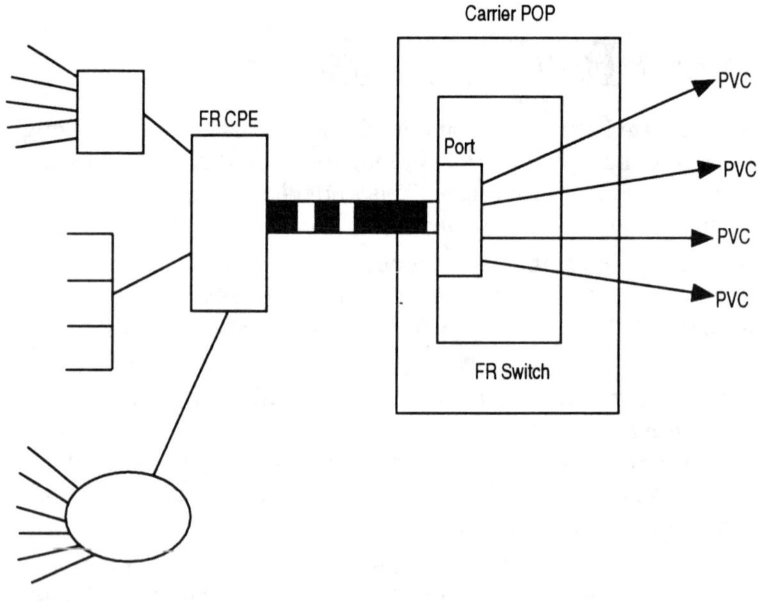


*Fig. 4.1: Three of the elements in a public frame relay service are the access, port connection, and PVC.*

## The Role of the Port Connection

The port connection is the point of entry into a frame relay network. It is typically associated with an individual site. In most networks, for most sites, only one port connection is needed, even though many different users, applications and protocols may need network access.

A single port connection will support multiple logical connections (i.e., PVCs) to many different remote locations. Once again, all the users, applications and protocols will share these PVCs in most cases.

The port connection's primary function is to provide dynamic allocation of network capacity to meet the changing needs of the users sharing the network.

The port connection is defined in terms of capacity/speed. In other words, you will choose a port connection's speed, and that choice will depend upon the amount of information that will be sent to/from that location at any given moment in time. We will discuss design considerations and criteria for selecting the port speed in Chapters Six and Seven.

You can typically choose from many different port connection speeds, including: 56/64K, 128K, 256K, 384K, 512K, 768K, 1.024K, and 1.536M bps. Some vendors do not offer all of these speeds. For example, local frame relay service providers may have a smaller selection.

*The Port Connection*

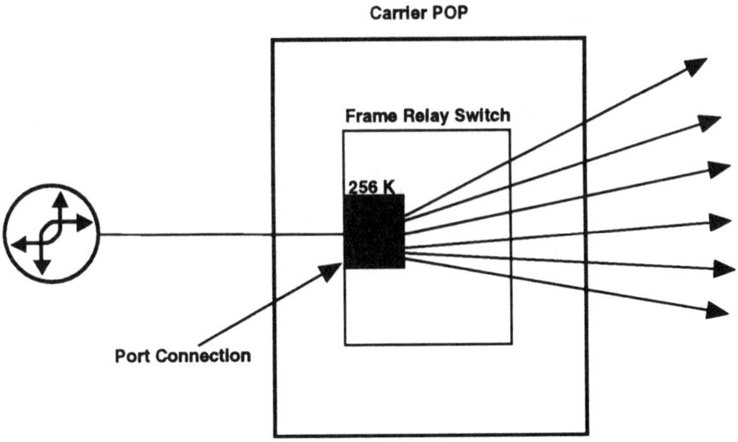


*Fig. 4.2: Many users and applications at a given location will share the port connection's network capacity. The role of the port connection is to dynamically allocate the capacity to the users and the PVCs that send information.*

The capacity of the port connection becomes the bottleneck for that location. Whatever the port connection's speed, you cannot send or receive information faster than this at any given point in time for that location. If you are used to thinking about bandwidth in terms of space (not speed), then conceptually you cannot receive or send more information to/from the site at any given instant in time than what the port connection allows.

The port's capacity is allocated depending on what applications need to send data out on to the network and where that data needs to be sent. The port connection will dynamically allocate its capacity, in real time, as the needs of the network users at that site change. This idea of dynamic capacity allocation of the port's capacity is discussed in more detail below.

## The Role of PVCs

Permanent virtual circuits (PVCs) are the logical connections, or paths, between port connections on a frame relay network. They operate like a dedicated network connection, only they are more intelligent.

PVCs are "permanent", in that the PVC is there all the time — once it is assigned between two port connections. The information traveling on a PVC will take the same path each time, and will flow in sequence, meaning that the frames do not have to be reordered into correct sequence at the far end.

Like a traditional dedicated circuit, a PVC is "owned" by the company that assigns it, and no other company will be able to send information across, or intercept information within, another company's PVC. These virtual connections are every bit as secure and reliable as a traditional private line. If the idea of a logical connection makes you uncomfortable, it may help to remember that a DS-0 is really just a logical connection within a digital cross-connection system (DCS).

PVCs are also "virtual", in that the PVC does not physically take up space on the port connection, or in the network, until information needs to be sent across it. Because it does not take up capacity when it is idle, this capacity is available to be allocated to other PVCs which are active and which may need additional bandwidth.

### *PVC Reroutes*

Most frame relay services build redundant physical network paths into the underlying network architecture so that in the event of a physical line failure, the PVC will have an alternate route available. The path of the virtual connection is constant, unless a major network failure occurs along that path. In this case, the PVC will be given an alternate route around the network failure, and will maintain that route until the primary route is recovered (or for some networks, until the PVC is manually returned to the primary route).

If information is being transmitted across the PVC at the time of network failure, it will probably be lost and will need to be retransmitted. However, for many frame relay networks the PVC reroute takes place very quickly, usually in a few seconds (i.e., less than 1 to 7 seconds after the failure occurs). This is an area where service providers can differ greatly, so discussing this topic with your carrier is important. If a few frames of data are lost, the end equipment will simply ask for a retransmission. The user of the application will very likely be oblivious to the fact that a service-related problem has occurred on the network.

*PVCs Reroute Around Network Failures*

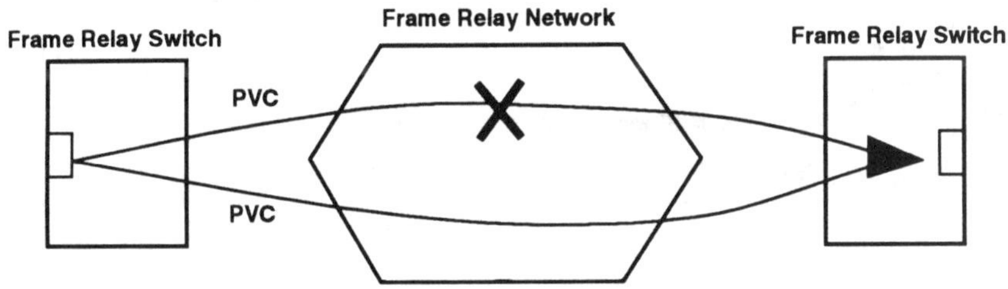


*Fig. 4.3: In the event of a failure on the frame relay network, the PVC will automatically route to an alternate path until the primary path is available.*

## *Assigning PVCs*

When setting up your network, you will assign at least one PVC between any two locations on the network for which direct interconnectivity is required. Typically, all the applications at the two sites will share this single logical connection, and the connection will be designed to adequately support these aggregated transmission needs.

There are some situations for which you may decide to assign more than one PVC between the same two locations. This is sometimes the case when a network manager decides to keep SNA traffic on a different PVC from the LAN traffic, perhaps for prioritization and performance reasons. In this case, the two PVCs will operate independently, but will still share the same access and port connection, providing better economies of scale than if separate dedicated connections were being used.

*PVC Connectivity*

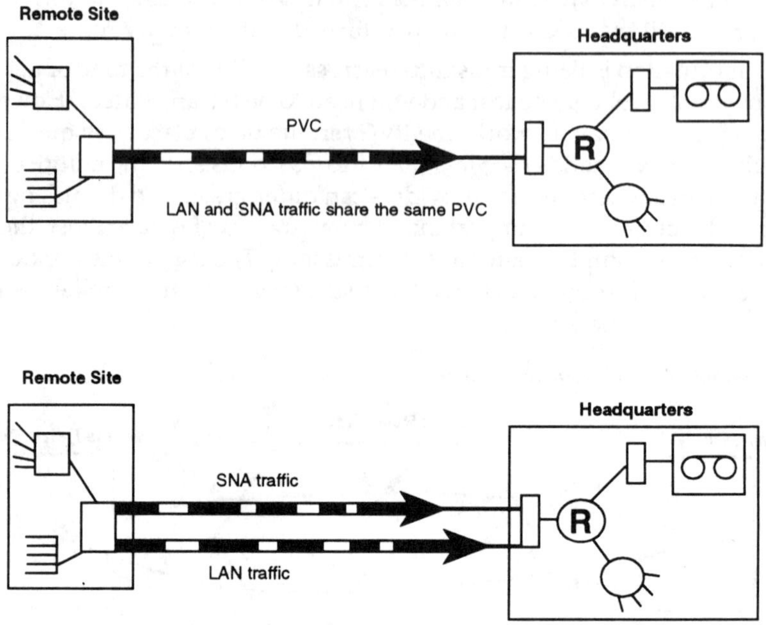


*Fig. 4.4: PVCs provide the logical connectivity between locations. Typically, all the applications will share a PVC; however, it is possible to separate applications onto different PVCs.*

## *Switched Virtual Circuits (SVCs)*

There is another form of virtual circuit that will soon be available with frame relay services. Switched virtual circuits, or SVCs, are connection-oriented virtual circuits that are intelligently negotiated and established between your equipment and a carrier's network when information needs to be sent. The primary application of SVCs will probably be connectivity to locations outside of the normal closed user group within which you would typically establish PVCs.

SVCs are not enablers of dial-up connectivity into the network, as they are often mistakenly thought to be. SVCs enable spontaneous connectivity between sites already connected into the network and will be most useful for applications needing infrequent connectivity to a given network site. They will combine nicely with dial up access options once they become available commercially in public frame relay service. SVCs will probably not be widely available until the mid part of 1995 at the earliest; accordingly, this book is concentrated on PVCs.

## Committed Information Rate

For each PVC you will need to determine its committed information rate (CIR). The CIR is a statistically guaranteed level of transmission that the network will provide to the logical connection when information must be transmitted. So, the CIR assignment should reflect the expected average traffic volume between the two sites that the PVC is connecting. The CIR is not always easy to estimate when first designing a frame relay network, but there are some guidelines, which will be covered in Chapter Six.

CIR is a statistical measurement of throughput over time. The standard specifies that CIR=Committed Burst Rate (Bc)/Time. The time interval can vary, but is typically a few milliseconds or tens-of-milliseconds.

The transmission of incoming frames in excess of the CIR depends heavily upon the network platform and the state of network congestion. In some cases, incoming frames in excess of the CIR will be stored in buffers. In other cases, excess frames are transmitted, but are the first traffic to be discarded if network congestion occurs.

While deciding on an initial CIR for each PVC can present a challenge in some environments, the beauty of frame relay is that once in operation, you will be able to see your average and peak traffic volumes on the PVC and adjust the CIR accordingly.

The PVC's CIR cannot exceed the speed of the port connection *on either end* of the PVC. So, if you have a 56K bps port connection at Site A, and a 384K bps connection at Site B, the CIR between the two cannot exceed 56K bps. You could not assign a 256K bps CIR between these two port connections, because the 56K bps port connection would find it difficult to buffer information coming into it at 256K bps, when it can only send the information out to the local loop at 56K bps. The result would probably be that the information overflows the buffer and is discarded — requiring retransmission. This is the reason for the rule on CIR assignments described above.

Committed information rates are available from zero K bps to 1.536M bps, and just about every size in between. Most carriers limit standard offerings to a few sub-64K choices plus any increment of 64K bps. This is done primarily to simplify the marketing message, not out of any technical constraint. Most carriers are capable of providing CIRs in any increment of 1K bps. You will probably find that the available selections of 64K bps increments are more than sufficient to effectively design your network.

Carriers are limited by the capabilities of the network platform (i.e., equipment). Consequently, some carriers do not offer zero CIR, and others do not offer simplex PVCs or user-defined burst rates. For some carriers, the highest

*CIR Alternatives by Port Speed*

| Individual PVC CIR Alternatives (K bps) | Port Size (K bps) 64 | 128 | 256 | 384 | 512 | 768 | 1024 | 1536 |
|---|---|---|---|---|---|---|---|---|
| 0 | ✔ | ✔ | ✔ | ✔ | ✔ | ✔ | ✔ | ✔ |
| 16 | ✔ | ✔ | ✔ | ✔ | ✔ | ✔ | ✔ | ✔ |
| 32 | ✔ | ✔ | ✔ | ✔ | ✔ | ✔ | ✔ | ✔ |
| 48 | ✔ | ✔ | ✔ | ✔ | ✔ | ✔ | ✔ | ✔ |
| 64 | ✔ | ✔ | ✔ | ✔ | ✔ | ✔ | ✔ | ✔ |
| 128 | | ✔ | ✔ | ✔ | ✔ | ✔ | ✔ | ✔ |
| 192 | | | ✔ | ✔ | ✔ | ✔ | ✔ | ✔ |
| 256 | | | ✔ | ✔ | ✔ | ✔ | ✔ | ✔ |
| 320 | | | | ✔ | ✔ | ✔ | ✔ | ✔ |
| 384 | | | | ✔ | ✔ | ✔ | ✔ | ✔ |
| 448 | | | | | ✔ | ✔ | ✔ | ✔ |
| 512 | | | | | ✔ | ✔ | ✔ | ✔ |
| 576 | | | | | | ✔ | ✔ | ✔ |
| 640 | | | | | | ✔ | ✔ | ✔ |
| 704 | | | | | | ✔ | ✔ | ✔ |
| 768 | | | | | | ✔ | ✔ | ✔ |
| 832 | | | | | | | ✔ | ✔ |
| 896 | | | | | | | ✔ | ✔ |
| 960 | | | | | | | ✔ | ✔ |
| 1024 | | | | | | | ✔ | ✔ |
| 1088 | | | | | | | | ✔ |
| 1152 | | | | | | | | ✔ |
| 1216 | | | | | | | | ✔ |
| 1280 | | | | | | | | ✔ |
| 1344 | | | | | | | | ✔ |
| 1408 | | | | | | | | ✔ |
| 1472 | | | | | | | | ✔ |
| 1536 | | | | | | | | ✔ |

*Fig. 4.5: With most services, CIR speeds are available in speeds up to, but not greater than, the port speed on either end of the PVC. With some services, the maximum CIR available on any single PVC is 1.024M bps.*

CIR that can be assigned to an individual PVC is 1.024M bps. These idiosyncrasies make a service review with carriers imperative as you begin the network design and carrier selection process.

The PVC will send information at its CIR. You need to be sure that the CIR you choose will handle the expected average traffic volume of the site in a way that is adequate to meet the needs of the users.

The CIR is the default rate of transmission across the PVC. For example, when there is heavy network utilization at your site and many PVCs are simultaneously contending for port/network capacity, PVCs will operate at the CIR. The PVC will also be limited to a transmission rate close to the CIR during network reroute situations, when overall network capacity contention will increase dramatically on the rerouted section.

PVCs are often able to exceed the transmission rate set forth by the CIR, via a technique called bursting. This is discussed later in this chapter.

Choosing the PVC's CIR is very important because the CIR defines the performance of the network and the experiences of the network users. Do not be afraid of making a wrong decision. The benefits of frame relay include a high degree of flexibility. Within limits, it is very easy to change a PVC's CIR. As you gain more and more insight into the traffic patterns of your network, the PVC's CIR can be modified to more accurately reflect the needs of the users.

## Simplex PVCs

Frame relay is a full duplex service, meaning that information can be transmitted simultaneously both into and out of a location/port connection. The flexibility of frame relay allows PVCs to be sized to meet the needs of the applications in each direction of the connection.

Data applications and traffic patterns are not usually homogeneous or symmetrical. Small requests can generate a huge amount of data being sent to the requesting party. Think of an advertising agency's request for a stock photo from a photo storage library; the request for the photo may be no more than 100 bytes, but the photo itself could be megabytes in size.

In a dedicated circuit environment, if you need about 1.5M bps in one direction because of the need to transmit large files, or large volumes of information, but only need 256K bps in the other direction, you must buy a DS-1 (i.e., T-1) circuit. This essentially means that you are paying for more capacity in one direction than what you really need or use.

With frame relay and simplex PVC assignments, the network can be designed so that each direction is given the level of capacity needed to support its applications, but no more. This means that you can save money by more efficiently designing your network, and not pay for more capacity, even in a single direction, than what you need.

Not every carrier offers this feature, but most do. Some call it asymmetrical PVCs. Initially you may not have enough information about your traffic patterns to take advantage of this feature. Once traffic pattern information becomes available, simplex PVCs can provide a path to cost savings.

*Simplex PVCs*

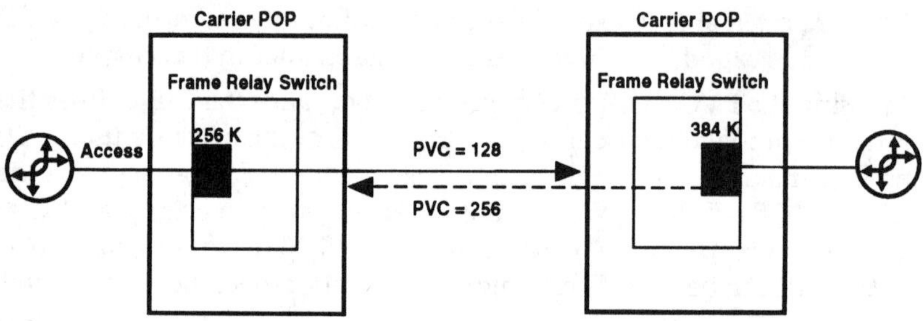


*Fig. 4.6: Simplex PVCs allow the assignment of different committed information rates in each direction of the logical connection.*

## Bursting

A PVC can exceed its assigned CIR when a large file or a large volume of information must be transmitted, and when excess capacity is available on the port connection.

The burst serves two main purposes. It allows information to be sent across the network more quickly, thus improving the response time of the application. It also eliminates congestion at the port connection more quickly, freeing the port and the PVC up to handle more incoming data.

If other PVCs sharing the port connection are active, excess capacity may not be available. The level of traffic, or congestion, on the public network will also affect the ability of the PVC to sustain a burst above its CIR.

The frame relay specification calls for data transmitted in excess of the PVC's CIR to be marked by the network equipment as "discard eligible" (DE). This means that in the event of network congestion, this data is the first to be discarded by the network, in a reactionary attempt to alleviate the congestion. The standard also specifies ways to avoid congestion and to decrease congestion as it begins to occur but before a problem arises, which would necessitate discarding frames.

*PVC Burst Capability*

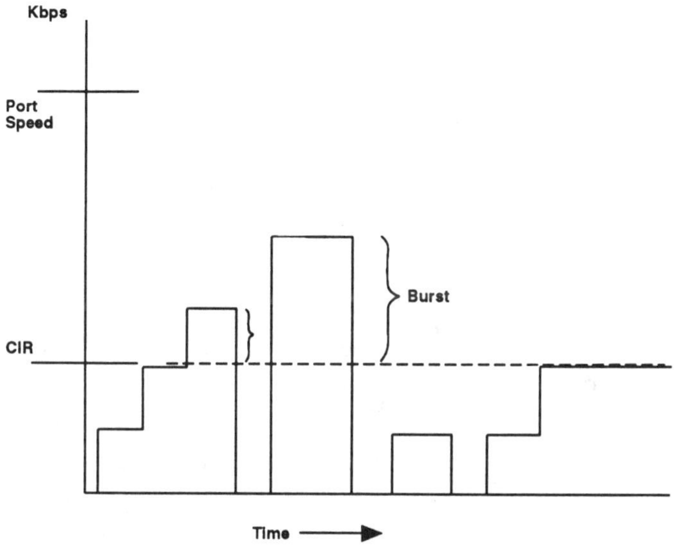


*Fig. 4.7: A PVC can exceed its assigned committed information rate when excess capacity is available on the port connection and the network.*

It is better for the network to proactively avoid congestion all together and in addition to the mechanisms specified in the standards, some equipment vendors have designed sophisticated algorithms to do just this. But even with this avoidance capability there may be cases when congestion is not prevented and must be contended with. In these cases, the first frames to be discarded by the network will be those in excess of the CIR. Think of it as jettisoning ballast to save a sinking balloon.

When a PVC is transmitting a large file and would benefit from a sustained burst, the increase in throughput may not immediately increase from the CIR to the burst rate (typically the port connection speed). Depending upon the carrier's equipment platform, the increase in throughput during a sustained burst may occur gradually, in a stepping fashion, as network congestion allows. For some networks, this gradual increase in throughput allows the congestion management systems within the network to more tightly control overall network congestion levels. If congestion begins to rise, the ability of PVCs to burst above the CIR will be quickly scaled back. Once again, a discussion with your carrier on this topic will provide information on how the PVC burst is handled and what relationship, if any, this has to the network's congestion management functions.

*Discard Eligibility*

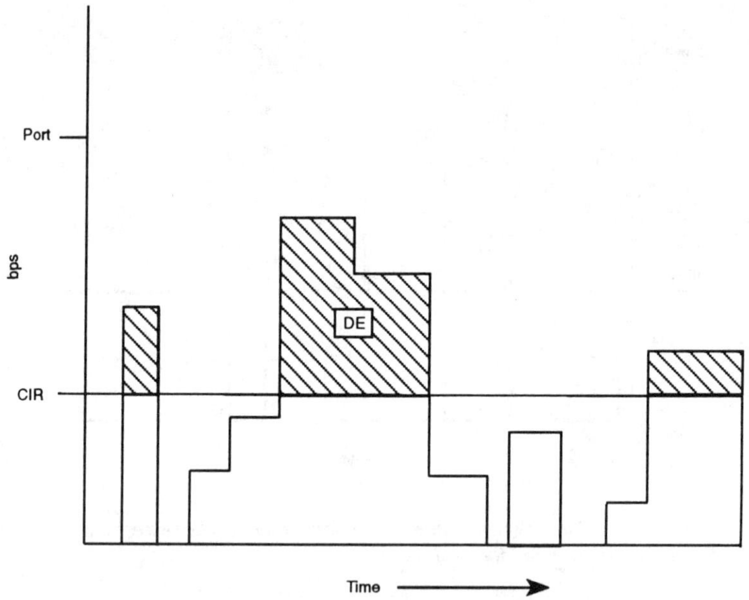


*Fig. 4.8: Transmissions in excess of the CIR are typically marked as discard eligible by the network and are the first frames to be discarded to reduce network congestion.*

Bursting has had its share of controversy, because a user could theoretically design a network with less predefined capacity (i.e., PVC CIR) than what the applications require, with the intent of letting the burst capability of the PVC handle the brunt of the data transfer. Frame relay service should not be looked upon as a way to get something for nothing. This strategy may work well early on in a service's life cycle, when the number of users on the network, and on your network, is relatively low. In the long term, you will probably be disappointed if your CIR is not adequate to meet the average traffic needs of your applications. The strategy may be appropriate for locations with low volumes of non-mission-critical traffic. Yet in such a situation, a dial-up solution may be more appropriate and more cost-effective.

The best way to insure network performance standards is to assign a CIR that can adequately meet the average traffic volume between the two sites which the PVC connects. The burst will then enhance the PVCs ability to meet the dynamic needs of the users, large file transfers, and busy hours.

## Dynamic Capacity Allocation

The issue of exceeding committed information rate and of dynamic allocation of port capacity is highly dependent upon the network platform being used by your carrier.

To begin this discussion, we will start with a conceptual description of dynamic allocation of a port and use a few examples. This description does not yet take into account the serialization output from the router or windowing of higher level protocols.

Consider a port connection with 4 different PVCs, each connecting with a different remote location, and each with a CIR of 64K bps.

*Example: Configuration*

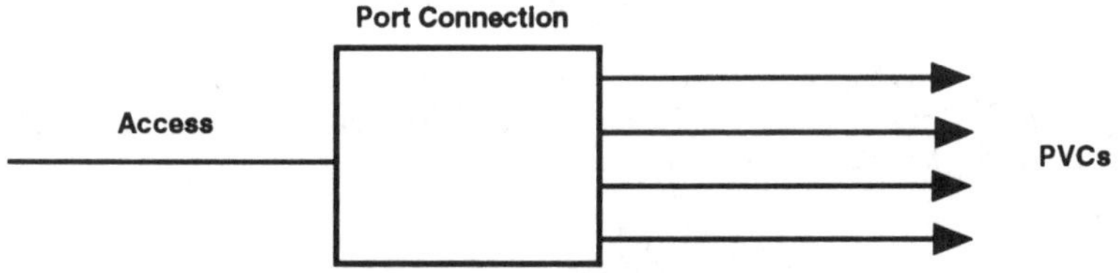


*Fig. 4.9: In this example, a port connection has 4 PVCs to which it can dynamically allocate capacity.*

In the first instant in time, $T_0$, no information must be sent. In the next instant in time, $T_1$, each of the four PVCs simultaneously needs to send exactly 64K bps worth of information to its respective remote location. The result of this is that in time $T_1$, all four PVCs are 100 percent active, each at the full CIR. At the next instant in time, no information needs to be transmitted. The diagram shows how the port connection has allocated this capacity.

Now take another example. Again at $T_0$ no information needs to be sent. In the next instant in time, PVC1 needs to send a 32K byte (256K bit) file. At time $T_2$, when the transmission begins, no other PVCs need the capacity of the port connection and network congestion is also low. In this case, the port connection will allocate the full capacity — 256K bps — to PVC1. The entire file will transmit in time $T_2$. This not only improves the response time for that application, it also immediately clears the network port connection of congestion and frees it up completely to accept more data. Of course, transmissions in excess of CIR are marked as discard eligible.

***Example 1: Dynamic Bandwidth Allocation***

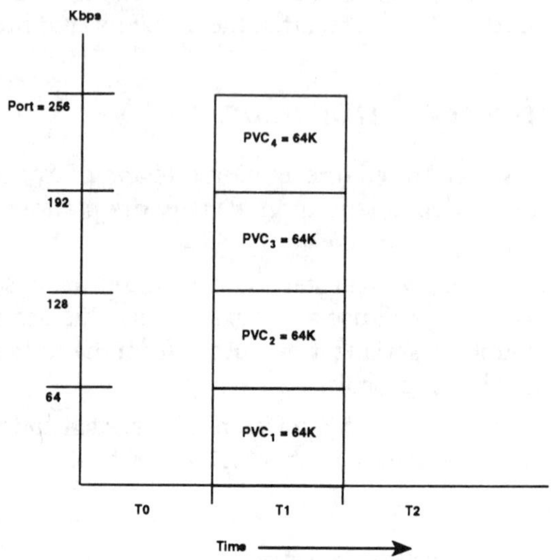


*Fig. 4.10: In time $T_0$, no information needs to be sent over the network. In time $T_1$, each PVC requires exactly 64K bps. In time $T_1$, no information needs to be sent. The port connection allocates its capacity to match these requirements.*

One last example. Assume that four different users are preparing to send data across the network, each using a different PVC. The first user will use PVC1, and needs to send a 48K byte (384K bit) file beginning in time $T_1$. The second user needs to send a file also, but it is only 4K bytes (32K bits) and it will not begin transmitting until $T_2$ over PVC2. The third user has a 16K byte (128K bit) file, which will begin transmitting in time $T_3$ over PVC3. The fourth user has a 32K byte (128K bit) file that will begin transmitting in $T_4$ over PVC4, but at the same time user two begins sending another 32K byte (128K bit) file over PVC 2. The diagram shows how the port connection will change the allocation of capacity to the PVCs in each time period.

*Example 2: Dynamic Bandwidth Allocation*

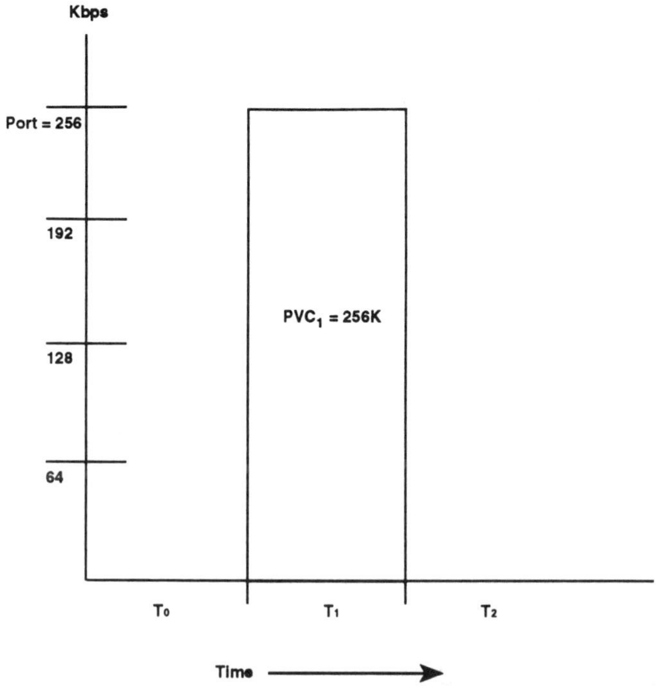


*Fig. 4.11: In time $T_1$, no information needs to be sent. In time $T_1$, PVC 1 needs all 256K bps for a file transmission, but no other PVCs need network capacity. The port connection allocates the capacity to meet these needs.*

Now, having worked through three conceptual examples, you should know that this view is not entirely correct. The examples represent the network bandwidth spatially. However, bandwidth is really a measure of network speed. If a port connection were to receive traffic simultaneously from both a router at your premises and other internodal traffic on your frame relay network, then this example of multiple PVCs being simultaneously active would be more correct. When just considering information coming to the port connection from a router, two additional concepts must be considered: router interfaces are serial ports, and higher layer protocols break files up into smaller segments and use sliding windows to control the flow of transmission.

*Example 3: Dynamic Bandwidth Allocation*

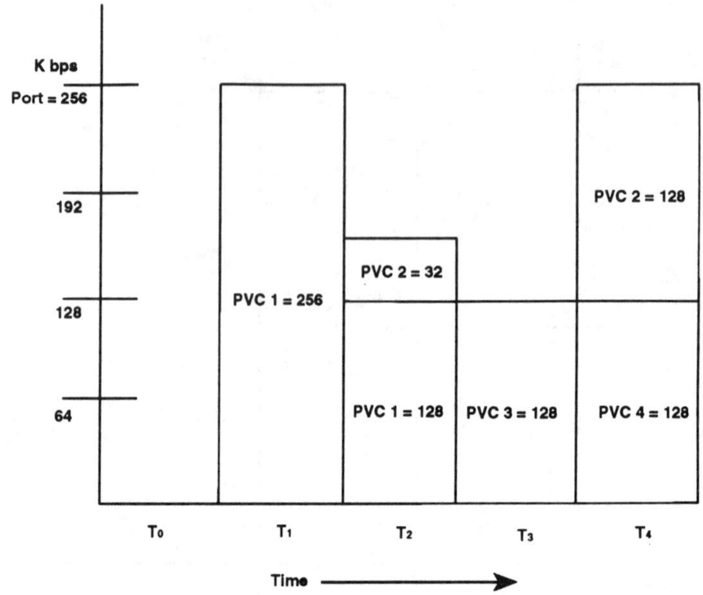


*Fig. 4.12: No information is sent in time $T_0$. A 48 byte file is sent over PVC 1 beginning in time $T_1$. A 4 byte file is sent over PVC 2 beginning in $T_2$. A 16 byte file is sent over PVC3 beginning in $T_3$. In $T_4$, PVC2 and PVC 4 both send a 16 byte file. The port connection dynamically allocates capacity to meet those needs.*

## *Serialization*

Your equipment will have a serial interface into the network over a local loop. The equipment can only send one frame out at a time (actually, one bit at a time). The equipment is clocked at the port connection speed, and it probably does not recognize an underlying CIR on a PVC. While some router vendors are working to address this, even when the premises equipment can recognize an underlying CIR, it may not be able to alter the flow of incoming and outgoing traffic in accordance. The result is that transmissions are sent to the port connection at the port speed.

Depending upon the network equipment, the port and PVCs might have buffers in which to temporarily hold incoming frames that are in excess of the CIR. Some network platforms implement congestion management schemes which will provide feedback to a switch and will throttle a PVC's output to the CIR instead of allowing DE frames through the network in a congestion situation where they are likely to be discarded. Frames that are not sent out immediately are held in the buffer until they can be sent as non-DE traffic. Other network platforms operate more in keeping with the frame relay standards. The violating traffic is allowed onto the network, but it is the first to be discarded in congestion situations.

An analogy for the allocation of PVC space based on CIR would be a voice application where a business person has three different phone calls waiting. The business person can jump between the different callers, giving each one a specific time segment in which to talk, depending upon the importance of the caller (i.e., the CIR for the PVC). When the business person is talking to caller one, caller one gets the whole line and all of the business person's attention. However, when time runs out for that caller the business person will put caller 1 on hold and move on to caller 2, and then 3, cycling back to caller 1 and so on. CIR is a measurement of committed throughput within a given time window. If you were to measure the total time given to each of the callers over some time window, this would be the amount of conversation (i.e., traffic) guaranteed to get through to the business person.

Bursting above the CIR would be like a speakerphone application, where each caller is given a specific amount of dedicated time, but where dead-spaces in the conversation could be filled in by anyone with something to add.

## *First Come, First Served*

In the above examples where simultaneous file transfers occur, the role of the router becomes critical in understanding what is really happening with your traffic and how it is sent out onto the network.

If the router receives several files at once, it will treat the files on a first come, first served basis, unless prioritization guidelines have been programmed into the router.

Each transfer is handled independently. So the first file is sent out, then the next, and so on. Because of this serialization, the PVCs out of the port connection are really not active all at the same time (unless other internodal traffic is being handled as well).

### *Prioritizing Traffic*

Instead of the simple first come, first served approach to processing incoming data, many routers allow you to set prioritization parameters by incoming port, protocol and even packet size.

This mechanism allows you to prioritize critical traffic, like SNA transactions, in front of other file transfers in the event that congestion is occurring at the router. This topic will be covered more in later chapters.

### *Window Size*

Another factor that further complicates the simple conceptualization used above is the intelligent protocol being used by the application. Many protocols today have "sliding windows." The protocol will break a large file transfer up into smaller packets for transmission. It will then release some number of these packets, say 4 to 8, out onto the network for transmission. The router will receive these and forward them as described above. The protocol will then wait to receive an acknowledgement from the receiving device before more packets are released.

This is one of the gaiting mechanisms by which transmission flow-control is matched with CIR, or with the effective throughput rate of the network. All of these elements work together in a single file transmission.

### *Putting The Pieces Together*

The end result of all of these elements, and the effect on your traffic and throughput, can be seen by walking through one file transfer example.

1. User sends a file using the TCP/IP protocol.
2. TCP/IP breaks the file into smaller packets, and sends out the first set.
3. The router receives the packets, encapsulates the information into a frame relay frame, and sends each out serially over the network to the port connection at the port connection speed.
4. The port connection places the incoming information onto the correct PVC after reading the address information.
5. If the PVC's CIR is less than the port speed, and the incoming frames are enough to violate the CIR, one of two things will happen:

    A. The information will be transmitted at the port speed, but some of the frames will be marked as discard-eligible; or

    B. The network will signal the port connection that congestion is occurring on the path, and the frames in excess of CIR will be buffered.

6. The end equipment will acknowledge receipt of the frames, and the acknowledgments will be sent back over the network (or if some frames have been discarded, will signal for a retransmission).

7. The protocol will calculate the effective throughput of the network based on the time interval of acknowledgements, and will adjust the window size accordingly. The result of this is that if there is congestion on the network and the effective throughput of the PVC is close to or equal to the CIR, the router will continue to send frames to the PVC at the port connection speed, but the number of frames being sent by the protocol to the router for transmission will not violate the CIR.

## What is CIR?

As stated above, the committed information rate of a PVC is really just a statistical average of throughput over time. The gaiting effect of CIR on realized throughput depends upon:

- The equipment being used by your carrier;
- How buffers are used and how large the buffers are;
- What protocols are being used and how windowing is handled by the protocol;
- The congestion management system between switches on the carrier's network.

In one sense, CIR is a measure of quality of service, a frame/loss ratio. In another sense, it is a measure of effective average throughput. One result is clear: If you are not getting the network performance that your users and applications require, either in response time or throughput, then you probably need to increase CIR.

## Effects on Network Design

What is most important is that you understand dynamic allocation enough to design your network and that you understand the benefits of dynamic allocation. For these purposes, the conceptualization of port capacity in spatial terms may be more useful, even though it is slightly inaccurate.

Unlike dedicated circuits based on time division multiplexing, PVCs do not take up capacity when information is not being sent over the connection. This frees up the port's capacity for allocation to active PVCs. The ability of the port connection to dynamically allocate its capacity to different PVCs over different time periods in response to real time changes in connectivity requirements is one of the reasons that frame relay network solutions can simultaneously improve network performance while decreasing costs.

## Oversubscription

Recall that we discussed the intermittent nature of data applications in Chapter Two. The fact is that most leased line connections between two locations have an average utilization of 30 percent or less. This means that 70 percent or more of the time, an individual dedicated connection is idle.

Frame relay services typically let you exploit this intermittent characteristic of data by "oversubscribing" the port connection. This means that you can actually assign more PVCs and *total* CIR to a port than the port connection's speed (the CIR of any individually PVC is still limited by the port connection speed on either end). Of course, the port connection is still the bottleneck, but oversubscription lets you gain a lot of connectivity for a lower price than a dedicated solution.

The purpose of oversubscription is to allow more cost-effective network connectivity. This is accomplished in two ways. First, because of oversubscription, you may be able to choose a lower port connection speed in a frame relay environment than what you would need in a dedicated environment.

Take the example of a headquarters location with 32 remote locations across different time zones, all of which need at least one direct connection at 56/64K bps. If traditional leased lines were used, the primary site would need two DS-1 local loops, one for the first 24 DS-0 connections and one for the remaining 8 connections.

*Private Line Network*

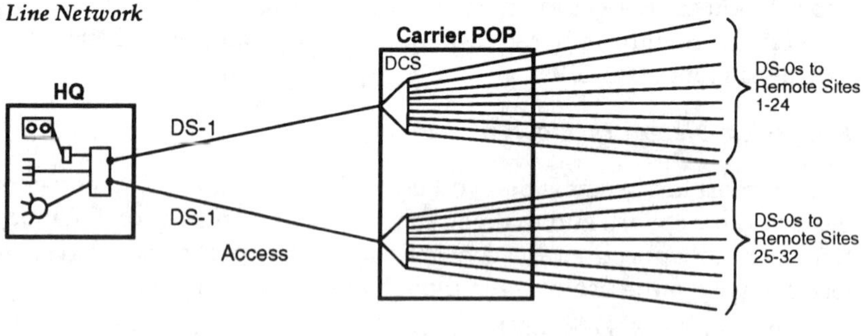


*Fig. 4.13: In this example, the headquarters location must have two DS-1 local loops to support a DS-0 connection to each of 32 remote locations.*

Oversubscription would allow you to purchase a single port connection and a single DS-1 local loop and allow all 32 remote sites to share the capacity. In fact, depending upon the likelihood of all the sites sending information into the port connection simultaneously, and the size of the port's buffers, you may determine that the port connection does not need to be a full 1.536M bps (a full DS-1). You may determine that because the applications are intermittent, only a 768K bps port connection is needed.

*Oversubscription Reduces Costs*

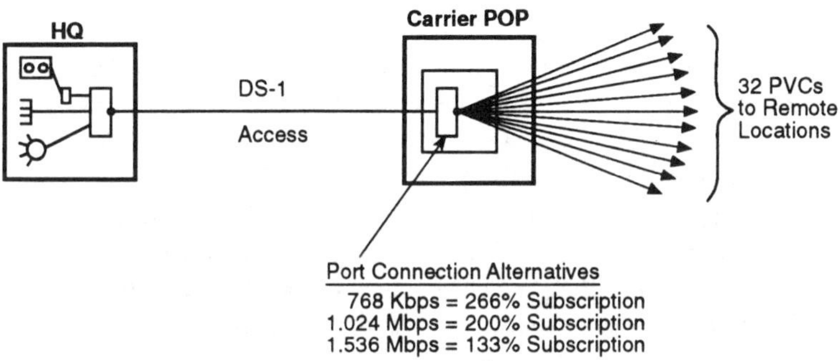


*Fig. 4.14: The ability to oversubscribe a port connection allows all 32 remote locations to be supported by a single local loop and a single port connection. One of several port speeds could be chosen depending on the CIR total of all the PVCs and the level of oversubscription desired. In this example, the PVCs are assumed to have a CIR of 64K bps.*

Oversubscription means you save money on both local access and on the cost of the port connection itself. You take advantage of the statistical multiplexing of frame relay and the ability of the port connection to dynamically allocate capacity.

The second way that oversubscription provides benefit is that it allows you to provide direct connectivity to and between remote sites that would probably not cost-justify a connection in a leased line network.

When combined with dynamic bandwidth allocation, oversubscription allows the capacity of a port connection to be shared over a larger number of individual network connections than would be possible in a dedicated environment. Since PVCs do not take up capacity until information needs to be transferred, the ability of the port connection to dynamically allocate its capacity across a large number of PVCs can result in significant cost savings.

In looking at a complete network, PVC connections are typically less expensive than leased lines, especially once a network site is connected to the service. The incremental cost of a PVC between two sites already on a public frame relay network can be as low as $50 or $100 per 64K bps per month, or less. With term and volume discounts this can be reduced even further.

Increasing the amount of direct connectivity between remote locations means that the congestion at primary and hub locations is reduced because less overall traffic tandems through the site. This increases the performance of all the applications on the network.

Oversubscription fits nicely with the dynamic allocation of network capacity discussed above. By increasing connectivity within the network and reducing the size of the port connection, you can increase the average utilization of the port connection. This means spending less money and getting more performance for the money that you do spend.

Where a leased line may have an average utilization rate of under 30 percent, a tightly engineered frame relay network should be able to run an average utilization of the port connection in excess of 30 percent and still result in better network performance for the users.

## Frame Relay over Cell Relay

Many frame relay services today do not actually use a frame-based switching fabric. Instead, cells are switched and incoming frames are divided up into cells by the network equipment, and then reassembled back into frames at the receiving end.

The reasons for this are the greater network speed and efficiency that cell switching enables, although other benefits result from this process as well.

One advantage of switching cells is that as soon as enough of a frame is received into the network equipment to fill up a single cell, that cell can be forwarded to the destination. The rest of the frame may not have been totally received yet, but already part of the information is on its way. Overall network efficiency is increased because the network is able to fill up capacity in a "tighter" manner that what would be possible if frames had to be forwarded whole.

This same efficiency is gained at any intermediate nodes. Cells are relatively small. The well-known ATM cell is 53 octets. Small cells can be quickly processed by the network equipment.

The term "cell" connotes a fixed length packet. Because the cell is fixed in length, the size is totally predictable, and therefore some functions, such as the cell-switching, can be done in hardware not software. This translates into increased switching speed.

The disadvantages of using cell relay are primarily the added overhead. Each cell contains approximately 10 to 12 percent, so there is a higher percentage of overhead on the backbone network than might be true with frame switching, where there are five bytes for the entire frame regardless of size.

However, since the carrier is responsible for the efficiency of the backbone network, and not you, this increase in overhead will not directly affect your applications or your expenses. The carrier may need to allocate more capacity to the network backbone to accommodate the increased overhead, but the carriers own the facilities in many cases, so this is less of an issue for them than it would be for you. Plus, carriers can better leverage the advantages of large numbers by using a cell relay backbone. This is because cells can be packed more tightly and processed more quickly and more efficiently than frames across a network.

The fixed length of a cell gives the switching equipment several advantages when it processes the cell. First, since the equipment knows exactly how long each cell is; it doesn't need to figure it out by reading flags that indicate the beginning and end of a cell. Every cell is exactly the same size. This means the cells can be switched in the hardware, which increases the speed of the switching process and the total number of cells that can be handled in a short time period.

The small size of the cell means that a large frame can be divided up, with some of the frame being sent towards the destination before the entire frame is even received by the first switch. Because the frame doesn't have to be completely received before some of its information is transmitted, total latency (delay) is decreased. Only at the last switch must all of the cells be stored until the last one is received so that the frame can be put back together again.

As it turns out, the additional overhead is more than compensated for by the increased speed and efficiency of cell-switching. The law of large numbers and the ability to statistically multiplex traffic on the network benefits the carrier, and the use of a cell-switching backbone improves a carrier's economies of scale.

So, the cell switching fabric creates a faster and more efficient service for both the carrier and the end users.

***Cell Relay Backbone On Frame Relay Network***

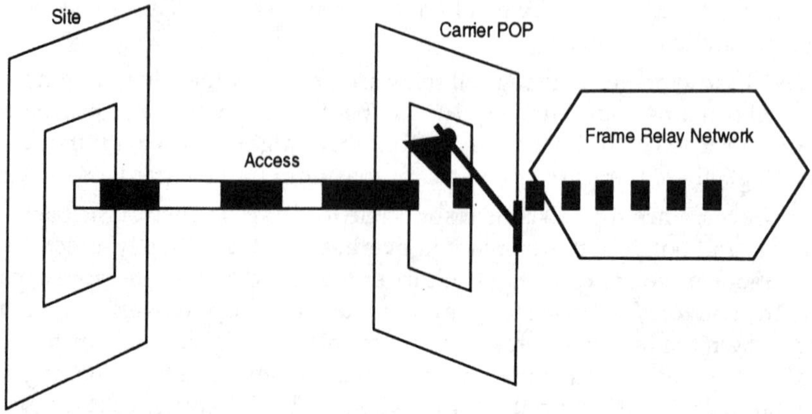


*Fig. 4.15: Most frame relay services accept incoming frames but then "chop" the frames into fixed length cells for transmission across the network backbone.*

# Congestion Management and Avoidance

As we have mentioned previously, there are times when the network does hit temporary periods of congestion, and not all data can get through. You should have a basic understanding of how congestion management and avoidance is handled by your carrier(s) in such instances.

You do not need to be afraid of using frame relay simply because your data may be discarded in periods of congestion. However, understanding congestion management will help you better determine the design of your network and may help you decide between carriers.

The place to begin is by describing the congestion management approach designated in the frame relay specifications. This is not the whole answer, and will only serve as a launching point for further discussion in this text and with your carriers.

The frame relay specifications are simple. If congestion occurs, get rid of it.

This means discarding DE frames. These are the frames that are in excess of a PVC's CIR and are marked as DE, or discard eligible. The underlying assumption is that the network has been designed to support the aggregate CIR, and discarding frames in violation of the CIR will bring the network back to stability. The assumption is a valid one. Public networks are designed using the aggregate CIR for guidance, and the action most probably will bring the network back to a non-contentious state.

There are several ways the standards specify for dealing with congestion before it occurs. If the network becomes congested and data is discarded, the user applications will recognize that a frame has not been received, and will implement correction procedures. In other words, the frame will be retransmitted.

Some network backbone equipment uses proprietary algorithms which build upon the congestion management specifications within the frame relay standards. The algorithms monitor the state of network congestion continuously and adjust the ability of the port connections to dynamically allocate excess capacity to PVC bursts (i.e., to let a PVC exceed its CIR). Doing so allows the network to proactively avoid a state of congestion.

You should understand how your carrier's network equipment manages congestion. If it is reactive and closely follows the frame relay standards, you may want to consider a higher CIR than if it is proactive and includes continual congestion monitoring. In either case, with most frame relay services you will see an effective throughput rate on each PVC at least equal to the CIR, and possibly above it.

Carriers offering public frame relay services are responsible for engineering the network so that users will be provided with a transmission rate equating to the CIR of a PVC, or greater. Since you are buying a service you do not necessarily need to worry about congestion management. However, if you choose to explore this area with your carrier, do not accept the following answer when you inquire about congestion management: "We are a carrier and capacity is free. Therefore, we simply throw a lot of capacity at the network, and in doing so we avoid congestion."

Carriers are in this business to make money. They are not non-profit organizations. Money is made in frame relay because the advantages of large numbers can be applied and the resulting economies of scale can allow the carrier to offer a highly effective transmission solution at a rate lower than a dedicated connection.

Frame and cell relay use statistical multiplexing to gain the resulting efficiencies. This is not a bad thing; in fact, as you have seen, it provides many advantages. Carriers have been using this same approach to designing voice networks for a long time. Most customers of voice products only notice problems with network capacity on such days as Mother's Day and Christmas. In these cases, network congestion may cause a delay in your voice application.

Frame and cell relay services work much the same way. Carriers will design the backbone network to support the aggregate CIRs, but they will rely on conservative design parameters that allow for the efficiencies of statistical multiplexing. The carriers benefit from the intermittent nature of data applications as well, which is one reason they can afford to offer frame relay services at such attractive rates.

Understanding the approach the network takes to congestion situations will help you understand how the network will handle your data in periods of congestion, such as network reroutes. This could impact some of your decisions when designing the network. One advantage of buying a service, however, is that you do not necessarily need to worry about technical issues, such as congestion management. You simply need to manage the carrier and insure that the carrier is delivering the level of service for which you have contracted. How this is achieved becomes an academic question.

## Pricing Structures and Alternatives

Pricing structures are varied across frame relay services. We will discuss the few constants and the many variations.

The vast majority of frame relay services are priced as a flat monthly fee per connecting location. In a flat rate scenario, the price is not sensitive to the mileage of the virtual connections, but instead to the port connection speed and either the CIRs of the PVCs, or the number of PVCs.

Appendices C and D outline the pricing approach of several providers, each of which puts a slightly different twist on pricing.

There are some general statements about the results of frame relay pricing that can be useful when designing a network and comparing frame relay solutions to other solutions.

With some services you are charged for the number of PVCs, while in others you are not charged for the number of PVCs in a network but are instead charged based on CIR. This means that the price for three PVCs each at 64K bps would cost the same as a single PVC at 192K bps. The impact of this is that it becomes very cost-effective to have more direct connections between remote locations.

In using leased lines, it is often most cost-effective to aggregate traffic to a few hub locations and buy larger/faster leased lines to connect these sites. This is not always the case with frame relay. And as discussed in Chapter One, more direct connectivity can result in better network performance for all users.

The average cost of CIR decreases as the amount of total CIR at a given location increases. This occurs in at least one of two ways. First, the price of the port connection is a fixed price and is usually relatively large compared with the price for the logical network connectivity between port connections. As you add more connections, or more CIR, you amortize this fixed cost across more capacity, effectively reducing the incremental cost of adding capacity by reducing the average cost per connection.

Most carriers allow you to oversubscribe the port connection, and may even charge less once you have reached this 100 percent subscription level.[1] This is a recognition of two things:

1. You cannot send more information into the network than what is defined by your port connection speed. But for many connectivity requirements, you don't need to connect two given sites all the time, you need to the ability to connect anytime information needs to be sent. This is an important distinction. The ability to connect is valuable. This is where oversubscription plays a role. Once you oversubscribe a port connection, you cannot connect to every location at the full CIR, all at the same time. With oversubscription, you leverage the fact that it is the connectivity itself that is valuable — the ability to connect when needed. The higher the level of port oversubscription, the greater the risk that there will be contention for the port's capacity among PVCs. Carrier's recognize the additional risk, but they also recognize that the connection is still valuable. Therefore, capacity can be assigned over 100 percent, but you will still pay a charge for this capacity. However, it does cost less incrementally, reflecting the higher risk that an application could be delayed. The result is that both you and the carrier should come out better than you would in a dedicated environment. You get a connection that you may not be able to cost justify in a leased-line network, and the carrier gets at least some revenue for giving you the ability to connect to this site.

2. The value of having a connection to some locations is much less than the value of having a direct connection to other locations. The same is true for all goods, and has long been recognized by economists as a downward sloping demand curve. Take water. If water were very limited in supply, the water you need to drink to survive would be very valuable, and you would be willing to pay a lot of money for it. However, the water that you use to wash your dog and your car is much less valuable. Even though it is exactly the same water, its value is less.

> The same holds true in networking. You are probably more willing to spend more for a connection from a remote site back to the primary site than you are for a connection between remote sites. For the most part, private line costs do not decrease, even though the relative value of the connections do. The decreasing cost of incremental network connectivity in a frame relay environment is a recognition of this fact.

Carriers are becoming very creative with pricing options. For example, some carriers allow you to designate zero CIR on a PVC (all the frames are eligible for discard). This is something like buying a bus ticket with no guarantee that the bus is actually coming, or flying standby on a plane. While this would not be recommended for high-volume sites or mission-critical applications, is does provide a very cost-effective solution for connectivity between remote locations and/or for low-volume sites with non-mission-critical applications.

Other carriers are allowing usage-based pricing. This allows you to only pay for the amount of traffic that you generate on the network. There are pros and cons to this approach. The good news is that most sites actually generate significantly less traffic than what most network managers estimate. Usage-based charging could significantly reduce your overall costs. The downside is that costs are not very predictable, and if your usage is high you may pay more than what you would if you were to preassign the CIR. Again, the ability to quickly modify your decision means that you have the flexibility to change your mind if your first decision ends up being less optimal than another approach.

Some carriers add a mileage-sensitive element. While many network managers prefer the simplicity and cost-effectiveness of non-mileage-sensitive pricing, networks that are concentrated into a tight geographical area can benefit from this mileage-sensitive alternative.

The bottom line is that you will probably have to compare bottom lines. This is easy if every carrier is made to price out exactly the same network. However, because of the options available from some carriers, the approach to congestion management or other design-affecting elements, the same network performance may be achieved from different network architectures by different carriers. It makes comparing prices between carriers a bit more difficult than what you might like.

It also means that elements other than price will probably figure into your final selection. These might include your comfort with the carrier, the carrier's ability to reach your network locations and offer the highest degree of network reroute protection in doing so, the ability of the carrier to offer

CPE and CPE support, provide configuration management, and provide other ancillary services and support options.

## Regional and Local Services

If the majority of your locations are within a concentrated geographical area, such a one LATA or a few states, you should consider using a local or regional frame relay services provider. These providers typically have very aggressive service pricing, and may offer an additional level of hand holding.

Regional and local carriers often take a slightly different, and simpler, approach to price structure. Once again, the pricing across carriers differs widely, but an example would be that you buy a connection into the network for a fixed price based upon the port connection speed. Additional PVCs are priced as a small, flat fee independent of committed information rate.

Again, in recognition of the fact that the relative value of direct connectivity suffers from diminishing returns, the service providers will often decrease the cost of PVCs as the number of PVCs increases. For example, the first PVC will typically be included in the price of the port connection, the next 5 PVCs might cost $10, the next 5 might cost $8, the next 5 only $6 and all the rest $5 each.

While the available port connection speeds from which to choose are often less than with national services, the prices reflect the fact that the distance of the average connection is less. Pricing for many of these services is typically very attractive, with a 56K bps port connection and PVC costing less than $100, and incremental PVCs a small fraction of this cost. Local and regional frame relay services are very often extremely cost effective for connecting four or more locations together.

Once again a note on congestion management is useful here. CIR is a way for a public network to police the traffic patterns of individual network users and fairly allocate network capacity in cases of congestion. If a carrier automatically sets the CIR of every PVC at the port connection speed, then you may want to explore how network capacity is fairly allocated during congestion periods.

Regional and local providers will usually have arrangements with other local, regional and/or national providers, so that you can connect to locations outside of the region. Some of these carriers even offer support for native protocols, including X.25, async and SDLC to cost-effectively connect locations with very low speed requirements into a frame relay network.

## Service Options for CPE Support

Most carriers will provide the option of a complete turnkey network solution, including the router and CSU/DSU, initial configuration of the equipment and ongoing maintenance. You may pay a slightly higher rate for this equipment than if you were to purchase it directly from the equipment vendor, but before you dismiss this option, consider some of its advantages. If you have staff that is not highly skilled in router-networking, or don't have staff at remote locations, you may find this alternative saves time, money and frustration.

When the carrier provides the equipment, it will often do the initial configuration of the equipment, including helping you to load in your wide area network router tables and set the router up for a frame relay environment.

It is important to understand where the line of demarcation for network responsibility resides. Even if you purchase a turnkey equipment or network outsourcing solution, the carrier is probably not going to be accountable for local area network or application problems unless that responsibility is specifically negotiated in a custom arrangement.

Many carriers will provide configuration management of the router as an optional service. The carrier will update the router tables to match the moves, adds and changes of devices on the LAN. This topic will be covered further in the chapter on network management and managed network services.

If your carrier provides a complete package including equipment, then when the network breaks you have only one number to call: that of your frame relay carrier. It is the carrier's responsibility to localize the problem and fix it. The advantage of this approach is that finger-pointing is significantly reduced. Once again, this should save you time, money and frustration.

More and more carriers will even take on a greater role in operating and optimizing the network, in a proactive manner, if you so choose. Before you cringe at the idea of giving up this control to your carrier, consider first what you might be able to do with the extra time. While this solution is not for every company, it can provide some network managers with the opportunity to concentrate their time, and that of their staff, on more strategic business concerns and applications instead of the daily firefighting inherent in network operation.

The next chapter will explore your alternatives for connecting to the public frame relay network by looking into different access alternatives.

[1] *For example, at least one carrier uses a nonlinear pricing structure in which the cost of each 64K bps of network capacity assigned out of a port connection is less than the previous 64K bps, encouraging the assignment of more network capacity and more direct connectivity between sites.*

CHAPTER 5:

# CONNECTING TO THE NETWORK

Your entire frame relay network may be within one LATA, in which case the "access" portion of the connection is typically included in the service. But when using a wide area public frame relay service, each network location must have a local physical connection into the wide area network. There are basically two main choices available: a traditional leased-line local loop or an intraLATA public frame relay service.

## Leased Local Loops

Within the category of leased lines, you may choose a low-speed circuit, a high-speed non-channelized circuit, or a channelized circuit that allows non-frame relay services to share the same local loop (i.e., DS-1 loop) as the frame relay service.

Each of these alternatives will be described below. You will probably find that you will use a combination of these alternatives throughout your network, depending upon the unique needs of each site.

### Low-Speed Connectivity

The most popular port connection speed, in terms of number of units sold, is the 56/64K bps port connection.

Over 50 percent of all public frame relay ports are 56/64K bps ports, and the most common way to access this port connection is through a 56/64K bps DS-0 circuit.[1]

The only downside to this approach is that if you should ever need to increase the port connection speed above 56/64K bps you would need to disconnect the DS-0 local loop and re-order a higher speed access connection. You will also need a new CSU/DSU. Therefore, the advantage of quick scalability is lost.

However, if you think the site will be adequately served by a 56/64K bps port connection for at least 6 months, then the savings gained from this approach will probably be well worth the hassles of upgrading the circuit, should this become necessary in the future.

When taken alone, the data applications at many remote offices will be well served by 56K bps connectivity. But, if you have other leased line applications, such as voice tie lines, you may want to consider a channelized DS-1 loop, to allow you to save money by integrating these applications onto a single access line.

Channelized refers to the process of breaking a DS-1 circuit down into its constituent parts, which equals 24 DS-0 channels, each operating at 64K bps. These individual circuits can then be split into smaller circuit bundles, which can be used by applications needing 64K bps or greater bandwidth. For more information on why this can be advantageous and how to channelize a circuit, see the sections on Non-channelized Access, Channelized Access, and Integrated Access below. This channelization can be accomplished by a channel bank, fractional CSU/DSU or multiplexer at your location.

The general crossover point between DS-0 local loops and DS-1 local loops is three circuits. This means that if you need three or more DS-0 local loops into a given location to support all the voice and data applications at that site, upgrading to a channelized DS-1 loop may save you money.

### Non-channelized Local Access

Non-channelized DS-1 loops would typically be used to support port connections of 1.536M bps.

With a non-channelized DS-1 loop, the entire local loop supports the frame relay application, and does not support other applications such as voice or traditional private lines.

### *Channelized DS-1 Local Access*

Using a channelized DS-1 means that you apply DS-1 formatting, in the form of 24 DS-0 channels plus one additional framing bit, to the DS-1 circuit. This function is performed by the CSU/DSU.

The channelization allows sub-DS-1 port connections to be supported by DS-1 local loops, by only providing the port connection with the number of DS-0 channels needed for the throughput purchased.[2]

The channelized DS-1 allows you to allocate a combination of 64K bps streams to one set of applications, such as those using the frame relay network, and allocate other 64K bps bit streams to different applications.

The carrier needs to terminate the circuit in a device that can support this channelization; this is typically a channel bank or digital cross-connect system.

A channelized DS-1 is probably the most common form of access into public frame relay services for port connection speeds above 56/64K bps.

### *Integrated Access*

Many customers limit their initial expenses with frame relay by making use of unused channels on existing DS-1s. In fact, one of the advantages of using channelized local access is that you can share loop capacity between different applications, such as frame relay, traditional private lines, voice and video. Most carriers term this "integrated access."

Integrated access is a function of both your CSU/DSU, or multiplexer, and equipment in the carrier's point of presence, or POP. Many CSU/DSUs today offer the ability to support a T-1 input port and two or more V.35 ports (for a total of three input ports). This means that you can achieve an integrated access solution without having to invest in a multiplexer. A multiplexer is more expensive, but it will allow you to have a greater degree of flexibility in allocating the 24 DS-1 channels to different applications, because it will support more than just three input ports.

By using integrated access, you can economize on loop costs. The carrier will terminate the loop into a channelization device, such as a digital cross-connect system. The DCS will allow the carrier to partition groups of DS-0s to the correct service platform.

Planning will become important if you select integrated access. For example, contiguous slotting of the DS-0s may be critical to the operation of some of the applications. Contiguous slotting refers to placing individual DS-0 circuits in contiguous, or adjacent, time slots. The purpose is to limit the delay variation between arriving data across different DS-0s. When one application uses 256K bps, for example, then four DS-0 circuits would be used (4 x 64K bps = 256K bps). Delay variation can be minimized by keeping the DS-0s on adjacent time slots such as channels 5, 6, 7 and 8; as opposed to using channels 5, 9, 14 and 24. In fact, contiguous slotting would be recommended, although not absolutely necessary, for the DS-0s supporting the frame relay port connection.

*Integrated Access*

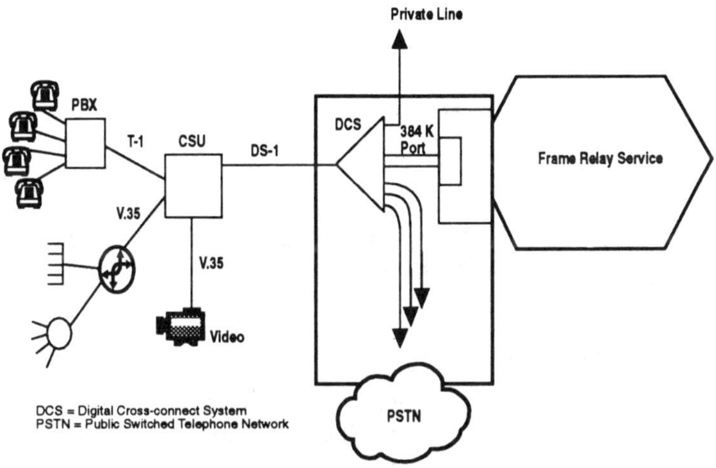


*Fig. 5.1: Integrated access allows voice, data, and video applications to share the same physical access facility. Applications are assigned specific time slots, or DS-0s, on the DS-1 loop. The loop terminates into a DCS where circuits are broken out and cross connected to the appropriate service offering.*

With this being the case, you will need to think about future network growth trends and perhaps plan for the expansion of contiguous channels for one or more applications. In doing so, your initial DS-0 slotting on the DS-1 might look like figure 5.2.

This will also mean that your loop will be underutilized, until the predicted growth begins to occur. However, when the higher capacity is needed for one of the applications, it can be easily and quickly added, without a major re-engineering effort.

Contiguous slotting of DS-0s and planning for this network growth will require coordination with your carrier(s). In fact, you should acquire a circuit layout record to verify that the slotting is consistent with your requirements prior to actual service installation. This will help you to avoid future application- and growth-related problems.

*Contiguous Slotting and Growth Planning*

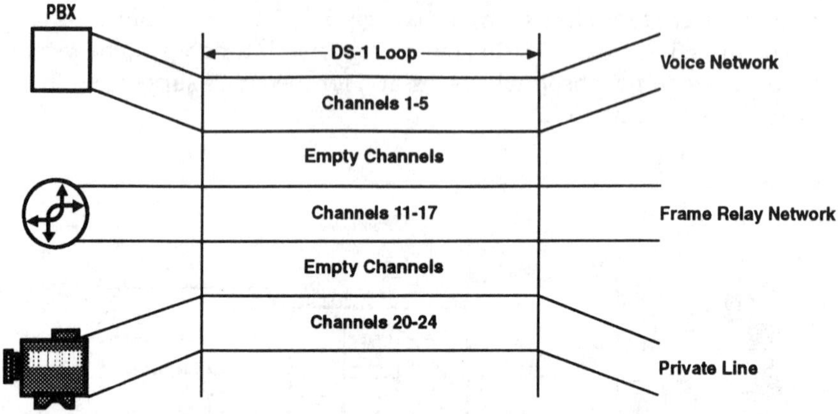


*Fig. 5.2: Leaving open channels on the DS-1 loop allows future expansion of contiguously slotted circuit groups as network requirements increase. In the diagram, channels 6-10 and 18-19 are open for future growth.*

### *Pros and Cons of Integrated Access*

There are positive and negative aspects to integrating several applications onto the same local access facility. Consider both sides carefully for each location before making your decision.

The positive aspect is obviously the savings that you can achieve with this approach. Sometimes this is the overriding concern, especially at less critical remote sites.

The negative aspect is increased vulnerability. With all your eggs in one access-basket, you are subject to a single access failure affecting all the communications at a location. You may decide that you want your voice applications on one local loop into one carrier's network, and your data applications on a different loop into a different carrier's network. This provides some added protection, even though the last mile of both loops may be in the same physical conduit.

Either way, you should think about how you can recover connectivity to the applications in the event of a network outage. These considerations and some potential solutions are covered in Chapters Six and Seven on Designing the Network.

Another potential negative: a lack of choice for the carrier. If you use an existing circuit for integrated access for frame relay, you are choosing your current carrier to be your de facto frame relay service provider.

## *Metropolitan Fiber Rings*

There is also a growing number of alternative access solutions. These solutions involve metropolitan fiber rings. These networks offer fiber into and out of select buildings — usually in the business districts of cities — with geographically diverse points of entry and exit.

While Competitive Access Providers (CAPs) are the most prominent providers of these high-speed networks, many RBOCs are also constructing metro fiber rings.

The services available on these rings vary by provider, but will often include speeds as low as 1.536M bps, or even below.

There are several advantages of this type of access. The quality is higher because the entire facility is fiber. Automatic network restoral following a fiber cut is typically built into the network, offering subsecond response times to failures and higher network availability. Scalability is also easier. Once the connection is in place, providing your application with more capacity is usually a logical assignment, not a physical one. This speeds up installation intervals for incremental capacity additions.

*Metropolitan Fiber Rings*

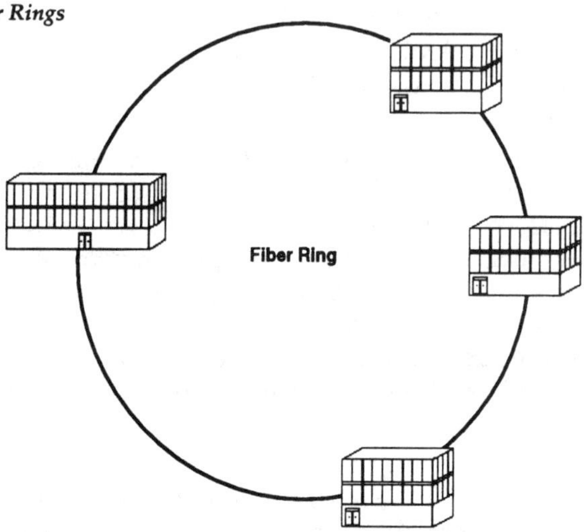


*Fig. 5.3: Metropolitan fiber rings offer geographically diverse points of entry and exit from a building. This decreases access circuit vulnerability and, when combined with automatic network restoral, increases service availability.*

### *Timing*

Regardless of your local loop choice, you will need to draw timing from the network. One of the reasons for the ones-density rule imposed by AMI line coding (as discussed in detail below) is to provide a mechanism for recovering timing. Successive zeros don't produce any electronic signal — or voltage. The "1" pulses provide the timing information.

You will configure your CSU/DSU for loop timing — so that it draws timing from the local access facility.

### *Line Coding*

When using a DS-1 local loop, you will need to choose your line coding algorithm. Line coding affects the way the CSU/DSU and the network will handle the least significant bit in every byte (the eighth bit). The two most popular forms are AMI (alternate mark inversion) and B8ZS (bipolar eight zero substitution) line coding.

With AMI line coding, the least significant bit will be forced to a "1," and will not be available for the transportation of user data. This process, called "bit robbing" or "bit stuffing," limits the effective throughput of each 64K bps channel within the DS-1 to only 56K bps.

If you choose to use AMI line coding to support a high-speed port connection, then you will need to make a choice. This choice is best explained through an example.

Assume that you decide upon a 256K bps port connection. You will use an existing CSU/DSU, which does not support B8ZS, to save capital expenditures. In this case, you can either use four DS-0s, each a 56K bps effective throughput, for a port connection of 224K bps. Or, you can use five DS-0s, each at 56K bps, and clock the CSU/DSU at the full 256K bps port connection speed (280K bps of capacity is actually available if you add up all the local loops, but most carriers do not offer this as a port connection speed. Only a few CSU/DSUs support this type of configuration, so you are better off just using B8ZS line coding.

B8ZS line coding, often called clear channel, allows the full 64K bps of throughput to be used. To use B8ZS line coding, you will simply need a B8ZS CSU/DSU. This is the recommended approach when connecting to a frame relay network service.

Unless you face a situation where for budgetary reasons you cannot afford a B8ZS CSU/DSU, it is strongly recommended that you use B8ZS line coding on the access links to your frame relay port connections. The added throughput and efficiency are worth it.

*Line Coding Affects Local Acces Planning*

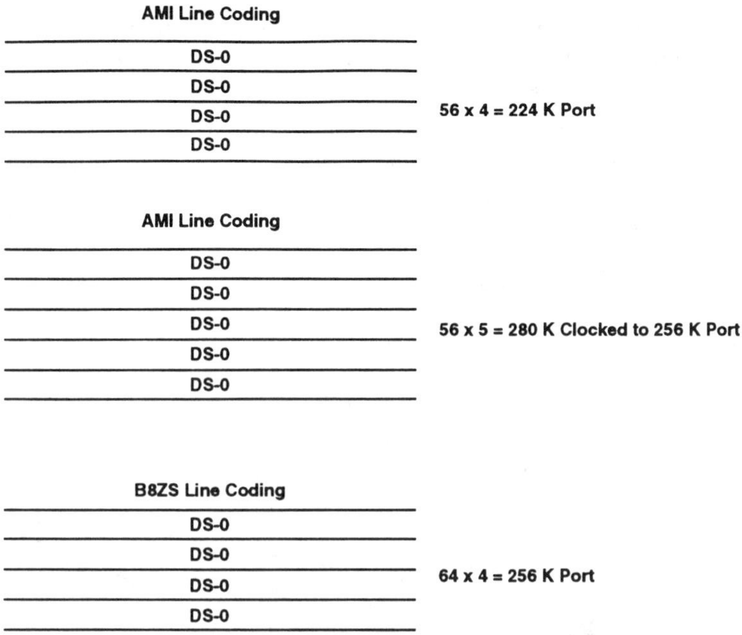


*Fig. 5.4: Three choices are available to support a 256K bps port connection. If AMI line coding is used, then either 4 DS-0 circuits can be allocated for an effective throughput of 224K bps or 5 DS-0 circuits can be used. If 5 are used, the CSU is clocked at the port speed of 256K bps. If B8ZS line coding is used, 4 DS-0 circuits are needed.*

## *Formatting*

You will also need to choose the formatting option on your DS-1 loop. This is once again a function of the CSU/DSU. Older models will only support Superframe formatting (SF, sometimes called D4), while newer models will support Extended Superframe (ESF).

ESF is recommended because it will provide a higher level of visibility into the performance of the DS-1 local loop. Its ability to segregate a loop by direction will also speed the process of trouble localization and identification.

## Local Frame Relay Services

It is entirely possible that you could use a local frame relay service to access a wide area frame relay service. You should consider several issues when evaluating this approach.

As a rule of thumb, it will usually take about three locations within a given LATA before local frame relay service becomes a cost-effective access alternative. This means that you need connectivity from three (or more) sites within the same LATA into the wide area network. If you also need direct interconnectivity between the sites in the LATA, the cost-justification could be positive with as few as two sites.

*Private Line vs. IntraLATA Frame Relay Access*

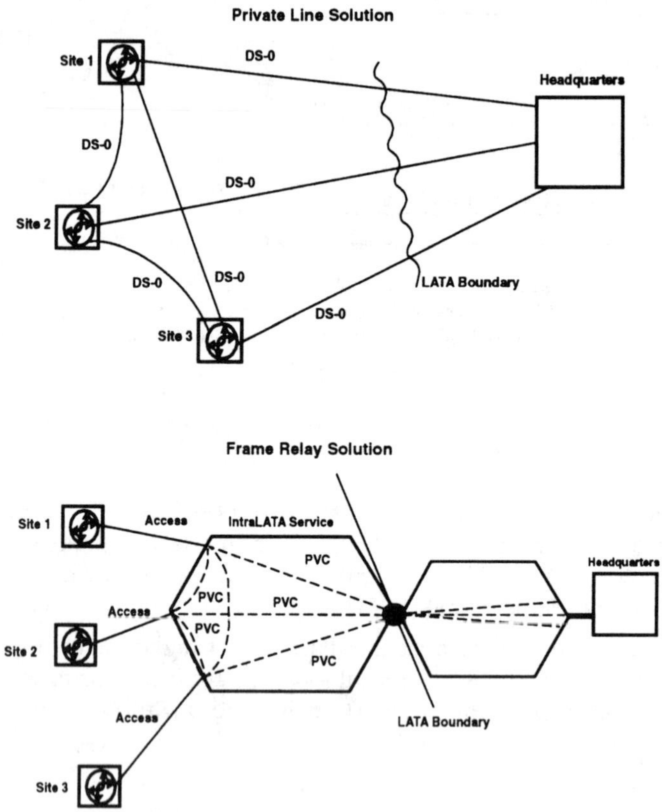


*Fig. 5.5: In configurations with three or more sites within a LATA, a local frame relay service could be a cost-effective alternative to private lines.*

If you have just a single location within a LATA that must have access to the wide area frame relay service, you will probably find that it is more cost-effective to use a traditional private line — we say "probably" because most local frame relay services are non-mileage sensitive in price structure. If you have a very long loop (greater than 15, 10 or possibly even 5 miles), you may want to at least evaluate the economic trade-off between using a dedicated leased line and a frame relay service.

It is worth mentioning that this rule of thumb varies greatly by port speed and by region. In some LATAs, a 56K bps frame relay connection is less expensive than a DS-0 local loop for even one location, even for very short mileage.

### *Network Architecture and Service Implications*

Local access frame relay services can be a bit different in underlying architecture than wide area network services. Be careful in making assumptions about the LEC's architecture. You may assume you have automatic reroute protection from network outages when this may not be the case, or may only be true for a portion of the loop. (This same caution applies to wide area services, as mentioned in Chapter Six).

In a best-case scenario, a local access frame relay connection will look like figure 5.5. This is "best case" because the local frame relay service provider has a frame relay switch in your serving wire center and several others within the LATA. This reduces the length of the more vulnerable "access" portion of the service and also provides automatic routing around network failures.

Of course, a true best-case scenario would include fiber into and out of the building at different physical locations. As mentioned above, this alternative is becoming more widely available.

With most local services and for most locations, access to these fiber rings is either not available or involves using an access line to reach the ring. In these cases, the access portion is just as vulnerable as standard leased-line services.

If the access line is cut, the effect will be the same as a local loop failure for that location. Unless other alternatives have been established, the location will be isolated from the network until the problem is resolved.

In figure 5.6, the frame relay switch is located in the first central office into which the access line terminates. This may not always be the case, and just as with IXC services, your connection may be backhauled to the nearest switch. Again, this backhauled portion will be vulnerable to cable cuts. Until your connection is actually on the frame relay network, you probably do not have

*Network Configuration for IntraLATA Service*

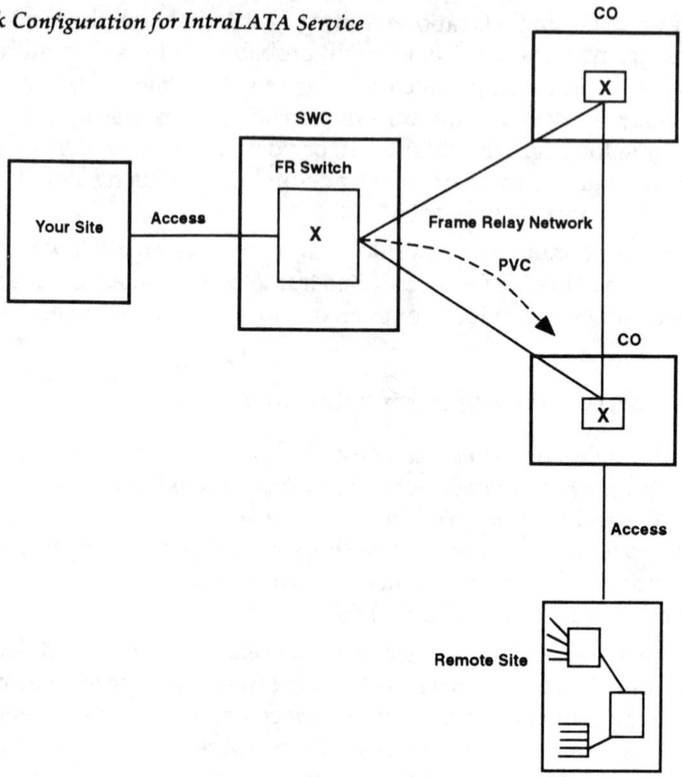


*Fig. 5.6: In this example, the carrier's frame relay switch is located in your serving wire center. Combined with the automatic network restoration capability made possible in this LATA by connecting several frame relay switches together, the service availability should be higher than standard private line loops.*

automatic routing around network failures. The same is true for interLATA frame relay services as well as intraLATA.

Many local services are still in early stages of deployment, and there may be only one (or possibly two) frame relay switches within a LATA. This means that little, if any, automatic rerouting will actually be achievable should a cable cut occur. Consult with your frame relay provider to understand the level of network protection the underlying platform can provide.

Keep in mind that you are no more vulnerable by using frame relay services than you would be if you chose a dedicated leased line access; you just may not be any better off. Take the time to evaluate and understand the circuit routing before you make qualitative assumptions. Economics may be the single biggest driver for this decision, at least until the intraLATA network's architecture includes two or more switches for alternate routing.

## Network to Network Gateway

In using an intraLATA frame relay service in place of a dedicated leased line to access your wide area frame relay service, you may see a price structure for this access option that includes both the standard LEC frame relay port and PVC charges, as well as an additional "gateway" charge for connectivity between the two networks.

With dedicated private line local loops, you are typically charged two channel terminations plus mileage for the connection between your location and the carrier's POP. In using intraLATA frame relay service, you will see a similar charge for this portion of the network connectivity; the name may just be different. For example, it could be called a "gateway charge," referring to the fact that the traffic is leaving one carrier's network and entering another carrier's network.

All of the locations within a LATA can share the same gateway and the same wide area network port connection. Each site will still need its own set of PVCs to each of the remote locations to which it needs direct connectivity. The sites will not be able to share PVCs.

If you have more than one location in a LATA and plan, this approach could prove very cost-effective. If leased lines were used instead of intraLATA frame relay, each site in the LATA would need its own wide area frame relay port connection. By using an intraLATA frame relay solution instead, the sites can share a wide area port connection. This will reduce expenditures.

If all three intraLATA sites interface into the local frame relay service using a 56/64K bps port connection, then the IXC port connection they share could be a 56/64K bps port connection or a higher speed port such as 128K or 256K bps. The first example of three 64K bps ports sharing the same 64K bps wide area port connection would not be recommended, due to the problems you may encounter in contention for the port's capacity. However, allowing all three to share a higher speed port connection is an ideal scenario when you have several locations in one LATA, as well as several locations in other LATAs.

*IntraLATA to InterLATA Frame Relay Service Connectivity*

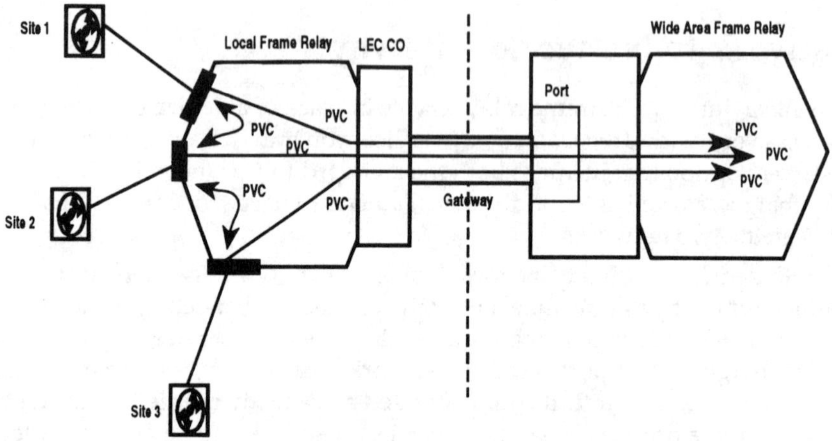


*Fig. 5.7: Each location shares the gateway and wide area network port connection.*

# Provisioning and Maintenance Coordination

Some of the biggest obstacles the carriers have been working to overcome to provide interconnectivity between frame relay services are operational in nature. Provisioning, installation, and maintenance procedures must be established between the local and wide-area frame relay service providers, and in many cases new relationships and rules must be developed.

With traditional local loops, an interexchange carrier can often gain visibility into the local loop and all the way to your CSU/DSU. With ESF formatting, the carrier can evaluate the performance of the local loop in real time and identify the direction of potential problems. The carrier can remotely control the CSU, putting it into a loop-back mode for circuit testing if needed.

Once two carriers interface frame relay networks, a great deal of this traditional visibility and control for a single carrier is diminished, making coordinated procedures between the carriers even more critical. The ability to know if a problem is on the local frame relay or interexchange frame relay service exists, but a change in diagnostic procedure for further isolating the problem is required. The good news is that the local frame relay provider will have a better view of the access link in an intraLATA frame relay environment than they would probably have with low speed private lines. If the IXC carrier is your single point of contact for all problems, then communication between the IXC and LEC becomes the critical link. To their credit, many local, regional and long-distance providers have done a good job putting communications channels and procedures in place. A few stragglers remain.

Visibility for one provider into another provider's network is still possible. For example, a wide area network frame relay provider would have visibility into the performance of a PVC directly connecting your site with the WAN frame relay port. However, the wide area carrier will not be able to see any PVCs that directly connect two sites within the same LATA over the intraLATA frame relay service, even though that carrier may be providing you with a single-stop solution and a single number for maintenance. In this case, the carrier would have to coordinate procedures for maintenance of these facilities with the local service provider.

A solution is for the IXC to provision a PVC into the local frame relay provider's SNMP agent and extract Management Information Base data about the health of your frame relay network. While this is not yet common practice, it soon may be. It is also probable that carriers will develop additional ways to provide partner service providers with greater visibility into each other's networks.

## Location-by-Location Decisions

What you will probably discover is that a mix of DS-0, channelized DS-1, non-channelized DS-1 and even intraLATA frame relay services will be used throughout your network. The best approach is to evaluate each location on a case-by-case basis and choose the solution that is most appropriate or that site. Mix and match.

[1] *The term DS-0 is used here instead of DDS because DS-0 options are becoming more available and typically cost much less than a DDS circuit. The difference in quality is minimal, if anything. DDS is an older term which refers to hubbing the channel through a special data-only channel bank - no longer a necessity for high quality data transmission. Most access providers now offer a hubless 56K bps access option, which is generally called a DS-0. Depending upon the carrier's capabilities, this may be clear-channel 64K bps, but is more likely limited to 56K bps throughput.*

[2] *The option of using a fractional T-1 will not be covered because so few access providers currently offer this alternative. However, the salient points covered under channelized DS-1 would apply, and line coding and formatting would need to be determined.*

## CHAPTER 6:

# DESIGNING THE NETWORK

The process for designing a frame relay network can be a bit different than for designing a private line network. The traffic profile information that you must consider is largely the same as for a private network, but the ultimate network design that information suggests will probably be very different. Your underlying, site-to-site traffic pattern can be more closely matched by a frame relay network than by a private line network. In designing a frame relay network, you will need to consider the level of mesh connectivity required for each network location and the bursty nature of your data applications.

Many companies do not have a good feel for the underlying traffic patterns, the average and peak utilization of individual network connections or individual applications. This means that your initial network design may be based on indirect indicators, and will then be fine-tuned over time as more direct traffic pattern information is gathered.

This chapter will provide guidelines and suggestions for what to look at when designing your network, and how to use the information that you do have available to determine your port connection speeds, your connectivity requirements (i.e., PVCs), and the required speed for each connection (i.e., the PVC's CIR).

## Network Objectives

While it may sound too academic and theoretical to say that the place to begin is by understanding your network objectives, this is in fact the case. The reason for this is that these high level objectives may provide guidance when choosing between alternative topologies, determining CIRs, deciding upon oversubscription allowances and burst assignments, etc.

For example, you may want to set an objective that any user accessing the network anytime from anywhere will experience a consistent look, feel and network performance. Another goal may be that the network manages itself, with as little human intervention as possible, and/or that carrier service options are used for daily management instead of your internal resources. While these may seem like obvious niceties, they may represent very specific objectives, or they may just be general guidelines. While most network managers will say they want these characteristics, they may not follow through on the network design to ensure them, especially if it means increased network costs. You need to determine, up front, what objectives will guide your design. If you can put hard numbers around these, such as "no more that one second response time for the interactive applications from any network point," so much the better.

For example, realistic numbers might be:

- 1 second for block-oriented applications such as SNA
- 80 ms at the outside for interactive TCP/IP and X/Motif applications
- 100 ms for screen-update-oriented client-server
- 60 ms for general interactive, character-based applications
- Availability of 99.996 percent

The basic threshold for human response on average is 20 ms. At this delay, type-ahead becomes apparent for moderate typists. As a practical matter, delay influences the location/distance in milliseconds for clients and servers. The network topology, the computing server characteristics and the application designs become interlinked. Therefore, the whole picture must be taken into account when designing the network for a given location.

One network manager at a large computer manufacturer, which happens to use a public frame relay service as part of a public/private hybrid network configuration, spends very little time "managing" the network, and much more time on strategic business projects. The entire network is managed and maintained by three people, although it spans over 20 locations worldwide. More importantly, this manager and his staff spend an average of 90 percent of their time on projects that are strategic to the core business. This decreased level of day-to-day management can be one of the big benefits of a public frame relay network service compared to a private network.

You need to determine your availability objectives for different sites, as well, because this could also have a big impact on network design and cost at a given location. For example, you may determine that no amount of network downtime is acceptable for the business at the primary data processing location. In this case, you may be willing to spend more money for geographically diverse local loops into geographically diverse frame relay port connections. This same requirement, and the added expense that goes with it, may not hold true for your remote sales offices.

## Making a List and Checking It Twice

There are two main steps to beginning your network design. The first is to understand your current network topology and do a detailed site inventory. The second step is to collect information about the underlying traffic patterns of the applications being supported.

The inventory will help you to know what network elements are under design consideration. You wouldn't want to overlook a necessary part of the network design, like hardware or access, at a location. In addition to the frame relay network elements, each site must also have a local loop, a router (or some other type of frame relay equipment), and a CSU/DSU. Sometimes the hardware you have, or will buy, includes integrated CSU/DSU functionality. The point is to inventory each location separately, to determine which elements are already in place and which are not. The inventory should include a review of the existing network topology.

Your frame relay carrier will provide the local access as part of the service, but if you already have DS-1 local loops in place with spare capacity at several locations, then the use of integrated access (see Chapter 5) could influence your choice of vendor. The carrier can also provide an equipment package that includes the router and CSU/DSU, if you are in need of either or both of these devices. Having a single carrier provide all the service elements can help reduce finger-pointing between vendors when problems arise. Using a carrier to provide a more complete, integrated solution is covered in detail in the chapter on network management and managed network services.

It is helpful to keep a specification sheet on each site so that you can record information about that site that might affect the network design. This could include whether the site is critical enough to warrant the evaluation of local access diversity for network protection, whether the site will operate as a backup data center during a disaster scenario, whether the site will need to change its network configuration during a disaster scenario, etc. Other information that can be helpful in designing the network into each site is discussed below.

There could be some small sites that could either connect directly to the frame relay network or be indirectly connected to the network by using a short tail circuit (i.e., a private line) to hub into another, larger site. It is also possible to use dial-in connectivity, as covered in greater detail later, for locations with very low traffic volumes. Your specification sheet for the small site could indicate which configuration(s) you plan to consider for a site. If you use a tail circuit design, the configuration will affect the connectivity and equipment requirements at the hub site. Therefore, you should also make a notation on the specification sheet for the potential hub site so that the incoming tandem traffic can be accounted for in the network configuration.

While frame relay is designed to help cost-effectively flatten network architectures, you may find that not every site will cost-justify a direct connection. This is especially true for low-volume sites that are geographically close to larger locations which themselves will cost-justify a direct connection. The branch location will inherit all of the connectivity of the hub site by connecting directly to that hub site and using the hub location's PVCs. You will want to evaluate the economic trade-offs of different network topologies before making a final decision.

In order to design a network that will meet the needs of each site, you and your carriers will need an understanding of the applications, protocols, and other environmental factors at each site. Therefore, the specification sheet should include any information you have on the following topics:

- Network applications, including average file size, transaction frequency, time of day utilization pattern, number of users, and relative priority level of the application
- Protocols
- Other existing equipment, such as SNA devices that might be under lease (and amortization/cost status if applicable)
- Existing network facilities serving the site/application and average performance. For example, are you seeing congestion problems as slow response times with the current network? When?
- Non-frame relay applications at the site

This last point, the non-frame relay applications, might include applications that could someday migrate to the frame relay network, and those that will probably never migrate. Both could affect the network design at that site.

For example, you may begin by not consolidating SNA applications onto the frame relay network, but plan to do so once the network is proven. You may also have voice and other leased-line applications that will not be on the frame relay network, but could share the access facilities.

Just be sure that any and all information that could affect the network's design is captured somewhere. Even if you do not yet know, or will not be able to discover, some of the traffic detail, just having the issue identified on paper for the site will allow you to make some working assumptions as you begin the design process.

Many frame relay users find that the paper work created during the design process serves as historical reference in the documentation package that supports the network. Archive notes, saved simulations, charts, and graphs, and assumptions used to design the network can be used later to validate the assumptions, answer questions about process or calculation. They can also be used for network modification.

## The Tail Wags The Dog

When designing the frame relay network configuration at a location, the tail wags the dog. This means that the port connection speed for a given location should be decided last, after you have determined the PVCs needed and the CIRs of the PVCs. The aggregate of the CIRs will then determine the port connection speed.

You need to know the PVC requirements to determine the port speed. But to know the PVC requirements, you must understand the connectivity requirements of the site, which means understanding the users and the applications.

### *The PVC Map*

Begin by simply plotting all your locations on a map so that you have a general idea of the relative proximity of each location. This will help you to "locate the edges" of the network. These are the sites requiring connectivity. You then "connect related edges." In this stage, you design paths from one edge location to a related location, as defined by a need to exchange information. This graphical representation can form the basis of a PVC map developed at later stages.

When you design your frame relay network, you will do so by designing each site individually and then stepping back and putting it all together to make sure the final design makes sense.

In putting together the PVC map, look at each network location (i.e., each edge site on the network) separately. You will first need to determine the other remote locations to which a *direct* frame relay connection (PVC) is probably required. Notice that it says "direct connection." You may need the ability to communicate with a lot of other remote sites, but the volume of traffic may not justify a direct connection.

Just like with other network architectures, frame relay will allow you to create a logical mesh of connectivity without creating a physical mesh. This is cost-effective when a very small amount of traffic volume exists between two locations, like two remote sales offices. Some traffic between some locations, like E-mail between remote sales sites, may first be routed through one or more intermediate locations before reaching the final destination. The advantage of frame relay is that a greater number of direct connections are affordable, and this greater level of direct connectivity can improve overall network performance. Still, there is no reason to have a direct connection between two sites that only send each other infrequent e-mail messages.

Deciding the remote locations into which a site will have a direct PVC connection is a matter of estimating traffic volume between the different sites. At this stage, you can probably go by instinct if nothing else. For example, a small field sales office probably needs to communicate to the headquarters location, possibly one or more primary data processing sites, and perhaps a regional sales headquarters site. Unless some other special application is being used that would require additional connectivity, these would be good beginning assumptions. Do not fall into the trap of thinking a remote sales office only needs a connection to its regional sales office simply because that's the way the private line network was designed. The majority of traffic may actually be passed along to the headquarters location. With frame relay, you will assign a PVC that correlates with the underlying traffic pattern. That could mean a PVC directly between the small remote site and the headquarters.

### *Determining PVCs*

When deciding on the size/speed (i.e., the committed information rate) of the PVCs at a network location, you may want to treat PVCs as one way, or *simplex*, connections. This means that you look at each direction of the traffic separately. If you suspect that you have one or more applications in which the volume of traffic in one direction is substantially different from the volume of traffic in the other direction, then this approach is warranted. Looking at each direction of a connection separately is fairly easy and can be done systematically throughout the network by looking at the *outbound* connectivity requirements from one site to each of the other sites to which it will have a direct PVC connection. Outbound means the traffic volume *from* that site *to* other sites. The return connectivity requirements are actually outbound PVCs from the other locations back to the first site, and would be designed when you design the outbound network requirements from each of those locations.

PVCs are logical, full-duplex connections. Some carriers will allow you to purchase a different CIR in each direction of the PVC to more cost-effectively support asymmetric traffic patterns. The reasons for approaching the design by looking at each direction of a connection is that many applications actually have CIR requirements in the outbound direction that are different than for the return direction.

Traffic patterns are often not homogeneous across a network. Private lines don't allow you to buy differing capacities in each direction, which means you may be paying for more bandwidth, at least one way, than what you really need. You may be able to save money with a frame relay network by only purchasing the level of CIR that your applications need in each direction of a connection, assuming that the carrier supports simplex PVCs. Even if your carrier does not support this feature, you will still want to design your network by looking at each direction of the connection separately. You would then choose the higher of the two committed information rates as the CIR for that PVC.

Initially, you may not have enough information about your traffic pattern to tell if you need more or less capacity in a single direction. Once you are up and running in a frame relay environment, the network can provide you with this information. You can then go back and fine tune the frame relay network design.

You may want to consider some of the emerging network design tools for frame relay, which will allow you to run network simulations under different design assumptions and topologies. This is not necessary, however, as the carriers will help you with designing your network during the proposal process (See Chapter 13).

The specification sheet for each site will help you determine the CIR for each PVC. Look at your list of applications, current network facilities, etc., for each site as you determine direct PVC needs. In this stage, you are better to err on the side of too much direct connectivity, as opposed to too little. Doing different "what-if" pricing in designing a frame relay network is very easy compared with private line networks. You will probably have two or three different designs that could be used at each site, with differing levels of direct connectivity. You can either begin with a best case design and scale down if needed, or a least-cost design, and add connectivity if your budget allows. You will find that once a site is connected to the public frame relay network, adding incremental PVC connections and capacity is relatively inexpensive.

Remember, one of the advantages of frame relay is that the network should match the traffic pattern, instead of vice-versa. While traffic pattern information is difficult to come by in many cases, you can at least begin to get a sense of traffic flow by looking at who needs to send information to whom.

### *Determining CIR*

Deciding the committed information rate can be easy or hard, depending on how much information you already have about traffic patterns, average and peak volume, and how much "guess-timating" you are comfortable doing for the initial design.

Again, if you don't have hard numbers, don't be alarmed. Common sense and some basic mathematics can take you a long way in this process. You may need to make working assumptions about file size and frequency if you don't have specific numbers to go by. Record any assumptions on the specification sheet. Keeping track of your working assumptions will help you when working with different carriers to communicate your needs.

Rule of Thumb guidelines can be helpful as you design the CIR. These "rules" are typically company-specific and based on previous networking experience. For example, you may have already developed a rule of thumb that says "no more than five order-entry users per 56K bps of available network capacity."

Look at each PVC out of a site individually, and choose a CIR that will support the expected average traffic volume from the first site to the second. The burst capability of the PVC should not be counted on for transmissions when designing the network. The burst should simply be looked upon as a way to more quickly clear congestion from the port connection, handle busy periods for a given application or PVC, and get large files through the network more quickly. Since the burst may or may not be available, depending upon overall port and network contention, you should design the CIR to meet the average requirements and response time objectives of the supported applications.

The burst capability has a "smoothing" effect on application performance and protocol errors at the application level. Sometimes this effect is also achieved at the transport level and the frame relay level. More advanced designers should be aware of the effects of serialization delay, packetization and queuing delay and the effect of the burst capability on the network and the application.

To illustrate the process of determining the actual CIR for a PVC, we will use a couple of different network examples. Before we do this, one last vital piece of the puzzle still needs to be discussed: the port connection.

### *Determining Port Connection Speed*

The port connection speed at a network location should be determined after you know the total of the CIRs out of and into that site. When you design the PVCs at a site, look at the outbound traffic needs. Once all of the PVCs have been determined, and a CIR for each PVC chosen, you then go back to each location and determine what port connection speed makes sense, balancing performance and financial considerations.

This may now sound strange, but as a general rule in determining the port connection speed you will look at the inbound CIR total for that site and begin your design with the minimum port connection speed needed to support the traffic volume. This is because the outbound PVCs can rely on buffers at the router and port connection site when contention for network capacity is occurring. The inbound PVCs are not afforded this luxury. Therefore, when too many inbound PVCs are all simultaneously contending for the same port connection space in an oversubscribed environment, some data may be discarded and require a retransmission.

If the inbound and outbound CIR totals are very different, and the outbound total is significantly higher than the inbound's, you may want to adjust the port connection speed upwards until you reach a point where the oversubscription level for the outbound traffic is at a level with which you are comfortable. In most networks, the traffic patterns are symmetrical enough that the total inbound versus outbound CIR will not be much different. It is only in the case of highly asymmetrical traffic patterns that you need to double check the port's ability to meet the needs of traffic in both directions.

Don't total both the inbound CIRs and the outbound CIRs to determine your port speed. If you do, you will choose a speed that is much greater than what you need. Look at each direction of traffic separately and make sure that the port connection speed you choose can handle each direction.

It is difficult to conceptualize, but *the inbound and outbound traffic streams do not contend for the same port capacity.* Think of it as really being two separate port connections, one that is dynamically allocated for the inbound traffic and one that is dynamically allocated for the outbound traffic. You only pay for one port connection, and you only choose one port connection speed for both the inbound and outbound traffic, but the traffic itself does not mix on the same port connection.

In determining the port's speed, consider a 100 to 200 percent subscription level depending upon how intermittent the applications are and the likelihood of every PVC being simultaneously active. If you will remember from Chapter Four, oversubscribing a port connection means assigning more total CIR, across all of the PVCs supported by the port connection, than what the port connection could actually handle at any given point in time. For example, you could assign a 256K bps port connection eight PVCs, each with a CIR of 64K bps, for a total of 512K bps. Oversubscribing a port connection will save you money at the site, because it means a lower port connection speed can be utilized. In the example above, if a 256K bps port connection is used for all eight PVCs, the price could be about 25 percent less at that site than if a 512K bps port speed were used.

Some carriers will define oversubscription of the port connection, for pricing purposes, to be the ratio of the port's speed to the *outbound* PVCs. Don't let this pricing approach confuse you during the network design stage. How you choose a port connection's speed and how that port is then priced are two different issues. They are related only in that you want to balance network price with network performance. Regardless of how the carrier prices the service and defines oversubscription, from a design perspective you want to check the oversubscription levels for both the inbound traffic, and then for the outbound traffic, to ensure that the port connection speed can adequately handle the CIR totals in each direction.

## Pilot Network

Piloting is a technique you may find very useful as you launch into your first frame relay network experience. In setting up a pilot network, you would choose two or preferably three network locations for initial frame relay installation, and would then proceed to install and benchmark test the network before installing frame relay to other locations.

During the pilot stage, you can test some of your rule of thumb assumptions you may have brought from the private line network and determine if they are still appropriate in a frame relay environment. Experiments on the pilot network serve as reference for building the real network or as feedback for network design.

The pilot network does not have to be a time-consuming or costly project. It can simply be the first phase of your overall network implementation. If you run the pilot network in parallel to your existing network for a short time, say 30 days, you can benchmark the two networks initially to determine any change in application performance.

You can then use the parallel configuration as a safety net by rolling existing applications onto the frame relay network before the leased line is disconnected. This will allow you to quickly switch the application back to the previous network should any performance-affecting problems arise.

In this example of migrating applications from a private network on to a frame relay network, you can actually use frame relay to steer, or "shape," the traffic patterns from undesired existing patterns into more ideal patterns in some cases. This can be done through the way in which you design your PVCs and your routing tables. Additional information on this topic is discussed in the chapter on network implementation.

## Network Examples

Looking at a few different frame relay examples will be helpful in order to illustrate some different design principles and guidelines. Keep in mind that while these examples will be as realistic as possible, they will also serve to demonstrate certain design techniques such as using two different PVCs for different application types, using asymmetrical PVC rates and using dual homing for access protection. In your initial network design, you may want to begin as simply as possible, and then enhance the network once you have more experience.

Beginning with a very simple environment, we'll consider a six-site network with only LAN traffic to support. Then we'll look at a much more complicated and much larger network example.[1]

### *Example 1: A Simple Network*

The most simple frame relay network is one in which every site is similar to other sites, and where either a star or a full mesh network configuration is needed. A good example is a large law firm with several locations nationwide and partners and researchers at each site. We will use a firm with six locations, Ethernet LANs already installed at each site, and the need to share documents of cases and research material over the network.

Given that these files are large, the lawyer's time is expensive, and clients are billed back for expenses incurred on their case, this law firm does not need to be overly concerned with network costs. What they need is a very reliable service that supports any-to-any connectivity.

A situation like this is a bit unusual, because in this example every network site may actually need a direct connection to every other site. The organization is fairly flat, and the number of lawyers, and amount of traffic, at each site is about the same.

*Determining CIR*

Determining CIR is a matter of deciding how big the average file is, how often files are transmitted, and how rapid a response time is needed.

The specifications for each site look about the same.

- Each location has five to eight lawyers plus five to eight research assistants, a secretary and some interns.
- Ethernet LANs are already in place.
- There are no routers or CSU/DSUs installed, because the company has been using dial-up connectivity with modems.
- The response times are several minutes or more per file transfer, and it is costing the firm money in lost time.
- TCP/IP is the only protocol. E-mail is used extensively within an office, and sometimes large files are attached. The firm wants company-wide E-mail.
- No technical network expertise exists at any of the sites.
- The documents range from a single page up to several hundred pages. The average size is 10 to 40 pages.
- Each lawyer sends five to eight large documents across the network on an average day. There is no specific pattern for traffic between certain offices; it is very homogeneous.
- The research assistants use the network much more frequently, but the files tend to be smaller. They will average 10 to 20 document exchanges per day.

## *E-mail*

*E-mail is such a growing network application, a quick word on the topic is in order. E-mail in the Novell Netware environment or in the Internet environment is usually demand-based, with files sizes less than 4K bytes unless large files are attached. Unless special application software is used, E-mail messages are queued up, and dispatched one at a time over the network until the queue is empty. The queue service interval (i.e., run interval) determines the busy percentage of the channel more than the size of the E-mail message.*

*Because cost is not the primary issue for our law firm, and response time is, we will assume for this example that each site has a PVC to the other five locations. The CIR for each PVC would probably be between 64K and 192K bps. Here's why:*

*If the average document is 10 to 40 pages, then this equates to about 15,000 to 60,000 bytes (1500 characters per page). There are eight bits in every byte, so multiplying this number by eight will give the total number of bits in the average small file. In this example, the files are 120,000 to 480,000 bits. At 64,000 bits per second the file would transfer in 1.875 to 7.5 seconds, assuming no propagation delay by the network.*[2]

*If a 192K bps PVC were used, the response times would decrease by two thirds, to .63 and 2.5. If a 128K bps PVC were used, response times would decrease by half, to .94 and 3.75.*

*If the application is a store and forward design, then this difference in transfer time may not matter much. If the applications include real-time desktop collaboration, or if someone is likely to be waiting on the files as they are transferred, then there could be a business impact from the additional transfer time.*

### *Port Connection Speed and Access*

Since any of these transfer times are acceptable, the firm could make a choice based on cost. For example, the firm could choose to use a single DS-0 local loop from each site into the network, with a 56/64K bps port connection.[3] The firm could oversubscribe this line by 500 percent, by giving each of the five PVCs a CIR of 56/64K bps. The down side to this solution is that if more than one PVC is active at any one time, they will be contending for the same port connection space and will operate at less than the 56/64K bps CIR.

Since cost is not the most important issue, but response time is, an alternative would be to use a DS-1 local loop and a higher port connection speed. Some level of oversubscription is acceptable, because not all the PVCs will be active at the same time.

If a 192K bps PVC were used from each site to every other site, then the total inbound (and outbound) CIR from each site would be 960K bps (192K times five PVCs). If a 128K bps PVC is used, the total in/outbound CIR would be 640K bps.

If the firm chose to use the 192K bps PVC, a 384K or 512K bps port connection would make the most sense. Since the CIRs would be relatively high and the likelihood of the PVCs all being active at once relatively low a higher level of oversubscription would not be a problem.

The 384K bps port connection, with the PVCs, would equate to 250 percent subscription and about $1200 to $1500 per month per site, before local access. If the access is about $300 per DS-1 loop, the entire network would cost about $10,000 per month, before term and volume discounts are applied.

Of course, if the DS-0 loops with the 56/64K bps port connection were used instead, the entire network would be less than half that amount per month.

#### *Carrier-Provided Equipment and Management Options*

Since this law firm is not in the network business and has little expertise with routers, using the frame relay carrier to provide all of the equipment, and possibly a managed network service, should be strongly considered. With a managed network service, the carrier will monitor the network around the clock and will take responsibility for fixing any problems with the wide area network addressing. They will provide a much higher level of technical support than if the standard frame relay service were purchased without this option. Of course, this costs more. However, in the case of the law firm, it would make sense.

### *Example 2: Complex Network*

The next example will be as complicated as the last was simple. Assume that a nationwide manufacturing company has 18 locations consisting of a headquarters site in New York, three remote regional sales offices, three remote warehouses and eleven remote sales offices. The network design will be different at the small locations, the regional sites and the headquarters site. By examining the differing needs at these sites, some important design principles and considerations can be illustrated.

*Simple Frame Relay Network*

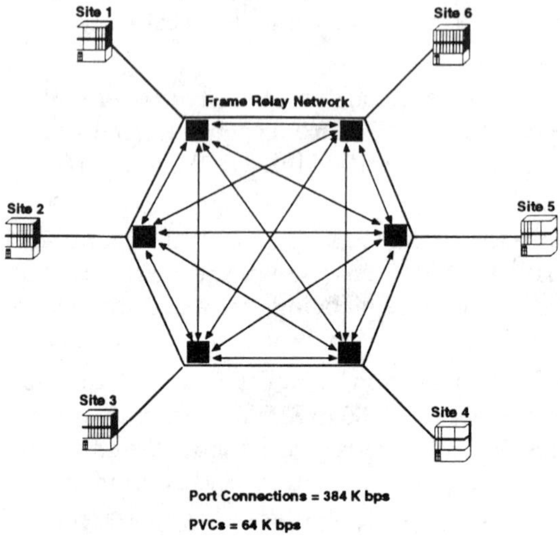


*Fig. 6.1: In this simple example of a law firm with six locations, each site has a 384K bps port connection and a 64K bps PVC to every other site.*

## *Small Remote Site*

For small remote sites, the design process may be as simple as estimating the CIR based on the level of connectivity in place today. For example, assume that today one or two 9.6K bps circuits support interactive applications from the Washington, D.C. sales office back to headquarters in New York, and one DS-0 circuit supports the LAN traffic and file transfers. You determine that aggregating the applications onto a single network could save money,[4] and you work out a migration plan for the local equipment environment and the applications.

### *Port and PVC Choice*

In the case of a small remote site, a good place to begin is to assume that a DS-0 local loop will be the most cost-effective alternative. Therefore, a 56/64K bps port connection would be needed. Traffic is generated primarily to and from headquarters so a 56/64K bps PVC would be assigned back to the central site. [5]

Initially, you might determine that traffic to other locations does not warrant additional PVCs; however, additional PVCs to other locations could be added later at a small incremental cost. For example, you may need to add

*Private Line Network*

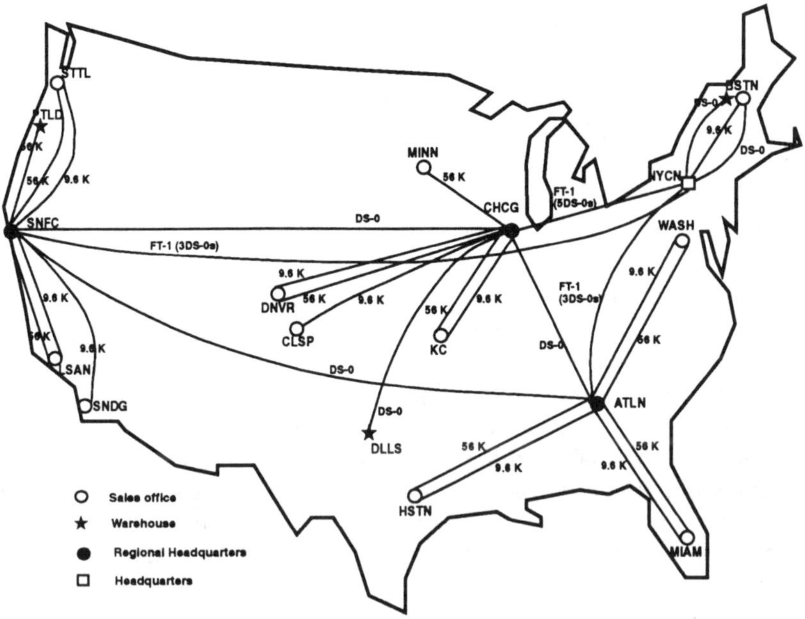


*Fig. 6.2: This private line network connects 18 locations nationwide and supports both LAN and SNA applications. Many of the small remote sites support parallel networks, while excess capacity has been added between required headquarters for added network protection.*

a PVC from a remote site to its regional headquarters, to a warehouse or to another data processing center.

You may be wondering how the conclusion was reached that two 9.6K bps lines and a 56K bps line resulted in a 56K bps port connection. Simply, most leased lines are significantly underutilized. By using a 56K bps port connection and a 56K bps PVC back to the central data processing site, both the interactive applications and the file transfers have full use of the capacity when they need it. If they both need it at exactly the same time, they can share the capacity momentarily. When one application stops, the other takes all the capacity.

As a rule of thumb, take the total of the CIR and choose a port connection speed that will provide a subscription level between 100 and 200 percent. For small remote sites, depending upon the applications and the protocols being used, it is not uncommon to see subscription rates of 300 to 500 percent. The effects of routing protocols on network design are discussed in detail in the chapter on network implementation.

*When Interactive and LAN Networks are Consolidated*

In collapsing two or more networks as described, the interactive applications will probably experience improved performance due to the higher bandwidth now available. The file transfer applications will probably not notice a lower level of performance, since the same amount of capacity has been assigned. The total capacity available at the site has actually decreased, but the network can now dynamically allocate the capacity to the applications that need it, thus increasing overall performance and decreasing costs.

For mission-critical response-time sensitive interactive applications, sharing capacity with applications that transmit large files can cause longer delays if an interactive transaction gets trapped behind a large file transfer. One way to deal with this is through prioritization in the router, perhaps by protocol type. This can slow overall router processing down, but at a small site the effect could be minimal. A different approach, or a complement to prioritization in the router, is to assign two different PVCs to the two types of applications. For example, the interactive PVC might be assigned a 32K bps PVC, and the file transfer applications a 32K bps PVC (or 64K bps if you want to oversubscribe the port).

It is worthwhile here to at least mention that the effects of queuing and buffering in the framerelay switch may decrease the effectiveness of router-based priority-queuing mechanisms as frames cross the router-to-frame relay UNI boundary. Holding times of frame fragments in the switch buffer, aggregation operations within the switch used for buffer memory coalescing, and link optimization of the carrier can have impact in this area. The best method to determine how your frame relay carrier's network will work with your applications is through the pilot network approach discussed above.

*Network Price at Remote Sales Sites*

The price, whether you use one 64K or two 32K bps PVCs will probably be around $200 to $300 per month, not including access or equipment. And if all your network locations and connectivity needs happen to be within the same LATA or small geographical area, using a local or regional carrier for the frame relay service could bring the total price down to as little as $100.

If you want to add another PVC, say, connecting the remote sales office to the nearest regional sales headquarters, the cost for a 32K bps PVC would increase the cost at this site by about $50 per month. The return PVC would also have to be figured in, but you will probably find that the result is fairly inexpensive incremental connectivity to any location nationwide.

*Connectivity to Small Remote Sites*

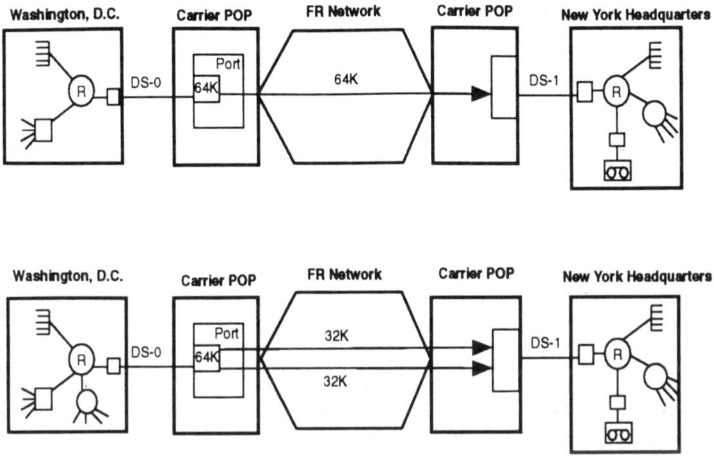


*Fig. 6.3: If both LAN-based and interactive applications will show the frame relay network, then either one PVC can be used to support both application types, or the applications can each have a separate PVC but still share the access link and port connection.*

## *Tail Circuits and Remote Sites*

For some small remote sites you will need to determine if the site should directly connect into the frame relay network, or should instead use a standard private line (i.e., a "tail circuit") to connect into the network through a hub site. This hub site would itself connect directly into the network.

The cost trade-off to be evaluated is whether a direct connection would be more or less expensive than the private line. This may be the case if the private line were a very short connection, such as within the same LATA or in a nearby LATA. Another cost impact to evaluate, although the impact will be a one-time, is the effect on the router at the hub location. It will need to support the tail circuit connection, which could warrant a larger and more expensive router.

In the sample network, a good candidate for this configuration would be the small sales offices in San Diego and Colorado Springs. Both sites are very close to larger sites that will connect directly into the network. A low-speed private line to the next-nearest location in both cases will cost around $100 per month, versus around $300 for a direct connection into the frame relay network. Therefore, unless these sites must directly connect with several other sites, this could be one way to save money.

As another rule of thumb, if you are using a flat-rate national frame relay service, you should look at small sites that are within 200 miles of other, larger locations as candidates for using a private line to frame relay hubbing architecture. If the small site itself needs high bandwidth or connectivity to several other locations it will probably warrant its own network connection. But if the capacity requirements can be met by a 56K bps connection or less, and most of the traffic is to one or two other locations on the network, then aggregating the traffic at a hub can be a way to save money.

The performance trade-off to be evaluated should include the effect on application performance at both the remote site and the hub site. The remote site's applications will tandem through the hub location, and this will add latency compared with a direct connection. The hub location's applications could also be impacted by the higher level of congestion, and added contention for the network capacity.

Also note that at the hub site, such as Denver, one of two alternatives is possible for access. Either a DS-1 local loop can be used to support both the tail circuit(s) and the frame relay port connection, or two different DS-0 local loops will be needed. The solution you choose will depend upon the port connection speed needed at the Denver location, the cross-over price between DS-1 and DS-0 loop prices at that site, and whether or not any other applications could share the access.

### *Regional Sites*

The term "regional sites" is used here as a general reference to any medium-sized or large locations that are not headquarter sites. These may include manufacturing locations, data processing centers, and regional sales offices. Typically, these sites would have greater networking requirements than small remote sites, but smaller than major headquarters sites.

In many cases, these are the sites used as networking hubs in private network configurations. You may find that these sites no longer need the same level of bandwidth once you move to a frame relay environment, because the site may no longer be functioning in the role of traffic aggregator.

Regional sites used as network hubs in a leased-line environment are often part of a backbone network that includes the use of ring network topologies and/or geographically diverse circuit routing from one or more IXC carriers. For reasons explained below, the network between regional hub sites may change drastically in a frame relay environment.

In designing the frame relay network to support these sites, several items are of importance. Typically, the leased line circuit routing and design between regional sites bears little relation to the actual traffic pattern of the applications being supported. The network topology is designed to protect

*Tail Circuits*

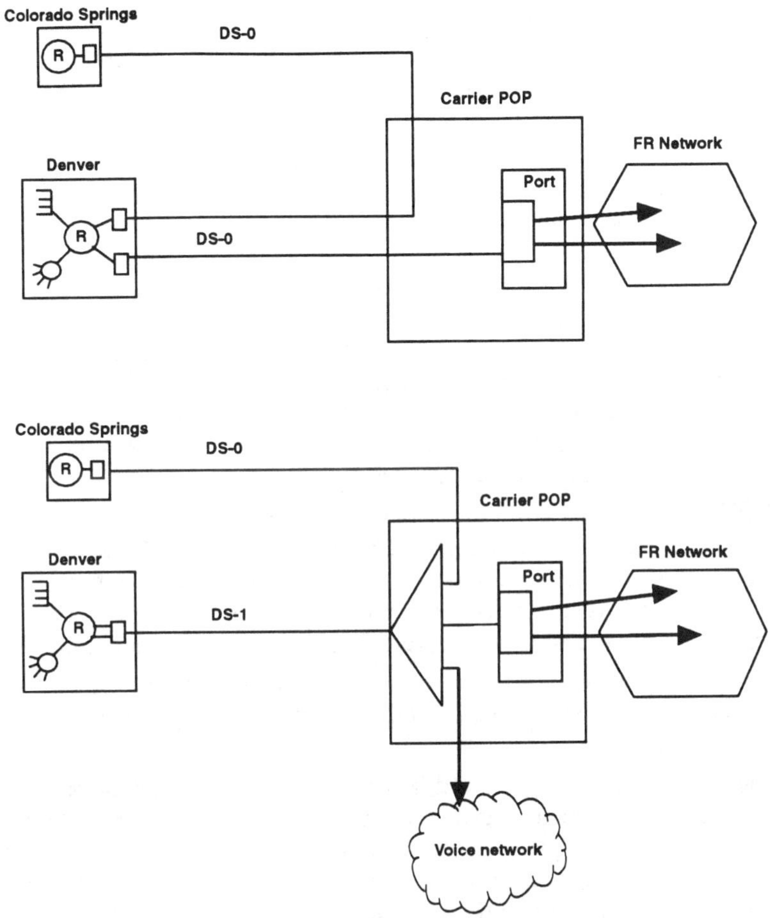


*Fig. 6.4: The hub location, Denver, could either support a tail circuit to Colorado Springs by terminating two local loops or by using a DS-1 circuit with integrated access.*

regional network sites, and the other sites they support, from isolation in the event of a major circuit failure.

The implication of this network design is that nearly double the amount of needed capacity may actually be purchased between the hub sites than what would ideally be required to support the applications. But, since the result of this is that the network can survive a cable cut by routing the affected applications to the "spare" capacity on the network, the extra capacity can be cost-justified.

The frame relay network is capable of automatically routing around an IXC network failure. This means that ring topologies between regional network sites *may* not be necessary. It also means that the amount of excess capacity on the network might be reduced.

The main caveat to this statement is that the carrier may backhaul some of your network connections to its nearest network switch. This backhauled section will not be protected by the automatic restoration capabilities of the frame relay network, and could be vulnerable to major cable cuts. The ubiquity of the carrier's network and frame relay switches in relation to your network locations might be an important selection criterion as you evaluate alternative carriers. Many carriers are also implementing digital cross-connect system (DCS) and/or SONET (synchronous optical network)-based self healing networks. In such a case, even if your carrier did not have a frame relay switch in your LATA, the backhauled portion of the circuit could automatically route around an IXC network failure.

The lesson here is that in designing the network you should find out the actual circuit routing of your connections in relation to a carrier's switch locations. Are you being backhauled or not? Does the carrier have SONET- or DCS-based network restoration capabilities in place for the portion of the network your connections will traverse? Check each network location.

You will probably find that many of your primary network hub locations are in major metropolitan areas and that the frame relay carrier will have a switch in the LATA.

The automatic routing around failures on the frame relay network could save you money, because you will not have to purchase and maintain diverse IXC network facilities between remote sites. You will no longer need to build in your own rings, with excess capacity available on the ring, in case of a network failure. The carrier does this for you when building the public frame relay network.

Local access protection may still be an issue. Alternatives for protecting access lines and increasing network availability are discussed later in this chapter and in Chapter Five.

You may also find that the criticality of network availability to former "hub" locations decreases if the site is no longer playing a traffic aggregation role, or if it is playing a much smaller aggregation role. More of your small remote locations may be directly connected into the frame relay network instead of connected through hub locations.

The network connecting regional hub sites together and back into the central site should be designed to match the flow of traffic of the underlying applications.

Consider the regional headquarters in Chicago for the sample company. Some information is known about the traffic volume and characteristics, as summarized below. Assume for this example that the voice and data applications share the same local access facilities and are split out in the carrier's POP. If you are concerned about single points of network failure, or if your voice provider is not the ideal carrier for your data needs, then you may want to use two different local loops.

The applications at the Chicago site are summarized below:

- **LAN traffic.** There are 2 LANs at the Chicago site. The LANs support the remote engineering and design personnel and the sales department.

    - **Engineering.** The engineering department sends both text files and diagrams (CAD and other) to other engineering and design departments at headquarters as well as to the Atlanta office where another design team is located. E-mail is used heavily by the organization as a whole and by this department. All corporate communications from headquarters is done via E-mail, so that a heavy volume of traffic goes from New York to Chicago, with a slightly lighter level of E-mail traffic from Chicago back to headquarters.

    - **Sales.** The sales and sales support departments use the LAN to send customer proposals to and from headquarters. Sometimes, the proposals are also sent to other remote sales locations, but this is rare. Sales management at all the sales locations use the network to share sales figures. Monthly contests are run and the standings are broadcast in near real-time to all locations on the LAN. The level of E-mail between sales offices is relatively light, with much heavier traffic back to headquarters. Documents are often encapsulated in E-mail.

- **Interactive applications.** Many of the regional sites have SNA applications for order entry and tracking, payroll and accounting, and other administrative applications. This is true for

Chicago. These interactive SNA applications will now share the frame relay network.

- **Customer Support.** Regional customer support groups enter orders, track orders and provide status updates to customers by using IBM SNA-based applications. Some of the customer service reps have 3270 terminals, but more and more are being provided with personal computers running 3270 emulation. The site is only operational as a customer support center from 7am to 6pm local time. After that, phone calls are automatically forwarded to a 24-hour support center at headquarters. When an order is entered into the system an electronic copy is sent to headquarters and to the nearest of the three regional warehouse locations. The flow of traffic from the warehouse back to the regional office is very light, and includes only acknowledgements of order receipt and a planned delivery date.

- **Accounting.** Payroll, accounts receivable and payable and other accounting data are sent over the network to headquarters.

Based on the following overview of the applications, what is generally known about the network before frame relay, and the characteristics of the traffic generated at this site, the following topology designs might result.

- **To Headquarters.** Either one or two PVCs are needed from the Chicago regional site to headquarters in New York, depending upon whether the interactive and file transfer applications will share a single PVC or be assigned separate ones. Assume that two different PVCs will be used.

- **To the Warehouse**. A PVC is needed to the warehouse location in Dallas, since a copy of orders is sent to this location.

- **To Atlanta.** A PVC is needed to the Atlanta regional headquarters where the other remote engineering and design department is located. In this way, the Chicago regional office is different from the San Francisco regional office, which does not have a remote engineering team.

- **Other Locations.** PVCs are really not needed between Chicago and the other remote regional sales offices because the traffic flow is light and can be routed through headquarters. However, it may be that in the future you would want to add direct PVCs to each of the smaller remote sales offices supported by the regional headquarters site, due to the low cost of this incremental connectivity.

## *Specification Sheet:*

***Chicago Existing Equipment:***

*Router (frame relay capable)*

*CSU / DSU — including 2 V.35 ports, a T-1 port, and 1 WAN serial port*

*Ethernet LAN (2)*

*Token Ring*

***Other non-Frame Relay Applications:***

*Voice - will consider integrated access*

*Hub - Will act as hub site for Minneapolis Sales Office*

***Applications:***

*SNA Interactive*

*Users: Customer Service, Sales Support - CAD file - 5 users*

*Average File Size: 1 screen (500 bytes)*

*Frequency: To New York = 4 to 8 screens per minute per person ; delay sensitive; heavy hours - 9:30-11:30am, 2-4pm*

*To Dallas= 2 to 5 screens (copies, not delay sensitive)*

*Architecture: Token Ring LAN with PCs (3270 emulation): 4M bps, SDLC to LLC2 protocol*

*LAN — Two LANs: Engineering and Sales*

*Users: Engineering, design and development teams, text and CAD files - 15 users*

*Average File Size: 24,000 to 56,000 bytes - file transfers, 1,500 bytes - E-mail (without attachments)*

*Frequency: To New York = 18 to 34 file transfers per day (no pattern), 225 E mails per day; heavy traffic - 8-9am, 1-2 pm*

*To Atlanta = 10 to 17 file transfers per day, 70 to 100 E-mails; heavy traffic - 8-9am, 1-2pm*

*Architecture: Ethernet, PCs and Universal Workstations, TCP / IP protocol*

*Users: Sales, proposal generation - 18 users*

*Average File Size: 17,000 to 25,000 bytes - file transfers, 1,500 bytes - E-mail (without attachments)*

*Frequency: To New York = 6 to 11 files transfers per day (no pattern), 360 E-mails per day; heavy traffic - 8-10am, 1-3pm*

*Architecture: Ethernet, PCs, TCP / IP*

## *Math for Chicago Design*

***SNA traffic to NY:***

*500 bytes times 8 bits = 4,000 bits*
*x8 per minute/person*
*134,400 bits/minute/person*
*x5 people*
*160,000 bits/minute*
*divided by 60 seconds*
*2,666 bits/second*

***LAN traffic to NY:***

*E-mail = 1,500 bytes times 8 bits =120,000 bits*
*x585 per day*
*7,020,000 bits/day/8 hours = 877,500 bits/hr avg or*
*14,625 bits/sec avg*

*File Transfers: Engineering*

*24,000 to 56,000 bytes = 192,000 to 448,000 bits per file*
*448,000 bits/CIR = transmission time (no propagation delay)*
*448,000 bits/128,000 bits/sec = 3.5 seconds*

*File transfers: Sales*

*17,000 to 25,000 bytes*
*136,000 to 200,000 bits*
*200,000 bits/128,000 K bps= 1.56 seconds*

Looking at possible committed information rates, the PVC to the warehouse probably only needs to be 32K bps, because just copies of the orders are being sent, and response time is not critical.

The PVC to Atlanta should be between 64K and 256K bps because of the size of the engineering files. The company places a very high level of strategic importance on these new product designs, and the delay time for transmission must be minimized so that the engineers do not sit idle. It is suspected that more interaction between the groups would occur if network performance were improved, and this could help speed time to market and generate improved relations between the groups. We'll use 128K bps for the first network design.

The PVC supporting the LAN traffic back to headquarters could be 64K to 256K bps. The interactive traffic warrants at least a 32K bps CIR, but a 64K bps CIR might further improve response times during peak traffic periods. Since the volume of traffic is heavier from Chicago to New York than the return traffic for this application, you would probably use the 64K bps. However, in designing the New York site and the return PVC from New York to Chicago, you would probably use a lower CIR, such as 32K bps.

The Minneapolis sales site could use a short 9.6K bps tail circuit to hub into Chicago, and this site's traffic would share the PVC back to New York.

The total of the inbound CIRs to Chicago is 384K bps, which is the sum of 32K + 128K + 192K + 32K. Given this level of inbound traffic, a 128K to 384K bps port connection could be used, depending upon your comfort level with oversubscription . As a sanity check, the outbound CIR total is 416K bps, which would lead you to the same range of alternatives for the port connection speed.

Since the applications are very intermittent, the first pricing cut should probably assume a moderate level of oversubscription. For this network at this stage, a range of 125 to 175 percent subscription for both inbound and outbound traffic would be recommended to start. This can then be adjusted once the performance of the applications and the utilization of the PVCs can be measured. This level of oversubscription is a good place to start because it leverages some economies of scale for the site, while still giving room for growth and modification. This logic would lead you to choose a 256K bps port connection for Chicago. From an inbound traffic perspective, this provides a subscription level of 150 percent (384K/256K = 1.5). The outbound subscription level, which is the one that could influence the pricing at this site (depending upon your carrier's pricing approach) is 162.5 percent (416/256 = 1.625).

The resulting network would look like Figure 6.5.

A similar process would be done for each of the regional sites, and the warehouses. For regional sites with the same applications as Chicago, you may simply copy this design. For regional sites with different connectivity needs, or completely different applications and traffic patterns like the warehouses, you will need to design a new network configuration.

*Chicago Network Configuration*

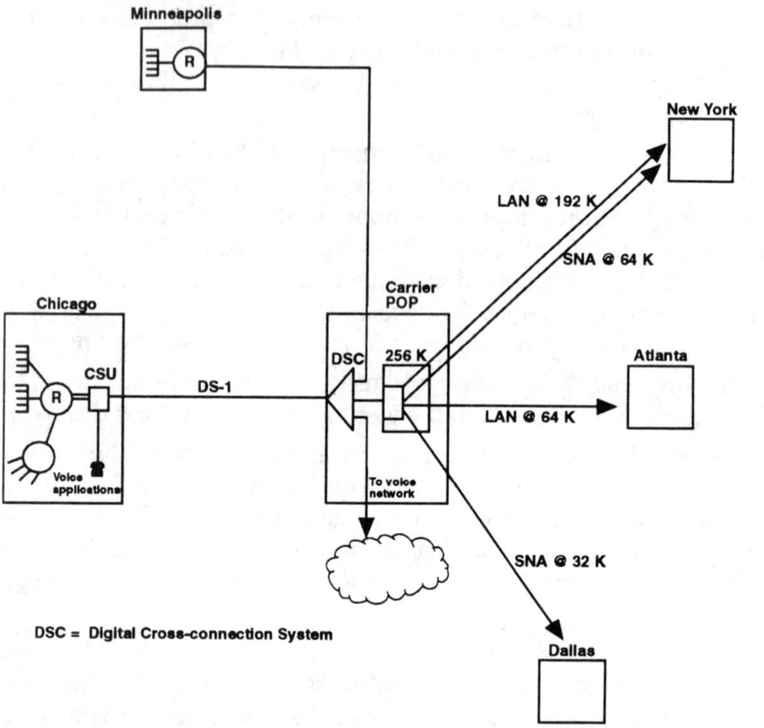


*Fig. 6.5: In this configuration, integrated access is used at the Chicago site to support the tail circuit to Minneapolis and the voice application. The frame relay port connection would be about $1100 per month or less before access.*

## *Corporate Headquarters*

The corporate headquarters needs direct connectivity to all of the major regional sites. Direct or indirect connectivity is needed to the remote sales offices as well. A decision about local access protection, and the form it should take, will need to be made for this location. We will look at both network designs, one without access protection and one using dual homing.

Without examining every application as done for the Chicago site, we can quickly discuss the general needs and show a resulting configuration.

### *Applications at Headquarters*

Large files are transferred between the proposal group and remote sales offices, and between the main engineering department and the remote engineering and design groups. E-mail is used to communicate general company information to all employees, and is used substantially among employees as a means of communication.

The central order processing system receives all the orders entered from field offices, but sends very little information back out to the field offices, unless an update on a particular order is being requested.

### *Choosing PVCs and CIRs*

One likely network design for the headquarters site would look like Figure 6.6.

We have assumed that headquarters would require a 128K to 192K bps PVC to each of the three regional headquarters in Chicago, Atlanta and San Francisco to support LAN traffic. This is because remote engineering and design teams, plus sales people, use the network to transfer large files and to exchange E-mail.

A 32K bps PVC is needed to these same regional sites to support the interactive SNA sessions. Traffic includes primarily acknowledgements and screen updates, and is lower in volume than the incoming traffic from each of these locations, which is 64K bps.

A 64K bps PVC is needed to the warehouses for both the interactive applications and the database reconciliations that occur in off-hours.

A single 64K bps PVC could be used to each of the remote sales offices. As with the design of the Washington, D.C. sales office, the interactive traffic could instead use a different PVC from the file transfers. If this is the design approach you decide upon, then two PVCs would be needed from New York to the small remote sales offices. A 32K bps PVC could be used for the file transfers and to keep it simple, assume that the interactive transactions will also have a 32K bps PVC.

### *Choosing the Port Speed*

Since the inbound CIR total of 1664K bps is greater than the outbound total of 1568K bps, the inbound total will be used to choose the port connection speed. In this case, a port speed of 768K bps to 1.024M bps is probably a good choice. Since the applications across all of the locations are expected to be highly intermittent in terms of the statistical likelihood of all the connections being simultaneously active, using a 768K bps port connection is probably fine. This gives an inbound oversubscription rate of 216.6 percent and an outbound subscription rate of 204 percent, which should provide advantageous pricing. If you are initially uncomfortable with oversubscription and would prefer a more conservative approach, a 1.024M bps port connection could be used.

Using the 768K bps port connection, the price for the New York site, excluding access, will probably be around $4000 per month. If the higher port speed of 1.024M bps is chosen, the price for the network at the New York site will increase by approximately 10 percent, to around $4400 per month. These price approximations do not include term and volume discounts. For a network of this size, at a two year term, you should be able to find discount levels ranging from 20 to 30 percent off standard pricing.

*New York Network Configuration*

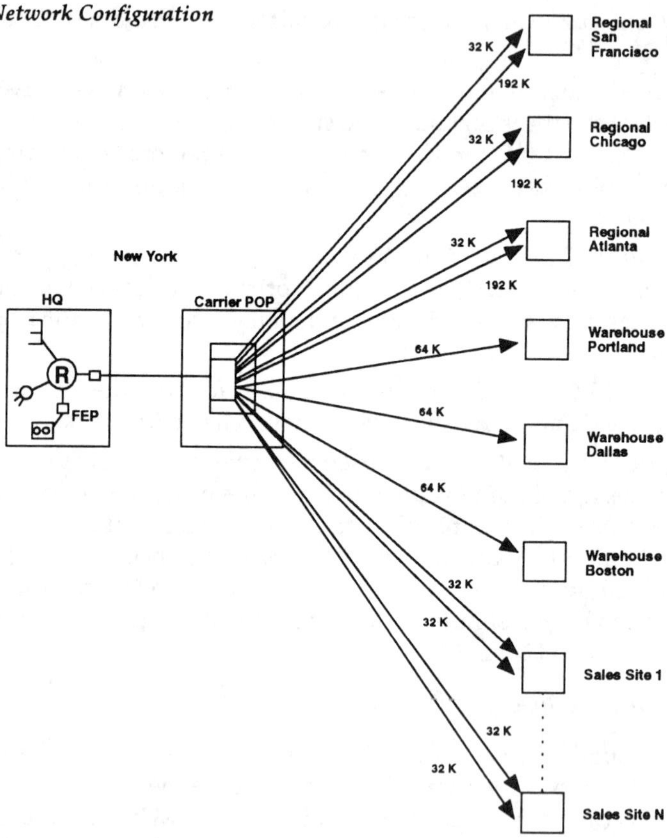


*Fig. 6.6: One possible configuration for the New York location is to separate the LAN file transfers from the interactive transactions by using two separate PVCs. In this example, two PVCs are used between New York and the sales offices, as well as the regional headquarters. The cost would be about $4000 per month before access.*

### *The Complete Network*

The complete network design could look like figure 6.7. The design does not include using tail circuits, as previously discussed. However, it is possible that tail circuits could be used to reduce the overall price slightly. Given this network design, the savings from using frame relay instead of private lines would be between 15 and 58 percent, for an annualized savings of $33,000 to $112,000.

*Complete Network Configuration*

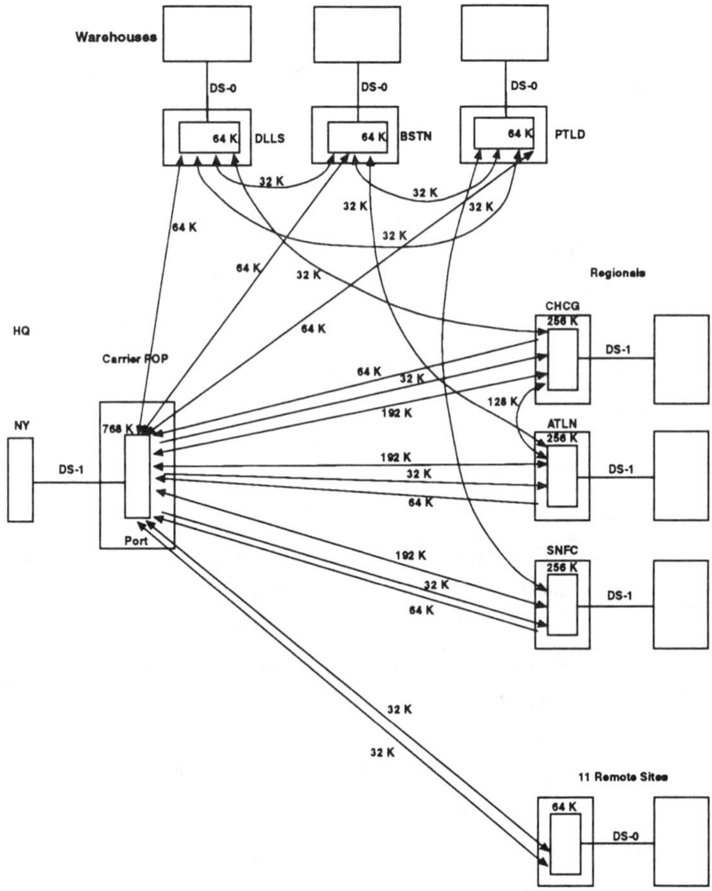


*Fig. 6.7: One possible network configuration is shown above. The configuration does not include the use of tail circuits or the use of dual homing. It does include the use of asymmetrical CIR assignments on some of the PVCs and a separation of the LAN and SNA traffic between headquarters and some of the remote locations.*

## *Before and After Network Pricing*

*We sent the specifications for this hypothetical network out to four national carriers for bid. We asked that they provide month-to-month and term pricing for both the private line network, and the frame relay network, as designed. Three of the four carriers were able to respond within the allotted time frame, and the results are summarized below. In all cases, the frame relay network provided significant savings over the private line network.*

*One caution is in order. The frame relay network bids do not necessarily represent the same quality of service across the carriers. For example, one of the carriers bid the CIR, but bid it with a "minimum usage" assumption while the other carriers bid the same connections with "unlimited usage" assumptions. These are the qualitative differences you must discover as you work with different service providers.*

*Carrier 1*

| | *2 yr Price* | *Base Price* |
|---|---|---|
| *Private line network* | *$16,300* | *$19,200* |
| *Frame relay network* | *$16,400* | *$15,400* |
| *Frame Relay Savings* | *15 %* | *6%* |
| *Annual Frame Relay Savings* | *$33,600* | *$10,800* |

*Carrier 2*

| | *2 yr Price* | *Base Price* |
|---|---|---|
| *Private line network* | *$16,300* | *$14,670* |
| *Frame relay network* | *$ 6,900** | *Not Aval.* |
| *Frame Relay Savings* | *58 %* | *Not Avail.* |
| *Annual Frame Relay Savings* | *$112,800* | *Not Avail.* |

**price does not represent unlimited use of CIR*

*Carrier 3*

| | *2 yr Price* | *Base Price* |
|---|---|---|
| *Private line network* | *$15,200* | *$13,000* |
| *Frame relay network* | *$ 11,800* | *$9,700* |
| *Frame Relay Savings* | *22%* | *25%* |
| *Annual Frame Relay Savings* | *$40,800* | *$39,600* |

In addition to the monthly savings, network availability at remote locations and network performance should both increase. The savings shown here do not reflect any equipment savings that may result from eliminating leases on SNA-related equipment and licenses, multiple CSU/DSUs, multiple wide area network router ports, etc. They also do not reflect the operational and administrative savings typically associated with consolidating separate networks into a single facility and using public networking solutions instead of a private network configuration.

### *Dual Homing at the Headquarters*

Dual homing could be considered at the headquarters site to provide local loop protection in the event of a circuit outage. If dual homing is used to protect the site from local access failure, then a decision must be made about whether the second port connection will be in the same POP as the first, or if a DS-1 private line will be used to access the carrier's next-nearest city with a frame relay switch. The first configuration would obviously drive the cost of the network connection up by the price of the DS-1 local loop, while the latter configuration would drive the price up by the DS-1 loop plus the IXC circuit.

Backhauling to another city to get geographically diverse port connections is usually not provided by the carrier without an extra charge, as it is if the carrier *has* to backhaul the circuit to the nearest switch because it doesn't have a switch in that LATA.

Assume for this design the use of two port connections on two different switches in the same city.[6] In using a dual-homing configuration, the port connection speed for each of the two ports would be half of what you would use if only a single port were being utilized. Therefore, the ports in this case would be 384K bps. The PVCs would each have a CIR of half as well.

The return PVCs must also be split into two. However, each of the remote sites needs only a single port connection. Since splitting the PVCs in half in terms of CIR is required in a dual homing configuration (unless you want to pay for twice the network capacity), this example will not include breaking out the LAN and SNA traffic onto different PVCs. For one thing, this would make the diagram more complicated. It would also complicate the network routing and could have a negative effect on network performance as the CIRs for each PVC, after being halved two times, would be very low.

Figure 6.9 shows an example of the PVCs between New York and San Francisco in a dual-homing arrangement. In this example, we are showing one 256K bps PVC between New York and San Francisco, where both the LAN and interactive applications share the same PVC (assume that traffic prioritization is occurring in the router). After dual homing, two PVCs are used, each at 128K bps.

*Before Dual Homing*

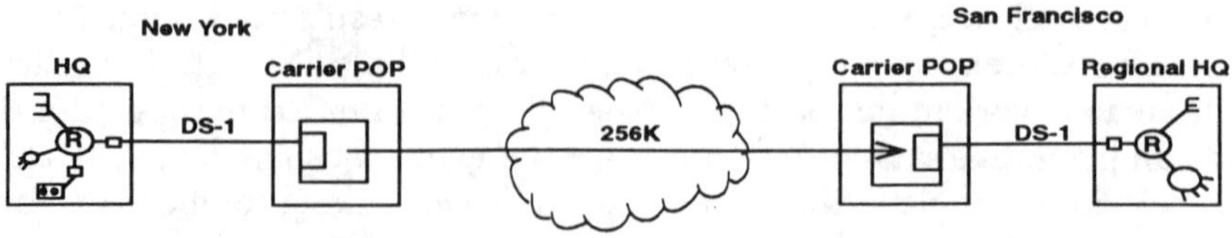


*Fig. 6.8: Connectivity between New York and San Francisco before dual homing might consist of a 256K PVC shared by both the LAN and interactive applications.*

*After Dual Homing*

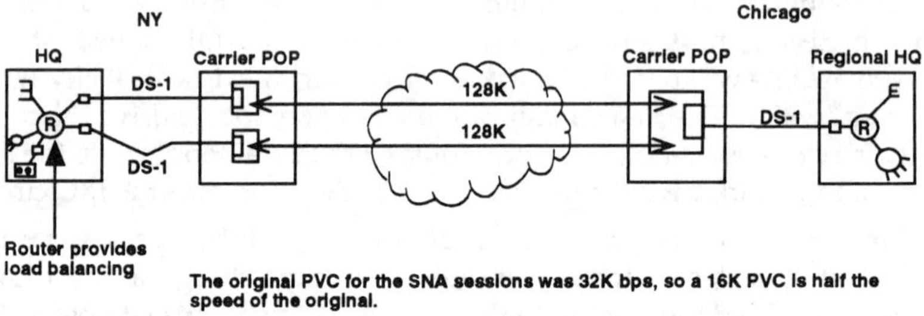


*Fig. 6.9: With dual homing, two port connections with two local loops would be used, but each port connection would be half the speed compared to using a single port. A PVC is assigned out of each port and would also be half the CIR. The routers would load balance the traffic.*

The router will load-balance the traffic until one connection is lost, after which the router will use the surviving PVC to carry traffic, and the applications will probably see a slow-down in network performance. Once the failed connection is restored, the router will again automatically balance traffic between the connections, and network performance will return to the status quo. If network availability is enough of a concern that you are using a dual-homing configuration, you will probably want to use two routers, and not just one (as briefly discussed in Chapter 7).

The cost for the dual-homing configuration increases the price of this site by 10 to 12 percent, before local access is considered.

One note of caution on dual homing. Dual homing complicates network routing, and potential problems with split horizon and network partitioning must be considered. Dual homing by itself is used by many frame relay network users today, when local loop protection is needed and other solutions, such as a local frame relay service or an access solution over a self-healing ring network, are not affordable or available.

When dual homing is combined with using separate PVCs between locations for interactive versus file transfer applications, the network design and routing get complicated. The relative CIRs for the PVCs, as they are divided and then redivided, decrease, and this can cause throughput constraints for the applications using the PVCs. As with any tool, dual homing and dual PVCs between the same two sites should be used by experienced people and with caution. They are excellent problem-solving tools, but if not applied properly, can create more difficulties than they alleviate. Rely on your carrier for guidance in this area.

## Design Overview

As you have seen, designing a frame relay network takes a few guidelines and a lot of common sense. If you have information of actual traffic patterns and applications available, then get out your calculator! If not, don't worry. Just design an initial configuration that seems logical given your current network facilities and performance and your near-term growth forecasts. Then, if the design is not optimal once you have traffic statistics to examine, change it. It's really pretty simple.

[1] *Actual user case studies are provided in Appendices C and D.*

[2] *Speed of light propagation delay over a fiber optic network equates to about 4 to 5 microseconds per kilometer, or 10 usec per mile. Simple delay is computed by summing transmission delay (10 usec/mile), fixed switching delay, and the maximum of queuing and packetization delay in the network.*

[3] *In some LATAs only a 56K bps DS-0 loop can be purchased, while in other LATAs, a full 64K bps loop is available.*

[4] *Alternative approaches for consolidating LAN and SNA applications are discussed in later chapters.*

[5] *The alternatives for handling SNA are covered in Chapters 8 and 9. You may decide on two PVCs, one for SNA and one for LAN traffic.*

[6] *Many carriers have more than one switch in the same POP, and you can take advantage of this by having each port connection terminate into a different switch for added protection without having to backhaul the second port to a different city.*

## CHAPTER 7 - DESIGNING THE NETWORK:

# ALTERNATIVE APPROACHES AND TRADE-OFFS

The previous chapter walked through a specific network example and derived a network topology and a configuration for PVCs, committed information rates, and access. This chapter will discuss general alternatives in network design approaches with frame relay, and the elements to consider for each approach.

Once again, many of the decisions discussed here should appropriately be made on a site-by-site basis. There is no single right or wrong answer; there are trade-offs to be made between network cost and network performance, as hinted at in the prior chapter. The flexibility you gain with a frame relay network will allow you to defer many of these decisions until you actually bring a site or an application onto the network. It will also allow you to change the configuration easily, if you find that more or less direct connectivity within the network is required.

## Topology Alternatives

The real world is never as clean-cut as the text book. In the real world, there will be many more issues to consider based on your unique situation. The most cost-effective network design for you will depend upon your existing network infrastructure, existing network equipment, the way in which your underlying applications have been written, and other organizational considerations.

Relatively small networks, and even many medium-sized networks, are often pure frame relay environments with no private lines in use. Networks this size would typically include from three to 20 sites. Sometimes they are fully meshed; however, as the number of sites increases, so does the probability that partial mesh environments are used.

Larger networks are often hybrid configurations using private lines and frame relay, or they use all frame relay but in a hub arrangement. The hub networking approach is often much flatter than what would be seen in a pure leased line environment, with less traffic aggregation at the hub sites. The hybrid networks leverage the best attributes of private lines and public frame relay, and often utilize the existing infrastructures already in place for network connectivity.

### *Star Configurations Versus Full and Partial Mesh Configurations*

Many applications on today's networks are written for centralized environments. Therefore, adding mesh connectivity doesn't really make sense, because the application is not designed to be distributed. As the application is cycled up for rewriting, the underlying computer code and application design may be modified for a distributed environment if it makes business sense to do so.

In many networks, a fully meshed configuration of PVCs is neither necessary nor cost-effective. Frame relay can save your company money, even if mesh connectivity is not required. Most frame relay network implementations fall in the middle — some mesh connectivity will improve network performance compared to a star configuration, but a fully meshed configuration is not needed. However, there are still many cases where the underlying applications only need connectivity to a central site and a simple star configuration is appropriate.

How can frame relay save money in a star configuration? Two reasons: the mileage cross-over[1] point between frame relay and private lines, and the ability to oversubscribe a frame relay port connection.

The first is a result of the non-mileage-sensitive nature of frame relay pricing. Many IXC tariffs make frame relay more cost effective if your average leased line interexchange connection is greater than about 400 miles. Regional frame relay service providers will often have a leased line-to-frame relay cross-over point of 100 miles or less. If your network is all (or mostly) in a single LATA, intraLATA frame relay cross-overs may be just a few miles. There are also some carriers that use mileage bands, providing alternatives for both geographically concentrated and geographically disbursed locations.

The second way in which frame relay can save money in star configurations is by oversubscribing the central network connection and thereby reducing the local access requirements at the central site.

If you currently support 150 remote locations with direct low-speed connections, then you would need seven DS-1 local loops (150/24). A frame relay solution, where a port is oversubscribed by about 220 percent, could reduce the number of local loops to three. If the average DS-1 loop is $600, the resulting savings would be nearly $30,000 per year in just access costs. The number of wide area network equipment ports would also be reduced, as would the number of CSU/DSU units.

Of course, many existing low-speed networks use multipoint, multidrop leased lines to save money and reduce access. In this scenario, you may not see such a large savings from reduced loop requirements However, you may find that you can afford to upgrade these 9.6K bps multipoint connections to direct connections at 56K bps. This would improve network performance and increase network survivability, while costs stay relatively stable.

### *Partial Mesh Configurations*

If a pure star configuration is not quite enough, then a partial mesh of PVCs may be appropriate. You probably do not need a PVC between every remote location to every other remote location, because the traffic simply does not justify this. Instead, you should try and match the PVCs to the underlying traffic pattern.

The process of determining where PVCs should be deployed is equivalent to laying sidewalks on a college campus. When new buildings are added, no sidewalks are put in, just grass. Then, after a semester, you go back and lay sidewalks where the grass has been worn down, because this is the traffic pattern. If you put the sidewalks in first, you will just end up with paths worn in the grass.

*Star Network*

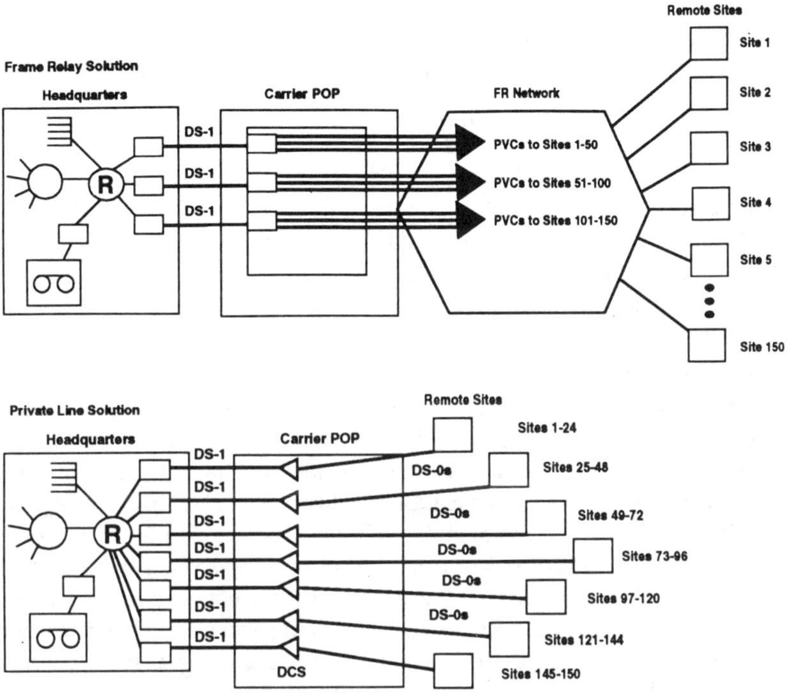


*Fig. 7.1: In a large star network configuration, the ability to oversubscribe a frame relay port connection can decrease the number of CSU/DSUs and local loops needed at the headquarters location.*

This same design approach is actually possible with frame relay networking. You can begin by putting PVCs everywhere (or everywhere you think they need to be) and then after a few months, redesign the connectivity based on actual network utilization.

If your network is so large that using a full mesh of PVCs initially is impractical, you could rent a protocol analyzer to determine the underlying traffic patterns in your network. Some carriers will even work with clients to provide this analysis as a service, complete with technicians, protocol analyzers and network design assistance.

If neither of these approaches is practical for your situation, then you should use the design approach outlined in the last chapter. Take a look at your applications and make the best estimations you can. Then adjust the configuration later based on network performance and utilization patterns.

### *Concentration and Nodal Architectures*

Most private networks are based on nodal architectures, where small sites hub traffic into larger regional sites, which themselves may be hubbed into other sites, or which may be connected directly to a network backbone. The backbone network has built-in diversity for survivability. This is a hierarchical approach to network design and is done to save money on expensive leased lines.

Frame relay can flatten the network architecture, but this may not necessarily mean that the network is 100 percent flat. Many frame relay networks still use some network hubbing. This is especially true if there are many small sites that are geographically concentrated and have relatively low volumes of traffic. Leased lines can be used for the short connections, and frame relay for the longer connections. Of course, this could drive the equipment costs up at the hubbing location, and also increases contention for network capacity at these sites. Overall performance may be slightly lower, depending upon traffic volume. A hub configuration should be considered if you have a very large number of small sites that are geographically concentrated, because it could save you money without negatively impacting overall performance. There are many concentration (i.e., FRAD) alternatives available.

### *Public Frame Relay, Private Lines — or Both?*

You don't necessarily have to choose between operating a private network using dedicated leased lines and using a public frame relay service. You can mix and match both types of services in your network to gain optimal cost and performance.

Many corporations today are using both private lines and public frame relay services. A typical network configuration might look like figure 7.2.

In this configuration, the frame relay equipment (in this case the router) is acting as the gateway device between the public network and the private network. The router will forward incoming traffic to the correct WAN port, based on its addressing tables, which will indicate the outbound connection to which an incoming packet should be allocated.

*Hybrid Network*

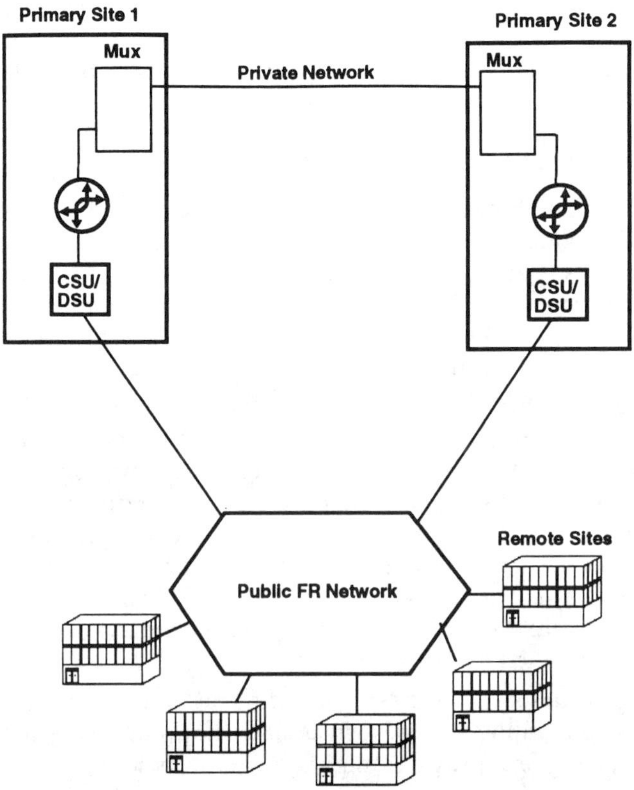


*Fig. 7.2: A public/private hybrid network allows you to maintain control over the private network between primary locations and use a frame relay solution for connections outside the private network. The router, or other frame relay equipment, at Site 1 acts as the gateway between the networks.*

Many intelligent multiplexers today have frame relay interface cards. If this is the case with your equipment, the multiplexer itself could act as the network gateway. It would be connected into the public frame relay network in addition to its standard leased line connections to other multiplexers. Once again, traffic would be routed to the appropriate network based on the destination address.

One thing to look for in considering this configuration is that sometimes the multiplexer frame relay cards are more costly than just buying a low-end router or using an existing router port. You will also want to compare the functionality of the two approaches and be sure that your are not losing any critical functions or decreasing your future design and growth flexibility. FRAD/concentrators can be another alternative.

### *Local, Regional or National Frame Relay Service?*

As previously mentioned, frame relay services are offered by local service providers that concentrate services within a LATA, regional providers that concentrate on a specific geographical territory, which may cover a few states, and national providers. There are even consortia and partnerships that link many providers together to extend network ubiquity (which could be termed "virtual ubiquity" in a frame relay world). Here's a general set of guidelines for thinking about which type of provider might be best for your network.

If most of your locations are within a single LATA, or are highly concentrated within a few different LATAs, a local frame relay service provider might be the best bet from both a cost and service standpoint. If you have locations concentrated in more than one LATA, then connecting the LATAs together can be accomplished using private lines or using a regional or national frame relay service. The local services might be provided by the same company in each LATA, or by different local frame relay providers, depending upon the jurisdiction.

If most of your locations are spread across different cities, but in a tightly concentrated geographical area, such as all in the Southeast or the Northwest, for example, a regional provider might be a good choice.

The advantage of a regional provider in this case, compared to a national/global provider, is that you might get a better price and you might get more built-in network redundancy. A national provider might place one switch in each of the major metropolitan areas in each state. If your locations are in smaller outlying cities, the carrier will backhaul to the nearest network switch.

Regional carriers, however, might have a half-dozen or more switches within a single state, all connected using geographically diverse facilities. This means better network protection from failures and higher availability. Regional pricing is typically very aggressive, as well. Most regionals have agreements with other carriers for terminating traffic to locations outside the region, so you are provided with a single point of contact and billing for your complete frame relay network.

National providers would then be used when you have lots of locations, most of which are not highly concentrated in any one area.

If you have both concentrated and disbursed locations, you have one of two alternatives. You could use a combination of frame relay services, such as both a local service and a national or regional service. You can also just choose one provider, after evaluating the economic and service quality/ubiquity trade-offs.

## CIR, Bursts, and Setting Burst Levels

Most carriers do not allow you to choose whether or not you can burst on a PVC, and to what speed you can burst. In many services, the burst level on a PVC is automatically set equal to the port connection. However, a few carriers do allow choice, and others may follow. There may be reasons why you do not want a PVC to exceed its committed information rate, so we will briefly discuss bursting and its effect on network design.

There are really two different types of burst specified in the frame relay interface standard. How these are implemented in each carrier's service is dependent upon the platform and the service definition. CIR is equal to Bc/T where Bc is the committed burst rate and T is some (arbitrary) time interval. If you exceed the throughput level during some time interval, the excess frames are either Bc or Be, where Be is excess burst (are you confused yet?).

To make things as simple as possible, simply know this: Some carriers deliver traffic up to the CIR. Anything above the CIR is a burst, and all bursts are created equal. What the carrier does with bursts is highly dependent upon its network platform and congestion management system. The bursts may always be sent through the network, but marked as discard-eligible (DE). Or the excess traffic many only be allowed through if the individual network path, the PVC, is not congested. If this is the case, the PVC can slowly begin to exceed its CIR, expanding all the way to the port connection. If the network is congested, or becomes so during the burst, the PVC will be throttled back towards the CIR and the excess frames will be delayed in buffers. Once again, frames in excess of CIR are marked DE. In many cases, Bc is either equal to the CIR and Be is equal to the port connection speed. Or, Bc equals the port speed.

Finally, still other carriers set Bc above CIR, and Be above that (usually Bc is between the CIR and the port speed and Be is the port connection speed). In this case all frames in excess of CIR are still eligible for discard, but some are prioritized differently than others. When network congestion occurs, the Be frames, which are those frames in excess of Bc, are discarded first. Then the Bc frames are discarded if the first measure doesn't bring the network back to stability.

Incidentally, how the CIR is defined and how and when a PVC can exceed its CIR is often tied closely to the overall congestion management system within the frame relay network. If you have mission-critical applications on your frame relay network, then either discuss these topics with a few carriers until you can make an educated decision, or sign up for a service-level agreement that places responsibility on the carrier for delivering a specified quality of service, throughput and availability to your applications. Then leave it up to the carrier to figure out the best way to deliver it.

As stated above, with some services, you can define a burst rate for your PVCs. Carriers don't typically charge for burst capability on PVCs, so you may think that you would always want to take advantage of the maximum allowed (i.e., as limited by the port connection speed on each end). While this may be the case, it is not necessarily so. Factors such as network predictability and end-user expectations can influence this decision.

### *Predictability*

If the PVC bursts above its committed information rate when excess network capacity is available, the performance of the applications using the PVC will actually vary over time. Sometimes this is fine, and other times it is not.

Some applications perform better if the network response times are highly predictable. One simple example of this is the customer service rep (CSR) working to take an order from a customer over the phone. The CSR will develop a very specific rhythm for entering information, waiting for screen refresh, and performing other tasks. If the network responds slowly on some occasions, and faster on others, the entire rhythm is disrupted and the actual productivity decreases. *Network predictability* is actually more important than getting information across the network as quickly as possible.

In certain situations, whether because of the application, the underlying protocol, or both, it may be better that the frame relay connection supporting the applications functions as much like a leased line as possible. In these cases, it may be better if the PVC is not allowed to exceed its CIR. In other cases, you may want the supporting PVC to burst as high as the port connection will allow.

### *Managing User Expectations*

There are two schools of thought on managing user expectations for network performance. As you might expect, both schools have pros and cons. One school says, take what you can get when you can get it and "don't worry, be happy." This is really the basis for the Internet community and LAN networking. These environments are not designed like the traditional hierarchy with strict rules and monotonously consistent performance. They are dynamic, chaotic and at some times the network is faster than others. Users with this mentality understand fluctuations in performance characteristics over time.

The other school advises keeping the network performance consistent and predictable, where possible, regardless of time of day, day of week , or geographic location. This gives users a consistent expectation benchmark and allows the network to perform up to this benchmark.

Which philosophy is right for your network may be highly dependent upon the applications you are running and the types of users you are supporting. In fact, you may find that some departments and applications are more suited to consistency, while others want what they can get when they can get it.

Managing the expectations of network end-users for network performance is one factor in deciding whether or not to allow PVCs to burst above its CIR. Once again, not all services allow you to set this parameter, but either way the following information might be useful to consider when designing your network and determining CIR levels and port speeds.

SNA network designers learned long ago that the actual network performance is not nearly as critical as the consistency of network performance over time. The resulting implication of this discovery is that new networks are brought on line with network response times specifically imposed upon them that are slower than what the network could really achieve. This is done because the network manager knows that more and more users will be added to the network at the location and that eventually adding users will degrade the response times of the initial users.

To protect the initial users from experiencing this degradation in performance, the network manager designs the initial network so that the first user and the 100th user experience exactly the same network performance. Since the performance does not change over time, every one is relatively content.

It may initially seem like you should take advantage of any and all "free" network capacity. However, you may want to think first about the implications on end-user expectations and consider which users might most benefit from this "burst" and which users may prefer consistency.

Take, for example, a remote office with several LANs. The remote engineering team is using the LANs to send large files and diagrams to other remote engineering teams. When the frame relay network first comes on line, the supporting PVC is given a CIR of 64K bps. However, because the site is new and only a few users are up on the network, there is plenty of spare capacity. The PVC consistently sustains a transmission rate above the CIR.

The result is that the engineering team's files are transmitting at a much greater speed, and instead of taking 30 seconds for the average transmission, they are only taking four seconds. The engineering team is very happy, and you are very happy.

Then, you begin to bring new departments and new applications onto the frame relay network. You are very happy, because the frame relay solution allows you to do this at a fraction of the cost of a dedicated network. As new users come onto the system, they are very happy, because the network performance is as good as, if not better, than the previous network. The contention for the port's capacity increases, but the applications are intermittent enough that most of the time the supporting PVCs are sustaining a transmission rate slightly in excess of the CIR assigned.

But the engineering team, and other users who initially used the network before contention began to rise, are very unhappy. These users have watched the network performance slowly degrade as more users were added. While the network may still be delivering an average performance in excess of the CIR for which you are paying, in relative terms it is not nearly as good as what the PVC was sustaining prior to the growth in users.

The engineers call you to complain about the degradation. Their expectations have been benchmarked, and the only way they will really be happy is to increase the CIR of the PVC(s) supporting them. This costs more money. If you increase the CIR, you are not happy because the network now costs more. If you do not, you are still not happy because your customer is complaining. This is like the Kobayashii Maru, (for the uninitiated, this is the no-win scenario in Star Trek).

This example can also apply if you choose to use a "zero CIR" service or a lower CIR than what your application really requires. It simply highlights the fact that you should consider the trade- offs and make an educated decision. The moral to this story is that there are many reasons to use frame relay, and many ways in which it can save you money and improve network performance. Bursting is only one of many benefits that frame relay offers, and depending upon your networking situation, you may want to consider the amount of bursting that would be most appropriate.

Of course, the first school would say that it is just such control-oriented thinking for which frame relay offers an alternative. If the status quo were maintained, we would not advance. Galileo and Copernicus brought us new ideas by stretching out of the old mold and reshaping previously held beliefs. This is really how and why internetworking was started in the first place. Both sides have good points, and balance is the key.

*User Expectations*

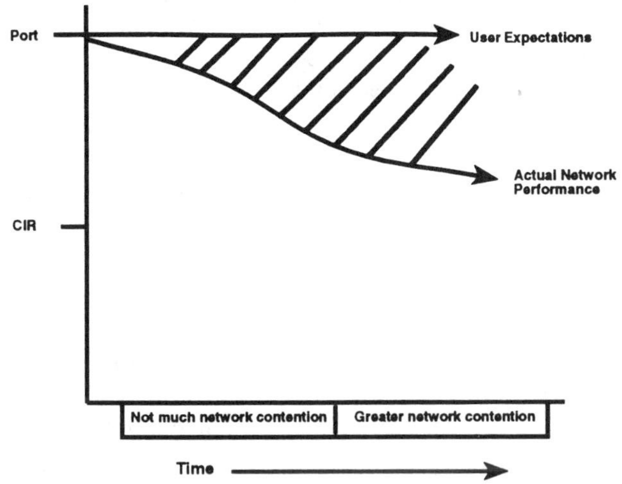


*Fig. 7.3: As contention for network resources increases over time, initial users may begin to experience slower network response time and lower effective throughput. Even if, on average, the effective throughput is in excess of the CIR, the initial network users could be dissatisfied. This effect should be considered during network design.*

# Small Sites, Telecommuters and Roving Users

We have discussed star, partial mesh and full mesh environments. Companies with hundreds, or even thousands, of locations cannot practically consider a fully meshed network topology. Direct connectivity to and between all of the smaller locations is not feasible, but the ability to pass electronic information to them is no less important.

Some of these sites are so small that they cannot justify the cost of a direct connection into the corporate network because the volume of traffic is very intermittent and very low. Still, connectivity in some fashion is necessary, and becoming moreso as new data applications are being deployed.

For example, more and more sales forces are being given portable computers, with the ability to dial into the corporate network to access sales tools, E-mail, phone books, etc. Telecommuting is also becoming more and more popular, especially in densely populated cities.

There are a couple of solutions for these types of locations in a frame relay context, including dial-up frame relay and using terminal servers and modems. Dial-up ISDN services will be available soon, but at this writing there is little available information. Suffice to say that if you are considering dial-up frame relay, talk to your carrier about the available alternatives.

### *Dial-Up Frame Relay*

Users can access frame relay networks via dial-in ports to a carrier's network. The objective of dial-up frame relay is to allow cost-effective connectivity to the corporate backbone for low usage sites, such as small field offices and telecommuting locations. It also allows mobile workers, such as sales people, to access the network.

Few carriers offer dial-up today, but more carriers are expected to offer this service over time. Some interesting new ISDN solutions are emerging. This may be an important decision criteria as you evaluate potential carriers.

With dial-up frame relay, several alternative configurations can be used. A modem could establish a standard dial-up analog connection into the carrier's network. Depending upon the service, the underlying protocol might be X.25, SLIP, TCP/IP or one of several others. The carrier's network will terminate the connection into equipment that will perform a protocol conversion into frame relay.

The carrier may have one or more modem banks that are shared by all dial-in customers and are connected into network servers in the carrier's POP. You would be given a phone number to dial, perhaps a nationwide 800 or 950 number, to establish a dial-in connection.

The party dialing in would enter a user ID and password to establish the connection into the public network. This serves as a security point to keep unauthorized parties from utilizing your frame relay backbone. It will also provide the server with the information about which port connection and PVC the call should traverse.

In this dial-up configuration, the underlying network is static. This is not a switched virtual circuit. You would establish a particular port connection on your backbone network to which all dial-up connections are routed. The carrier would ensure that a PVC exists between the dial-in server and this port connection. The terminating equipment on your premises would then route the incoming packets to the correct on-net address.

Your carrier may also offer ISDN access. In this case, you would be able to dial into a port connection that is dynamically established upon verifying your incoming phone number. You would predefine one or more PVCs, which would be automatically provisioned by the network once your dial-in ISDN call is established. As long as the session is active, you would have access to all of the PVCs. Once the session is terminated, the PVCs are deactivated until the next time you call into the network.

*Dial-Up Frame Relay*

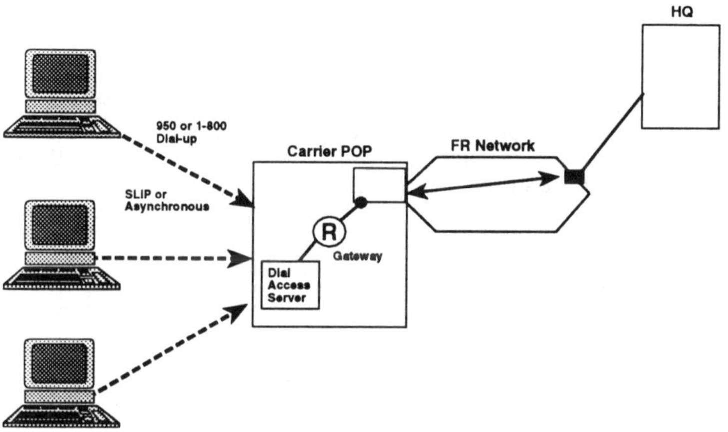


*Fig. 7.4: Carriers offering dial-up frame relay connectivity will typically provide a 950- or 1-800-number. In establishing a dial-up connection, the call is terminated in a dial access server that connects to a frame relay gateway. Your connection is routed to a PVC that terminates into an existing frame relay network location.*

## *Terminal Server and Modems*

You can set up your own dial-in capability by establishing a modem bank connected into a terminal server. In this case, the same type of connectivity as described above will occur. You — not the carrier, are responsible for maintaining the configuration.

You should compare the cost of this alternative to using a dial-up frame relay service. In some cases, you may find that one approach is significantly less expensive than the alternative.

A variation on centralized modem banks, or as a complement to centralized facilities, is to place a small modem pool at remote locations. Local users, telecommuters, and others, could dial a local number and then access the corporate backbone in this manner.

***Dial-Up ISDN***

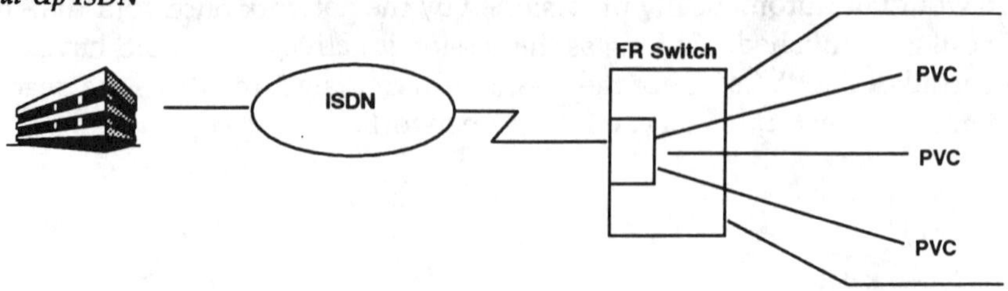


*Fig. 7.5: Dialing into a frame relay network over ISDN will provide access to multiple PVCs, which are predefined and then dynamically provisioned by the network upon verification of the incoming number. This capability will provide cost-effective connectivity for low utilization sites, and could also be used as a dial back-up solution.*

***Modem Bank and Terminal Server***

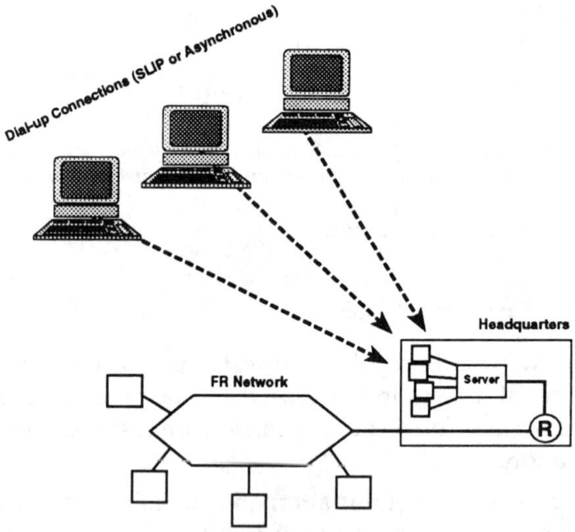


*Fig. 7.6: Dial-up connectivity can also be achieved by setting up a modem pool connected to a terminal server which is then connected to the frame relay network through a router.*

## The Internet

Connectivity into the Internet used to be reserved for academia and computer nerds (i.e., experts). It is now not only commonplace, but an important element to the corporate backbone.

Many frame relay service providers are offering users the alternative of leveraging the existing connection into the frame relay network for Internet access. This saves the cost of a dedicated Internet connection.

The carrier must have a connection into the Internet. This "gateway" is then shared by many different companies. To connect with the Internet, you would simply assign a new PVC from one or more sites into the carrier's Internet gateway.

*Connecting To The Internet Using Frame Relay*

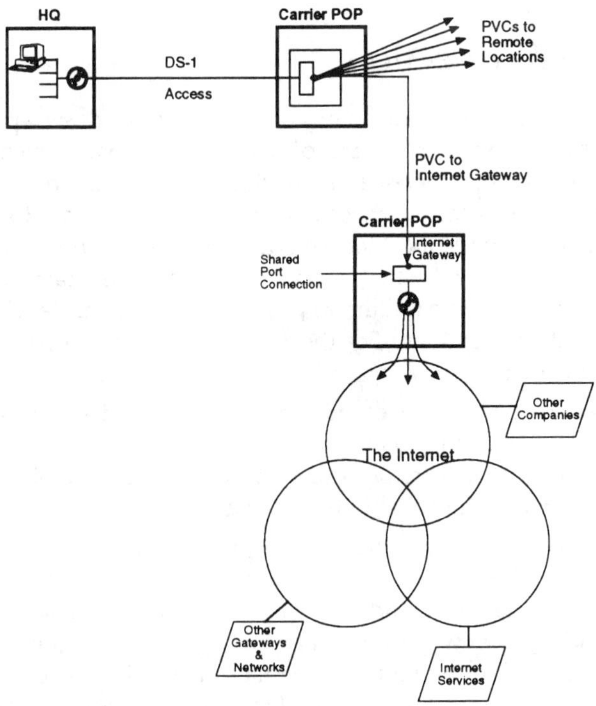


*Fig. 7.7: Many frame relay providers offer the option of assigning a PVC into an Internet gateway for cost-effective Internet access over the frame relay network.*

The carrier will normally charge an incremental monthly fee for this service. The price will probably be about the same as what you would pay by using an Internet access provider's service, except that you will not be paying for another dedicated local loop.

Users on your network would all share this connection for Internet access. If the volume of Internet-related traffic at one location is high, it may warrant its own PVC into the carrier's Internet gateway.

As with any Internet connection, whether you leverage an existing frame relay service for connectivity or you use a direct connection, you will need to consider security implications. Your router can be set to filter unauthorized incoming and outgoing addresses. You can also establish user ID and passwords. Security measures can include setting different filter configurations for the PVC to/from the Internet than what you would use within your corporate frame relay network. The topic of security is itself the focus of many books, and won't be extensively covered here.

## Local Access Protection

Access protection is another issue to be considered in the design process. This would be protection from natural disasters, like floods, which affect access service, or from the fiber-seeking backhoe. Some network sites are more critical than other sites. In these instances, you may want to design greater redundancy into the local loop environment to ensure communications. While you would prefer that every network site maintains 100 percent availability, you may only be willing to pay to guarantee this level of availability at a few critical locations. For those locations, local access protection will need to be evaluated.

If the local access provider uses an underlying transmission system that is ring-based and is self-healing, and if your local loop resides on that ring, then you have the most reliable form of local loop protection available. Unfortunately, this alternative will probably not be available at all of your locations.

The next best way to achieve local access protection is by using a fiber ring on the loop or through the dual-homing configuration discussed in previous chapters. The critical factor would be insuring that the loops are geographically diverse, and the best way to that may be by purchasing the loops from different suppliers (or having your frame relay carrier do this for you). If for some reason this is not a feasible solution for you, perhaps one of the following will be.

### A/B Switch

One alternative is to use an A/B switch in the carrier's POP in front of the port connection.[2] An A/B switch is a small device that demarcs two (or more) different network connections, but only cross-connects one of the connections at a time to the third port. The switch can then be activated to switch the cross connection to the other circuit by dialing into the switch and using DTMF (dual tone multi-frequency) signals to control the configuration.

With this solution two local loops terminate into your router, one of which is active, and the other which is held in reserve. If these lines are not completely diverse in the circuit routing, including separate entrance and conduit facilities, you do not gain much survivability. Therefore, you may want to consider using two different local access providers.

In the POP, both loops terminate into an A/B switch. The switch is then connected into the frame relay port connection. In the event that the active local loop is cut, you would have to dial into the A/B switch and reconfigure the switch to the backup local loop.

*Loop Protection*

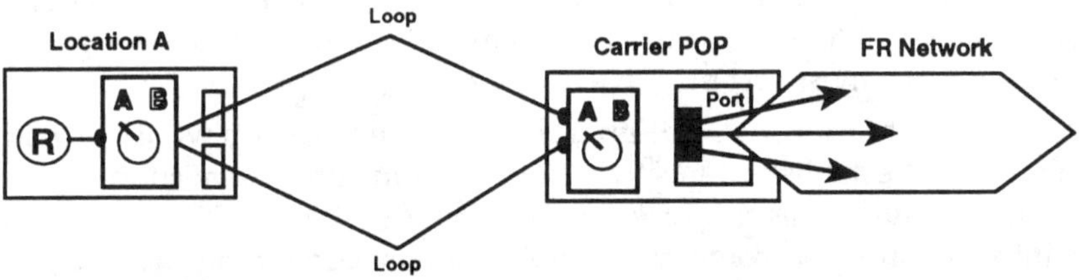


*Fig. 7.8: AN A/B Switch, or Automatic Protection Switch (APS), can be used between the router and the port connection to protect the network from a loop failure.*

One of the weaknesses of this configuration is that it is manual. You must be aware of the circuit failure, and then dial in and reconfigure the connection. The router will automatically attempt to switch to the second line upon the failure of the first line, but the second line will not yet be terminating into the port connection. Until you dial in and reconfigure the switch, the second loop will be in loopback.

Another problem can be that the backup loop may go down, and because active traffic is not flowing across it, the failure is not noticed and is not corrected.

Overall, this configuration is far from ideal. Though, if it is all that is available at a location, it may be better than nothing at all.

### *Automatic Protection Switch*

An alternative to the A/B switch configuration is to use automatic protection switches (APS) on both ends of a local loop. This overcomes the weakness of the manual intervention and delay in the A/B switch configuration.

In this configuration, APSs are placed in front of the router and in front of the port connection. Again, one loop is active and the other is for back up. In the event of a failure of the active loop, the switches will automatically, and in a synchronized fashion, switch the traffic to the backup local loop. This configuration would look just like figure 7.8, except instead of an A/B switch, and automatic protection switch would be used.

Some APS equipment will only switch on a hard circuit failure, while other equipment can switch if a performance threshold is exceeded due to circuit degradation.

Not all carriers will support this option, and even those that do may not necessarily offer the service at a cost-effective price.

### *Dial Backup*

When all is said and done, you may find that a simple analog dial backup connection, which totally bypasses the frame relay network, is less than perfect but is the most cost-effective solution.

Not to be confused with dial-up frame relay, dial backup would provide the ability to re-establish connectivity into the same port connection following a local loop failure. *This service does not currently exist today.* You cannot dial back into the same port connection. The reason is because the local loop is "blocking" this port connection and will not automatically move aside to make room for a dial-up connection into that same port. There are some emerging solutions, including ISDN connectivity, which may soon address this problem. A discussion with your carrier on this topic is recommended.

Dial-up frame relay could be used to reconnect a site into the corporate network by providing connectivity back to the site that accepts dial-in frame relay connections. This would re-establish network connectivity until the problem is resolved.

The ISDN solution could also be used. Once available, this will prove the most attractive solution to dial backup, because you could gain access to the same set of PVCs, with the same DLCIs, as what had been provisioned from the primary path. Therefore, you would not have to make any router table changes, and the connection would be nearly seamless.

*Dial Back-Up*

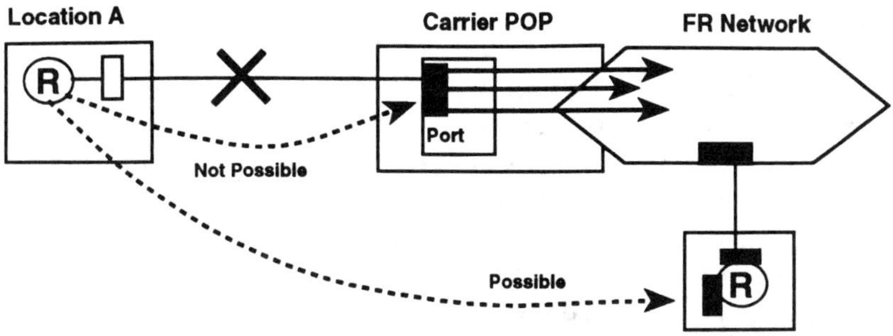


*Fig. 7.9: If a loop fails, it is not possible to dial back into the same physical port connection; however, it is possible to circumvent the frame relay network entirely, or use the ISDN dial-up access solution.*

## Dual Facilities

The most concrete way to ensure complete network availability would be to use two routers, two CSU/DSUs and two local loops that are geographically diverse at all network points. You would then use two port connections, probably in two different carrier POPs.

This level of protection is expensive and is only justifiable at a small percentage of network sites. If a ring-based local loop is available that can automatically route around a network failure, then you can achieve very high levels of availability without the added expense of completely duplicate facilities.

*Dual Routers, Dual Homing*

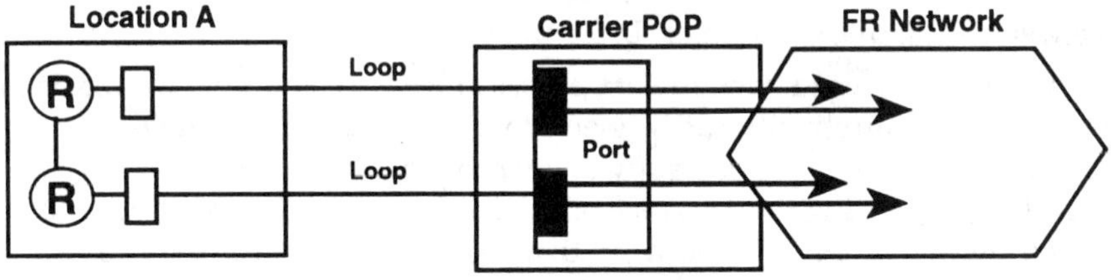


*Fig. 7.10: The best all-around protection would be to use two different routers, two loops, and two port connections. This provides total redundancy, but may not be cost-effective for all network sites.*

## Designing for Disaster Recovery and Back-Up Sites

Certainly, if a company is putting mission critical data over any network, disaster recovery must be part of the design process. Disaster recovery in this instance refers to the recovery of a primary data processing center in the event of a catastrophic failure at that site.

There are two main types of disaster recovery that need to be considered, site recovery and network recovery. Site recovery is very different from network recovery, although both play an important role in creating a highly available network.

Network recovery is provided as part of the frame relay service, in that the service can intelligently route traffic around an IXC network failure. Network recovery capabilities can be extended through the local loop, and any backhauled network segments, using the alternatives discussed above. Site recovery, on the other hand, is a very different type of problem.

Most site disasters are not precipitated by the highly visible and headline-grabbing natural disasters that make worldwide news, such as earthquakes, tornadoes, flooding and hurricanes. However, these highly visible disasters often cause a temporary rise in the concern of network managers for site recovery planning. Most disasters are more localized. A toilet flooding in the floor above a major communication center. A fire. A faulty sprinkler system. Even intentional sabotage or unintentional user error.

Since every day is filled with figurative "fires" that must be fought, the longer term planning for site recovery, although very important, may not ever make the daily prioritized list of events to which you allocate time. That is, until it is too late. If a primary data processing center is down for a few hours, or a few days, it can cost the company millions of dollars. If it is down for a week, it can mean complete bankruptcy.

If you do not have a backup data processing center and plan for recovery, then that is an entirely different project from building your frame relay network. However, you will be happy to hear that connecting into the backup site and implementing the recovery plan can be much easier, and more cost-effective, with a frame relay network than with dedicated leased lines.

You may have one of two popular backup configurations. Either you use a hot or cold site facility from a disaster recovery service provider, or you use one of your own networking locations to act as a backup site in the event the primary site fails.

The term "hot" site is used to refer to a backup recovery center in which all the necessary hardware, software and information components necessary to conduct your business are present and ready to activate in real time or near real time. This could be a second facility that you own that keeps a copy of all your ongoing business information so that in the event of a disaster at the primary site, people can be moved to the hot site and can resume normal business functions. Or, you can contract for a service from a company specializing in providing hot-site facilities.

The term "cold" site refers to a similar type of arrangement, but the facility not as quickly engaged as the hot site. It may simply be a building, or room, with some of the necessary equipment, but in the event of a disaster you may have to load your software, bring in tapes of business information, etc.

Regardless of which of these two alternatives you have, you must be able to divert traffic to the backup site if the primary site is no longer operational.

Take a small star network with just six locations as an illustrative example.

*Disaster Recovery Before*

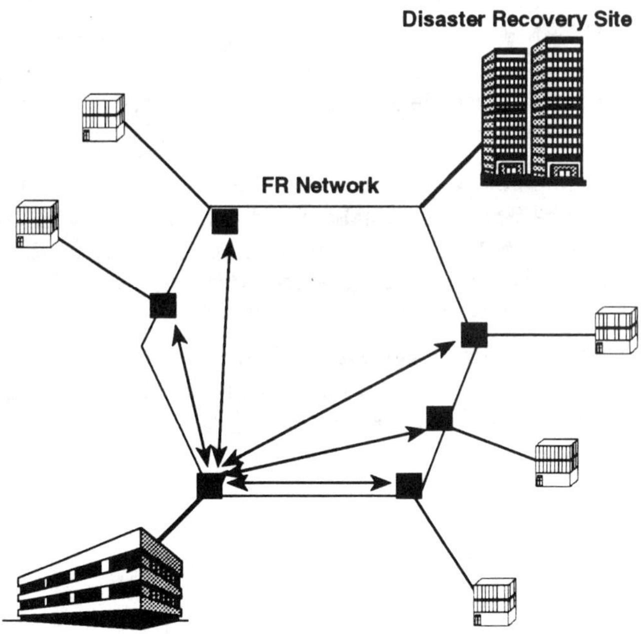


*Fig. 7.11: In the event of a catastrophic failure at the Primary Site, all data processing functionality and connectivity would move to the Disaster Recovery Site.*

In the event of a catastrophic failure at the headquarters location, all of the functionality of that location must be recovered at the disaster recovery site. In addition, all of the connectivity must be recovered. Depending upon what services your carrier has available, one of three alternatives is most likely: our network can be reconfigured by you, the carrier, or in some automated fashion; you can use a dedicated leased line or bandwidth on demand configuration; or you can pre-establish PVCs into the recovery site so that no change must occur to the network following a site disaster.

### *Network Reconfiguration*

The most logical approach is to simply reconfigure the network. Following a disaster, the PVCs that were terminating in the headquarters site would be reconfigured to terminate into the backup site. This reconfiguration could be accomplished in one of three ways:

- **Carrier Manual.** You and the carrier may have worked out a plan up front that in the event of a site failure you can notify the carrier and it will reconfigure your PVCs, as pre-designed, within a certain number of minutes or hours.
- **User Manual.** Carriers will eventually be giving users the ability to control the provisioning of PVCs in real time. You would access the network using a network management tool and reconfigure your PVCs into the backup site.
- **Automatic.** Conceivably, an alternate configuration for PVCs can be stored in a database and automatically activated in the event that the primary site is no longer active on the network. It might be automatically triggered (not yet available) or manually triggered by the carrier or by you directly.

Some carriers can support at least one form of reconfiguration today, while others cannot. Over time, these options probably will be supported by nearly all carriers and will become the default option.

*Disaster Recovery After*

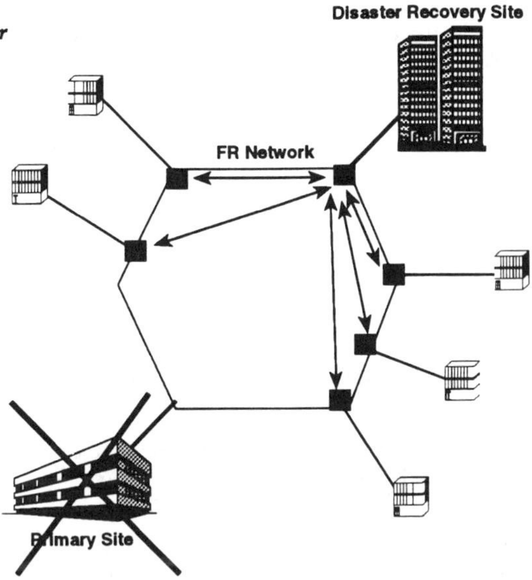


*Fig. 7.12: After a disaster at the Primary Site, connectivity is re-established to the Disaster Recovery Site.*

## *Scheduled Dedicated Capacity*

Another alternative is to use a dedicated connection from the port connection at the primary site to the backup site. The connection would only be activated in an disaster, and while you might pay a small monthly recurring

*Disaster Recovery Scheduled Dedicated Connection*

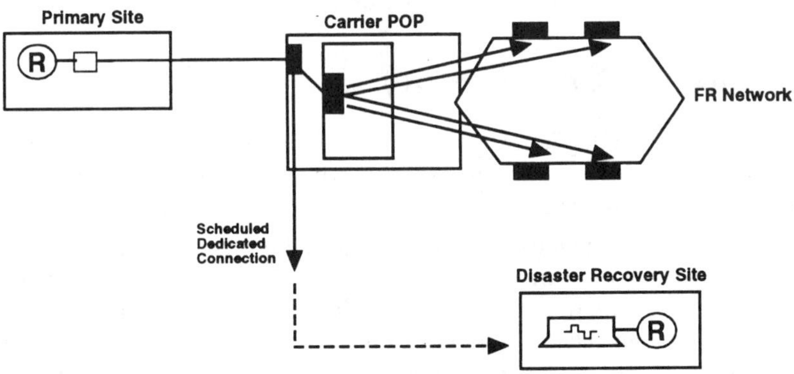


*Fig. 7.13: A scheduled dedicated connection could be used to gain connectivity to the Disaster Recovery Site.*

charge for the configuration, you would only pay for the actual connection if and when it is used.

Most carriers do support this type of service. They utilize bandwidth-on-demand service to allow you to schedule the capacity to the backup site following a disaster. The carrier may not normally sell the bandwidth-on-demand service to support the configuration shown above, but may be willing to work with you towards this end.

The other possibility is using an A/B switch in front of the port connection, instead of the carrier's bandwidth scheduling system, to switch to the backup connection to the disaster recovery site. The disadvantage here is that you would be paying for the backup connection on a full-time basis.

Another disadvantage is that the dedicated connection may not be protected from network failures, which could leave the entire network vulnerable to a cable cut when operating in this configuration.

### *Full Time PVCs*

The last alternative we will discuss may seem excessive, but you may find that the cost is actually less than the dedicated solution and offers advantages over the reconfiguration service. These include being able to conduct tests at any time without modifying the network.

With this alternative, you provide every network site with a PVC to the backup location's port connection. The incremental cost of this can be less than $20 to $50 per site per month. The backup site would need its own port connection, but regardless of the solution you choose, you will have fixed monthly costs for network connectivity at the backup site.

In the event of a site failure, or when disaster recovery testing must occur, the PVCs are already in place and can be utilized.

## International Connectivity

International frame relay is really taking off, and managers will find global frame relay networking becoming easier to purchase and manage as carriers and users alike become more familiar with international frame relay.

If you have a domestic frame relay network, then connecting to international locations can occur in one of several ways. The most optimal decision will probably be decided — as always — on a per site basis. The country to which you need connectivity, the type of infrastructure in place within that country, and the availability of alternatives will all impact your decision.

*Disaster Recovery Full Time PVCs*

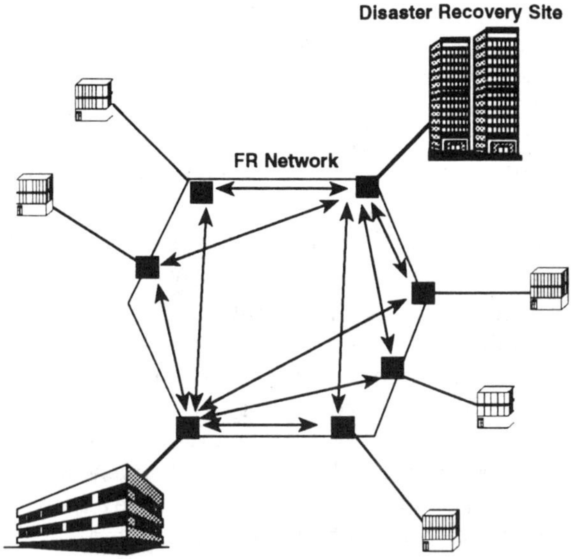


*Fig. 7.14: PVCs can be assigned from each remote location to both the Primary Site and the Disaster Recovery Site.*

If you already have an international network in place, and you migrate your domestic network to frame relay, the best choice might be to leave the international connections alone, at least in the beginning. Over time, as the domestic network is stabilized and you become familiar with managing the service, you can begin to look at how different international sites can be most cost-effectively handled.

## *International Leased Lines*

You may want to maintain direct leased line connections to some international locations, especially if these connections are already in place today. The configuration would look much like the public/private network hybrid scenarios discussed above. The router, or other frame relay equipment, would act as the gateway between the leased line and the frame relay network, allowing full connectivity between the users on each.

This solution might be optimal where only a low-speed point-to-point connection is needed, where the connectivity is already in place and proven to be reliable, or where other alternatives are less cost-effective.

### International Public Data Service

Another alternative for connectivity to international locations is to use a non-frame relay public data service, such as X.25 or TCP/IP. Many times, these services are more easily acquired and more readily available. They may also have error correction functionality to help compensate for inferior network quality in those countries where fiber is not ubiquitously deployed. Remember, frame relay functions best when the underlying network is virtually error-free.

This is just another example of a hybrid configuration, with your premises equipment acting as the gateway between the networks.

At least one carrier today is offering interworking between X.25, TCP/IP and frame relay, and other carriers will soon be offering this service. By interworking, we mean the network provides transparent protocol *translation*. Each site interfaces into the network using one of the three protocols supported. If the underlying data needs to be forwarded to a site using a different interface protocol, the network will recognize this and translate it to the required protocol. Translation is different, and more advanced, than encapsulation because the network is literally changing the packet header information and format to match the requirements of the interfacing equipment.

With encapsulation, the network simply takes the incoming packet and adds the overhead, such as addressing, of the protocol into which it is being encapsulated. The disadvantages of this approach are that you now have two layers of overhead, where only one is needed, and you must be able to unencapsulate at the receiving end.

Translation between two protocols means that the overhead from one protocol is replaced with the correct overhead and addressing format needed by the next protocol. It also means that the packet, or frame, can now be immediately received and read by the equipment to which it is being sent; it does not have to be unencapsulated first. This added level of network intelligence is what allows you to mix and match different network interfaces within a single network architecture for optimal cost-efficiency.

### International Frame Relay

The final alternative is to use a public frame relay service to reach international locations. Many carriers are offering this alternative today, and it can be a viable and cost-effective solution, especially to major world trading centers such as London, Hong Kong, and Tokyo.

In this configuration you can have the same carrier provide both your domestic frame relay network and the international connectivity. This means that the "cloud" simply expands to a global scope.

The only reason you might take this approach is that one carrier can provide more economical domestic service, while another provides more economical international service.

If international connectivity is a requirement, then this could be a major decision criterion for choosing among frame relay service providers.

One important criterion to consider in connecting to international locations is the level of technical and service support you will need at that site. You may want to choose a carrier that can provide you with remote support for all the equipment, maintenance and even round-the-clock network monitoring and management. The time, language and cultural differences of networking in a foreign country can increase the normal networking frustrations. Your carrier can help alleviate you of some of these responsibilities with managed network services (See Chapter 11) or with equipment and maintenance packages.

## Design Considerations in the Local Environment

This chapter, and the one preceding, have dealt primarily with design considerations and issues for the frame relay service. However, when you implement a frame relay network you will also need to consider the local architecture.

- If you are running SNA, which of the many architectural approaches should you consider?
- What equipment alternatives are available and what are the guidelines for choosing among new-generation IBM platform upgrades, FRADs, and routers?
- What hardware alternatives are most cost-effective for small remote offices?
- What alternatives are available for traffic prioritization when mission-critical applications will use the network?
- Which routing protocol should you choose, and how do different network protocols work over the wide area network?
- How will you manage the network once it's implemented? Should you pay your carrier to provide expert operation or configuration management in place of, or in addition to, your own staff?

- ☎ If you use frame relay now, where does this leave you in the future? Do you maintain the flexibility to grow and migrate the network over time, or are you locked in to a frame relay solution that requires new hardware investments as your networking needs change and as new services become available?

These questions will be answered in the second half of this book. Read on.

[1] *The non-mileage sensitive pricing of frame relay results in a flat rate per connection. Leased lines are mileage sensitive in price structure. There is some point where a leased line becomes more expensive than a frame relay connection, within the context of a network, because the leased line increases in price as the length increases. The crossover points vary by carrier, and are roughly estimated here.*
[2] *Not all carriers will support this configuration.*

CHAPTER 8:

# SNA, FRAME RELAY, AND IBM

Throughout this book, we have attempted to be vendor-independent, not mentioning or highlighting specific carriers or equipment vendors, although we have tried to cover both the standard and unique capabilities of the leading players. We are not really making an exception in this chapter, although we specifically discuss IBM. In this case, we are interested more in addressing "IBM" in terms of its network architecture and set of widely used protocols, due to the high number of installed SNA networks worldwide.

This chapter will cover some of the available migration paths and alternatives for using a frame relay network service. In Chapter 10 other protocols such as TCP/IP, AppleTalk, Novell IPX and DECnet are discussed. This chapter will concentrate on the SNA protocol suite, and will present alternative strategies for routing SNA over frame relay. Many different vendors' equipment can be used to successfully implement the strategies discussed below. These general configuration alternatives are discussed in the next chapter, which covers LAN and SNA integration.

There is, however, a deviation in this chapter from the rest of the book. Many of the migration strategies discussed are in the earliest stages of implementation. In other parts of this book, both theoretical and real-world viewpoints can be provided, with a splash of advice based on the three years experience so far amassed with frame relay. More theory and less practical advice can be offered here, simply because a pool of experience for many of these migration strategies has not yet been formed.

If you have a significant amount of hierarchical SNA traffic, and just a few LANs, then you may want to consider one of the migration strategies and LAN/SNA consolidation approaches discussed in this chapter. If you have a more balanced distribution between LAN and SNA traffic, and/or the LAN traffic is growing rapidly, then you may also want to consider some of the approaches discussed in Chapter 9.

This chapter is not designed to give you the full IBM migration blueprint, and if you are an SNA expert, the information discussed here may not be new. The purpose of the chapter is to present IBM's set of alternatives for migrating traditional SNA architectures to frame relay so that you may consider this information in light of the consolidation strategies presented in Chapter 9. The broad overview will give you a feel for the issues involved, the trade-offs, and the questions to ask.

The best place to begin is with a very quick review of the controller family and the network roles played by this equipment. Then we will look at where frame relay fits into the overall IBM network strategy, and finally discuss the different ways you can integrate LAN and SNA applications over a frame relay network.

## The Controller Family

Historically, IBM's SNA has been a single line protocol environment: SDLC. Recognizing this as an inhibitor and that most networks today support multiple protocols, IBM has developed a migration strategy for current SNA users, which includes support for multiple protocols and for "routing" SNA traffic.

The controller family is IBM's bread-and-butter networking platform. The family consists of three primary products: the 3174 cluster controller, 3172 controller, and the 3745 front end processor (FEP). The family has traditionally communicated SNA traffic using SDLC.

It's important to recognize the role that each of these devices plays within a network so that in planning your migration strategy you can assure that no critical functions are lost in the migration.

The 3174 consolidates traffic from multiple terminals at a site, and interfaces with a front end processor (either locally or remotely). The 3174 controller accepts information from and sends information to the terminals and handles all direct communications with the front end processor. It temporarily buffers information/requests going from the terminals to the mainframe until it is polled by the front end processor. It then responds to polls by forwarding the packets. The traditional controller accepts SDLC formatted data.

The 3172 is designed to be channel-attached to the mainframe, and it is not typical for this to occur over a wide area network (unless remote channel extension is being used). This chapter will not deal with the 3172 controller.

The front end processor not only controls the polling sequences to remote controllers, it also "routes" the SNA traffic. You often hear the phrase "SNA isn't routable." This is not actually true. FEPs route SNA traffic much like a router routes TCP/IP traffic, by reading the destination address and selecting the best path. It also acts as a traffic concentrator for the mainframe, supports "group polls" and performs other functions.

## Where Frame Relay Fits

If you have a wide area network environment that can only accommodate a single protocol, regardless of what that protocol is, this can be a bit limiting. If the subnetworking protocol happens to be SDLC this can be a real problem as you grow and expand the network, because SDLC can only transport SNA traffic. SNA is not an "open" protocol allowing a network device to look at the header information and determine the destination address. Therefore, the SNA traffic can either be routed by the FEP, or it can be passed through to a single path with no "routing" as done today in many non-IBM routers and FRADs.

In the local environment, the Token Ring LAN already supports multiple protocols. IBM has even expanded the controller family to support TCP/IP and Ethernet LANs. But in the WAN, IBM needed to develop a solution for handling traffic other than, and in addition to, traditional SNA over SDLC. IBM chose frame relay as its multiprotocol WAN solution.

The reason for the choice of frame relay, instead of another WAN protocol, are several:

- **Software Solution:** The similar data packet structure enabled IBM to migrate communications links from SDLC to frame relay without hardware changes. The changes could all be done in software.

- **Capital Investment Evolution:** The software migration path provides the 60,000 installed SNA networks a high level of investment protection, and also gives users of these networks a strong reason to stay with IBM as their networks grow and change. Upgrades to frame relay are available as new software releases, and in many circumstances there is no additional charge.

- **Multiple Protocols and Interoperability:** Frame relay provides multiprotocol support and provides IBM an interoperability path between the controller family and multiprotocol routers, including IBM's own router as well as other leading routers, which will support the new IBM protocols.

At this writing, IBM supports frame relay on the following products:

- Controller family: 3745/6, 3172, 3174
- RouteXpander card (within PC)
- AS/400
- 6611 router and 2210 router

## The Future of SNA

Up until recently an FEP could route SNA traffic but other non-IBM devices could not. This made integration of LAN and SNA traffic over a single frame relay network difficult. IBM is giving SNA a face lift, opening up the protocol to other vendors and providing a path to application and network convergence. These modifications are important to the overall frame relay migration strategy because they provide alternatives for handling the SNA traffic over the network.

### *Client-Server Evolution and APPN*

In the subarea, hierarchical SNA environment, there is a clearly defined master-slave relationship between devices. The mainframe, or host, reigns and all other devices are subservient. The controller family acts as the intermediaries between VTAM (virtual telecommunication access method) in the mainframe and the dumb terminals on users' desktops. The NCP software in the FEPs takes the input from many 3174s and routes the traffic to the correct VTAM.

In the evolution to client-server, the master-slave relationship dissolves. A remote PC can directly communicate with another remote PC, with the mainframe, or with many other types of devices on the network. Polling is not used in this environment to control when and where information is transferred.

APPN is IBM's Advanced Peer-to-Peer Network protocol, which supports any-to-any connectivity on a network and provides the ability to "route" SNA traffic. The APPN protocol is open so that non-IBM vendors can either duplicate or purchase the code.

Today nearly 50 vendors, including the leading internetworking equipment vendors, participate in the APPN Implementers Workshop. It also allows a more dynamic relationship between devices. This means that instead of having to bring the network down for an NCP regeneration or initial program load (IPL), relationships between devices can be transparently and automatically updated. When combined with the flexibility for physical reconfiguration provided by frame relay service, this makes for a highly dynamic network environment.

APPN is the architecture for routing SNA. It is simpler than the NCP used by FEPs for subarea traffic routing and therefore can be accommodated by smaller, and less expensive, networking devices. The result of APPN migration should be a reduced cost of network ownership and operations.

Within APPN there are three types of devices: low end node (LEN), end node (EN), and the network node (NN).

The EN and its less sophisticated counter part, the LEN, generate APPN traffic. Most PCs have enough memory and processing power to be easily upgradeable to ENs. Just like a PC is provided a TCP/IP protocol stack for TCP/IP applications like file transfers, the PC is given an "APPN protocol stack" where APPN becomes the transport and network protocol. The EN runs native APPN, and perhaps other protocols as well.

NNs route the traffic generated by the ENs and LENs. Because APPN is an open and portable protocol, non-IBM equipment can become NNs, ENs or LENs. In fact, routers are available today that are NN-capable.

NNs exchange topology information using Control Point-to-Control Point (CP-CP) sessions. The NN then uses this information to calculate optimal paths between logical unit (LU) devices. Each NN keeps a database reflecting the entire network topology of every other NN in the network. In large networks, the overhead generated by this information exchange can be significant. The advantage of this approach is that network definition is automatic and dynamic.

*APPN Network Architecture*

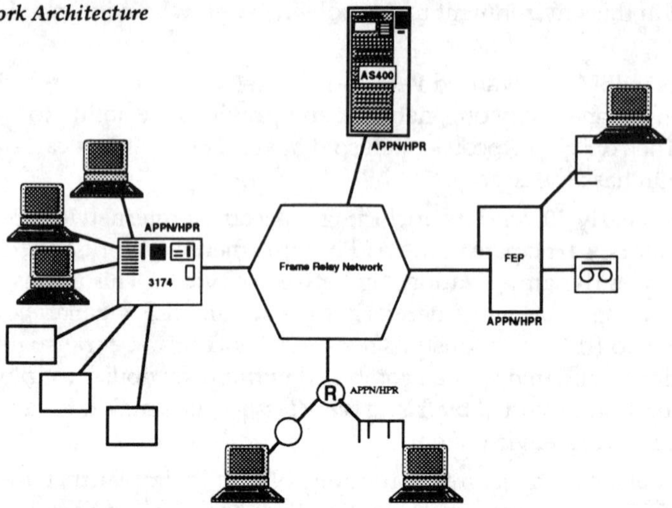


*Fig. 8.1: Many IBM and third-party devices can function as an APPN network node. The network node in an APPN/HPR network can "route" SNA.*

APPN provides for segregation of networks into network domains to keep this problem of overhead generated from topology exchanges in check. You can set up border nodes and firewalls for topology updates.

Today, IBM's FEP and 3174 controller are APPN network nodes. Both also support frame relay. The result of APPN is that SNA traffic can be routed over a frame relay network.

APPN has some weaknesses, such as the inability to route around network failures and the ability to provide improved congestion/flow control. As you move to high speed networking, congestion must be tightly managed and these issues are being addressed by IBM with APPN's successor protocol, HPR, discussed below.

## *Second Generation APPN — HPR*

High Performance Routing, HPR, is an extension of APPN and is sometimes referred to as "APPN+." It is an "industrial strength" version of APPN suitable for tomorrow's interworking environment. It adds significant improvements to the protocol in much the same way that frame relay improved upon X.25.

APPN provides both error checking and error recovery services. It assumes that the underlying transmission facilities are not reliable, much the same way as X.25. Each APPN NN stores a copy of each packet it transmits until it receives a positive acknowledgment from the network node. This takes time and space, and is not necessary for digital networks.

HPR moves error correction to the edges of the network, making it faster and more efficient than APPN. This is a significant architectural advantage. HPR operation is like a link-state routing protocol, in that each network node has a topology map of the entire network.

When a packet is received for routing, the first NN defines the end-to-end network path that the packet will take. This allows the intermediate NNs to simply read the routing information in the HPR header and route the packet accordingly. This totally new, connectionless routing scheme is based on two new IBM architectures, Rapid Transport Protocol (RTP) and Automatic Network Routing (ANR). The end-to-end route as preestablished by the first NN is appended to a Routing Information Field (RIF) within the HPR packet header. In contrast to the Layer 4 routing of APPN, most HPR routing takes place at layer 2. The HPR protocol will support other connection-oriented and connectionless protocols.

HPR will also provide non-disruptive rerouting to an alternate path when one path fails. PVC reroutes in frame relay are not instantaneous, and can sometimes take several seconds. The SNA sessions could be lost during this interval. The HPR should be able to establish a new connection prior to a session time out. HPR does offer a user-configurable retry count before an alternative path is established. If you are using a frame relay network, this would allow you to give the PVC a chance to reroute before the HPR rerouting is initiated.

At this writing, HPR is only just becoming available on IBM products. It is certainly IBM's best effort to offer a viable network alternative to TCP/IP. However, you will probably find that with TCP/IP being so entrenched for LAN internetworking, HPR will become one other protocol within a multiprotocol network — albeit a potentially important protocol for internetworks supporting a high level of transaction-oriented processing. While IBM is intending for HPR to rival TCP/IP and become a default-standard for SNA traffic, the company is not precluding support for and interworking with TCP/IP. Both protocols can be natively routed on the same equipment.

HPR will support only LU 6.2 traffic. This is where the software for dependent LU server and requester (DLUS/DLUR) figures into the migration equation. It provides a mechanism via APPN/HPR to support traditional 3270 subarea traffic as explained below.

HPR is part of RFC 1490 (multiprotocol encapsulation over frame relay), allowing it to run in parallel with other protocols over a frame relay network.

### *Keeping Subarea Traffic*

Recognizing that a large majority of networks will continue to support very traditional subarea SNA, including dumb terminals and intelligent PCs, a migration strategy has been developed to allow both traditional traffic and APPN traffic to share the same physical network infrastructure and frame relay network service.

Dependent LU Server (DLUS) and Dependent LU Requester (DLUR) allow hierarchical SNA to be converted to APPN and routed over an APPN/HPR network. This helps to reduce inhibitions for migrating to HPR, because the migration can occur in stages throughout the network, with some network sections remaining traditional hierarchical SNA.

A dependent LU server, such as VTAM, and a dependent LU requester, such as a controller workstation or router, communicate to initiate session requests and for the exchange of network management information. The data traffic (LU1, LU2, LU3) from dumb terminals or printers is natively routed across an APPN network to the mainframe without modification to the device or mainframe application.

The DLUR can be installed in APPN equipment to allow the equipment to accept traditional SNA traffic and convert the traffic to APPN. In this scenario, an old 3745 model FEP or a remote controller, which, for some reason, you do not want to upgrade, could interface with an APPN device with a dependent LU requester installed. That device would route the traffic to VTAM, over an APPN network, which would be equipped with DLUS.

The result is that you can migrate your network in stages, and even choose not to migrate some portions of the network, and still use a single frame relay network service to support all of the traffic. This provides network savings through consolidation of LAN, subarea and APPN/HPR SNA onto a single network, improves performance for the SNA traffic because polls are handled locally and line speeds are faster, and delivers a more flexible and dynamically configurable network architecture.

One possible downside to this strategy is that DLUS/DLUR is currently not planned for availability on the AS/400s, which support both 3270 emulation traffic and 3174 attachments.

In addition to IBM's implementation of DLUS/DLUR, third party implementations of DLUR emulation are expected to provide the same migration path offered by the IBM approach.

*APPN With Subarea SNA*

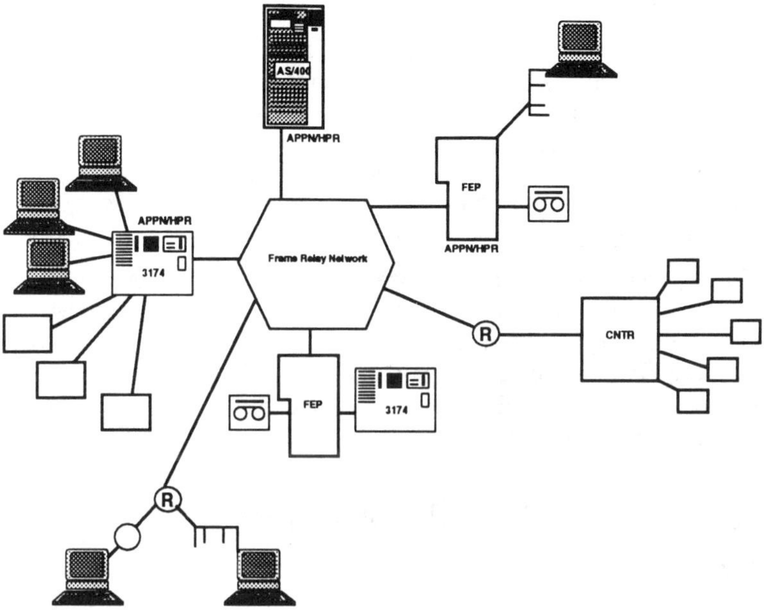


*FIg. 8.2: APPN/HPR combined with dependent LU Server and Requestor allows the network nodes to support traditional, subarea SNA traffic.*

## *AnyNet Product Family*

The AnyNet product family is a software approach to multiprotocol networking based on IBM's emerging Multiprotocol Transport Networking (MPTN) architecture. The objectives of AnyNet is to allow a customer to:

- add new application types independent of the existing network;
- extend the reach of an application over multiple networks;
- consolidate and simplify multiprotocol networks while preserving investment in existing applications.

This application and network independence is achieved by the implementation of the MPTN architecture, which separates the application support and transport network.

The AnyNet gateway allows customers to concatenate unlike networks into one logical network. The software gateways are currently implemented on OS/2 and MVS.

Instead of having the conversion between different applications and different protocols reside on the desktop and in the operating system, the AnyNet Gateway provides a single piece of equipment that can convert between TCP/IP and SNA. The gateway allows SNA application to run over connected SNA and TCP/IP networks. It also allows Sockets applications to run over connected TCP/IP and SNA networks. An IPX to SNA gateway is a future direction for IBM. IPX is Novell, Inc.'s network layer protocol.

These gateways operate at the transport layer (layer four) and do not provide protocol conversion. Native protocol data is put in an MPTN connection command and then sent across a new network type. The AnyNet access node on the second network receives the MPTN command and forwards the native data to the matching application. The native system can be any vendor's SNA or TCP system.

## Integrating LAN and SNA Traffic Over Frame Relay

There are several alternatives for integrating LAN and SNA (both subarea and HPR) traffic over the same frame relay network. Each alternative has both pros and cons. The most important thing to realize is that each of the alternatives is maturing at a very rapid rate. Implementing one solution does not preclude you from taking advantage of other alternatives as they become available. In fact, by integrating the applications over a single frame relay network now, you can buy yourself time to reengineer the local topology, choosing a migration path that best meets the needs of your organization. If one of the consolidation solutions available today makes sense for your network, you might even be able to finance SNA equipment additions or upgrades from the network savings achieved from the consolidation.

### *Frame Handling*

One of IBM's first steps into the world of frame relay networking came in a Release 6 upgrade for the FEP. Called "frame handling," it allowed the FEP to act as a frame relay transport provider over a private corporate network in support of attached routers running a frame relay protocol.

In this configuration, a frame relay router can be connected to a FEP with frame handling capability. The FEP can accept incoming frames and route the frame over a private network to its destination by reading the DLCI

*Frame Handling*

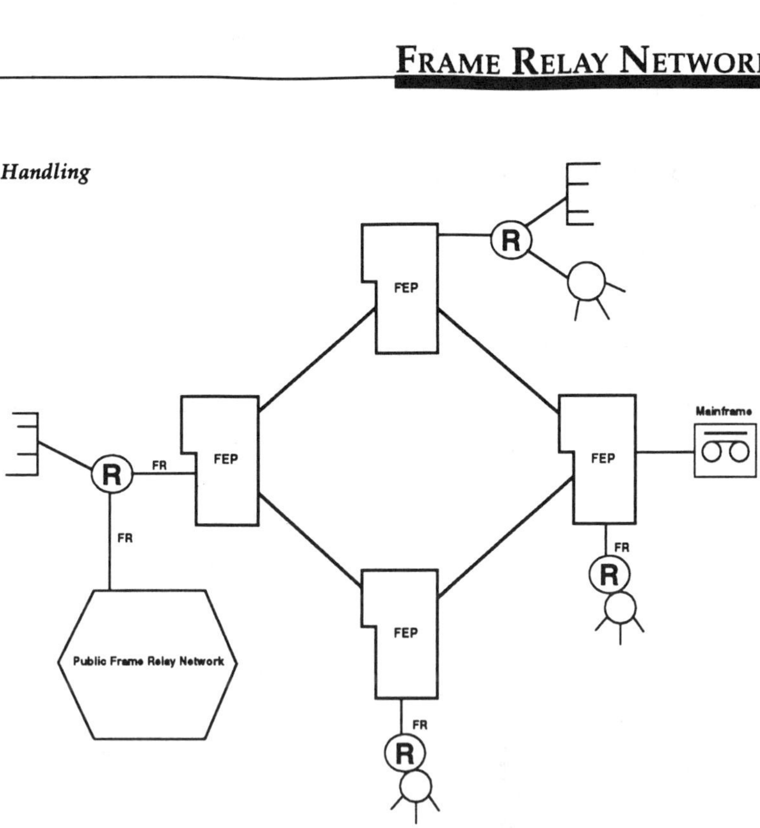


*Fig. 8.3: Frame handling allows routers and other frame relay equipment to pass frames over an FEP private backbone. It was one of IBM's first moves into frame relay services support.*

address. The same router could also be connected to a public frame relay service in a hybrid network arrangement.

The frame handling solution was only a first step. The next step was to enable the FEP to fully support frame relay, including allowing the FEP to be a user of public frame relay services. Since the FEP supports both Token Ring and Ethernet interfaces, it can be one path through which to achieve network consolidation.

If your company has a substantial investment in SNA systems, if the architecture supports many mission-critical applications and/or if the percentage of LAN traffic relative to SNA is small, then this migration path may offer you the ability to achieve consolidation without jeopardizing your network applications.

If, in addition to upgrading some of your FEPs to frame relay you also want to explore alternatives for reducing the number of remote FEPs in your network, this topic is discussed more below. Using routers to support SNA and LAN traffic is covered in Chapter 9. Depending upon what functions the remote FEP performs, a router (with or without APPN) can sometimes take its place.

### Frame Relay Support

IBM now supports direct connections into a public frame relay network on the entire controller family, including the 3745 FEP and on the 3174 controller. It also supports frame relay on the AS/400 and the RouteXpander card, which fits within a PC. This means that these devices can directly interface with a frame relay network, without being front-ended by a device such as a router.

*Frame Relay Support*

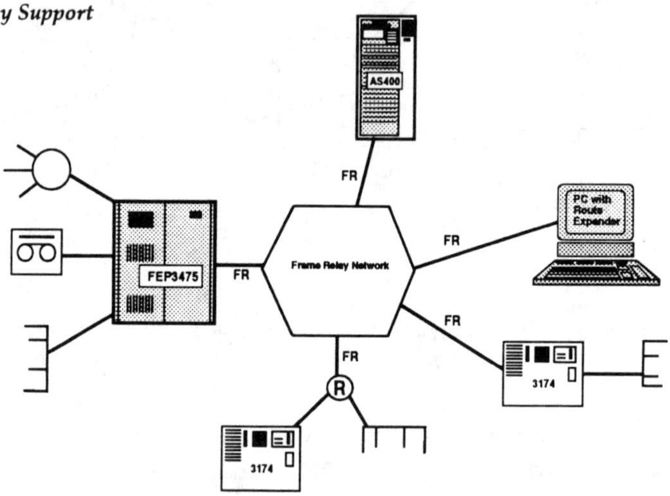


*Fig. 8.4: IBM's 3475 Front End Processor, 3174 Controller, AS/400, and RouteXpander card support direct connections into a frame relay network.*

### SNA over LANs

IBM now widely supports both Ethernet and Token Ring LANs on the 3174 and 3745 controllers. The protocol for using LAN transmission media for SNA traffic is the LLC2 (logical link control) protocol. LLC2 is the SDLC equivalent in a LAN environment.

LAN-attached PCs running SNA applications can use LLC to send data to the mainframe. A LAN-attached router will either source route bridge, data link switch (DLSw), or route the traffic via APPN/HPR.

With source-route bridging, the LLC session passes transparently through the router and is not locally terminated. In large networks, especially, this can cause an unacceptable level of congestion on the wide area frame relay network. There can also be time-out problems with the sessions because the polling is not locally terminated. This is exacerbated if the number of network hops is greater than two.

The use of bridging over a frame relay network has been cautioned several times in this book, due to the inefficient use of network capacity, the added congestion, and session time-out problems. Bridging should only be used in small networks and/or where no other alternative is available, such as for handling protocols such as DecLAT.

Data Link Switching is covered more below. It works the same whether the SNA equipment is LAN-attached or directly attached to the router. With DLSw the router will terminate the polls locally, improving network response time and decreasing the congestion over the WAN by filtering out most of this polling traffic.

The last alternative is to have the router actually "route" the SNA traffic. This requires that the APPN/HPR be implemented, and that the router be acting as a NN with DLUR support. This is also covered in detail below.

### *Routers and Data Link Switching*

DLSw is an IBM-developed approach to encapsulating SNA and NetBIOS within TCP/ IP. It can be found under RFC 1434. The link controls are terminated locally (i.e., spoofed) to enhance overall network performance and keep wide area network congestion down (see Chapter 9 for a discussion of spoofing). Serial tunneling was initially developed by several router vendors as a mechanism to transport SNA traffic over an IP backbone, but each vendor had its own approach. An RFC should be available soon that standardizes DLSw.

The router is directly connected to the 3174 controller and creates a TCP/ IP packet from the SNA or NetBIOS packet. This is done by placing the SNA packet into the payload of a TCP packet, then into the payload of an IP packet and finally into the payload of a frame relay frame. At the other end of the connection, a router is also attached to the FEP. (If the router and the FEP are both running APPN, then the remote router could directly communicate with the FEP).

The TCP/IP layer controls the session and assumes full responsibility for delivering the packet. If a packet is dropped by the network, the router and not the SNA devices assume responsibility for error recovery. The TCP/IP protocols will take responsibility for routing the packet, insuring transmission

*Data Link Switching*

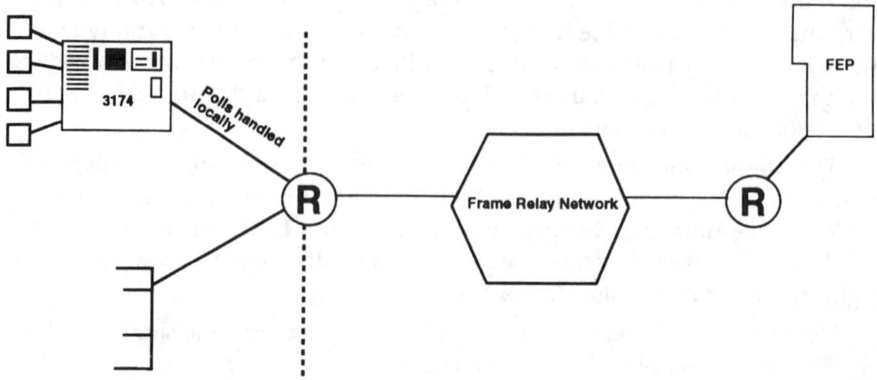


*Fig. 8.5: With DLSw, the subarea SNA traffic is encapsulated first into TCP/IP, where session control and error recovery are managed for the transmission. Then the packet is encapsulated into frame relay and sent to the wide area network. Polls are terminated locally to improve performance and reduce network congestion.*

integrity and even routing around network problems. Do not consider an implementation for tunneling in which a protocol other than TCP/IP is used unless it has the same error correction capabilities.

This approach allows the router to consolidate the traditional SNA traffic onto the frame relay internetwork without modification to the underlying SNA architecture. A standard controller can be directly attached to the router, and the router will perform protocol encapsulation. The advantages of this approach are that you can replace parallel leased line networks with a single frame relay infrastructure that is probably faster, more easily reconfigured, and less costly while deferring decisions on upgrade paths for the SNA network itself. Controllers are also upgradeable to support direct interfaces into a frame relay wide area network, providing an alternative path.

The disadvantages of this approach apply mostly to large SNA networks with a fairly heavy level of SNA traffic and response-time sensitive applications. The solution has difficulty scaling up to very large networks, and the unpredictable response times can cause session time-outs. If you can engineer your network so that you do not exceed two hops per logical link carrying the DLSw traffic, this solution can provide a viable alternative. When you tunnel SDLC through IP, you lose sight of the SDLC management information. NetView visibility into and control over the TCP/IP environment is just becoming available and is not as advanced as SNA management.

When using DLSw, the SNA traffic from a given controller is not routed but instead mapped through to a single virtual connection back to a primary mainframe. By implementing customized modifications at the application layer you can allow a single user/workstation to choose between different destinations, but the network really doesn't apply this level of intelligent routing itself. For many networks this solution is adequate for today and can buy migration time for converting the SNA subarea traffic to HPR in the future.

### *Routers and FRADs versus the FEP*

Can a router or FRAD replace a front end processor? The answer seems to be both "yes" and "no," depending upon which FEP functions you rely upon and for which you have replacement strategies. The NCP provides boundary insulation to the applications and VTAM, allowing you to move applications without affecting dependent devices. However, changing the relationship of devices often requires an NCP regeneration, meaning the network is physically down. This is one of the areas where a combination of APPN/HPR and frame relay can benefit an SNA network.

The FEP also provides routing for the SNA traffic, a method of traffic concentration, prioritization, load balancing, and transmission groups. As Chapter 9 discusses, some alternative solutions are available that provide concentration in networks with a single mainframe, even without implementation of APPN/HPR.

APPN/HPR can provide the "routing" functionality performed for SNA traffic by a remote FEP. DLSw can provide a tunneling approach if, once again, you are not ready to implement APPN/HPR.

So, a router or FRAD can replace some of the functions of the FEP but not necessarily all, making the answer to the initial question highly dependent upon your network configuration. Many current frame relay customers have achieved significant network savings though the elimination of at least some remote FEPs from the network.

### *Consolidation Using APPN and HPR*

The long term strategy by IBM for SNA is HPR. The controller family and other APPN/HPR devices are able to route the SNA traffic and also provide traffic concentration, prioritization and load balancing. Both APPN/HPR traffic and traditional subarea traffic can be simultaneously supported over the same frame relay network by implementing DLUR/DLUS. In addition, other protocols such as TCP/IP, SPX/IPX, DECnet, and so on, can be supported by the NN.

***Remote FEPs***

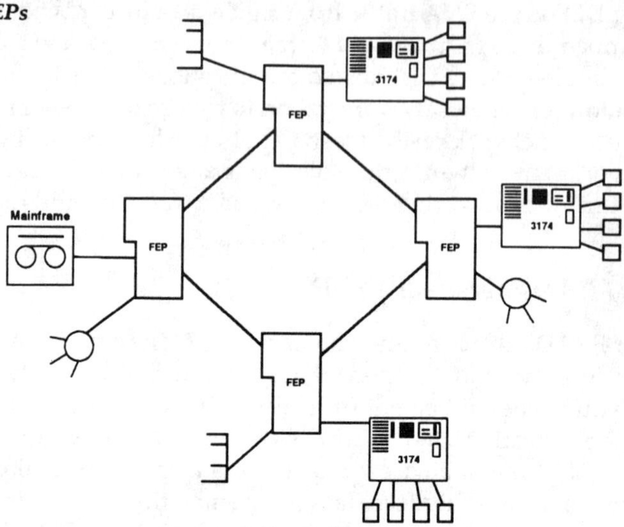


*Fig. 8.6a: Remote FEPs concentrate controller data and route SNA. Some functions of the remote FEP can be replaced by routers.*

***Remote Routers Replace FEPs***

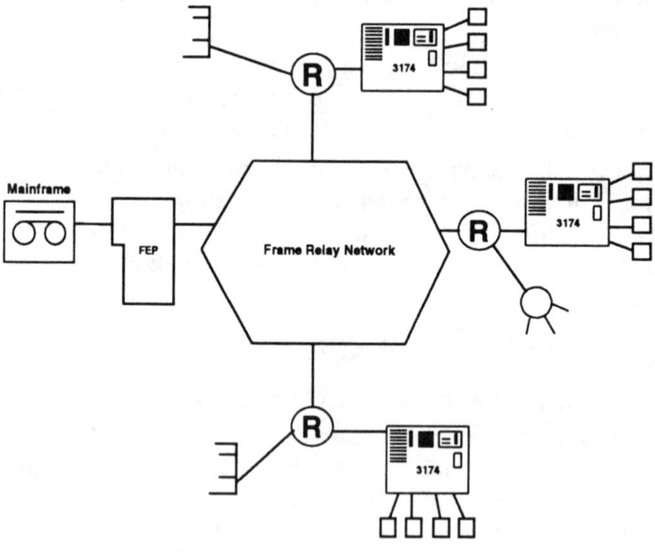


*Fig. 8.6b: For some networks, it may be possible for routers to replace FEPs at more remote locations, especially if APPN/HPR is used.*

The consolidation of the LAN and SNA traffic lowers the cost of network ownership and operation. It is a simple architecture and allows you to leverage your existing investment in both hardware and skills. Since APPN/HPR is an approach that is supported by many vendors, not just IBM, you will have alternative equipment platforms from which to choose. The implementation of HPR within RFC 1490 (multiprotocol encapsulation) provides interoperation between different equipment vendors' products.

The HPR over frame relay solution allows dynamic configuration and definition of relationships between devices, dynamic configuration of the network and dynamic rerouting, while also providing a higher level of response-time consistency than what could be achieved over an internetwork without HPR.

The biggest disadvantage right now is the limited deployment and support for HPR and DLUR/DLUS. This problem should be quickly overcome now that the standard is complete and both IBM and non-IBM equipment supporting the protocol is being introduced to the market.

### *Network Management*

Network management is covered in detail in Chapter 11, although a quick discussion of NetView and NetView/6000 (now called NetView for AIX) is appropriate here. Regardless of the migration and convergence approach(es) you choose, you will probably find that you will continue to use NetView to manage the SNA/APPN/HPR devices and traffic. Then you may use another LAN management solution, such as NetView/6000, for the LAN/SNMP devices. These solutions can also work together to create a hybrid management solution for LAN and SNA networks.

The NetView management system uses SNA protocols for communication with network devices. You will continue to need NetView to manage the traditional IBM devices, including the controller family.

Most routers are monitored via SNMP (although configuration of the device is typically via a vendor-specific application). There are many network management alternatives for managing SNMP devices, including NetView/6000, SunNet Manager, and OpenView. You will need one of these solutions for managing the routers and other SNMP devices in your network.

IBM has enabled the NetView and NetView/6000 systems to exchange information, with NetView assembling the data into a single integrated view of the network. Several leading equipment vendors are developing NetView/6000 interfaces to allow the NetView/6000 (and thus NetView through an information exchange) to view alarms and monitor the health and status of SNMP network devices.

Some IBM equipment, such as the controller family, can be configured to support monitoring using SNA protocols, SNMP, or both. In fact, parts of the device can be monitored using NetView, and other parts, like the IP routing functions, can be monitored via NetView/6000 (or another system) using SNMP.

The down side is that you may need different management system components, plus another system that allows you to remotely configure your routers and other internetworking equipment if these are non-IBM devices. NetView and NetView/6000 can be tied together through command and control functions so that you can create a single focal point for management. Recent innovations with NetView, called the Resource Object Data Manager, are layering additional intelligence on top of data collection functions to provide automation for responding to alarms and other network situations.

## No Single Solution

In LAN and SNA consolidation and migration, as in many other areas, IBM does not offer a single clear cut path for users of its System Network Architecture. IBM has traditionally offered several, sometimes competing, networking strategies and implementation alternatives because it recognizes that there is not a single solution that will meet the diverse needs of all SNA users.

Frame relay migration is no different. You can choose one of many alternatives, depending upon the size of your network, whether you want to maintain some subarea traffic, and whether you want to truly "route" SNA over the internetwork.

The standard approach for integrating LAN and SNA traffic over a frame relay backbone has been to use a router that implements source-route bridging, DLSw or other SNA tunneling, or SDLC-to-LLC conversion. Many router vendors support these solutions (as discussed in Chapter 9), and IBM has been no exception. If you have traditional SNA subarea traffic, then these solutions may work fine for your network, and allow you to gain the economies and other advantages offered by a frame relay network without having to modify any of your SNA infrastructure or applications.

IBM sees a flaw in these approaches because they are TCP/IP-oriented and therefore do not provide the same level of SNA-based routing or congestion control and traffic prioritization. If you already have large-scale APPC based applications, then IBM offers another solution to provide SNA-based routing and SNA-style congestion control.

IBM's solution is HPR and all of its supporting elements, including DLUR/DLUS and APPN. Since the APPN/HPR protocol is open, many different equipment migration paths to achieving the end goal of "routing" SNA will be available.

The result, in theory, is an environment that supports subarea SNA, next-generation client-server transactions based on HPR, and LAN applications including protocol support for TCP/IP, IPX, and other protocols. If you implement one of the strategies discussed above, perhaps you can share your experiences and advice for inclusion in the next edition of this book.

CHAPTER 9:

# LAN AND SNA CONSOLIDATION

Throughout this book, it has been stressed that consolidating LAN and SNA applications onto a frame relay network is a viable strategy. Obviously, there are both pros and cons involved in migrating the SNA traffic from a leased line network to a frame relay network. Savings and improved response time are the biggest benefits; predictability of network performance and establishment of prioritization and network management can be the biggest challenges.

But in the end, it makes sense to consolidate data applications on to a single network. This means not only consolidating the LAN and SNA networks, but other file transfer, imaging and transaction-oriented data traffic as well. The terms "LAN" and "SNA" are just a catch-all for both emerging and legacy data applications within the business.

The optimal network configuration and migration strategy will depend largely upon:

- The legacy networks and equipment you already have in place;
- The percentage of SNA/transaction applications compared with LAN/file sharing applications;
- The relative speed of growth in each area.

It will quickly become apparent that there are many paths and alternatives to physical consolidation. As shown in the network design chapters and as discussed more in chapter 10, there are ways to maintain logical traffic separation if this is a characteristic you desire.

Over 50 percent of the installed frame relay networks today handle at least some SNA traffic, and a few of these networks support only subarea SNA traffic. Some frame relay solutions require changes to the existing SNA topology while others require minimal, if any, changes to the SNA system or underlying equipment currently in place.

There are several different topologies for supporting SNA in a frame relay network. This chapter will cover topology alternatives and migration strategies for consolidation over frame relay using both router and FRAD approaches. Thanks to IBM's new "open" peer to peer architecture, you will find that the configurations discussed below can be complements to and/or replacements for IBM approaches to migrating SNA and LAN applications to a frame relay network.

Looking ahead, the core challenges of implementing frame relay for LAN, SNA and consolidated networks are further dissected. Chapter 10 discusses in detail the alternatives for prioritizing SNA and other transaction processing over file transfers. Chapter 11 deals with network management and managed network services in general.

In general, there are three major areas to discuss with LAN/SNA consolidation:

1. Polling considerations
2. Router configurations
3. FRAD configurations

These are discussed in turn, followed by a brief discussion of migration issues with LAN/SNA consolidation.

## Getting Started with Spoofing

In delving into the issues of topology and migration, it is necessary to start with one of the core principles of SNA: polling. Polling is a critical element of an SNA network, and the issue of how to handle the polling over an integrated LAN/SNA network must be considered. This isn't specifically a frame relay issue; you would face the same trade-offs if you decide to use a private-line-based router internetwork. If you allow the polls to travel the wide area network, you will increase network congestion and impact application response times. The alternative is local termination of most of the polls, a procedure known as "spoofing."

Spoofing improves network response times because most of the polls do not actually travel across the Wide Area Network, WAN. For example, if a FRAD or router is handing SDLC traffic at a remote location, the requests to send information from the attached concentrator (or 3270 emulator) are acknowledged by the router instead of being sent across the network in response to the FEP poll. The router/FRAD plays the roll of a local (or remote) FEP in this respect.

The router attached locally to the FEP at the other end of the connection is performing the same function. It is responding to the FEP polls as if it were a remote cluster controller, sending information or replying that no information needs to be transmitted.

A small percentage of actual polls are allowed through the network, just to ensure that devices remain attached and operational — a "heart beat" monitoring process. However, the majority of the polls are kept off of the wide area network.

The benefits of spoofing are that WAN congestion is decreased and response times on the network are improved. Most of the consolidation approaches available today, using either routers or FRADs, offer the ability to spoof the polling. These consolidation approaches are discussed below.

## Consolidation Via Routers

The router vendors offer several alternatives for consolidating LAN and SNA traffic over a single frame relay network, and the sophistication and breadth of these options increases each month. The basic configurations that will be discussed here include Token Ring bridging, SDLC tunneling and Data Link Switching (DLSw), which is also mentioned in Chapter 9, and APPN Network Node support from routers.

The information presented in Chapter 10 regarding protocol prioritization is a critical complementary element for consolidating LAN and SNA traffic using a router.

While we will discuss the basic configurations in the following sections, know that there is no single "best" configuration for all network environments. Each has its pros and cons, and you will probably use a combination of solutions within your network.

## *Token Ring Bridging and LLC2*

In this scenario, SNA devices, either controllers or 3270 emulators, are LAN-attached. The SDLC packet is translated into LLC (Logical Link Control) packets. The router intercepts the LAN packets and handles them as it would any other LAN packet on the network.

*Token Ring Bridging*

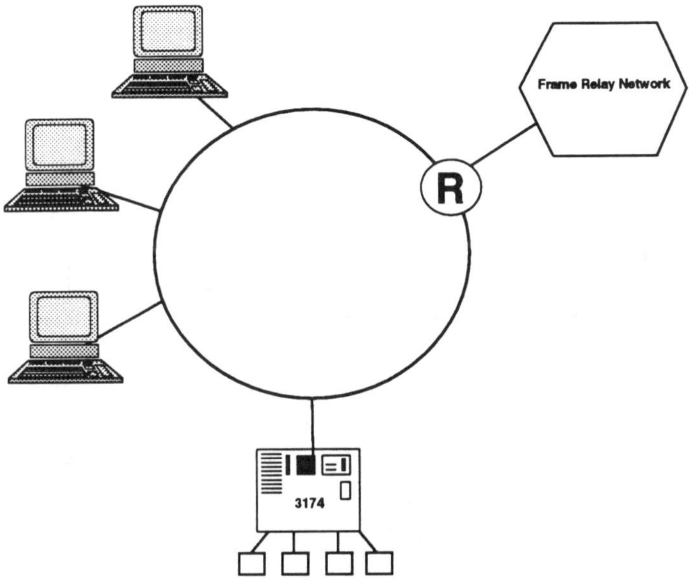


This approach is adequate in networks where routing on the WAN is not needed and where devices are LAN attached. The advantage of this approach is that, because the SDLC packet is actually converted to LLC2, traditional SNA network management, via NetView, can be performed. It also reduces the nondeterministic time delays that characterize TCP/IP-based routing alternatives, and preserves IBM system investments. Source route bridging does not recover well from link failures, and the number of hops is limited to between two and seven, depending upon time-out sensitivities. While this is a less-than-ideal solution in large networks with high traffic volumes due to the bridging and high levels of polling overhead that will traverse the WAN, it is a good interim solution, especially in smaller networks.

## *SDLC Serial Tunneling and Data Link Switching*

SDLC tunneling is another alternative. Router vendors initially developed their own approaches to serial tunneling. Today, several router vendors also support DLSw, which is IBM's proposed approach to SDLC tunneling.

Most serial tunneling implementations provide local termination of SNA polls. The SDLC packet is then encapsulated into a TCP/IP packet. This provides the ability for the router to handle all of the flow-control and standard error recovery processes as it would with any other TCP/IP packet. The TCP/IP packet is encapsulated into frame relay and sent across the frame relay network.

*SDLC Tunneling and Data Link Switching*

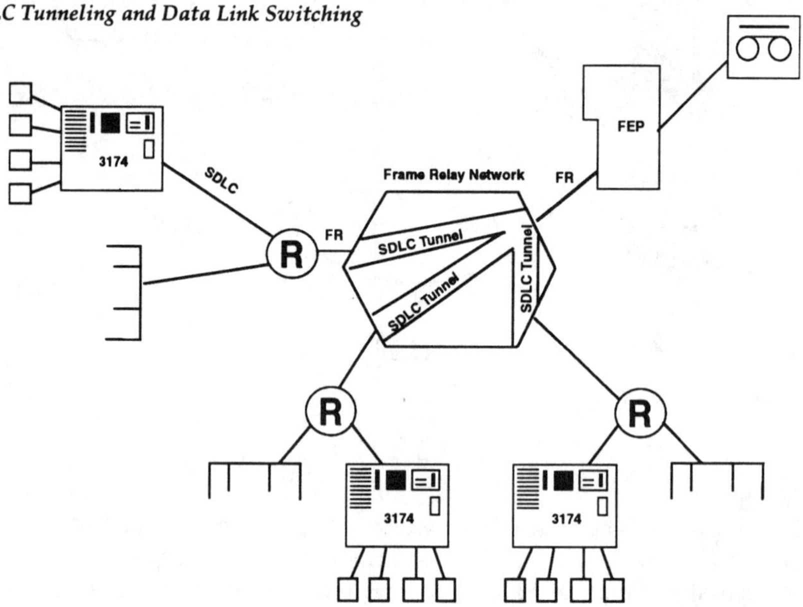


*Fig. 9.2: By using SDLC tunneling, a router can send SDLC information across a frame relay network to a central mainframe. The SDLC data cannot be "routed," in that all the SDLC packets from a given source will be sent to the same PVC, and thus a single mainframe. Data Link Switching (DLSw) is one approach to SDLC tunneling.*

The biggest disadvantage of tunneling/DLSw is the unpredictability of response times, which is a function of the TCP/IP environment. This disadvantage can be overcome, at least partially, by prioritization techniques within the router (see Chapter 10) and/or with segregated and prioritized PVCs (see Chapters 6 and 7). In relatively small networks, the problem of session times outs, which results from unpredictably high response times, is less of a factor because the number of intermediate network hops can be kept at a minimum. Even in larger networks, frame relay can offer a greater level of direct connectivity than leased lines so that the number of hops can be minimized and so too can potential problems with session time outs.

Another downside to this configuration is the added 40 bytes of overhead the combination of TCP/IP and frame relay add to each packet. However, a new method of TCP/IP overhead compression has been defined in RFC 1144, which decreases the TCP/IP overhead to 5 bytes.

*SNA Over LANs with DLSw*

A combination of the above solutions is also a possibility, especially where LANs and multiprotocol routers are already in place. The SDLC frame can first be converted into LLC2 and then encapsulated into TCP/IP. This allows the packet to be routed (not bridged) across the WAN, and provides for automatic link recovery from failure.

## LAN and SNA Consolidation with FRADs

When consolidating LANs and SNA traffic, you can either use a router or a FRAD. The term "FRAD" is used in the frame relay standards to mean any frame relay access device, be it a router, concentrator/multiplexer, or bridge. However, the use of the term FRAD has also grown to have a more specific meaning in the industry. FRADs are frame relay concentrators, or frame relay assembler/disassemblers, which are cousins to PADs (packet assembler/disassemblers) in the X.25 world.. They are typically premises devices, which are both more than, and less than, a router. FRADs and routers are converging in terms of functionality. Most of the capabilities described below will very soon be a standard part of routers. Similarly, the FRAD vendors will continue to expand their routing capabilities.

FRADs can support multiple native protocols, including legacy protocols like bisync, async and SDLC. They can often provide routing functionality and traffic prioritization. And many are equipped specifically to support traditional subarea SNA over a frame relay network, including the ability to support the class of service differentials to which SNA network managers are accustomed.

When routers were first developed, they were used as part of a leased line network in which many LANs at one site could communicate with many LANs at other sites. The process of routing traffic was complex because of the multiple protocol environments and because of the complexity of the physical networks. Many routers had more than one wide area network interface, and the router could use sophisticated algorithms to choose the best available route, or path, for each packet being sent on to the wide area network. Thus, routers were able to help keep network traffic optimized and keep costs down.

Bigger and bigger routers were developed to support more and more LANs with more and more wide area network connections.

Frame relay changed this, at least for a segment of the market. With frame relay, only a single physical interface and a single wide area network port on the router are needed to support connections to many remote LANs. Frame relay also simplified the process of routing; as more connections were available, fewer network "hops" occurred, and the network itself added intelligence and a layer of management.

Just as routers have expanded to meet the changing needs brought about by frame relay, so too has the traditional packet assembler/disassembler been modified to allow the consolidation of LAN and legacy traffic over a frame relay network.

### *Advantages of FRADing*

One of the advantages of using a FRAD is that you can add this new layer of wide area networking equipment in front of your existing controller, PAD, bridge/router, etc., and allow all these applications access to a frame relay network without modifying the underlying network architectures.

Using a FRAD lets you keep the existing equipment and logical configuration of your SNA and other networks, in place. For the SNA network, multipoint/multidrop leased lines and point-to-point leased lines can be replaced with a frame relay network almost transparently.

### *Basic FRAD Configuration*

The basic configuration in using a FRAD is shown in Figure 9.3. Sitting behind the FRAD is a router, cluster controller, X.25 PAD, asynchronous terminal, etc. The FRAD concentrates all the traffic together and maps each incoming port to an outgoing PVC. The FRAD will also spoof the polling protocols, providing rapid response time to polls and decreasing congestion on the network.

*FRAD Configuration*

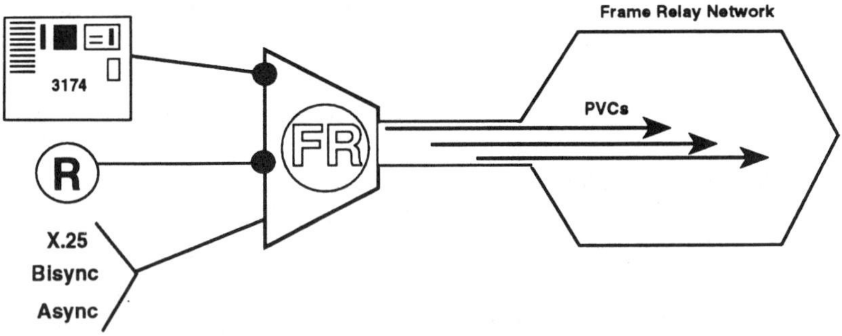


*Fig. 9.3: FRADs will typically support a wide variety of interfaces and at least some basic "routing" functionalities. If you already have controllers, bridges, PADs, and other equipment in place, the FRAD can encapsulate all the input data streams onto a single wide area channel and into a frame relay network.*

With this basic FRAD design, you may not have full routing functionality. In other words, each incoming port might be mapped to a single PVC. Some FRADs have developed capabilities well beyond this basic configuration level; however, for many network locations with the need to connect SNA traffic and maybe some LAN traffic to a single central location, this is all the functionality that is really needed.

## *FRAD Routing*

FRADs are available today with routers and CSU/DSUs built right into them. You can not only connect your controller to the FRAD, but directly connect your LANs as well. If you have more than one LAN at a site, you might use an inexpensive bridge behind the FRAD for the intrabuilding traffic, and let the FRAD be the router interface into the WAN.

For sites that don't need big fancy routers, native support for multiple LAN protocols and lots of LAN input ports, FRADs can offer an alternative to support LAN and SNA applications and gain connectivity to a frame relay network. The cost differential between FRADs and routers is narrowing, so functionality becomes the critical differentiator.

### *Multipoint/Multidrop*

FRADs can allow you to swap out the old multipoint/multidrop leased lines for the more flexible frame relay virtual connectivity. This is accomplished by defining logical groups of PVCs, and presenting the PVC group to the front end processor as a string of sites on a multipoint line. Since everything in the frame relay environment is "virtual something," this could be termed a "virtual multipoint."

Take an example of four multipoint leased lines, each with eight locations being supported. Two of the lines are supporting several sites with heavy transaction rates. These leased lines are running very high utilization rates, the network is congested, and applications are suffering long response time delays. The other two lines support a very light traffic load.

Ideally, you would like to redesign the network to more equally balance the load, putting some of the highly active sites on the same circuit with less active sites, instead of having all the heavy traffic sites on the same two circuits.

Modifying a multipoint leased line network is difficult and time consuming. It is also costly.

Now assume that at each remote site you install a FRAD between the controller and the wide area network. You also install a FRAD between the WAN and the FEP at the primary site. The FRAD is connected into a frame relay service, and uses PVCs for connectivity back to the central site. Each FRAD provides local termination of polls, again providing more rapid response times and decreasing overall network congestion.

The FRAD at the central site can group bundles of PVCs together into a logical multipoint/multidrop circuit. The FEP polls the FRAD, and the FRAD delivers the frames from each site in the order of the multipoint configuration.

If you discover that too many of the highly active locations are on the same "multipoint" circuit, you would simply rearrange the logical PVC groupings. In fact, if you have locations that experience cyclical trends in processing volume, you can rearrange the network regularly to ensure that the network and response times are always optimized.

Performance increases for applications on the network can increase in this configuration, and not just because the polling is terminated on the local connection. The access and transmission speeds of each site into the network can increase from 9.6K bps to 56K bps. In fact, at the central site, since the connection is a V.35, you could increase the speed to 128K bps, or the maximum speed supported.

*Multipoint Circuits — Before Frame Relay*

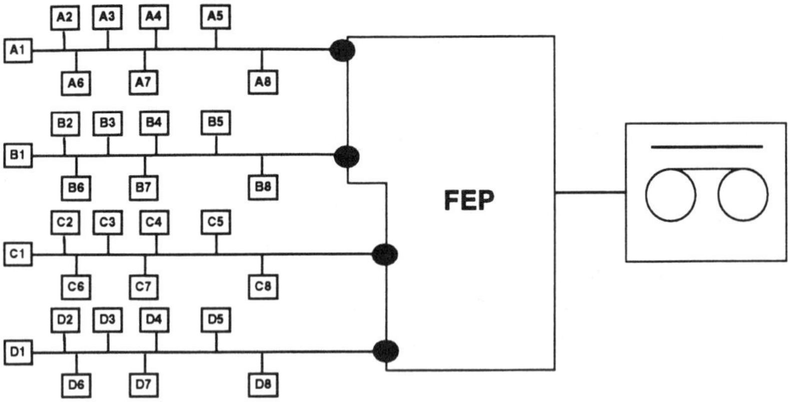


*Fig. 9.4a: Multipoint groups are physically connected, and making changes to group configurations difficult.*

*Virtual Multipoint Circuits*

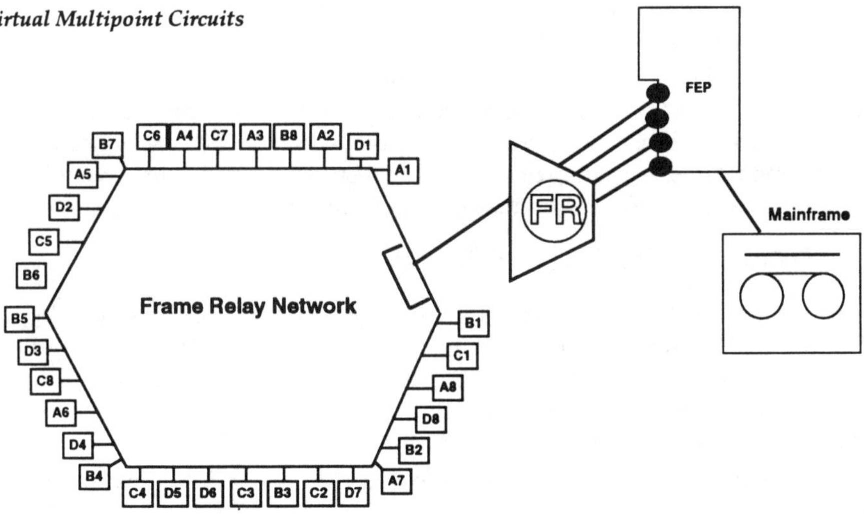


*Fig. 9.4b: Frame relay allows the FEP to receive logical groupings of multipoints. Changing the assignment of a location from one logical group to another is easy and rapid; you simply change its logical group assignment.*

### *Token Ring Interface Connection*

Just like a router, FRADs can also be combined with a TIC (Token Ring interface connection) to the FEP, instead of using a serial port. This increases the speed of communication between the two devices from 56K bps to 4M or 16M bps. All the PVCs are logically bundled to the single Token Ring interface. You don't need the virtual multipoint configuration and grouping of PVCs, as discussed above.

The biggest disadvantage of this configuration is the cost to upgrade the FEP, which can be several thousand dollars. For networks with a hundred or more sites, the amortized value of the upgrade cost per site may be low enough to justify the move. For smaller networks, the justification may be more difficult.

### *FRADs to Concentrate Traffic*

The initial application of the FRAD was as a traffic concentration device where many small locations reside within a close geographical area. This might include multiple sites within the same campus, metropolitan area or state.

Instead of each location having a unique connection into the frame relay network, the small peripheral sites can connect into a FRAD at one central location. This FRAD can provide a single interface into a frame relay service.

The rapid emergence of local and regional frame relay services, and even mileage-band pricing from some of the IXC carriers, has somewhat diminished the need for this concentration function. However, for many network environments this can still provide a cost-effective alternative for providing comprehensive connectivity to many small locations within a region.

### *FRADS and Native SNA in the WAN*

There are at least a few regional frame relay service providers that have incorporated FRADs into their offerings. The advantage of this configuration is that if you have a large number of traditional devices, such as async terminals, you can directly interface these into the frame relay network without any upgrades, additional equipment, or modifications at your site.

Each remote location's traffic is given a single PVC back to a central site, which is also connected into the frame relay network. The advantages of this approach are that you gain speed, and thus performance, on the network; the ability to automatically route around network failures; the ability to dynamically reconfigure the network topology; and network savings associated with the change without any investment or modifications on your part.

*TIC Connection*

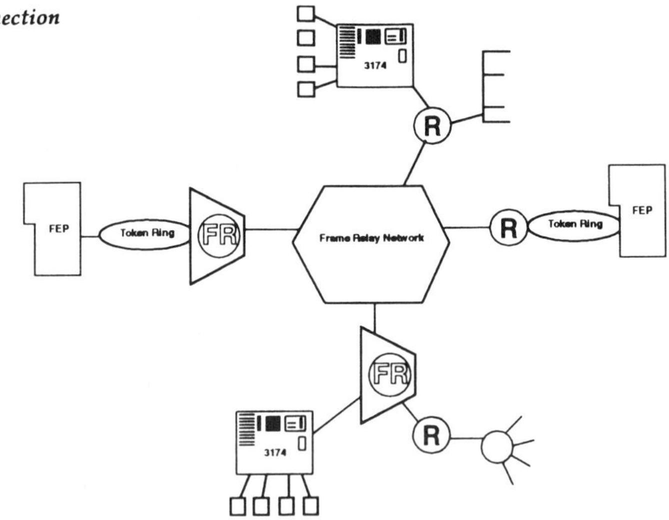


*Fig. 9.5: A FRAD can support a 3745 FEP which is token ring attached. The same is true for routers. The advantage is the speed of communications between the frame relay device and the FEP.*

*Concentrating Traffic*

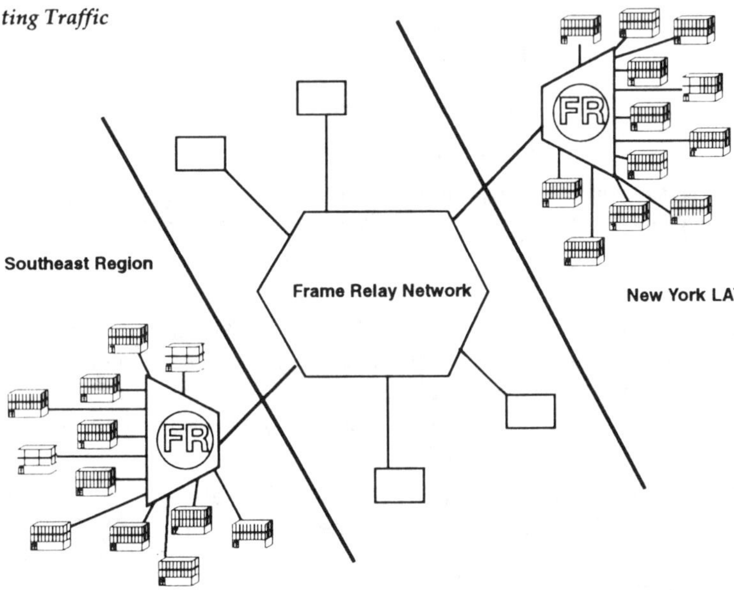


*Fig. 9.6: If you have many locations within a metropolitan area or a small geographical region, FRADs offer one alternative to cost-effectively concentrating the traffic onto a frame relay service.*

## *Interfacing FRADs (or Routers) with FEPs over a WAN*

There is not time in this book to cover every variation of possible configuration. However, one other configuration deserves brief mention. Both IBM's FEP and many router and FRAD vendors support RFC 1490, which is the agreement for multiprotocol encapsulation over frame relay.

*Multi-Vendor Configurations*

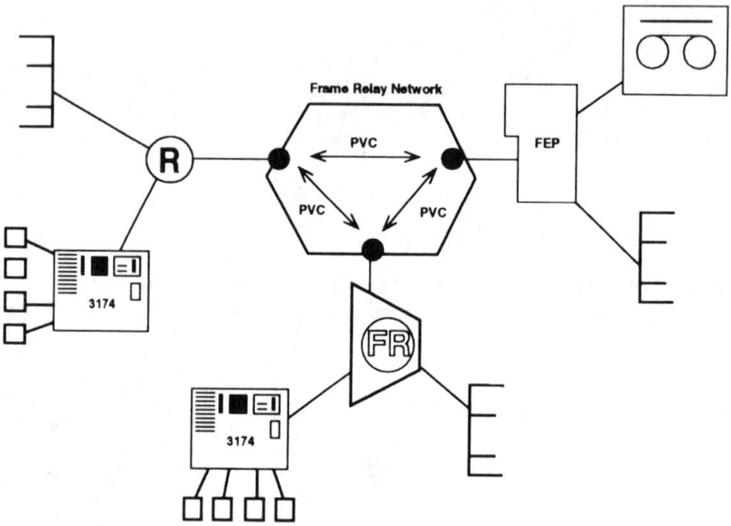


*Fig. 9.7: The multiprotocol encapsulation implementation agreement allows frame relay devices from different manufacturers to transparently communicate over a frame relay network.*

It is possible to allow a remote router/FRAD to place SNA traffic (such as LLC) onto one PVC that terminates directly into a frame relay-capable FEP. A router/FRAD is not needed in front of the FEP in this configuration. Separate PVCs can be used for non-SNA traffic to the same and other locations, terminating into a router/FRAD.

The SNA traffic is not encapsulated into TCP/IP first. The session is handled directly between the FEP and the remote router/FRAD. The disadvantage is that once again, without APPN/HPR implementation, the SNA traffic is not routable. It is simply sent to a single VTAM. Another disadvantage is that there is no local termination of the FEP's polling.

## Routers FRADs and APPN Support

Several router and FRAD vendors are active participants in the APPN Implementer's Workshop (AIW). Routers and FRADs that support APPN, and eventually HPR, can be configured as a standard APPN Network Node (NN) and as such are capable of "routing" SNA/APPN traffic. Acting as NNs, the devices function as peers to other IBM devices directly attached to the frame relay network. This means that a router at one site can communicate across a frame relay network to an APPN FEP at another site.

If the router or FRAD is also equipped to support dependent LU requester (DLUR), it can support the subarea SNA traffic alongside the APPN traffic for consolidation over a frame relay network. The APPN traffic is routed, while the subarea traffic is tunneled to a specific VTAM. The handling of polls in both cases is local. (See Chapter 8 for a more complete discussion of APPN, HPR and DLUR/DLUS).

Some of the benefits associated with APPN include "routing" SNA traffic, allowing peer to peer communication, dynamic configuration and reconfiguration of the network without having to regenerate the NCP, and the ability to dynamically route around network problems. It should be noted that many of these benefits can be achieved through a migration to an internetwork environment without having to actually upgrade to APPN by using one of the alternatives discussed above for transporting SNA traffic over frame relay. This can buy time to plan the upgrade paths and to upgrade sections of the network in a phased approach.

## Migration Using Parallel Networks

In determining your overall network migration plan to frame relay, you may want to consider operating two networks for the first month or two, as you get the bugs worked out and gain experience with frame relay.

If you currently have a private line or X.25 network that supports production applications, then you could ease into your frame relay network by operating the networks in parallel, while you test the frame relay network with non-critical applications. As you migrate production applications onto the frame relay network, you could change them back to the existing network should you encounter a problem.

In planning for parallel networks, remember that the equipment must have enough WAN ports to support the existing configuration plus an additional port for the frame relay interface. If you have small routers at remote sites with only a single WAN interface, then these sites may not be chosen for the initial implementation if you plan on running parallel networks, unless you want to ship out a second router and tie the two together.

## Integration Behind the Scenes

The integration of LAN and SNA environments is more than just a physical and logical process. It is also a political and cultural one. The traditional MIS department culture is one of centralized control, rigidity of rules and architectures, sophisticated management information and relatively slow incorporation of new technologies and applications. The LAN environment is nearly opposite in every area, a culture that finds its roots in the impatient and heretical department manager attempting to quickly and cost-effectively implement business-enhancing applications. Topologies and protocols are varied, the pace of change is rapid, flexibility is required and management systems have not quite caught up. As these two disparate cultures begin to acknowledge not just the presence of the other, but the zones of advantage of each approach, the organizational structure is impacted.

The alternatives for SNA over frame relay presented in the chapter can either complement or replace the different configurations for LAN and SNA consolidation discussed in Chapter 8 The deciding factor will probably come down to the relative levels of SNA and LAN traffic and your comfort with routers, APPN/HPR and the other elements involved with the various migration strategies.

One important item to remember is that changing the wide area network solution can occur independently of any changes to the underlying data architecture. You can first move to frame relay, and then concentrate on upgrading or modifying the SNA protocols and applications.

CHAPTER 10:

# MATTERS OF PROTOCOL

Thus far we have dealt primarily with understanding frame relay and frame relay services, and designing your frame relay network. There are a few other issues that will impact the performance of your frame relay network and could influence your choice of vendors and your network architecture.

The issues covered next deal with the application and routing protocols you might use and their performance over the WAN.

As with nearly every topic discussed in this chapter, and in the book as a whole, different vendors' implementation's and support for the topics discussed vary widely. You will need to discuss these topics with your carrier and/or equipment vendor in detail. This chapter will give you a good idea of what topics are important and why, so that you will know what questions to ask and be able to interpret the answers you receive.

## Role Playing: Equipment Issues

The role of the router, or other frame relay access devices, has been described in earlier chapters as being responsible for accepting incoming packets and encapsulating them in frame relay for transmission to a public frame relay service. In fact, the frame relay equipment can play a broader and more intelligent role, as discussed throughout this chapter.

## *The Role of the CSU/DSU*

Before moving on to these more advanced routing topics, do not forget that unless you are using equipment with an integrated CSU/DSU function, the router will first connect into an outboard CSU/DSU. The role of the CSU/DSU is to apply the necessary line coding and formatting to the outbound data stream, such as that needed for a 56K bps or DS-1 local loop. This line coding and line formatting are then stripped off at the carrier's POP, and reapplied at the far end before the frame is sent to the CSU/DSU at the destination premises. For the greatest transmission efficiency and visibility, it is recommended that for DS-1 local loops you use B8ZS line coding, not AMI; and extended superframe (ESF) formatting, not superframe.

CSUs, like routers, can also play a larger more complex role should you so choose. Many CSU/DSUs today are also mini-multiplexers. They might have three or more input ports such as V.35, RS232 and/or T-1 for example. This allows you to integrate many different applications, including voice and video, onto the same local loops being used by the frame relay applications. Once at the carrier's POP, the traffic streams can be segregated and partitioned to a private line or public voice network.

## *Controlling and Prioritizing Traffic*

Up until this point, we have talked about the issue of traffic prioritization mostly in terms of the solutions available for logical partitioning of traffic within the frame relay network. While traffic prioritization within the router has been mentioned briefly, it has not been examined. Now is the time.

Most router vendors today support one or more alternatives for prioritization of traffic within the router. Remember, the router has a serial interface into the wide area frame relay network Multiple frames are not simultaneously transmitted, but are transmitted in a serial fashion at the speed of the port connection. Therefore, if you have mission critical transactions that require rapid response times and you have LAN file transfers that are not mission critical and are not as response-time sensitive, then you will want to prioritize the mission-critical traffic in front of the LAN. The question is: HOW?

### *Use Your Qs*

One alternative is priority queuing. Depending upon the router vendor you choose, you may be able to assign differing priority levels by protocol, by TCP/IP port number, and/or by packet size.

For example, you may have personal computers on the network that support both high priority Telnet sessions and lower priority file transfers, both over TCP/IP. In such a case, you could use the TCP/IP port number prioritization mechanism to prioritize the Telnet sessions in front of the file transfers. In other cases, you may want to prioritize small packets ahead of larger ones, or SNA in front of TCP/IP, etc.

The number of priority levels which you can assign varies somewhat by vendor. Probably you will have three or four levels, such as high, medium and low; or high, medium, normal and low. The buffers associated with each queue may also be configurable. The high priority queue might have a buffer of 20 packets; the medium, 40 packets; the normal, 60 packets; and the lowest, 80 packets.

*Priority Queues*

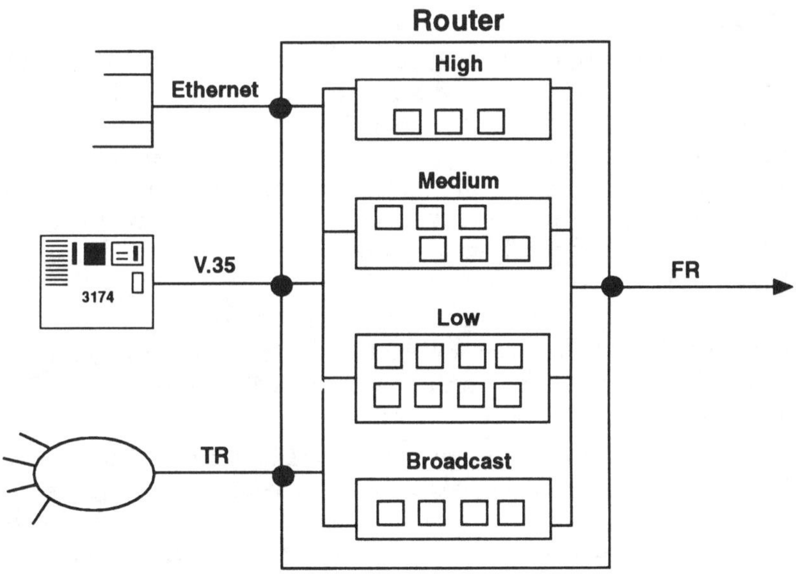


*Fig. 10.1: Routers provide prioritization of traffic through the use of priority buffer queues. Prioritization can occur by protocol, port number, packet size, etc.*

The router will empty the waiting packets in the high priority queue before moving on to the next queue, and then empty it, and so on. The only way a lower priority packet would be sent is if there is no other higher priority traffic in queue at that time.

When implementing this type of prioritization, be sensitive to how the higher level application protocols will respond if acknowledgments delays are incurred. Also be sensitive to the traffic — average and peak — assigned to each priority queue. If the buffers overflow, the packet will be discarded and a retransmission to the router will need to occur.

### *More Prioritization Control*

Priority queuing is a great mechanism for insuring that the important, response-time sensitive traffic doesn't get stuck behind less important traffic at the router. In the above example, however, you will notice that the packets in the lower priority queues are not transmitted until the queue(s) above it are empty. There is another option available from some router vendors that complements priority queuing.

In addition to the priority queues, you can define a guaranteed level of throughput, or sampling time, for each queue. Even if all of the packets in the higher priority queues are not transmitted, the router will still allow a specific amount of information from lower priority queues into the transmission stream. By doing this, you guarantee at least some level of throughput to all of the applications on the network, even if the lower priority applications have a relatively lower throughput level during periods of congestion.

### *The DE Bit*

The discard eligibility bit can be controlled by you and can provide yet another mechanism for prioritizing traffic. Setting the DE bit would typically be done in conjunction with priority queuing.

Many routers allow you to designate that the DE bit be set to indicate a packet is discard eligible, if that packet is within the low priority queue, or in any queue but the high priority queue. The reason for doing this is that when the router has a lot of data to transmit to the frame relay network, the high priority traffic will be counted towards the CIR level, while the lower priority traffic will already have the DE bit set when it arrives at the frame relay switch. The switch will treat it as burst traffic. This increases the probability that all the high priority traffic will be sent through the network as non-discard eligible.

*Using DE For Low Priority Traffic*

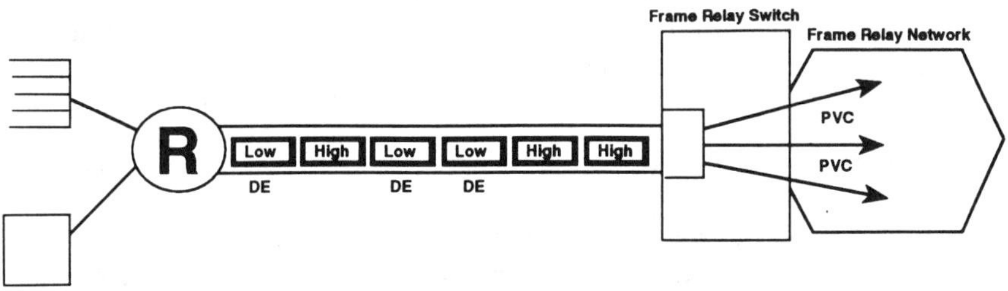


*Fig. 10.2: Routers can also set the discard eligibility bit within the frame relay header to indicate that the frame is discard eligible. This means that when the frames are received by the network switch, only the high priority traffic will count against the CIR. This decreases the likelihood of the frame relay network marking a high priority frame as discard eligible because the CIR on a PVC is exceeded in a given time period.*

The result is that the high-priority traffic has a very high likelihood of getting through the network without being discarded, even during congestion periods, because it is more likely to be within the CIR.

## *Implementation of Prioritization*

Prioritization of traffic at the router can be used alone, or in combination with logically separate PVCs, as a mechanism to insure that mission critical traffic is delivered across the network in a timely and reliable manner. The router can use a high-priority DLCI just for the mission-critical transaction traffic, and the network can also prioritize the associated PVC as high priority. The traffic is kept logically separate from lower priority traffic and is treated as high priority on an end-to-end basis.

One of the biggest keys in implementing prioritization is that you know the relative priority of different applications, protocols, and/or users. It might not be as simple as SNA over LAN. For example, some of the transaction traffic could be SNA delivered via a Token Ring LAN interface to the router, while other mission critical transactions could be hiding in TCP/IP-encapsulated Telnet packets.

Also, prioritization within the router is only one part of the answer. The router interfaces with the carrier's frame relay service, which is another area of potential traffic congestion. So once again you may want to understand how your carrier manages congestion on the network and how CIR is delivered, at least if you plan on putting mission-critical applications across the network.

As with nearly every topic discussed in this chapter, consulting with your frame relay provider and/or router vendor could provide valuable guidance when it comes time to implement a prioritization scheme.

## Recognition of CIR

Routers don't generally recognize the underlying committed information rate on a logical path. The router always transmits to the network at the port connection speed. What happens to the traffic at that point becomes a matter of the carrier being used and the underlying platform.

Some carriers pass all traffic through at the port speed and mark any frames over the CIR as eligible for discard; other networks mark some as more eligible than others, depending upon how much the CIR is being exceeded. Others throttle the throughput to the CIR and slowly allow the PVC to exceed the CIR based on the level of congestion on the PVC at the time, still marking packets in excess of CIR as discard eligible. Still others have almost no policing mechanism for traffic at all; everything goes through the port to the network and it is simply a big free-for-all.

Because all CIRs are not created equal, it might be argued that recognizing a CIR is a qualitative decision in addition to a quantitative one. Nevertheless, the router does not recognize this underlying parameter within the wide area network. It relies on the higher-layer application protocols, such as TCP/IP, to stabilize the transmission of packets to be transferred based on the number and rate of acknowledgements received.

Unfortunately, not all applications have a protocol that uses acknowledgements to control the rate of transmission. In fact, packets are just sent and sent, and there is no slowing down, even if one or two packets go AWOL. Some video over frame relay applications are an example.

In the case of a video application, having the router help out with traffic policing could be advantageous. Some of the vendors are working in this direction. The idea would be to police the application, with WAN network information like CIR taken into account. As it stands now, the router would probably just drop packets exceeding some threshold (like CIR) or set the DE bit on all video traffic. The purpose would be to keep the video application from affecting other, more mission critical, network transmissions.

One lesson to be learned here is that since the router doesn't recognize the CIR of a logical connection but instead always transmits at the port connection speed, choosing a CIR that will adequately meet the average traffic volumes is a critical component to achieving stable and acceptable network performance.

## Split Horizon

Using a partial mesh configuration of PVCs may make economic sense, but the initial designers of frame relay equipment didn't plan for this topology. Router vendors were accustomed to private line circuits and LANs. In thinking about frame relay, they envisioned a LAN model, and assumed a fully meshed PVC environment. They did not initially plan for a partial mesh network, although the limitation of DLCIs and the tariff structures have resulted in most networks using partial mesh configuration. This presented a problem because a split horizon develops in such a configuration.

It will help to first explain the problem, before we explore the solution the router vendors have developed in response to partial mesh configurations.

### *Causes of Split Horizon*

Before public frame relay services, there were two main approaches to designing internetworks. There was the LAN model, and the leased line model. With the LAN model, one router could assume that each router on the network was connected with every other router. In this configuration there is no reason for router A to pass on the routing information learned from router B to another router, because that router (C) is assumed to have a direct path to router B as well.

In a leased line network model this is not the case. The router does need to pass routing information to other routers because even though a physical mesh of leased lines was probably not in place, a logical mesh allowing any-to-any connectivity and optimal routing would be created — like a "virtual LAN" environment.

Since the router in a leased line environment had one physical port to associate with each leased line, a rule called "split horizon" was established. The default configuration with leased lines is to "enable split horizon" by prohibiting an incoming packet from being placed back onto the same network interface from which it was received. This prevented an instance where data was bounced back and forth across the network in a big routing loop.

A diagram will help to illustrate the problem that surrounds split horizon in a leased line network.

*Split Horizon*

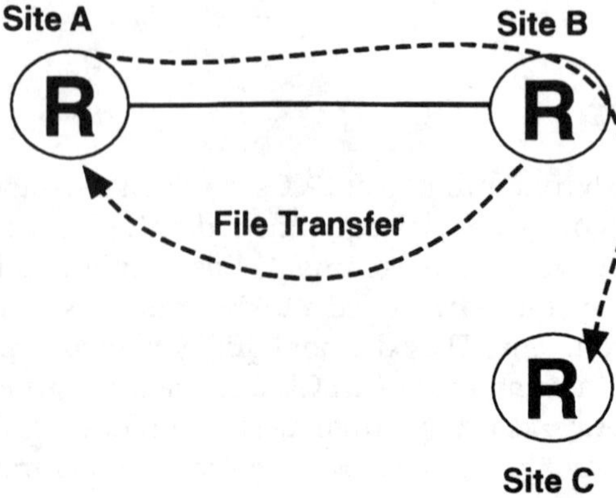


*Fig. 10.3: Routing loops can occur if a router is allowed to send an incoming packet back out the same interface over which it is received. In a private line environment, "split horizon" is enabled within the router to prohibit this from occurring.*

As mentioned, the reason for the prohibition on not allowing a packet back out over the same physical link is to prevent routing loops. If Site B has a direct connection with Site A and Site C, then routing tables will be exchanged between these routers. Site B will tell site A that it can communicate with Site C. Site A would therefore perceive that it could reach Site C even though it does not have a direct connection, because it can route traffic out the WAN port to Site B, which is connected to Site C. The routers will all exchange routing tables. Once Site A had a path to site C (through B) it would advertise to Site B that it could reach Site C. It would not be apparent to Site B that this information actually reflects Site B's own route to Site C, to which A has been given access.

The problem arises when the connection fails between Site B and Site C. Site B would recognize the connection failure, and would try to reach Site C through Site A, which has advertised that it has a route to Site C. In fact, this route does not actually exist, and the router at Site A would accept the incoming data from B, and attempt to forward it back out the same port, because this is how Site A reaches Site C. The result is a routing loop, and the result of this loop would be increased network congestion as the files are sent back and forth between Sites A and B.

Enabling split horizon makes perfect sense in a private line network environment, but not in a frame relay network. In a frame relay network, you want a single physical interface to support many remote connections. If a partial mesh network is used, then a frame has to be able to be sent back out on the same physical port over which is has been received, just on a different DLCI. However, you still don't want to create routing loops. The solution is the virtual interface.

## *Solution to Split Horizon: The "Virtual" WAN Connection*

In connecting to a public frame relay service, the whole idea is that the router will have one physical interface, but will have many logical connections to other remote locations. Thus the router would need to place the packet on the same physical connection over which it was just received. This presents a problem, because in a partial mesh environment, it is a hybrid of the LAN model and the leased line model. If a partial mesh of logical connections is being used and a router updates the other routers on its routes, then a routing loop could develop. If the router doesn't update, then optimal routing can't be achieved. What do you do?

If you are planning to use a partial mesh of PVCs and want optimal routing, the solution is a "virtual WAN connection." The router vendors developed the concept of virtual WAN connections to allow the router to treat each DLCI as if it were a leased line, recognizing each independently. So the rule would now read "don't send a packet back out the same DLCI over which it was received." Voila! Problem solved. Just be sure your router vendor can support this virtual approach to a partially meshed frame relay network.

***Virtual Interfaces Solve Split Horizon Problem in Partial Mesh Networks***

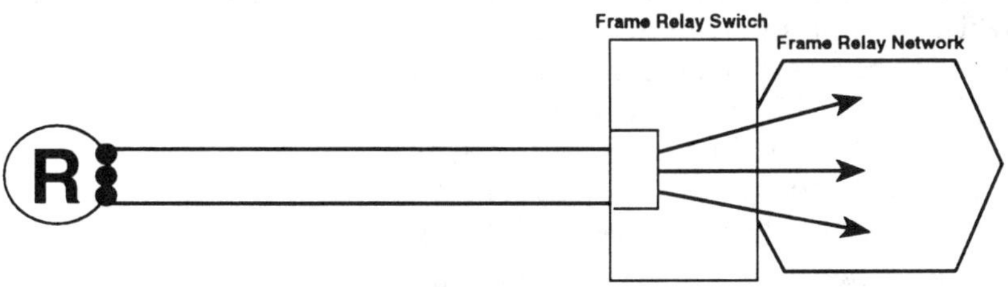


*Fig. 10.4: The router has only one physical interface into the frame relay network, but has a separate "virtual interface" for each DLCI/PVC. Therefore, in a partial mesh configuration, the router would not be able to send a frame back out across the same PVC over which it was received.*

### *Assigning Costs to Each Virtual Interface*

Before moving on, it is worth noting that with some routers you may be able to assign each DLCI its own routing metric, or cost, in order to facilitate optimal route selection. For example, PVCs with low CIRs might be assigned a much higher "cost" than PVCs with higher CIRs. If a router needs to send a frame, and either PVC will provide a path to the ultimate destination, the router would choose the "lower cost/higher CIR" PVC. The logic here is that you want to keep the traffic on the faster PVCs where possible, to keep congestion on the slower PVCs minimized. Therefore, you can assign a "high" cost to the slow PVCs, and a "low" cost to the high PVCs. The router will weigh this cost information, in addition to other information on number of network hops, etc. and will make an intelligent routing decision between available paths. The result is a more optimized traffic pattern.

If you decide to use this type of tool, it is very important to establish a standard within your own network and adhere to this standard when assigning relative values. In other words, the value of a kilobit of transmission speed should be consistent throughout your network.

## Routing Protocols

Throughout this book, the term "protocol" generally references a transport and/or network layer protocol operating at layer three and above of the OSI model, such as SPX/IPX or TCP/IP. The other main category of protocols is the routing protocol, which operates at layer three. There is a working relationship between the two protocol types, and not all network/transport layer protocols work with all routing protocols. The routing protocol you choose has important implications in the design and performance of the frame relay network.

Routing protocols are what the router uses to select the best available path on which to route an individual frame for transmission. This book is not intended to be an explanation of routing protocols, except in how they relate to implementing a frame relay network. The routing protocol you choose can impact your ability to implement a successful frame relay network, depending upon the protocols you need to support, the number of sites and LANs in your network, and the logical network configuration you design.

There are two ways to categorize routing protocols. The first main category for protocols is based on the method(s) the router uses for selecting a route. The main types of routing protocols are distance vector, DUAL (distributed update algorithm), and link state. DUAL is like a hybrid between link state and distance-vector, providing many of the advantages of each, but without some of the disadvantages.

The second protocol category is based on the method by which — and how often — the routers must exchange routing table information. In this category you find a distinction between more traditional periodic, and the newer update-only, routing protocols.

### *Distance Vector, DUAL, and Link State Protocols*

Distance-vector protocols, such as RIP (routing information protocol), use a hop count to determine the best available path. They choose the path with the fewest number of intermediate hops.

DUAL routing protocols are a sophisticated version of distance vector protocols, yet having internal metrics that allow the router to consider cost information, much like the link-state protocols, explained below.

The most popular link state routing protocol is OSPF (open shortest path first). Link state protocols look at many metric factors in determining the most direct, open path to an end destination. It is often referred to as the successor to RIP.

Distance vector and DUAL protocols do not keep a real-time comprehensive view of every connection in the network. Link state protocols do keep a complete real-time picture of every route in the network.

One approach is not necessarily better or worse than the other. It is a matter of trade-offs between how much information is regularly updated and stored in each router and what other indirect indicators of optimal routing can be used. Simple distance vector protocols, like RIP, are less ideal than the more sophisticated DUAL and link-state protocols, which take other network information into account and therefore are better able to make optimized routing decisions. RIP has other disadvantages that make it less attractive in a frame relay environment, as discussed below.

### *Updating Routing Tables: Periodic or Update-Only*

Routing updates refer to how often, and how, your routers routinely exchange information. You do not want your network to be congested with routing table updates to the detriment of the user traffic being carried on the network. The updates provide the most recent view of the network topology, including any DLCIs (and local loops) that might be unavailable, newly added DLCIs, etc. You want the routers to have this information. However, the status of the network doesn't really change all that often so there is a trade-off between "real time" status updates and the amount of added network traffic generated by these updates.

In large networks, performance problems can result when a large number of DLCIs are supported by one or more routers. When a router updates the other routers to which it is connected, it replicates its own routing table and transmits a copy over each DLCI. Lots of DLCIs mean lots of traffic on the local loop and lots of packets in the interface buffers. The traffic is of a high priority because network instability could result if the information is lost or damaged. The broadcast transfers occur in set time periods, and hence are called "periodic." Examples of periodic routing protocols are RIP and Novell's Service Advertisement Protocol (SAP). SAPs announce to every other server on the entire network the network services it provides.

A high volume of these broadcasts can impact user transactions. Some periodic routing protocols might broadcast a full route table update every 30 or 60 seconds over each DLCI. The bytes per routing table entry could range from 4 to 16, depending upon the routing protocol. SAPs might approximate 85 bytes per table entry. Each complete update must be sent over each DLCI. In large networks, this can create a problem.

An alternative to sending a full copy of the route table periodically is to send only the updates, or changes, to the tables on a required basis. This approach is called "update-only" and it significantly reduces the amount of broadcast traffic on the network. Examples of update-only protocols are OSPF, EIGRP (Enhanced Interior Gateway Routing Protocol), Novell's NLSP (NetWare Link Services Protocol), Apple's planned AURP (Apple Update Routing Protocol), BGP (Border Gateway Protocol) and IS-IS. By setting the timer to 0, it is also possible to have RIP send updates only.

Wherever possible, you will want to use update-only routing protocols over your frame relay network.

With update-only protocols, a keep-alive signal is sent between routers, every 10 seconds or so. Any change in the routing information would be broadcast when it occurred. Then, every 30 minutes or so, the router would broadcast a full update of its routing table information. The result of this is a much lower level of network traffic generated from the exchange of routing information.

As a general rule of thumb, try and keep the level of routing table update traffic at 20 percent or less of the access link speed. The lower, the better, in terms of performance impact on user throughput and latency. Again, many variables affect overall performance on the network, and this is only one. The bigger your network and the slower the connection speeds, the more of an impact routing updates and broadcast traffic will have on overall network performance.

*Update-only Routing Protocols*

| Network Level Protocol | Update-only Routing Protocol Choices |
|---|---|
| IP | OSPF, IS-IS, BGP4 and EIGRP |
| Novell | NLSP and EIGRP |
| AppleTalk | AURP and EIGRP |
| OSI | IS-IS |
| DECnet | IS-IS |

*Fig. 10.5: Update-only routing protocols reduced congestion from routing table updates over the wide area network. When possible, choose an update-only routing protocol to support the network level protocol.*

## *Choosing Routing Protocols*

You may think that since routing is simplified in a frame relay world that the advanced routing calculations of DUAL and update-only protocols are not needed. Not so, for two reasons.

First, the router may still be required to choose between two or more alternative paths for getting a packet to its ultimate destination. Optimizing this choice will keep traffic congestion levels lower and overall performance higher.

Second, distance vector protocols typically update the routing table information in a periodic fashion. The DUAL and link-state routing protocols typically use an update-only approach.

Isn't is amazing how each topic is another "link" in the chain? So we can now expand the rule of thumb to read: If you have a large, multiprotocol network, implement intelligent routing protocols such as DUAL or link-state, update-only routing protocols where ever possible, especially if the transmission rates are low.

Since not all network level protocols work with all routing protocols, you don't always get your choice. But where you do have a choice, these guidelines will help you to improve network performance.

## *Broadcast Traffic and Broadcast Queues*

Broadcasting in this chapter refers to the process of taking a single packet and making a copy of the packet for distribution to every DLCI router supports. A broadcast can also refer to a specific business application that requires a single file/packet to be distributed to a list of pre-defined destinations. You may not be able to limit the latter, but you may want to limit the former because when router tables "broadcast" their routing table information to every DLCI to which they have access, the result is a lot of traffic being transmitted over the network. Certain routing and bridging protocols and SAPs are notorious for a high level of broadcast traffic, as are some multimedia and groupware applications.

Handling broadcasts over any wide area network requires consideration and pre-planning, and frame relay is no different.

Some router vendors have implemented a special queue in the router, with its own buffer, for broadcast traffic such as routing and SAP updates. The objective is to increase the performance/throughput of user traffic and to keep the network more stable. You control the size of the buffer and the rate at which the queue will be serviced by the router. For example, the buffer size might be 300 or 400 packets. On a 64K bps interface, 44K might be assigned for user data and 20K bps for servicing the broadcast queue. During implementation, discuss this configuration with your carrier or router vendor. You will probably want to configure the buffer sizes and service rates for a worst case scenario and assume that period routing protocols are in use.

*Relative Broadcast Traffic Levels in Large Networks*

| Network Protocol | Routing Protocol | Relative Broadcast Traffic Level |
|---|---|---|
| **IP** | RIP | High |
| | OPSF | Low |
| | IS-IS | Low |
| | IGRP | High |
| | EIGRP | None |
| **IPX** | RIP | High |
| | SAP | High |
| | EIGRP | Low |
| **AppleTalk** | RTMP | High |
| | EIGRP | Low |
| **DECnet IV** | DE Net Routing | High |
| **DECnet V** | IS-IS | Low |
| **Banyan Vines** | RTP | High |
| | Sequenced RTP | Low |
| **ISO/CLNs** | ISO-IGRP | High |
| | IS-IS | Low |

The router identifies all broadcast traffic, allocating it to the special queue and managing it independently of the normal user data queues. The original broadcast packet will initially pass through the standard user queue, but the copies of the original be transmitted over each DLCI are stored in the broadcast queue. Because of timing sensitivities, spanning tree and bridged broadcast packets typically use the normal user queue.

As discussed above, one of the best ways to manage broadcasts is to use update-only routing protocols where possible.

## Network Level Protocols Over the WAN

The way transport and network level protocols perform over the network is obviously tied closely with the routing protocol being used. This book cannot hope to cover each protocol's idiosyncrasies in depth; however, there is now an accumulated body of experience for some of the protocols' performance over frame relay (actually, internetworks in general). This pool of wisdom is continually being expanded upon, so once again you are reminded to discuss these topics specifically with your equipment vendor and your carrier. In the meantime, here are a few crumbs of advice.

### *TCP/IP*

This is the easy one, because TCP/IP is designed specifically for internetworks and for functioning over a wide area environment, which may have a lower transmission speed than the local environment. It has built-in flow control mechanisms, including a sliding window for packet transmission/acknowledgements. For all practical purposes TCP/IP works transparently over the frame relay network.

It is wise with any protocol to consider an intelligent routing protocol, especially if the network is large (i.e., more than 20 DLCIs per router), there are a lot of users and LANs, and/or the logical connections speeds are low (i.e., 64K bps). For TCP/IP, this would include OSPF, EIGRP and dual-stack IS-IS. This means that RIP should only be considered if the network is small, LANs are few and/or speeds are relatively high.

### *Novell IPX*

It is estimated that 70 percent of internetworks support at least some IPX traffic. There is a long and painful story about routing IPX over a wide area network. Whether the network was made up of private lines, X.25, frame relay, or cups and strings, IPX made little discrimination. It performed horribly over them all.

The long story made very short is that IPX was not initially intended for low-speed wide area network connections, or the relatively long response times these connections provide (even at the speed of light, there is measurable propagation delay over the fiber in traveling cross-country). IPX was designed to operate over very high speed *local* connections. Because it was initially designed for the local environment, the IPX required one acknowledgement packet per transmitted packet. Over the WAN, this caused severe throughput limitations.

The great news is that the problem has been overcome very successfully by software upgrades (called Netware Loadable Modules, NLMs) Novell has since released for NetWare 3.11 servers. If you plan to run Novell IPX over your frame relay network, make sure you have the latest software release and are not using the "old IPX."

The first upgrade by Novell, and the one that most directly affects wide area networking, is called Packet Burst Mode, or P-Burst for short. This gives IPX a dynamically adjusted sliding window for sending/receiving packets/acknowledgements. With the upgrade, IPX can send several packets for transmission before expecting to see an acknowledgement. This significantly reduces the excessive overhead that would otherwise ping-pong between client and server and reduce network performance.

Novell also released an upgrade that allows you to increase the maximum packet size. Large packets may be better suited to local and campus environments, not wide area networks. Once again, there are different schools of thought on this topic. The default packet size of 512K bytes works well over the WAN, you may want to experiment in a non-production environment to determine the optimal packet size based on your networking situation. The packet size can be negotiated between client and server at the time of transmission, based on the smaller buffer.

Finally, Novell has introduced a SAP filter. Without this filter, SAPs telling about the server's services are typically broadcast every 60 seconds or so. In a frame relay world, or in any wide area network, this level of broadcasting can make things uncomfortable for network users due to the congestion resulting from every server doing this every minute — not to mention that it is really unnecessary, because new services are typically not added every minute to the server.

The SAP filter NLM prevents excessive SAP broadcasts and in doing so significantly reduces the congestion on the WAN.

In choosing a routing protocol for IPX, RIP may be your only available choice depending upon your router vendor. While this is less than ideal, the SAP filter will at least help matters. Intelligent routing protocol choices include EIGRP, and a new routing protocol from Novell NLSP (NetWare Link Service Protocol). This link state algorithm will also provide support for load-balancing traffic, sorting network addresses, more intelligent selection of routes and update-only route table exchanges.

### *AppleTalk*

AppleTalk is a routable protocol, but it is less intelligent and proactive than other protocols over the WAN. For example, AppleTalk does not have the same sophisticated implicit flow control mechanisms at the network level, and its routing algorithms are not as advanced, compared to TCP/IP and DECnet.

First the problem, then the solution. AppleTalk has its own routing protocol called RTMP (the routing table maintenance protocol). When two AppleTalk networks are connected, the periodic updates of routing tables occurs every 10 seconds. This could be a 10K byte file hitting your wide area network six times every minute — not good news if you would also like to use this facility to transmit user data.

Apple is developing a new routing protocol, which will be update-only. Called AURP (Apple Update Routing Protocol), the protocol will function like other update-only protocols as discussed above. It will also provide automatic address mapping, which will help to eliminate duplicate addresses and allow AppleTalk encapsulation into IP. EIGRP is the other update-only routing protocol that supports AppleTalk.

AURP doesn't address some other problems for routing AppleTalk over a WAN. Routes are still chosen based solely on the number of network hops, and a metric for connection cost information is not supported.

AppleTalk networks can also be prone to ZIP storms. ZIP, or zone information protocol, is used to maintain accounting of the network zone name to the network number. Devices on AppleTalk networks will typically have both a zone name and a network number, and ZIP helps to match the name with the number. The table is updated by the network's old nemesis, the broadcast message, which occurs when a new AppleTalk network is initially connected to the WAN. The broadcast will keep occurring until messages are received back. If the acknowledgement timer expires, another broadcast is sent. If the network is large, these ZIP storms can cause congestion problems.

Finally, AppleTalk will support automatic address discovery (see RFC 1293 below). This makes configuring the frame relay network less manual and reduces the propensity for human-error.

### *DECnet*

The only conventional DECnet related wisdom to share is that there is just one update-only routing protocol available right now for DECnet: IS-IS. This means that you may be using a less intelligent routing protocol, like RIP; if so, you have the standard considerations for network design that accompany a periodic routing protocol.

### *Bridging Protocols*

In general, vendors and carriers alike will discourage bridging protocols over any wide area network, including a public frame relay service. This is because they are: much less efficient in conducting business over the wide area where, compared to a local network, capacity is limited, round-trip delays are longer, and partial mesh configurations are likely. Advanced routing protocols assume that there could be congestion on the network and that packets can be dropped. They are designed with error correction capabilities and flow control mechanisms. Bridging protocols do not provide for either contingency.

However, like any general rule, there are certainly exceptions. Networks with only a few locations; a small number of LANs, routers or users; and using relatively high-speed connections can get away with bridging protocols. The bigger the network and the lower the access and logical connection speeds, the more likely it is that bridging protocols will affect overall network performance and efficiency.

Protocols that should be bridged include NetBIOS (Network Basic Input/Output System), DECLAT and SNA without APPN/HPR. One approach to handling these protocols over a wide area frame relay network is to first encapsulate them into TCP/IP before encapsulating them into frame relay. The downside is that this adds about 45 bytes of overhead per packet. However, the overhead compression technique of RFC 1144 (discussed later) can significantly reduce this added overhead.

The upside is that it provides some congestion management and flow control. The TCP/IP protocol will handle error recovery as well. The network will be more stable. The router will provide local acknowledgement on the Token Ring, so maintenance of sessions will be more robust.

Some routers can handle DECLAT by first translating it into Telnet TCP/IP. The translation means that you don't have the "double" overhead you get with encapsulation. However, the configuration can be complicated, so if you have DECLAT, discuss alternative approaches with your vendor or carrier first.

## How Many Routes Should a Router Route?

The number of DLCIs/PVCs you assign to every router depends upon a great variety of issues, including all of the factors discussed in earlier chapters plus the protocol issues discussed above. How many is too many? is a difficult question to answer, because the level of direct connectivity and connection speeds you have designed and the protocols you are using, impact the answer. So, too, does the number of users and LANs on the network.

As a rule of thumb, 10 to 20 DLCIs per router should at least raise a yellow flag. If you are using periodic routing protocols, have lots of LANs and lots of users, a closer look is probably in order. Each network is very different, so work with your router vendor or carrier to double-check these design considerations. If your network is smaller, you are using update-only routing protocols, and the number of DLCIs per router is less than 10 to 20, you will probably not see an effect on user traffic from the exchange of routing table information.

Since the DLCI address space is 10 bits, the maximum number of DLCIs (not considering the as-yet-unused extended address bits) is 1000. The LMI (local management interface) protocol generally limits the number of DLCIs to less than 800 and requires that all status reports fit into a single packet.

## RFCs

RFC stands for request for comment. RFCs are precursors to, or in some cases replacements for, standards. They are often widely agreed-upon implementation "standards," which many vendors' equipment will then be modified to support. And there are a few RFCs of which you should be aware because they improve internetworking capabilities.

- **RFC 1490/1294.** RFC 1294, now renumbered RFC 1490, is for multiprotocol encapsulation. The bottom line benefits are to increase interoperability between frame relay devices from different vendors. This means that you can use one vendor's routers (or other equipment type) at some locations, and a different vendor's equipment at others. This ability to mix and match allows you to pick the best and most cost-effective tool for the job.

And it really does work. The only downside is that each vendor will typically have its own configuration and management tools, its own solutions to specific networking problems, and its own idiosyncrasies. Managing two vendors is twice the work, but keeping up with two vendors' products as they grow and change is twice the fun. If one of the benefits you would like to achieve in migrating to frame relay is a simplified network architecture and lower administration and maintenance costs, then keep the number of vendors as small as possible. You may even want one provider to handle, equipment and network.

- **RFC 1293.** This is Inverse ARP, which allows the automatic discovery of the addresses on the router at each end of another router's DLCIs. Right now, the RFC only applies to IP, but some equipment vendors have already expanded the protocol support to include Novell IPX, AppleTalk, Banyan Vines, and DECnet. The benefit of the RFC is to simplify network configuration.

  If you use equipment that supports RFC 1293, then during initial network configuration you would only need to define the LMI type, identify which protocols will be supported and enable frame relay on the interface. The router will use the LMI to discover what active DLCIs are available. It will then use RFC 1293 to contact each of the routers to which it is attached and populate its own routing tables through the exchange of address information (at least for any of the protocols for which your vendor's equipment supports 1293). This significantly limits the amount of manual configuration needed.

- **RFC 1315**. This is the frame relay MIB (management information base), which standardizes what management information is made available on frame relay devices and where/how that information is accessed. This simplifies the process of integrating frame relay devices into your network monitoring and management process and programs. More information on frame relay network management is covered in the chapter on this topic.

- **RFC 1144 .** This RFC will provide overhead compression for the TCP/IP protocol down to five octets. It does this by anticipating that the next packet in a file transfer sequence will have the same address as the previous one and will have the same sequence number plus one. This compression technique will be useful where SDLC encapsulation, or other bridging protocol encapsulation, is being utilized with low-speed PVCs. In these cases, the slight increase in processing power to perform the compression is more than balanced by the increase in application performance and throughput.

## Branch Offices

The newest area to explode in terms of frame relay developments is in connecting the branch office to the frame relay network in a manner that is cost-effective and provides high performance. Some of the dial-up solutions discussed in an earlier chapter provide wide area network solutions for connectivity. The equipment vendors are also doing their part by making low-cost, easily managed alternatives available.

### *Routers: All Shapes and Sizes*

Remember the Dr. Seuss book "Inside, Outside, Upside Down?" Routers are like that these days. In the old days, say three years ago, you had only a few router vendors to choose from and they each had only a few router sizes (mostly big and bigger). Not so today. Routers come in small packages, too, and can be inside a computer or server or standalone as an outside unit. The selection ensures a cost-effective alternative for connectivity to the small office.

The process of routing is actually made simpler by frame relay. The routing protocols do not need to be as intelligent because a higher level of connectivity (virtual paths) are available. The router can cross-reference the destination address on a packet with the correct DLCI and off it goes. The process of routing is being incorporated via software into servers and PCs.

This means that for a small investment, usually less than $1000, you can upgrade a remote site's server to also act as a router for its supported devices.

The availability of low-end routers begins to complement nicely the emerging wide area frame relay service alternatives for dialup, such as ISDN and X.25, which bring the cost of connectivity down by not requiring a dedicated local loop.

### *Small Sites: Bridging, Routing or a Hybrid?*

As discussed above, bridging over a wide area network is not efficient when the number of sites, users and protocols begins to increase. This is because a bridge forwards all traffic, including the broadcasts, to each of the end stations to which it is attached. As the number of users and direct connections increase, so does the level of overhead traffic generated on the WAN.

The good thing about bridging is that it is protocol-independent. It is a layer 2 device that requires less intelligence, less management and less ongoing administration than the router, which operates at layer 3. Routers are much more intelligent about what traffic is allowed on to the WAN and what routes are selected. But routers are more difficult to configure and administer. There are always trade-offs.

Normally, a layer 2 device cannot directly communicate with a layer 3 device over a WAN. So, you can't directly connect a bridge at a remote site to a router at a larger site.

At a small site you may not need the sophistication of a router, or want the added administration a router requires compared to the more simplistic bridge. New solutions are emerging in the market to simplify the type of equipment at remote locations with low volumes of traffic. The new equipment solutions resemble a "bridge," in that they function primarily as a data link forwarding device. It is therefore easier to configure and maintain, helping to keep in check both initial and ongoing administration costs. The devices are themselves cost-effectively priced.

The argument is that most remote locations send the majority of traffic to one other primary location on the network. For sites where this is true, a less intelligent device could be used at the remote site, in conjunction with a router at the primary site.

To make this solution of "bridge to router" work, the router at the central site must be able to divide a single physical port into separate virtual ports, and then designate each virtual port as either a "bridging" virtual port or a "routing" virtual port. This is all accomplished in software so that the router only needs one physical WAN interface to support many other remote locations.

The traffic at a remote site simply passes though a bridging filter, which determines whether it should be sent to the wide area network or kept local. If passed to the WAN, the receiving router will then process it and route it to a specific location on the network.

The router at the "larger location" accepts incoming traffic from the small sites and constructs a "firewall" to filter out the unnecessary overhead traffic that does not belong on the wide area network. It will then intelligently route any user data that must be transmitted over the network. This set-up means that routing tables are not needed at the remote site, but instead are stored centrally. (Do all these "quotations" remind you of a certain Saturday Night Live skit?)

This approach can help to simplify network administration and cut costs by reducing the number of routers and routing tables in the network. For example, if you add a new protocol to the network, you would have few routers to reconfigure.

As this solution to remote networking evolves, more dynamic filtering is being added to the new layer 2 devices to allow filtering of the SAP, RIP and other broadcast traffic. The router at the central site will probably control this function based on how it is configured, keeping administration centered on the routers and not on the remote offices.

The industry is still divided on the effectiveness and price/performance trade-off of this solution for remote site connectivity. It is worth looking into if you have several remote sites with low levels of traffic that can be forwarded to a single network location for processing. However, the decreasing cost of routers, and the automatic discovery capabilities, have greatly simplified the management for routers. You should compare both alternatives in light of your current, and future, networking environment.

***Bridge/Routing Hybrid***

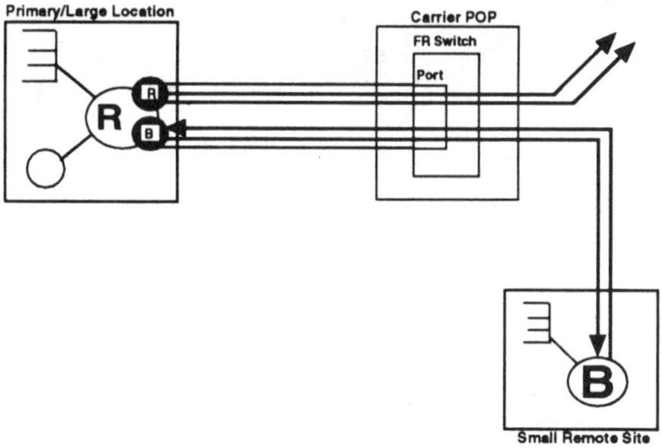


*Fig.10.7: Some emerging equipment solutions allow a bridge at a remote site to directly connect across the frame relay network to a router at the primary location. The router maintains one physical path into the network but can designate virtual ports within the physical port. Traffic is bridged from the small site to the large site where it is then routed to the rest of the network, or kept locally.*

### *Compression*

Compression in the data world is much more difficult than in the voice world. If a few compressed bits get rearranged or dropped in a voice conversation, it's no big deal. With data, the exact bits that are received must be delivered, no exceptions. The ability to compress a frame relay frame's payload, maintain data integrity and leave the important header information intact is being developed primarily for its application at small remote locations where line speeds tend to be low. It is expected that this compression technique will bring approximately a 2-to-1 increase in network throughput.

## Local Environment

As this chapter demonstrates, the local environment and the protocols you choose have an impact on how you initially design your network and on network performance. If you are not an expert in these areas, don't worry. And certainly, don't shy away from frame relay. These same topics will be influential in network design and performance regardless of the wide area networking solution you use. If you have a small network, say 10 sites or less, you may not have to worry about many of these issues. The larger the network, the more aware you should be of possible impacts. Fortunately, with frame relay, the carriers and the equipment vendors can help you to make optimal configuration choices.

CHAPTER 11:

# NETWORK MANAGEMENT OR MANAGED NETWORK SERVICES?

You must have visibility and control over the network to judge its performance and health. So how will you manage your frame relay network once it is in place?

The speed at which these networks operate, the incorporation of multiple protocols and multiple vendors' equipment and the geographical distances involved make comprehensive network management a difficult goal to achieve. The trend today is to move towards integration of management systems, but as you will soon discover, there is also still a place for specialization of tools and skills. The optimized network management solution requires a balance between integration and specialization. Fortunately, there are several alternative approaches from which to choose.

This chapter will discuss the objectives of a network management system, approaches for integrating frame relay network management into your existing solution, what to look for in establishing a system if you don't already have one, and where it makes sense to use segregated management systems. It will also cover the alternative of using a carrier, instead of your own resources, to manage the frame relay service.

One caution before proceeding. The best management system in the world, staffed by the most expert problem solvers, cannot make a poorly designed network function well. Network design is a critical element in network management. If the network isn't designed properly and the routers aren't configured correctly, the applications will not perform well, the routers or other equipment will not be able to optimize the traffic flows, and you will have ongoing network management problems.

With that said, we can proceed with the discussion on managing a well-designed network and keeping that network optimized.

## The Objectives of Management

There are several objectives, or layers, to network management. The ISO (International Standards Organization) model outlines them as follows:

- **Configuration Management.** This would include the management of physical and logical connectivity within your network, such as moves, adds and changes as well as ongoing planning and optimization.
- **Fault Management.** This includes the collection, management, and response to network alarms, and conditions that fail to meet a pre-defined performance threshold.
- **Performance Management.** This provides information with which to judge the quality of service, performance of individual connections and the network as a whole.
- **Security Management.** This includes management and control of access to the system and applications.
- **Accounting Management.** This provides information, monitoring and control over how communications resources are used and allocated.

Each of these five primary functions must be achieved for at least three major data network domains: the SNA applications and equipment, the LAN applications and equipment, and the wide area network.

Ideally, you could accomplish all five management objectives for all three domains from a single network management system. The reality is something less than this. As you will soon discover, you can probably integrate the monitoring over these domains on a single workstation and within a single management system. However, configuration management and the more sophisticated levels of performance and fault management may require augmentation with a separate tool designed for the specific network domain and/or equipment.

This book will not deal with the topics of security management or accounting management. Configuration management, fault management and performance management are discussed below *in relation to the frame relay service.* Management for the routers, intelligent hubs and applications is equally as important but will not be covered in detail because this could be a book onto itself. The options for establishing a network management system, and integrating it into your current management environment will also be discussed.

## *Configuration Management*

Configuration management includes both the physical and logical configuration of the network. This means everything from your network addressing and DLCI assignments to your port connection and PVC sizing. To manage the configuration, you must have information on the status quo and the performance of the status quo, as well as a tool to modify the configuration in response to the information you gather.

You will need a tool for remote configuration management of your routers, which may be a proprietary tool from the vendor. Capturing information on the status of the router can be done within an existing SNMP (Simple Network Management Protocol) management system, as discussed later in this chapter.

Most carriers provide a management system for the frame relay service that gives you a graphical depiction of the physical and logical network. This would be a PVC map, which would show each port connection and the PVCs it supports. You will probably be able to "window down" to a site level, or look at the complete network. You may also have intelligent graphics that will change the color of a loop, port or PVC if it degrades above or below a predefined performance threshold.

Configuring the physical PVCs directly is not really an option of any of the frame relay services at this time. SVCs, when they become available, will give an application real-time establishment of a virtual connection, and the carriers are working on tools to provide you with control over PVC connections as well.

## *SNMP: The Good, The Bad and The Ugly*

*SNMP is a triumph in that it is an open standard that is widely accepted and deployed within the LAN internetworking industry. There are many things that can be accomplished with SNMP and there are some that cannot. Both deserve mention.*

*SNMP is the SIMPLE Network Management Protocol. Its biggest advantage is this simplicity, and this is also the source of its biggest weaknesses. The protocol is simply a standardized set of messages that are exchanged between a network management system supporting SNMP and an SNMP agent within a network device. The agent maintains a database of information about the device's configuration, performance and status. This database is called a MIB, or management information base.*

*MIBs come in two forms, standardized and proprietary. (Actually, there is also a third form, called experimental, comprising of MIBs that are on their way to becoming standard). Many devices support both types, or a hybrid of the two. For example, the Frame Relay Forum has standardized a MIB for frame relay devices. Most frame relay vendors now adhere to this standard MIB, but many also add extensions for their equipment that provide information not specified within the standard MIB. Since there is one MIB per device (i.e., per router, switch, etc.), a large network can mean LOTS of MIBs.*

*With most frame relay services, the carrier collects information from the SNMP agents in each of the frame relay switches and centrally stores this information in a single MIB to be accessed for data retrieval. This allows the carrier to give you a single source, with security access, from which to collect performance statistics on all the port connections and PVCs in your network. You would also use SNMP to gather performance statistics and alarms from your own network equipment attached to the frame relay network. The result is lots of MIBs to manage and the potential for lots of traffic to be generated as you collect information.*

*Messages to the MIB take two basic forms: you either get information from the MIB, or change a value within the MIB. Getting information from the MIB is called a GET. You define up front what information to GET, and how often to GET it.*

*The second type is a SET message, in which you set a database entry. With most frame relay services, you can GET information from the service's SNMP agent to determine the performance and status of your port connection and PVCs. You cannot typically SET any values within the MIB to modify your configuration.*

*There is also an unsolicited message that can be sent from the agent to a management system, which is called a TRAP. TRAPs are issued in response to abnormal network conditions when an element of the network falls above or below a pre-defined performance threshold.*

*There are some other messages defined in the standard, but these are the basic ones to be concerned about at this stage.*

*As you can plainly see, SNMP is very simple. It is just a set of rules for exchanging information. It does not help you with interpreting that information, prioritizing the information, or viewing the information. It doesn't provide data in a very user-friendly manner, like graphs or maps. Applications must be written to take the information from the MIB, or the TRAPS from the agent, and intelligently process it. You can write this application, or you can use the applications written by your carrier and equipment vendor. You will probably do both.*

*SNMP doesn't provide very good security. Carriers have had to develop security systems for the public frame relay networks that allow each customer access to his network information, but not to another customer's information.*

*The next version of SNMP, called SNMPv2, will provide security enhancements. It will also define three different GET messages: get data from one or more entries; get a block of data; or get data from the "next" entry. This simply gives you the ability to get more information, more easily and with fewer commands than with SNMPv1. Most vendors and carriers are planning on supporting SNMPv2.*

*SNMP was designed to provide information on the configuration and status of network components. It was not intended to enable complex configuration, command and control functions. These functions are usually performed using a vendor-specific management tool.*

*Another important protocol that is used by many vendors and carriers to manage distributed environments is CMIP (Common Management Information Protocol). It works well in high-speed multivendor networks and many carriers use it to manage network devices. Today, there are no frame relay services that allow you to access performance information using CMIP, although some carriers are working in this direction. In the future, a choice of SNMP or CMIP may be available for gathering frame relay service information.*

### *Fault Management*

Accepting unsolicited network alarms can be done using your existing SNMP management system or a system provided by the carrier (or both). Interpreting the alarms and applying intelligent prioritization is another story.

If you are using your own SNMP management system, then you will configure it to accept unsolicited messages, called TRAPS in SNMP lingo, from the carrier's SNMP agent in the frame relay network.

How you then process these alarms depends upon your system and any applications you write, or intelligent prioritization and processing you apply. You will probably want to set some intelligent filtering based on alarm types and thresholds, again depending upon your preferences and environment. You may also want to prioritize frame relay service alarms with other alarms you are capturing so that when you have several from which to choose, you can prioritize and allocate your own resources to resolve the most critical problems first.

Basically, you are on your own with all of this, with the exception of any help your network management vendor might provide.

You can also use a carrier-provided network management tool to gather and report alarms. The carrier will already have written applications to filter and interpret the incoming data. The advantage is that you don't have to use your own resources; the disadvantage is that it is not customized for your network situation. Many carrier tools will also allow you to enter and track trouble tickets.

In the end, if you are managing your own network, you will probably use both approaches. Your own system will provide a high-level view of the frame relay service in relation to all of the other components in your network. The carrier's management system will give you more detailed information and processing, plus a direct link with the carrier to report and resolve problems. The integration of the two systems on the same workstation can help reduce the number of separate terminals and give your operations staff a single "footprint." Integration is discussed more later.

## *Performance Management*

There are two levels on which to judge performance. One is the overall network, and one is the performance of each individual component. Managing and evaluating performance requires information. There are several different statistics which you will use to evaluate the health and performance of your frame relay service. The primary ones include:

- ☎ Ingress/Egress frame counts, and discarded frames, for each port connection;
- ☎ PVC utilization as a percentage of the committed information rate, including average utilization and peak utilization in differing time periods;
- ☎ Discard eligible frames per PVC;
- ☎ Peak traffic period;
- ☎ Average/Peak utilization.

You can get this information in at least three different ways.

If you are using your own SNMP management system, you can set up a frame relay network MIB in your system that will periodically query the SNMP agent within the carrier's frame relay network and download the set of performance parameters you have elected to capture.

You will need to predefine the amount/types of information the management system will download from the MIB and the frequency of the downloads. The more information you gather, and the more often you gather it, the better view you have of the network's performance. The trade-off between this real-time information is the impact on network congestion. The more you poll the network devices for statistics, the more traffic congestion you create on your own network, which in turn impacts network performance.

We just never escape these trade-offs.

You can also use a carrier-provided tool for gathering, interpreting and displaying the performance information. The carrier will have already written applications that provide you with text and/or graphical depictions of network performance. They may also give you some flexibility for customizing the information and frequency and the report output.

*PVC Performance Over Time*

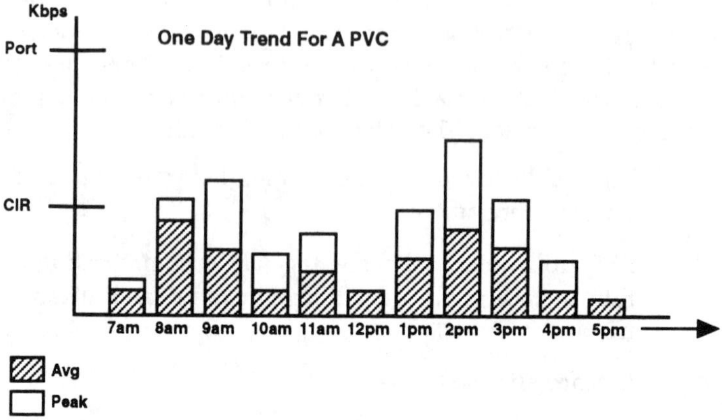


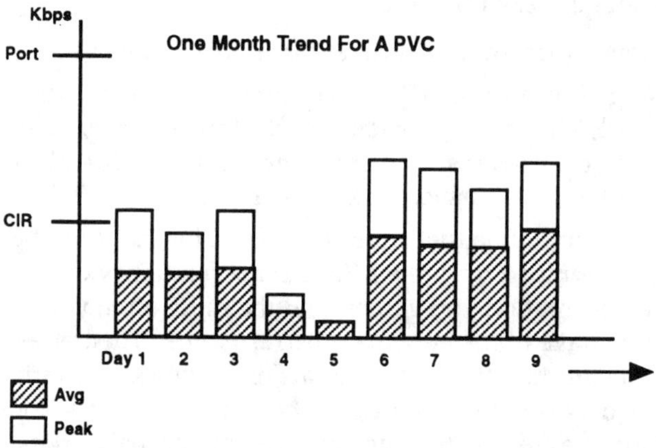


*Fig. 11.1: Graphical summaries of a PVC's average and peak traffic utilization, as a percentage of CIR, can be used to help judge network performance and fine-tune the network design.*

If you use your own tool, you once again have to develop an application to interpret the information and display it in a report. The up side of this is that you can customize your reports and make the frame relay report format consistent with your other network reporting formats. The down side is that you have to dedicate the resources upfront to writing the application.

## Setting Up a Management System

You will have three main alternatives for gathering the configuration, fault and performance information for your frame relay service:

1. You can gather raw statistics and alarms yourself, using SNMP, into your existing network management tool.
2. You can use a carrier-provided application, which may or may not include the associated workstation depending upon your needs.
3. If you do not have an existing management system and are not yet ready to deploy one, you can receive hard copy management and performance reports from the carrier. These could be delivered alone, or as part of a more comprehensive managed network service.

Of course, you may use a combination of these solutions.

### *Alternative 1: Doing It Yourself*

Most likely, you will approach management of your frame relay network from a beginning point based on an existing data network management system. IBM NetView dominates the existing management systems for SNA environments. HP OpenView, SunNet Manager, Novell NetWare Management System and NetView 6000 are the main management platforms for managing LANs, routers and intelligent hubs.

You likely have one of these or are looking at one for your LAN applications.

#### *Beginning With What's In Place*

If you have an existing management system in place, you will probably not want to spend additional resources buying and deploying a new management system for your frame relay network. If you only have an SNA management system such as NetView, you will have to either get a LAN management solution, use a carrier-provided system, or both. If you have one of the popular LAN management systems (like HP OpenView, SunNet Manager, Novell NMS or NetView 6000), then you are in luck and can build on this infrastructure.

You can gather raw network configuration and performance data, and alarms from a frame relay network into your existing SNMP-based LAN management system. This is made possible thanks to the standardization on a frame relay SNMP MIB, which nearly all frame relay service providers now support. You can access the MIB and pull raw data for your network (but not for any other company's network, obviously). There is considerable discussion about whether SNMP is the right short term, and long term, solution. Regardless of the answer, it is the only solution in place today. In the future you can expect carriers to expand to SNMPv2 and possibly CMIP (see sidebar).

As discussed above, the advantages of using your own LAN management system to monitor the frame relay service is a higher level of customization for the information gathering, interpretation and reporting. The disadvantage is the resources required to develop this customized application.

***What If Nothing Is In Place?***

If you do not already have a LAN/WAN management system but wish to establish one, here are some general guidelines. The biggest difference between management solutions is in how they scale up to effectively manage very large network environments with lots of devices and MIBs. For small networks (say less than 20 sites) the biggest difference will be price.

Sophisticated management platforms typically operate on high-end workstations and offer tools to let you customize applications. If you have a smaller network, you may want to consider a PC-based solution that operates on a DOS or Windows operating system instead of a Unix workstation. There is less functionality and customization for how you handle and prioritize different incoming alarms, view and present performance and configuration information, and fine-tune management parameters.

However, there is also a big price difference. The low-end systems can be purchased for $1500, while the high-end systems start at about 10 times this amount and increase to 100 times this amount depending upon the size of the network and the sophistication of the tools.

This is not to say that investment in a more sophisticated management is not a very good idea. Good management can be the difference between a well designed, well functioning network and a high-priced "not-work." The high-end systems will allow you to integrate more functionality into a single system. The price of this integration is resource consumption for developing customized programs. If you have a smaller network, you may want to use separate specialized tools with swivel-chair integration. You must weigh the benefits against the costs.

There are a few elements over which you will want control. If you are considering a low-end, PC-based system, choose a management system that allows you to determine the frequency with which you poll different MIBs and the MIB values that you capture with each poll. With a PC-based system, you can hit capacity quickly, meaning that if you try to gather too much information from too many points (MIBs) at a high frequency, the PC will quickly run out of storage capacity and could also have a hard time crunching all of the raw data into meaningful management information.

Using a PC-based system will probably mean that you will poll different MIBs (like the frame relay service MIB and each of the router and smart hub MIBs) less often, like once every 5 or 10 minutes instead of every 30 to 60 seconds. You will probably download less information with each poll as well. You must evaluate not only the tradeoffs between what information you retrieve and how often, but also the overhead traffic this generates on the network.

High-end workstation systems are designed for large networks with hundreds or thousands of MIBs. They are more expensive, but also provide more functionality both in terms of how much data you can collect and how often, as well as the degree to which you can customize applications for management and reporting. Regardless of which approach you think best meets the needs of your network, remember that gathering performance data from remote MIBs generates traffic across the network.

### *Alternative 2: Carrier Provided Management Systems*

In place of, or in addition to, using your own management system you may want to consider evaluating the carrier-provided management systems. Most of the frame relay service providers have developed management software that can be run on a high-end PC or workstation, or integrated into a Windows environment within your existing LAN management solution. The carrier's software will not only gather the raw data and alarms, but will also provide processing and manipulation of the raw information.

*Frame Relay Management Architecture*

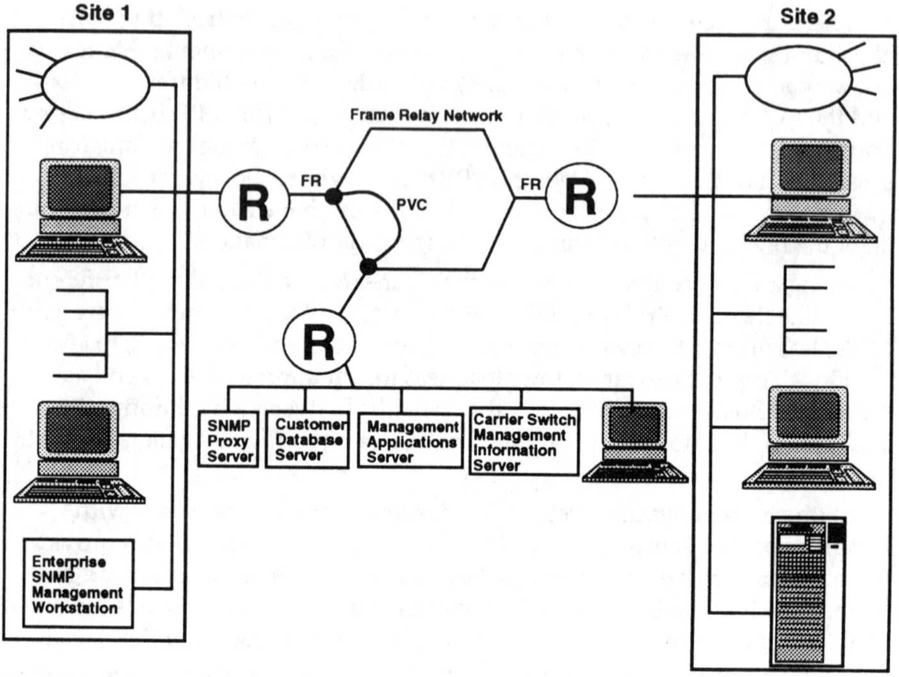


*Fig. 11.2: A PVC can be assigned into the carrier's network management interface to provide real-time alarm monitoring and ongoing network performance statistics.*

Instead of you gathering information from the carrier's frame relay service MIB and manipulating that information yourself, with this alternative the carrier will provide a turn-key solution. The point of using this alternative is that instead of doing all of this application development yourself, you use a system already developed by your carrier.

The carrier will load a new MIB into your workstation or PC. This MIB will be a smaller version of the one the carrier has developed for its frame relay service, and will already be programmed to gather information from the carrier's MIB and download that information into your MIB. In addition, you will receive a predeveloped application for interpreting and displaying the information. The system will provide most or all of the frame relay management statistics listed above, and will do so in a graphical format where applicable. The systems typically allow you to view historical network performance over some time period, such as the last 30 days. You can view the statistics in different levels of granularity, depending upon what you are looking to measure and evaluate.

For example, if you want to know the performance of an individual PVC and its ability to support an increasing number of applications, then you might look at both average and peak PVC utilization rates, as a percentage of CIR, in both five minute increments over a 24-hour period and one-day increments over a 30-day period. The carrier's management software would allow you to choose either or both of these alternatives, and would present the results in graphical form (e.g., a histogram).

One advantage of using the carrier's management software is that you do not need to build an application to interpret the raw SNMP statistics; it has already been developed for your use. The carrier-provided system may also provide additional functionality, such as the ability to enter and track trouble tickets, view and possibly enter new service orders and request changes to PVC configurations on-line.

If you do not already have a management platform, or do not wish to use your existing platform, many carriers will provide a turn-key management solution that includes the PC or workstation.

There is typically a monthly charge for access to these on-line systems which is usually two or three hundred dollars, or less. You should evaluate the cost advantages of having the information, with the price of attaining that information. Also look at the cost as a percentage of your overall network costs. Sometimes carriers will even discount the on-line services in exchange for your order, or for a term contract.

### *Planning a Wedding: Using Both Solutions Together*

The best approach for setting up management housekeeping for a frame relay service is probably to marry your current LAN management system with the carrier-provided management system. You can use your existing management workstation to run the carrier's application software, provided you have the available memory and processing power. This saves the expense and space consumption of another workstation.

With this approach, the carrier's software is loaded into your system and the application becomes another icon on your screen. For example, a cloud might be the icon for the frame relay network. By clicking on the cloud, you open the carrier's management application and gain access to the carrier's management applications.

In integrating the systems at the desktop, you can easily access both management applications from the same workstation. You may want to take this one step further by writing some customized applications for gathering SNMP TRAPS into your LAN management system so that you can be made immediately aware of problems from the LAN system's view and not from the carrier management system's view. This will allow you to keep the carrier's window closed until you need more detailed information, trouble ticket entry, performance reports, etc.

This hybrid approach allows you to be made immediately aware of alarm conditions without having to spend a large amount of resources customizing management applications. You can maintain a holistic view of the network, including the routers, hubs, LANs and frame relay service, from a single graphical depiction. The frame relay network is simply another icon on your management screen.

By windowing into the carrier's management system, you can generate management reports without developing a new application. You can explore alarms, enter trouble tickets when problems occur and track them through to closure.

Whether you use your own management system to gather alarms and performance data, a carrier's system, or both, you will still need to have a tool for remotely managing your network devices, like the routers and/or smart hubs. This will be a separate tool provided by the hardware vendor.

Overall, there is a balance between integration and specialization. You can integrate the administrative side, but you will still need specialized tools for control and manipulation of remote network elements.

### *Gathering the Data: Inband versus Out-of-Band Connections*

Whether you use your own management system, the carrier's, or both, you will also need to have an access mechanism by which to get to the network management data and alarms. You will probably choose between an inband or out-of-band connection. You can either assign a PVC within the frame relay network to access the carrier's SNMP and/or other network information, or you can use a standalone private line, X.25 connection or any other access method supported by your carrier.

There are trade-offs in terms of availability versus price. Assigning a PVC makes good financial sense and gives you a very cost-effective mechanism by which to gather network statistics and alarms. Of course, if the local loop fails and/or there is another outage affecting that PVC, your management system could be without its eyes and ears.

Using a separate private line or X.25 connection, however, may not be much more advantageous, even though it is "out-of-band." If a local loop failure is the cause, then a private line into your location would be equally affected unless it was being provided over separate entrance facilities.

*Inband And Out-Of-Band Connections*

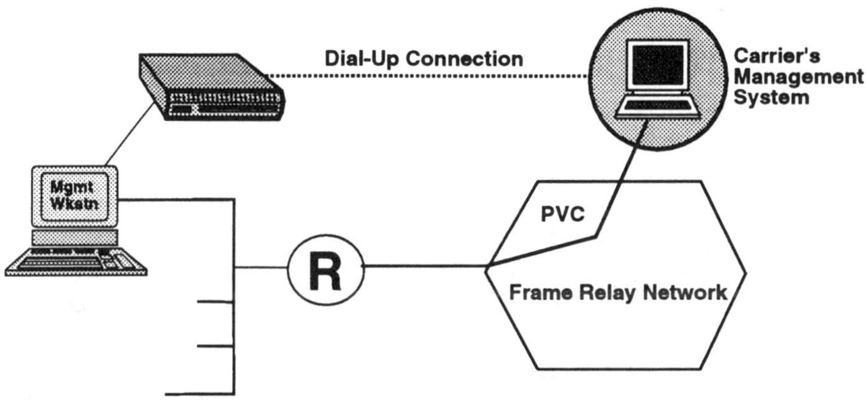


*Fig. 11.3: Information stored in the Carrier's Management Information Base can either be accessed by assigning a PVC over the frame relay network, or a separate dial-up connection, or both.*

One solution is to use a PVC, but to augment this with the ability to dial up into the network and directly into remote routers. You might use a modem and analog line attached to your management system, or use the dial-up port connections now available with many routers, for example. This provides the cost-effectiveness of the in-band approach while giving you a path to reestablish monitoring in the case of a failure of that in-band connection.

## *Alternative 3: None of the Above*

If you don't have a current management system and do not wish to deploy one at this time, then you have at least two alternatives. Most carriers will supply hardcopy monthly performance reports and graphics, just like what you can get with an on-line system. There is typically a monthly charge associated with this service.

The other alternative is to pay the carrier to monitor and manage the network for you. This topic is discussed in great detail below. By way of an overview, in considering this alternative, you should evaluate the cost of setting up a network operations center, staffing it with expertise for LAN/WAN internetworking over a frame relay network, and purchasing all of the related hardware and software. If you already have this in place, then you should evaluate the opportunity costs associated with using these resources for the daily management of the frame relay network as opposed to the management of other networks, or work on more strategic business-level or application-level projects.

## The Complexities of Managing a Multivendor, Multiprotocol Internetwork

In case you are under any false notions about the complexities of managing and maintaining a multiprotocol, multivendor internetwork, let's set your expectations at a reasonable level.

For a router-based network to function properly, the routers must work together as a group. They will exchange routing table, configuration and metric (e.g., cost) information and continually make adjustments in routing decisions based on these exchanges. You can fine-tune any single router with little impact to the overall network performance if the other routers are not properly configured and/or if the network design is poor.

Troubleshooting in an internetwork requires a special set of expertise. The carriers and vendors do not publish a manual. This information is something achieved through lots of experience or by secretly jacking into a highly secure and secret portion of the Internet at night when the moon is full and mind linking with an all-knowing artificial construct to absorb by osmosis the required information.

Few have ever personally experienced the latter, but it is rumored to exist somewhere — it's just a matter of stumbling upon the right location in cyberspace.

Without the osmosis, you must fall back on hardcore experience, which can be difficult to come by.

Isolating a problem in a dynamic routing domain can be challenging for the most experienced of internetworking engineers. The more protocols you support, the more special expertise is required and the more difficult problem resolution can become.

Adding a new site will usually require a look back at the existing sites and possibly a new round of router-tuning. The same applies for adding new protocols. It's like tuning and playing the guitar. Any one can do it, but few do it well.

## *Managed Network Services*

If any of the following conditions apply to your situation, you may want to consider evaluating a managed network service.

- You don't have networking management staff or your existing resources and staff expertise are not well enough developed in the LAN/WAN internetworking area to manage and maintain a router-based internetwork without significant investment and training.
- Your existing resources are capable of managing the internetwork but are fully occupied with daily management of other portions of the enterprise network and do not have the time to manage the internetwork properly.
- You have the resources and expertise for daily management of the network, but would like the flexibility to allocate these experts to more strategic network projects.

### *Elements of a Managed Network Service*

Managed network services provide a comprehensive, soup-to-nuts solution that can be purchased *in addition to* the frame relay transmission service and typically includes all of the following elements:

- Networking equipment: router, CSU/DSU, modem (for dial-up management access) plus initial configuration of the equipment and on-site equipment installation;
- Initial network design;
- Documented implementation plan;
- 24-hour-a-day, 365-days-a-year network monitoring and proactive network trouble isolation and correction;
- On-site equipment maintenance;
- Multiprotocol support;
- Ongoing router configuration management: address moves, adds, changes;
- Assistance with applying for NIC network addressing;
- Monthly performance reporting;

☎ Ongoing network performance evaluation and network design optimization.

Each of these elements requires further commentary.

*Networking Equipment*

Most of the carriers will provide you with some flexibility with regard to choosing an equipment vendor. They will support two or three of the primary router vendors' products. There are two benefits of this. The first is that you and the carrier can choose the router that best fits your environment, protocols, and requirements. The second is that if you have already standardized on a router manufacturer, and it is one the carrier supports, then you can continue using this vendor within the managed network service.

Most services also include a modem attached to the router. This is provided so that if in-band connectivity is lost for any reason, out-of-band connectivity with the router can be established. This will allow the managing technician to reboot the router and perform other configuration and/or management processes.

The carrier will typically provide either rack-mounted or standalone configurations of your preference. The equipment is pretested and preconfigured before shipping to your site. The configuration at this stage would insure that the correct number and type of LAN interfaces is included, all cabling is included, etc.

Some carriers provide the flexibility for you to supply your own equipment. This would be advantageous at sites where you already have a router in place and do not need another unit. In this case, the carrier is given complete responsibility for the router, and you will probably no longer have access to the pass codes, etc. You and the carrier can jointly decide who will control the maintenance of the equipment and the dispatch of maintenance technicians.

In most services, only two-port routers are supported. This means one LAN port and one WAN port. If you have a site with several LANs, then you would probably put a bridge or router behind the router provided with the managed network service. You would be responsible for this router, and the carrier would be responsible for the managed network services router. The reason for this is so that a definitive line of physical and logical demarcation can be established. If you are having problems with file transfers between the LAN on the second floor and the LAN on the fourth floor, this is not the carrier's responsibility.

You may then ask yourself why you would need a managed network service if you have to have responsibility for the local LANs? The answer is that the expertise for LAN-to-WAN internetworking over a frame relay (or other) network is quite different from the expertise for managing local routers and the attached LANs. Managed network services typically do not include the carrier taking responsibility for your LANs — only the interconnecting WAN and the attached LAN/WAN networking equipment.

*Network Design*

This is one of the most critical components to network performance. If the network is not properly designed, then it will not operate effectively. This includes the relationship between issues such as the routing protocols used, the configuration of the router buffers and prioritization parameters, the configuration of the PVCs, and sizing of CIRs and port connections.

All of the carriers will help you design and price out different network configurations. However, when it becomes the carrier's responsibility to manage and maintain that network, and when they will be held accountable to you for the network's performance, then the issue of design becomes very critical. As part of your managed network service, the carrier will become much more involved in the details of designing the network.

*Implementation Plan*

You will typically work with the carrier to develop a complete, written implementation plan for the network. This includes site-by-site planning of equipment and network installation within the context of the complete installation process.

This is typically a written document, which will specify those areas, such as site preparation and internal cabling, for which you are responsible. It should also specify what constitutes complete and satisfactory installation at each site. For example, the carrier is not responsible for helping you integrate each network application over the WAN. However, as part of the implementation plan, you may designate that each protocol will be tested by using one of your standard applications for that protocol, to one other site on the network.

*Network Monitoring*

Some carriers offer different grades of service for network monitoring and proactive trouble correction. For example, the standard monitoring package is usually seven days a week/24 hours a day, including all holidays and weekends. Some carriers offer different service levels, so that you can choose 24 hours a day all week long, or just 8am to 5pm business-day monitoring.

But be careful here. You may only operate your business during these hours, but if the network breaks in the middle of the night or on the weekend, you will probably want the carrier to detect the problem and get it fixed *before you reopen for business*. You don't want to come in on Monday only to find that the network has been down since Sunday morning. The 7x24 monitoring package is the only way to go if the applications are important to the business.

The network monitoring is typically done using SNMP. The carrier will keep a record of your complete network configuration and a real-time view of the status of physical and logical connections. Alarms on the network will trigger a proactive response in which the carrier will open a trouble ticket and will begin to isolate and resolve the problem. If you call in to report trouble, you may find that a ticket is already open and a technician is at work on the resolution.

You are also able to open a trouble ticket yourself. Keep in mind that there are certain things for which the carrier is responsible and other things over which you maintain control. LAN-to-LAN traffic within the same building and application level issues are in your domain.

Who closes the trouble ticket is a key question to explore with the vendor (regardless of if you are using a managed network service or just a frame relay service). You should be the one to decide when a problem has been solved.

### *Maintenance*

On-site maintenance is an area where you can exercise some latitude in terms of service level. The highest level of service typically offered is for four-hour on-site response times to hardware-related problems. Some carriers do offer a lower cost alternative for next-day response times. This might make sense at some non-critical locations and allow you to save money.

Make sure you choose a carrier that will provide on-site sparing (i.e., on-site spare parts) with a maintenance technician, in case the entire unit must be removed and repaired.

### *Configuration Management*

Configuration management is the management of the router address tables, including moves, adds and changes of attached device addresses and the addition/deletion of network protocols. You can typically submit your requests for moves/adds/changes either over the phone or via fax.

Configuration management also includes management and use of the router options for protocol prioritization, buffer queues and the issues for managing routing protocols and broadcasts over the WAN as discussed in Chapter 10. You should quiz prospective carriers on their knowledge of these issues and their plans to handle your protocols. If they are not prepared to discuss these issues with you, they may not have the expertise needed to manage and maintain your network.

*Network Addressing Assistance*

Some of the carriers offer a service to help you plan your addressing, and even apply for IP addresses with the NIC. A standard and well planned approach to addressing and naming will insure addresses are not duplicated and will make administration and problem resolution easier and more rapid.

*Monthly Performance Reporting*

If you choose to allow a carrier to manage your internetwork, you must have a way to evaluate and judge the carrier's performance. One of the tools for this is a monthly performance report that the carrier provides. The reports will typically include an outage and trouble ticket summary, including reason codes and resolution times. It should also include utilization reports for port connections and individual PVCs. You may want to get a trend report as well, for the ports and PVCs, showing a historical summary of utilization over time.

These reports are typically available either from an on-line system or in hardcopy format. Some services charge extra for these reports while others do not. Keep in mind that interpretation of the reports is not the same thing as production and delivery of reports, and interpretation is what is critical. Read on.

*Performance Evaluation and Optimization*

There should be both an ongoing informal evaluation process as well as a formal yearly evaluation process. Both are critical elements in maintaining a healthy network.

On the informal side, you should insist that a single, knowledgeable individual is in charge of evaluating your monthly performance report. This means reviewing the network in its entirety and making sure that the overall configuration continues to be properly designed as traffic patterns, applications and business environments undergo changes. This may or may not be done by the operational group supporting the standard moves/adds/changes within the router. It may instead be a project manager or network engineer assigned to your account.

Regardless of where the responsibility falls, make sure that someone looks at the monthly performance reports and *interprets the results in terms of potential impact on the network design*. It doesn't do any good to get a trend report that CIR utilization is averaging 80 percent, if no single individual has responsibility for interpreting the implications of the information. In this example, it may indicate that the CIR should be increased. If, on the other hand, CIR utilization has remained under 2 percent with peak utilization no greater than 50 percent, then the carrier should proactively suggest a downsizing of the CIR, unless some future application is expected to change the utilization pattern.

At least once a year you should have a formal evaluation with your carrier. This should be a planning session where you discuss both the past performance and the future network requirements.

On evaluating past performance, make sure that escalation procedures have worked properly and that problems have been addressed and resolved in a timely fashion. Also look for indications that the network design has remained consistent with the changing needs of the network and/or that the carrier has proactively suggested changes.

Future planning should include a site-by-site evaluation of expected business changes, new applications, new sites, sites being moved or deleted, personnel growth, planned protocols to be added/deleted, etc. This will allow you and the carrier to proactively plan how you will accommodate these changes as they occur. If you have a highly dynamic business, you may need a biannual or even quarterly review.

### *Choosing a Managed Network Service*

Each carrier defines its service a little differently from the next, but overall you will find amazing similarity in the descriptions of these services. The real key, however, is not in how these services are described but how they are provided. It is a bit like buying a diamond, in that it is a "blind item." You are not a diamond expert, so you rely on the experts to help you understand quality difference. Two different one-carat diamonds may be priced differently by several thousands of dollars. Can the untrained eye discern a difference? Managed Network Services can be much the same. The same solution applies to each situation: use a microscope.

Ask a lot of questions. Use the issues brought up throughout this book to guide your questions and judge the answers you receive. Also, look for a carrier that can provide the right level of service and type of equipment for your network. Some carriers offer ancillary services and equipment, such as intelligent hubs, LAN installation and other inside wiring, which could sway your decision.

Most notably, choose a carrier with whom you are comfortable working. You are in essence taking on a new employee or business partner, and the chemistry must be right.

## CHAPTER 12:

# DEVELOPING A REQUEST FOR PROPOSAL

In this chapter, we will discuss the process of carrier selection and provide a proven methodology for managing this process from the requirements-gathering phase through the request for proposal (RFP) to the actual selection of a carrier. Specifically, we will walk through the thought process that should go into the creation of the RFP and discuss the actual contents of the RFP and the chronology of the vendor selection process.

The important thing to remember in this exercise is that your end goal is not simply to discover the low-cost vendor. While cost will be a major factor in any decision, it is vital to use the process to further your own education and come out with the overall best network solution. The entire proposal process should be viewed as an opportunity to have carrier personnel, who probably have a lot more experience with the technology than you do, examine your data environment and provide guidance on everything from whether or not you actually have an application for frame relay, to topology, to network management strategies. This means sharing as much as possible about the network requirements as well as requiring the potential vendors to make a thorough and intelligent response to your request.

## Objectives

The first step in the process is figuring out what you want. After all, you can't know you are satisfied unless you know what you are asking for.

Each company considering a frame relay network will have a slightly different set of objectives in launching this process. It is crucial to develop and record these objectives, not only to include in your RFP, but also to use as a compass throughout the process. Remember that you will be dealing with several players with vastly different agendas. If things are not progressing toward your aims, you must take action to put them back on course.

Here are some objectives to consider:

- **Business Objectives.** These objectives relate to your organization's core business. If you make shoes, then you should clearly state how you hope this proposed network will help your company make or market shoes more efficiently, more effectively, or less expensively. You may want to specifically outline your tactical objectives as well as strategic objectives.
- **Performance Objectives.** Specify your performance objectives, including any existing benchmarks. This detail should be provided on an application-by-application basis. Many companies use metrics such as throughput, measured in packets or Kilobits per second, and screen response time.
- **Cost/Value Objectives.** While cost is seemingly clear-cut, the low cost vendor may also be proposing the lowest value network. Cost should be considered in both capital expenditures and annual service costs. If your organization has a preference or requirement for low capital costs, then this should be clearly articulated.
- **Training Objectives.** As mentioned, this process provides an excellent opportunity for you and your staff to learn more about the technology and how to design and manage a network. Determine what your goals are in this area, including which people you want to be educated and what you want them to learn. Areas might include sending your technical people to a carrier's network management center to discuss and learn about monitoring, having your engineers and designers work with the carrier's designers to understand the effects of different protocols, and visiting a testing laboratory to learn about simulations.

- **Scope Objectives.** How much of the network is under consideration? Do you need routers and CSU/DSUs only, or do you also need inside wiring, LANs and/or smart hubs? Do you want a single provider for both the equipment and the network, or will you consider separate providers?

- **Implementation Objectives.** How quickly must the new network be implemented? Will you want a phased approach, or will you want to bring the new network up at all sites within a few weeks? Are there any special implementation issues the carrier or equipment provider should be aware of that might impact network design or implementation planning? Will you be planning on-site inventories of your sites? Who will conduct these and when?

- **Expected Deliverables.** Clearly outline the output you expect from the process. Do you want each bidder to submit several different network designs from which to choose? Do you want each provider to outline several different support alternatives ranging from just network to a turn-key package? Do you expect an implementation plan developed as part of the design process? Will you expect the proposals to be submitted in a specific format? Will you require a formal presentation from all providers, or only those that make your short list?

- **Future Positioning Objectives.** Lastly, it is useful to take a look forward to where your business and network will be throughout the possible life cycle of this network. Which applications do you hope to migrate to the frame relay network in the future? Which networks do you hope to consolidate? Are there new applications or business processes you hope to enable? Do you foresee locations where other protocols, such as ISDN, SMDS or ATM, will be needed and will the ability to interwork protocols be important in your future network? Once you can outline your future vision for the network, you can look for business partners that share that vision.

During the proposal and implementation process, you will find it useful to refer back to this listing and compare your actual performance against these objectives.

## Evaluation Criteria

Many customers embarking on this process find themselves in the middle of the RFP process without any formal methodology for evaluating the potential network providers. The old adage, "Garbage In, Garbage Out," applies here. You must structure your process up front, because it is difficult to do this in retrospect.

While it is nearly impossible to transform the evaluation process into a completely objective exercise, it is possible to develop a list of evaluation criteria to be used as a common, agreed-upon guide for the evaluation of the vendors. Following is a listing of criteria commonly used to differentiate carriers:

- Price
- Reliability
- Customer service
- Operations support
- Technical field support
- Performance
- Network management alternatives
- Implementation support
- Equipment choices/support
- Number and location of switches
- Speed of backbone network (DS-1 or DS-3?)
- Cell relay or frame switching
- Proactive monitoring and trouble ticketing
- Protocol interworking
- Billing alternatives
- Flexible pricing schemes
- Internet access

- Disaster recovery
- Access recovery
- Integrated access
- Managed Network Service offering
- Flexible contract terms
- Service guarantees
- International service availability
- Future services and migration strategies (i.e., ATM, interworking)

Will you assign any criteria for the proposal process itself? Sometimes the ability of a carrier to respond in a timely manner with a complete and professional proposal can be an indication of corporate culture and method for doing business. You may want to give extra-credit points to those carriers that do a really nice job in the proposal process.

While this is a good start, it is vital to uncover the criteria important to your organization. This means doing your homework prior to the development of the RFP.

Your evaluation criteria should be rated on a numerical scale and put into a spreadsheet. Rating the criteria refers to the development of a system for weighting each criteria in terms of importance, and for numerically judging the vendors on each criteria.

Note: This is not the total solution. No RFP is awarded based solely on calculated numbers from weightings. However, usually these numbers are used to back up what ends up being a good gut-feel about the way to go. If the process is set up correctly, and you stay true to your goals, then the numbers and your gut feel should line up. If not, then this serves to highlight some things to revisit to validate the results and/or your choice.

Weighting the criteria can be accomplished in several ways. You can develop a weighting of the criteria from most to least important. This could simply mean designating the first most important, then second, then third, and so on. Or, you could weight each by critical (5), high (4), medium (3), low (2), extra credit (1), etc. The idea is to have an idea of which evaluation criteria carry more weight, pardon the pun.

Also, you need to determine how you will numerically evaluate each carrier on the criteria. Will you assign a 10 for perfect and a 0 for non-compliant, and then fill in the numbers between?

An example of how to use this numerical approach would be to rate the criteria on a 1-10 scale, where 10 is the most important. Then rate the carrier capabilities for each criterion on a 1-10 scale, where 10 is the most capable. Then you can get a relative assessment of how each carrier pans out by multiplying the two together, and adding up the total by element. You can have multiple people evaluating the bid do this, but the ratings of the criteria should be the same for everyone. In the end, you can total each carrier's score across all elements and use this as one piece of information in your final decision.

Again, while it is not advisable to make a decision solely on this kind of data, it is an excellent way to narrow down the competition and gain some peace of mind over final decisions.

## Writing the RFP

Overall, the RFP should provide enough detail for the carrier to make a complete bid, and should be organized in such a way that the carrier does not have to wade through a mass of information to get to the key points. For this reason, it is advisable to use bullets and tabular formats as much as possible and to provide a clear table of contents.

A sample table of contents for an RFP is provided below. This is just a suggested format, and while it has proven effective for several organizations, rarely can it be used without some level of customization.

I. Overview

- A. Summary of Business
- B. Listing of Objectives

II. Background

- A. Project Brief
- B. Ground Rules
- C. Time Line
- D. Corporate and/or Network Organization Summary

III. Current Network

- A. Overview (w/ map)
- B. Applications
- C. Site Information

D. Limitations

IV. Proposed Network

A. Overview (w/design if available)

B. New Applications or Changes to Existing Applications

C. Pertinent Business Factors (e.g., downsizing)

D. General Requirements

E. Benchmarks

F. Contract Provisions

V. Outline for Response

A. Proposed Network Design

B. Alternative Designs and/or Ancillary Services

C. Response to General Requirements

D. Costs

E. Implementation Plan

VI. Attachments

VII. Glossary

Below we'll talk about what needs to go into each of these sections to make your RFP successful.

### *I. Overview*

This section should be only a few paragraphs in length. It should provide a summary of your business, the service you wish to purchase and a listing of the key reasons and objectives for issuing the request. If you are considering the option of a managed network service, this should be clearly stated in this section, as should any other requirements that significantly affect the type of service you wish to purchase.

Depending upon what you are including in this proposal, some vendors may only be bidding on certain sections (such as equipment only, or the frame relay network only). It is important that everyone bidding have a clear idea of "the big picture."

### II. Background

This section should provide a more in-depth brief of the request with a summary of the number of locations, applications, and users to be served.

It will also lay out the ground rules for the entire process. Examples of nearly essential rules include:

- Carriers are expected to include final "best price" in proposal. Rebids will not be accepted.
- Carriers not able to complete a bid in the allotted time frame will not be considered.
- Bids will remain confidential throughout the process.
- Carriers are expected to use given contacts throughout the evaluation process (salespeople often try to speak only to the decision maker).
- Carriers will be expected to have the required technical experts at meetings.
- Presentations will be scheduled in the order of the arrival of the proposals.
- Proposals not meeting the format guidelines will not be accepted.

Your intended time line for the RFP process itself, and then for network implementation, should be clearly defined in this section.

This section should also include a description of your network management and support organization, including number of employees and levels of expertise. It is better to let the carrier know up front if you will need extensive assistance during the implementation. The carrier may choose to propose some outsourcing options based on this information.

You may want to provide specific detail on the management system(s) you currently use, the network analysis tools you have available, the staff's level of experience with routers and internetworks, and so on. After reading this section, the bidders should have a very good idea of the organization that will be supporting the network once it is in place.

## *III. Current Network*

The purpose of this section is to familiarize the carrier with your current network environment. The carrier needs to know and understand how you are using your current network and how it is performing. This tells the carrier what your past priorities have been and what shape your solutions have taken. It will also provide indications of where the current network is not meeting performance objectives.

A map of the existing network is critical. Most organizations have maps of their physical networks, and many have made logical maps as well. All of this information, as long as it is accurate, is useful.

Chapter Six discussed at length the information about your existing network that should be gathered to provide guidance for the new network design. Assemble any/all of this information and provide it as part of the RFP. If you want the carriers to help you design your frame relay network, they need every scrap of relevant information you can provide.

For each existing circuit in your network provide a matrix that lists:

- ☎ Carrier
- ☎ Applications being supported
- ☎ Access type
- ☎ CPE
- ☎ Average circuit utilization estimate
- ☎ Current performance or benchmark information
- ☎ Disaster recovery provisions
- ☎ Network/circuit recovery provisions, including diversity

This will provide a good "snapshot" of the current network. If there are statistics you cannot obtain through in-house measurement facilities, it is feasible to invite the carrier to perform testing.

Following the summary of the entire network, it is advisable to list each application separately. As you will recall, Chapter 6 provided further detail in this area. For each application include:

- ☎ Summary of application
- ☎ Platform (hardware, software, network, protocol)
- ☎ Number of users with location distribution

- Patterns of traffic by time of day or day of week
- Average size and frequency of transactions
- Availability requirements

You will want to include a similar overview for each site. Following is a listing of proposed information to include. Some of the information is duplicative with the above list. This is because for certain applications it might be more appropriate to provide the information on a network level, while in other situations it may be more useful to provide a site-by-site analysis. You will need to decide what is best for your network.

- Location
- Applications used at that site
- Number of users for each application and/or in total
- CPE (including smart hubs, controllers, etc.) and status of depreciation
- LANs
- Other network services used (e.g., voice, dial-up data)
- Special disaster recovery requirements
- Traffic patterns to/from other locations

You will need to include information on any new applications not currently supported, but will be once the frame relay network is in place. Provide any projections for traffic patterns and utilization that you can, the number of users for the applications, projections for implementation, etc.

While few vendors provide standard cross discounting of frame relay services with other services like long distance voice and private lines, sometimes a custom arrangement is possible. Also, you may want to explore the pros and cons of integrated access (as discussed in Chapter 5) to save money on loop facilities. These are some of the reasons why you should account for the non-frame relay applications at each site.

Finally, you will want to talk about the limitations of the current network(s), if any. This could be in terms of performance or availability, and/or in terms of flexibility and scalability.

### *IV. Proposed Network*

In this section, you will want to spell out exactly what it is you are planning on purchasing and what you will expect from the new network. Your objectives for the new network are an important component of this section.

You should have some idea of what the new network will consist of and provide as much detail as possible regarding your initial designs. Chapters 6 and 7 provide guidance on these issues and in designing a network. Carriers should very actively question your design to see if it is the best option. Be wary of the carrier who simply copies your specification and tags it with a price. You may simply have done a superb job at design, or the carrier may not be allocating appropriate expertise to your bid.

Note, in bullet form, your specific requirements for each site and/or application. Each chapter in this book is designed to give you information on requirements in specific areas such as the network itself, backhauling, loop recovery, site recovery, network management, and so on.

Provide a site-by-site and or application-by-application comparison of the current network requirements with your new network requirements. For example, if a site does not have loop recovery provisions in the current network, but you are wanting them in the new network, you would specifically point this fact out.

You may want to specify certain design alternatives that you will or will not accept, such as oversubscription of a port connection, use of "Zero" CIR PVCs. This can also include accepting equipment bids from carriers and other proposals for ancillary services such as network management packages and Internet access.

Provide any network benchmarks or performance figures for the new network. This should encompass items such as availability and throughput as well as mean time to repair and customer service availability.

Lastly , you will want to outline contract conditions you require and/or will consider. For example:

- A term contract in exchange for a price discount
- Service satisfaction warranty that will give you the ability to cancel the service for any reason during the first three or four months if you are not happy
- Credit provisions for non-performance and/or outages

- A technology or service migration clause allowing you to migrate to another service provided by that carrier without penalty

### *V. Outline for Response*

The carriers should be advised on exactly how to respond to your request. While it is not necessary to provide the carrier with a fill-in-the-blanks form, it is advisable to request specific point-by-point answers to each requirement and an overall format for the final proposal.

This is really critical to the success of the RFP. The carriers have their own boilerplate proposal responses for frame relay — where they tell you how great they are and how no one else compares. You need to structure your request for a response in such a way that breaks them out of that mold, or you will have to spend a lot of time sifting through sales pitches looking for answers to your questions. Some of the most successful RFPs have asked for specific summary pages on simple things including the following:

- Total installation expense — services
- Total installation expense — equipment
- Total installation expense — other
- Total monthly expense — services
- Total monthly expense — equipment
- Total monthly expense — other
- Total time to install

By forcing the carriers to specifically address your questions, you can better compare the final bids apples-to-apples. Let them put all the sales fluff up front, but when it comes to specific answers, make them follow format.

Your RFP can include a format outline, such as a section-by-section breakdown including:

1. Executive overview of proposal
2. Carrier overview/information
3. Pricing of *your* network design
4. Pricing for the ancillary services you specifically request in the RFP
5. Alternative designs, ancillary services and pricing

6. Implementation plan

You may want to provide detail on your objectives within each section, or provide specific section requirements.

When pricing your network design, you should provide information on the format of this pricing, as discussed below. You may specify that each carrier should provide pricing on certain ancillary services, such as network management or managed network support. If this is the case, also specify the format, such as pricing on a per site basis and not a network-level price. You may want to provide an open, or "other," category where the carrier can propose alternatives such as equipment or Internet access in conjunction with pricing for your network design.

Section 5 of this RFP encourages the carrier to challenge any of your design points or requirements and develop a new network design. There have been more than a few cases in which a customer puts out a request for a frame relay network and one or more of the carriers proposes a private line or hybrid network solution. Give the carriers a chance to optimize your network price, and then you be the judge of whether or not long-term flexibility or short-term performance would be impacted.

You should specify a format for the presentation of pricing. You should be able to get a complete breakdown of charges on a site-by-site basis. Each carrier prices the frame relay service component of the network very differently, so trying to fit them all into a rigorous format will just be frustrating for you and the bidder. However, you can specify a general format, such as site-by-site price breakdowns, which include the price for equipment, maintenance, management, access, and IXC detailed separately. You can also request a specific format for summarizing the network totals. For example, do you want IXC, access and equipment totaled separately, or each site totaled separately for all elements?

Require the carrier to provide a discount matrix based on different term contracts and volume levels. This should be separate from the base pricing.

While it is largely unfair to the carriers, few customers these days pay for installation charges. You should be able to negotiate a waiver of these in exchange for a term contract.

If there is a possibility of moving voice traffic to the carrier, ask for bids that reflect cross-product discounts or concessions.

You should note that you expect final prices from the carriers and will not necessarily allow changes to the bid once it is submitted.

Request an implementation plan, which includes a full Gantt chart of the proposed implementation schedule, a description of the progression of events, and information about the exact individuals who will be supporting each area/component of the installation.

### *VI. Attachments*

In this section, you should include any detailed performance and/or traffic data you have collected, simulation results you have run, and possibly the worksheets you used in developing your own design. The RFP process isn't intended to be a mystery game where carriers have to dig up clues and the best digger wins. You want the best possible network design, so provide as much information to all participants as possible.

### *VII. Glossary*

This may sound like you are writing a book, but many firms fall quickly into their own lingo, making it hard for carriers to fully understand what you are talking about. If you refer to sites in a particular way, or if you call your routers by a particular name that is non-standard, then this is the place to put some of that information. Since you have to respond in written format to all bidders for each question, you really want to minimize the problems up front, and confusion over terms is always a big issue.

## The RFP Process

At the outset of the RFP process, you need to know what you would like to get accomplished, and your time frame for completion. It is difficult to begin the vendor selection process without a clearly defined timeline. This timeline puts you in control of the order of events. Making this timeline known to all involved parties is one component of effective vendor management.

As an example, some carriers will request the option of rebidding services should another carrier undercut its price. If you do not allow for this rebid in your time line, the carrier will likely be a bit more careful in its initial price calculations. By establishing and managing to a time table, you are beginning to establish the ground rules for negotiation. As with any good guideline, you can also decide when to bend or break it.

Following is a proposed chronology for the RFP process. You should note that this schedule assumes that you have already gathered requirements and have at least a tentative idea of network topology and a complete site inventory.

### *Step 1: Getting Organized*

1. Identify and contact potential bidders.
2. Appropriate the staff to support the process.
3. Meet to clarify and record objectives.
4. Set up project Gantt Chart.
5. Determine tools for use in the process.
6. Assign RFP writing responsibilities for each RFP section to your staff.

One of the first tasks is to produce a letter expressing your interest in a frame relay network and asking for the carrier to provide a package of information on its respective offerings. This letter can be referred to as a Request for Information. This letter should go out to any carrier you might consider. Later, you can make a preliminary evaluation narrowing the process down to 3-5 service providers, if possible. If you will have the equipment vendors submit separate bids, then this might be another 3-5 vendors. The more players involved, the more difficult to the project is manage.

Depending on the size and complexity of your organization, determining the "tools" may simply mean choosing a word processing software package and/or making sure that everyone knows the preferred form of communication. In other cases, this may include network simulation tools, protocol analyzers, and other items.

You may want different experts within your own group to write different components of the RFP. Make sure that a common format is followed by all writers. While it may be tempting to have junior members of the staff put together the base information, it is crucial to have a few expert individuals who are responsible for the actual content of the document. This way, meetings with the carriers can be held in small groups with only these key people.

As discussed above in the section on writing the RFP, you may want to design your own frame relay network and insist that each carrier price out the design *without modification*. You might also specify a very strict format for this response, including a site by site pricing matrix you design and which the carrier fills out. In addition, you can give each carrier the option of including up to two (or whatever) alternative network designs/proposals. You may choose to require a specific format for these alternatives, or let the carrier choose the response format. Just remember: The more flexibility you give your carrier, the more work you have to do to figure it out and compare alternatives.

When developing RFPs, some organizations use fairly standard RFP templates based on past evaluations or available from third parties. One should use extreme caution in the development of the RFP, as lack of attention to detail at this stage can take the process back weeks due to a forgotten clause or misstated requirement. Also, an RFP format that is appropriate for private lines may not be wholly appropriate for a frame relay network. You may need to do some customization. "Garbage In, Garbage Out" again is an appropriate idiom at this stage. The RFP will communicate what you need, and will therefore be the primary basis for what you get.

This step is really a "gear up" week in which you put together the project plan and the project team, communicate the objectives and the time line, and set the ground rules. While the process is a lot of work, there is no reason why it cannot be fun.

### *Step 2: Drafting the RFP*

1. Produce and review draft copy of the RFP
2. Review materials from carriers
3. Decide on recipients of RFP
4. Plan any site visits

Once the process begins, your goal should be to make the carriers start working for you, instead of vice versa, as soon as possible. Set definitive time limits on discussions of who should receive the RFP and other issues that might slow down the process of delivering the document.

You will also want to make any plans for travel related to the bid during this week. Sometimes carriers will offer to take customers to see the network control center, to a network lab, or to a current customer site for a reference visit. While it is definitely helpful to visit a network control center, it is not constructive to do it the day after the board is scheduled to sign off on the decision. You will want to time these visits so that the findings can have an impact on your decision.

If you do get the opportunity to speak directly with a carrier's operations staff, ask lots of questions about how they manage and monitor the network, the level of proactive trouble monitoring and correction, their knowledge about different protocols, troubleshooting and escalation procedures, and so on. Some carriers also have network design centers and/or test laboratories in which engineers can model a potential network.

It is important to schedule any such visit as soon as is viable, so you need to decide if this will be part of your objectives, if it will be specifically required in the RFP, and how many such visits you will have the time to accomplish.

You should come out of this step with a clear idea of RFP recipients, a general plan for the travel schedule and the changes required to produce a final document.

### *Step 3: Sending the RFP Out*

1. Send RFP to selected carriers
2. Make site visits and/or contact references
3. Field initial questions from carriers

If you have constructed your RFP properly and included all necessary information, carrier questions should be limited to important issues and areas in which you have asked them to provide suggestions for alternate approaches. Having denoted contacts on your RFP, you should make sure that these people are available and are providing the required answers.

It is standard to give carriers two to three weeks to respond to the RFP. While it is possible to make them move faster, it does not really benefit anyone, as the proposals will reflect the haste with which they were prepared. If questions come in, it is customary to send out the answer in written form to everyone involved, again to make sure everyone is getting the same picture.

You do not necessarily need to visit a reference customer's site. You can gather plenty of information over the phone. Just make sure you have a complete list of the issues that you want to cover. At the end of the conversation, ask the person you are contacting what they would do differently so that you can benefit from their experience.

Following any on-site meetings or phone meetings, plan for a debriefing session. This can be E-mail or another meeting. The objective is to spread the information learned, and the impressions drawn, with the relevant decision makers and influencers.

### *Step 4: Evaluating Responses*

1. Review carrier proposals
2. Develop short-list if, appropriate
3. Develop list of questions and areas of clarification for each carrier
4. Conduct carrier meetings

5. Begin assigning evaluation ratings

As proposals are delivered, you and your colleagues should immediately begin reading them. You are looking for areas in which the carrier and/or vendor did not directly respond to the request and areas in which they have provided responses not meeting your requirements. The aim is to quickly develop a list of these issues, which is sent back to the carrier on the understanding that you will be expecting the bidder to address these issues in your scheduled meeting.

At some point, you should make a determination on the feasibility of going through with each meeting. We have had experiences in which carrier proposals are so far off the mark that the potential customer has simply told them they are no longer under consideration at this point. This usually sparks a rapid response from the carrier and it is at your discretion whether or not to allow them to amend the proposal. Historically, customers generally allow the carrier to make a recovery only to decide against them in the final analysis. If the carrier is really out of contention, it is a waste of everyone's time to allow them back into the process.

The next step is to have each carrier present its case in a face-to-face meeting. Carriers often see this as an opportunity to wow you with their multimedia slide show. Carriers will also attempt to jockey for position so that they are the first or last to present. For this reason, you should be proactive in setting up these appointments. Do not tell the carrier when the other meetings are. Also, make it clear that you will be sending them a list of issues to be covered in the meeting. Give negative marks to any carrier who insists on showing you their 45 minute Quicktime presentation, without regard to your specific network requirements and issues list.

Instead of having the carriers talk "at" you, you may want to consider designating this a working session. For example, you may want to schedule a half day for each carrier. Do not allow the carrier to set the agenda for the meeting. While it is acceptable for the carrier to make a presentation based on the issues you have raised, keep things on track and make the carrier respond to your specific questions about network design, support, implementation, pricing, and so on.

Have your sales person notify you prior to the meeting of the number of persons, including titles, attending. Don't allow more than two to five people or it becomes too difficult to manage the meeting. Make sure that the technical support person or the field engineer who will be supporting your account on an ongoing basis is present at this meeting. If this person has been instrumental in designing your network and will continue to provide ongoing technical support, you deserve the chance to judge his/her competency.

Make sure the carrier knows the agenda ahead of time, and the objectives to be accomplished in the meeting. This will save you from having to tell a person who has lugged an LCD projection screen from the parking garage that you would rather discuss issues than watch a "canned" presentation. Simple questions and answers should take up most or all of the agenda.

Use the meeting as an opportunity to understand what issues the carrier has considered in the network design and the implications of each on the final configuration. For example, after reading Chapter 10, you now know that running Novell SAPs over many PVCs can affect performance of the network. Therefore, if the carrier has designed a fully meshed configuration for your 30-site Novell LAN network, you may want to plan several questions regarding this design.

Begin to populate your evaluation matrix.

### *Step 5: Trimming It Down*

1. Complete evaluation of carriers
2. Select winner, or select finalists (no more than 2)
3. Compile list of remaining issues with each carrier

Once the meetings with each carrier have been completed, have each person involved in the evaluation process develop a list of strengths and weaknesses for each carrier. Have each person independently fill in the evaluation matrix. Also, each person should identify any deal "killers" which would, in themselves, prohibit the selection of a particular provider.

Once each person has formed his own impressions, you should consolidate all matrix information and present it in a single form. Develop a final rating for each carrier on each of the criteria, based on the average of all of the individual ratings. In a group meeting, you can discuss each carrier one by one. You may find a clear winner at this point, in which case you can begin focusing on implementation with that provider. However, in most cases, a few providers will be rated highly, necessitating a final meeting with the carriers on this short list.

### *Step 6: Picking the Winner*

1. Develop a further short list (if applicable)
2. Establish additional criteria for selecting a winner
3. Select your carrier
4. Notify other carriers of your choice and begin implementation

At this point, you should have the selection narrowed down to two providers at most. If possible, determine a few criteria that will be used to make the final determination of a winner. Price may or may not be one of these. If appropriate, communicate these final criteria for judgment to each carrier.

Do whatever is necessary to bring the decision to closure. If this means a trip to each carrier's network operations center (provided this hasn't already been done earlier in the process), get the trips scheduled and completed quickly. You may simply need to invite the carriers in for a final meeting in which they are asked to make any concessions on items still outstanding and to clarify any points with which you are not totally comfortable. Following this final round of meetings, make your choice.

It is possible that you are so torn between two providers that the best way to make a final decision is to provide each carrier with a network site at which to turn up service. This parallel implementation could provide you with the final puzzle piece that will allow you to choose the business partner that will provide the highest quality service and support. You can judge each carrier's ability to manage the implementation process on your behalf, solve implementation problems, test and establish your service.

Warning: This process of "parallel implementation" is guaranteed to drag out the RFP and network implementation process, so look before you leap. If you can establish a clear winner without this step, do it.

Once you have made your choice, the carriers not selected may make last-ditch efforts to win the business. Generally, it is not constructive to open up the process to these providers. Now is the time to get on with the implementation of your frame relay network.

## The Way Forward

Certainly, writing an RFP is a lot of work. It is an involved process, but with frame relay, a necessary one. In general, the more time spent up front with an RFP, the more successful your process will be. By defining and refining your descriptions, explanations, and structures in the RFP, you will provide the best guidance to the carriers. And that means the best output for your solution.

Best of luck in writing your RFP and implementing your frame relay network.

## CHAPTER 13:

# INTO THE FUTURE

Frame relay is only one of many new networking solutions coming of age in the 1990s. Network managers will be challenged to not only keep up with these new services and technology alternatives, but also to understand when, how and where each new alternative fits optimally into the enterprise network infrastructure.

This chapter will discuss future directions in new services and where frame relay fits in relation to these alternatives. It will look at carrier plans for allowing customers the ability to mix and match different solutions into a seamless internetwork.

Your objective is to insure that decisions you make today will not limit your flexibility in the future. Frame relay today does not limit other solutions tomorrow; in fact, your experiences with frame relay will improve your ability to evaluate and implement new services as they emerge. The carriers understand that users are concerned with technology obsolescence, and are taking steps to allow a smooth migration between services by supporting interworking between protocols and networks.

## Zones of Advantage: ATM, SMDS, Frame Relay

No single network protocol or service is going to be optimal for every site, every application, or every network. Ideally, you make decisions on a location-by-location basis. This means that each network site receives an optimized solution based on that site's needs, and continues to be optimized as the business environment changes.

Frame relay is one of three new public data networking services emerging in the 1990s, the other two being asynchronous transfer mode, ATM, and switched multimegabit data services, SMDS. There are at least three data networking alternatives, which have been brought forward from the 1980s: private lines, ISDN and X.25.

Where do these alternatives fit in relation to each other? Are they substitute technologies or complementary? Does implementing one mean that you are locked into that solution? How do the new services stack up against each other and how do they scale up and down?

Each different networking solution has certain advantages and disadvantages. Each service has a "zone of advantage." Within that zone, the service provides the most optimized connectivity solution. Some zones overlap.

These zones of advantage are typically best understood in the context of the number of sites, degree of connectivity, speed of connectivity, and type of applications to be supported.

It is difficult to draw a three- or four-dimensional chart that captures all of these attributes and, because of this problem, carriers often narrow down the attributes to two of the most important. Hence, the zones of advantage are expressed in two dimensions, as shown in Figure 13.1.

The applications, the speeds required, and the number of other locations in the network will all affect which service is optimal for your network. But often the needs of one site will be very different from the needs at others. For example, the applications, speed requirements and connectivity needs of your headquarters location is probably very different from a small remote sales office.

Not far in the future, you will be able to mix and match different networking solutions within the same network without losing connectivity. This will provide a very high level of investment protection and give you great flexibility in keeping pace with changing technologies and changing business needs.

However, when just getting started, it's best to start by implementing a single technology/service. This will provide experience and a point of reference for where other services can give you a relative advantage.

*Zones Of Advantage*

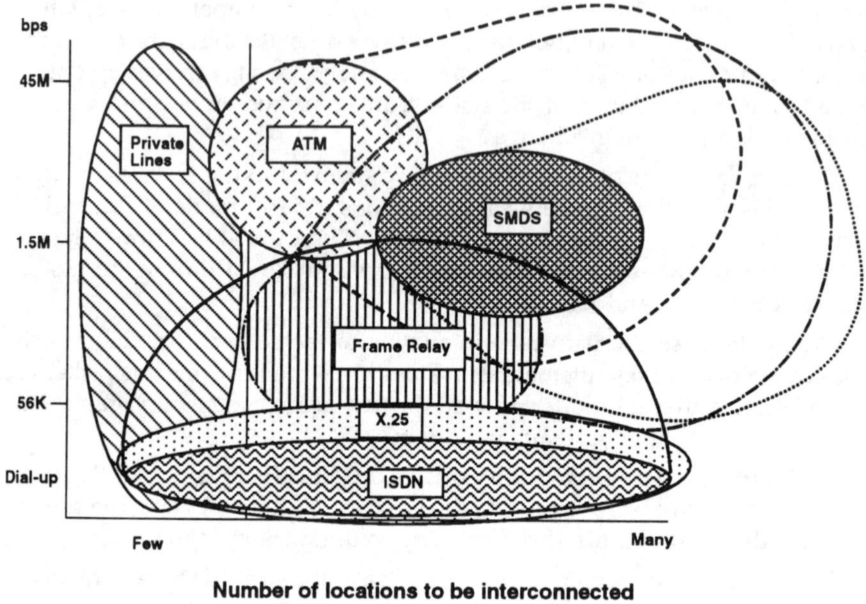


*Fig. 13.1: Each service has a unique zone of advantage for which it provides optimum network price performance. There is already some overlap in these zones, and new advances such as SVCs for frame relay and ATM, as well as expansions of the speeds addressed by each service, will increase the level of overlap in the zones.*

## *Meeting the Needs of Each Site*

The reason it is important to discuss the zones of advantages for different technologies and services is that within a corporate network there are many different types of locations. No single networking solution will meet the different needs of all these locations. You can take one of two approaches to network design. You can either try to maximize each location independently, or the maximization of the network as a whole can be the driver, even if a few sites have slightly sub-optimal solutions. You will probably begin with the latter approach, choosing a single network service that provides the best overall price/performance. Then, over time, as more services can be mixed and matched, you can begin to fine-tune each location's network solution.

Your small remote locations will need cost-effective connectivity into the enterprise network. Dial-up connectivity via analog data, ISDN, or X.25 might be the most appropriate solution at these locations. (See Figure 13.2.)

*Network Communication Needs Differ At Each Network Location*

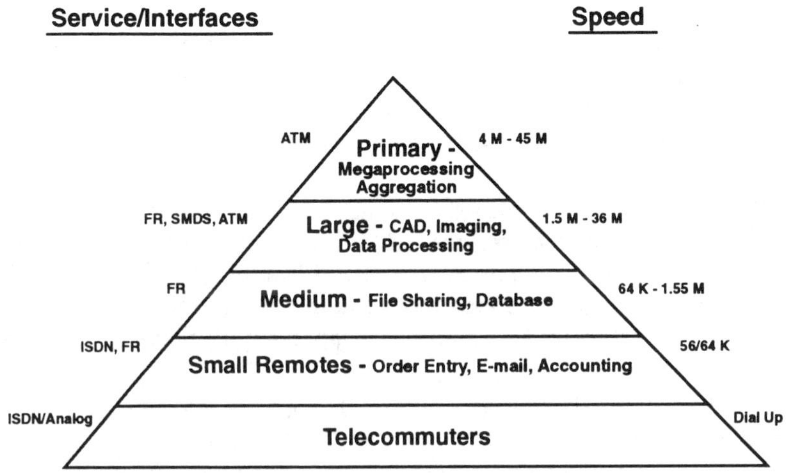


*Fig. 13.2: There is no single wide area network solution that optimally meets the needs of all the different business locations in an enterprise network. To gain an optimal configuration at each location, one would need to mix and match different services within the same network.*

A large number of your small sites might need 64K to 1.5M bps connectivity into the corporate backbone. The data applications at these sites might be best served by frame relay, especially if the user group is well defined as within an enterprise network. Other applications such as desktop video and multimedia applications, and even voice, can share the network given the correct equipment. While defined up to 1.5M bps today, there is already a 6M bps service available and a 45M bps frame relay standard under development.

SMDS is high-speed dial-tone for data and provides advantages where the user group is open and less-well defined, such as in the case of interenterprise connectivity. SMDS is like the postal service of data communications — you put an address on the data, drop it in the network, and it's delivered. SMDS' security protection would be like registered mail.

SVCs on frame relay will bring some overlap with SMDS, but SMDS offers standards for "addressing" and directories which frame relay does not. While the standard is defined for speeds of 1.5M to 34M bps, there are some SMDS offerings at 64K bps.

ATM is specifically designed to support voice, data and video applications. Eventually ATM services will offer differing quality of service parameters on different virtual connections to support the varying needs in each of these areas.

There will be variable bit rate services for data applications with guaranteed minimum throughput levels or with best-effort throughput. There will also be constant bit rate services that offer consistent delay and delay variance for applications, like voice and video, which do not tolerate variations in delay.

Overall, just as we have discussed consolidating different data applications onto the same frame relay service, ATM extends this further into non-data applications as well. To take advantage of this integration, you will need to integrate your voice, data and video either at the desktop through a multimedia application, or through using an ATM-capable multiplexer/concentrator on your premises.

Today, ATM is defined at speeds beginning at 45M bps, although some services begin at speeds as low as 1.5M bps. ATM, however, is not yet as well developed as frame relay or SMDS. There is still much work going on in the standards bodies and in the ATM Forum in defining traffic management, congestion management and different types of service.

Eventually, ATM will be a viable technology both as an underlying cell switching backbone with frame relay, ISDN, SMDS and other interfaces, as well as for end-to-end ATM services. At this writing, public ATM services are not yet ready to support production, mission-critical applications across the WAN. For locations needing speeds well in excess of 1.5M bps, private network solutions will remain the most viable solution for a while.

## *The Concept of Interworking*

Hybrid public/private networks provide a cost-effective solution to mix and match different network services. As we mentioned above, some locations will have frame relay; others switched digital data via ISDN; still others SMDS. To optimize the use of these services, you need to be able to seamlessly communicate from a site using one networking technology to a site using another networking technology. Carriers are working on a solution to allow you to mix and match different network services. Its called "interworking."

Interworking of technologies refers to the transparent protocol conversion or translation of those technologies. When performed by an intelligent network service, interworking gives you the ability to interface one or more locations using one protocol, and exit the network as a different protocol. The network performs the conversion based on the protocol of the destination location.

Best of all, a single network management system will provide visibility into all of the virtual connections, regardless of the protocol being used.

Interworking is still largely in test network implementation. Most service providers intend to eventually use an ATM backbone network to support frame relay, and possibly other interfaces such as SMDS, X.25, ISDN and TCP/IP and others. This service platform will allow complete interworking between locations, regardless of the interface protocol being used. (See Figure 13.3.)

*Service Interworking*

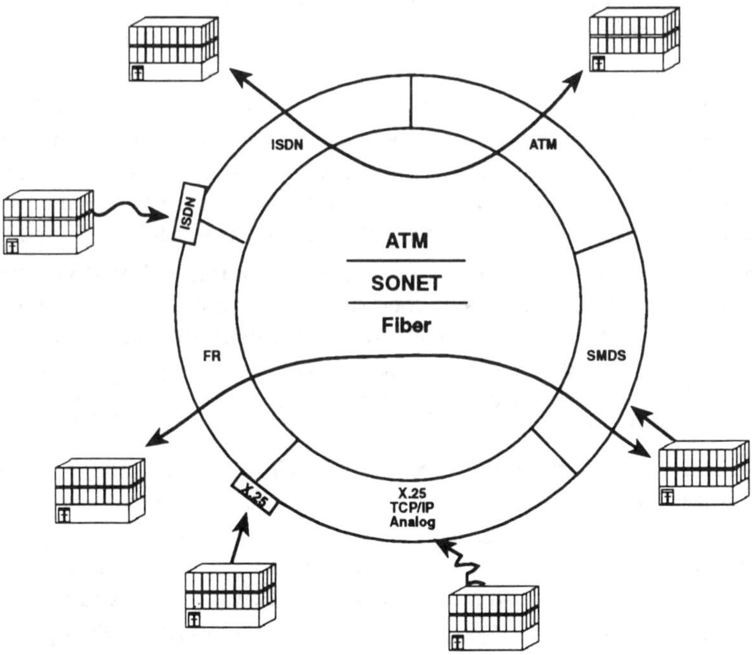


*Fig. 13.3: A cell relay backbone supporting different service interfaces and providing protocol conversion allows you to mix and match different solutions within a network to optimize overall price performance. Interworking means one can enter the network using one protocol and exit using a different protocol.*

When the interworking of different protocols, such as ATM and frame relay, is combined with emerging LAN emulation capabilities, a user on a traditional Ethernet LAN at one location can directly connect with a user on an ATM-based LAN, or ATM switch, at a different location. "Virtual LANs" can also be created with users spanning the country or the globe. Virtual LANs are logical groups of end users "assigned" to a particular local area network, instead of being physically connected to each other, or even being "local." A single user can belong to many collaborative work groups (i.e., virtual LANs), and receive all of the broadcasts, security features, and other services entitled to the users on that virtual LAN. The interworking of services means that a user at one location using a frame relay network interface can be part of the same virtual LAN as other users at different network sites using different protocols, such as ATM.

Private lines may also be one of the interfaces supported. This concept is often referred to as circuit emulation, because the virtual connection across the ATM WAN emulates a private line while still providing many of the automatic routing and dynamic allocation capabilities of ATM. The attractive element of circuit emulation is that the network performs the "cellification" of the information on the private line. You do not need to purchase additional ATM equipment.

The objective of interworking is to allow you to choose the optimal network solution at each network location and provide a smooth migration path between network services as the needs of locations change and grow. The reality of interworking as described here is not more than a few years away, with the first full products and services likely sometime in late 1995 or 1996.

In fact, some basic interworking services are available today. If you have some locations needing dial-up switched digital data connectivity, others better served by X.25 because of the existing equipment or underlying network infrastructure, and still others requiring frame relay, you are in luck. These technologies are already being interworked today to support certain classes of applications.

Two different carriers offer the ability to dial into a frame relay network, using X.25, and exit the network via frame relay (and vice versa). The network isn't yet performing the protocol conversion (it's more like encapsulation), but with a combination of your equipment and the carrier's network service you can achieve an end result that is very similar to interworking.

Recent announcements indicate that the interworking of ISDN and frame relay are imminent, adding additional service alternatives for cost-effective connectivity to small remote locations.

## Electronic Public Commerce

Some carriers are developing leading edge services that ride on top of a frame relay network and provide value-added network services to users. Some of the business applications these emerging public network services facilitate include:

- Image networking and the exchange of documents
- Electronic publishing
- Desktop videoconferencing and shared document and white board collaboration
- Electronic commerce and business transactions, including electronic billing, security services and audit trails
- Widespread use of the commercial, industrial-strength Internet

The advantage of using a public network service is that you decrease your initial investment and your ongoing administrative and operational costs. The service provider takes care of supporting security, bridging and connectivity, directories and the other necessary elements of applications, such as Lotus Notes, desktop collaboration, desktop conferencing and so on.

All you do is connect into the network using a dial-up, low-speed or high-speed connection. Instead of directly purchasing a new software application, you could use the public software available on the network. If you need to send a file or image to person in anther corporation, you use the public network to do so. If you want to establish a last minute conference with team members around the country or around the world, the network can handle all of the bridging and connectivity. The applications are endless.

Another example is electronic commerce. If your business distributes information, this distribution might be done electronically over the network. As multimedia applications hit the mainstream, even products such as car parts, fabrics or clothes, containers, and anything else you can imagine could be electronically "viewed" by potential buyers. The buyer could place an order over the same network, and either you or the carrier could bill the customer. You would receive an electronic copy of the order. This type of environment is sometimes referred to as a trader network. Trader networks can connect wholesale suppliers, retailers and customers together in a single electronic network.

Many of these value-added services and trader networks will be based on frame relay and cell relay infrastructures. One side effect of this trend to create value-added public network services for advanced business applications is that all businesses will have equal access. If your company doesn't have the staff or funds to constantly keep up with the newest technology advances, business applications and tools, you will no longer be at a competitive disadvantage. These applications will be available at your fingertips. You will simply need to decide which tools to take advantage of and how best to apply them.

### *Where Do SVCs Fit?*

As indicated earlier in this book, frame relay SVCs will probably not be widely available as part of public frame relay services until mid-to-late 1995 at best. It is unclear at this writing how the pricing for SVCs will equate to the pricing for PVCs. It is probably a fair assumption that for low volumes of traffic between two locations, or for highly intermittent applications, SVCs will be a cost-effective connectivity solution. SVCs will probably be more expensive than PVCs as the volume of traffic between two locations increases.

SVCs will likely be used for:

- ☎ Additional capacity to augment PVCs
- ☎ Support for highly intermittent applications, such as video/multimedia conferencing, or nightly/weekly remote database updates
- ☎ Connectivity between on-net locations where volumes are very low or highly unpredictable
- ☎ Connectivity between different corporations and other off-net locations
- ☎ Connections within trader networks and other interactive networks, such as shared multimedia databases, and electronic shopping/information services
- ☎ Back-up and reliability when used in combination with dial-up connectivity;
- ☎ Telecommuting in combination with ISDN access

You will probably use a combination of SVCs and PVCs within your frame relay network. Implementing frame relay with PVCs today will help you understand where and how to cost-effectively deploy SVCs when they become available.

## *Where Does SONET Fit In?*

You might be hearing a lot about SONET these days, in relation to high-speed applications. SONET stands for Synchronous Optical Network. It is a layer 1 (physical layer) technology that will complement and support the high-speed data services discussed above.

SONET will have a big impact on the way transmission streams are handled. It also will enhance network monitoring and maintenance, boost automatic network restoration from system failures and cable cuts, and allow smoother interoperation among carrier networks. It could also increase the supply side of the supply/demand equation for transmission services, eventually helping to reduce prices.

The need for SONET relates to the carriers' need for additional bandwidth and the desire to move to real-time provisioning. It will also help satisfy customer needs for high service reliability, through near-instantaneous re-routing.

### *SONET: From Electricity to Light*

In each carrier's point-of-presence, there is a lot of expensive equipment dedicated to multiplexing low-speed electrical transmission streams, like a DS-0 or DS-1 circuit, into high-speed electrical transmission streams, and then turning these high-speed signals into flashes of light that can be sent long distances over fiber optic cable. The low-speed channels are the basic building blocks for both public network services and private networks.

This multiplexing and demultiplexing process takes time. And the equipment adds points of possible failure, is expensive to maintain, and is always in danger of obsolescence.

SONET will eventually allow a single 64K bps DS-0 channel to be dropped out of, or inserted into, an optical transmission without bringing the entire signal down to the electrical level. Ultimately, this will save the carriers money in electronic multiplexing equipment and reduce the number of possible network failure points.

SONET will provide line and path performance information in real-time, in a way similar to extended superframe (ESF) monitoring on a DS-1, but better. The SONET equipment will not only calculate and report on performance; it will also react to the information it receives.

*Typical POP Architecture*

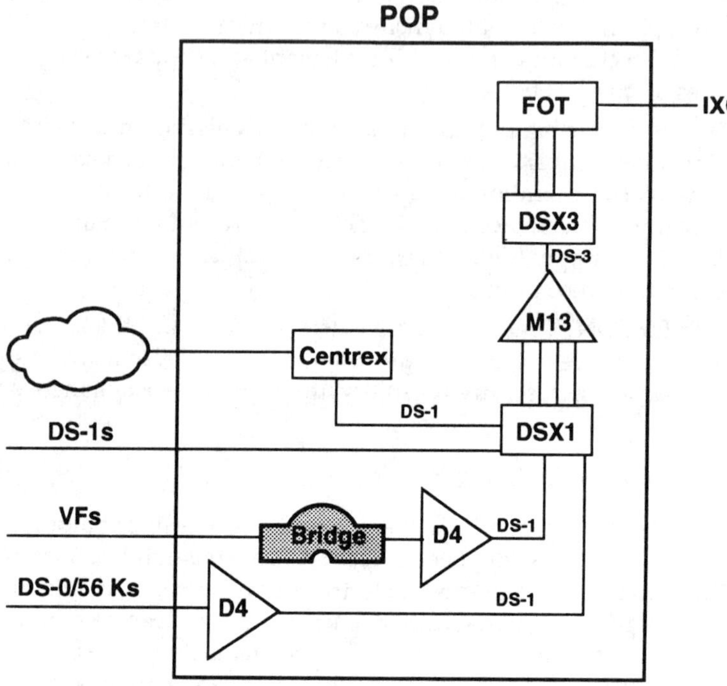


*Fig. 13.4: In the typical carrier point of presence there is a lot of equipment needed to multiplex low speed digital and analog electrical facilities up to higher speed electrical facilities and finally to a proprietary optical signal. SONET will eventually eliminate most of this multiplexing equipment.*

Today, the carriers each use proprietary optical transmission systems. This means that one carrier's network cannot interface with another carrier's network at an optical level. Once again, the transmission stream must be brought down to an electrical level. SONET offers an optical standard, which means that carrier networks will be capable of interfacing at very high speeds over optical interfaces.

### *Benefits of SONET*

SONET brings with it a range of user and carrier benefit. The manner in which SONET is implemented by a carrier can bring higher service availability. Carriers deploying SONET in ring, loop or mesh architectures will be enabling automatic routing around network failures. This is accomplished by reversing the traffic around these rings, or by intelligently selecting an alternate route. Each carrier will have its own unique SONET implementation plan, and the carriers will implement this survivability feature in different ways.

What does SONET mean in terms of new services? Initially, at least, very little. For those few users who require 155M or 622M bps between their locations (for scientific visualization or real-time animation applications, for instance), SONET is certainly one possible answer.

For the rest of the population, the deployment of SONET by the carriers will not immediately result in new services, but instead will trickle down in the form of indirect benefits. These will include higher network survivability and service availability, better network performance information, and eventually lower prices. SONET will be the backbone transmission system on which ATM and other data networking services will ride. Lower pricing would hopefully be the result of the carriers having more bandwidth available and spending less money on electrical multiplexing equipment.

So, SONET is something to be aware of, but is not a replacement for frame relay. Its more of a complementary technology.

## Should You Implement Frame Relay Now or Wait for Something Better?

If you are reading this book, then you are probably considering implementing a frame relay network. But with exciting new technologies such as ATM lurking just on the horizon, should you implement frame relay or wait for ATM?

Certainly, the answer to this question depends upon your networking situation. Most companies will find that frame relay is the most cost-effective connectivity solution today for the wide range of business locations and applications. It is well proven and available now. It provides many of the benefits associated with ATM at speeds and pricing that meet the current needs of most business locations.

Implementing frame relay now can bring you not just cost-savings, network consolidation, and flexibility today, but it can provide valuable experience for implementing other data networking services such as ATM in the future. You will gain experience with public data networking services, cost savings, and a migration path to ATM.

The interworking of technologies will provide the ultimate in network scalability, from dial-up to 45M bps. It will also allow sites using different services to maintain connectivity with other network locations, giving you investment protection and a smooth path of migration as business needs change.

If you're waiting for something better, more flexible, more scalable, or more cost-effective than frame relay, you may have a long wait.

So what are you waiting for?

Happy implementing!

# GLOSSARY

*3174*

IBM's cluster controller. It connects to terminals and other I/O devices on one end, and a mainframe channel on the other.

*3172 CONTROLLER*

IBM's network controller. It connects to the mainframe channel on one end and the LAN media (Ethernet, Token Ring, FDDI) on the other.

*3270 TERMINALS*

IBM class of terminals (or printers) used in SNA networks, often called "dumb" terminals when compared to their more intelligent cousin, the personal computer.

*3745 FRONT END PROCESSOR*

IBM's communications controllers, often called front-end processors. 3745 devices channel-attach to the mainframe and support connections to LANs and other FEPS.

*A/B SWITCH*

A switch that allows manual or remote configuration between one input and two outputs, where the input can first be cross-connected to the "A" output and later be reconfigured for cross-connection with the "B" output.

The devices are often used in disaster recovery or network recovery configurations.

*ACCESS LINK*

The local access connection between a customer's premises and a carrier's POP.

*ACCESS PROTECTION*

Refers to the process of protecting a local loop from network outages and failures. Access protection can take many forms, such as purchasing two geographically diverse local facilities, adding protection switches to the ends of geographically diverse local loops, or buying service from a local access provider that offers a survivable ring-based architecture to automatically route around network failures.

*AIW (APPN Implementer's Workshop)*

A group of vendors working with IBM to develop software and hardware consistent worth IBM's Advanced Peer-to-Peer Networking protocol.

*AMI (Alternate Mark Inversion) LINE CODING*

The line-coding format in T-1 transmission systems whereby successive ones (marks) are alternately inverted (sent with polarity opposite that of the preceding mark). Here's AT&T definition: A line code that employs a ternary signal to convey binary digits, in which successive binary ones are represented by signal elements that are normally of alternating, positive and negative polarity but equal in amplitude, and in which binary zeros are represented by signal elements that have zero amplitude.

*ANALOG*

Comes from the word "analogous," which means "similar to." In telephone transmission, the signal being transmitted — voice, video, or image — is "analogous" to the original signal. In other words, if you speak into a microphone and see your voice on an oscilloscope and you take the same voice as it is transmitted on the phone line and ran that signal into the oscilloscope, the two signals would look essentially the same. The only difference is that the electrically transmitted signal (the one over the phone line) is at a higher frequency. In correct English usage, "analog" is meaningless as a word by itself. But in telecommunications, analog means telephone transmission and/or switching which is not digital. See ANALOG TRANSMISSION.

*ANALOG TRANSMISSION*

A way of sending signals — voice, video, data — in which the transmitted signal is analogous to the original signal. In other words, if you spoke into a microphone and saw your voice on an oscilloscope and you took the same voice as it was transmitted on the phone line and threw that signal onto the oscilloscope, the two signals would look essentially the same. The only difference would be that the electrically transmitted signal would be at a higher frequency.

*ANNEX A*

The first of the frame relay standard extensions, Annex A outlines provisions for a local management interface (LMI) between customer premises equipment and the frame relay network for the purpose of querying network status information.

*ANNEX D*

The second frame relay standard extension dealing with the communication and signaling between customer premises equipment and frame relay network equipment for the purpose of querying network status information.

*APPC (Advanced Program-to-Program Communications)*

In SNA, the architectural component that allows sessions between peer-level application transaction programs. The LUs (Logical Units) that communicate during these sessions are known as LU type 6.2. APPC is an IBM protocol analogous to the OSI model's session layer: it sets up the necessary conditions that enable application programs to send data to each other through the network.

*APPLE AURP (Apple Update Routing Protocol)*

The network routing protocol developed by Apple for use with AppleTalk.

*APPLE TALK*

Apple Computer's proprietary networking protocol for linking Macintosh computers and peripherals, especially printers. This protocol is independent of what network it is layered on. Current implementations exist for LocalTalk (230.4K bps) and EtherTalk (10M bps).

*APPN (Advanced Peer to Peer Network Protocol)*

APPN is, according to its creator IBM, a leading-edge distributed networking feature IBM has added to its Systems Network Architecture (SNA). It provides optimized routing of communications between devices. In addition to simplifying the addition of workstations and systems to a network and enabling users to send data and messages to each other faster, APPN is designed to support efficient and transparent sharing of applications in a distributed computing environment. Because APPN permits direct communication between users anywhere on a network, it facilitates the development of client/server computing, in which workstation users anywhere on a network can share processing power, applications and data without regard to where the information is located. Workstations on an APPN network are dynamically defined so they can be relocated easily on the network without extensive re-programming. APPN also allows remote workstations to communicate with each other, without intervention by a central computer. Also, IBM's Advanced Peer-to-Peer Networking software.

*APS (Automatic Protection Switches)*

A switching device which automatically initiates the switching from a primary circuit to a secondary (usually geographically diverse) circuit when the error rate on the primary line exceeds a set threshold.

*ARCHITECTURE*

The architecture of a system refers to how it is designed and how the components of the system are connected to, and operate with, each other. It covers voice, video, data and text. Architecture includes the ability of the system to carry narrow, medium and broadband signals. It also includes the ability of the system to grow "seamlessly" (i.e., without too many large jumps in price).

*ARPAnet (Advanced Research Projects Agency NETwork)*

A Department of Defense data network, developed by ARPA, which ties together many users and computers in universities, government and businesses. ARPANET has been the forerunner of many developments in commercial data communications, including packet switching, which was first tested on a large scale on this network.

*AS/400*

IBM's mid-range mini computer. AS/400 stands for Application System/400.

*ASDS (Accunet Spectrum of Digital Services)*

AT&T's leased line (also called private line) digital service at 56K bps. MCI and Sprint have similar services. It is available in N x 56/64K bps, for N = 1, 2, 4, 6, 8, 12. The 56/64K bps POP-POP service (between long distance carrier central offices) costs the same as an analog line.

*ASYMMETRICAL PVC*

This terms refers to a PVC which supports simplex, or asymmetrical, assignments of committed information rates in each direction of transmission. A PVC transmission path is duplex, meaning that there must be a communications path in each direction between the two points being connected. However, with an asymmetrical PVC, the network capacity in each direction does not necessarily have to be equal.

*ASYNC or ASYNCHRONOUS TRANSMISSION*

Literally, not synchronous. A method of data transmission which allows characters to be sent at irregular intervals by preceding each character with a start bit, and following it with a stop bit. It is the method most small computers (especially PCs) use to communicate with each other and with mainframes today. In every form of data transmission, every letter, number or punctuation mark is transmitted digitally as "ons" or "offs." These characters are also represented as "zeros" and "ones" (See ASCII). The problem in data transmission is to define when the letter, the number or the punctuation mark begins. Without knowing when it begins, the receiving computer or terminal won't be able to figure out what the transmission means.

One way to do this is by using some form of clocking signal. At a precise time, the transmission starts, etc. This is called SYNCHRONOUS TRANSMISSION. In ASYNCHRONOUS transmission there's no clocking signal. The receiving terminal or computer knows what's what because each letter, number or punctuation mark begins with a start bit and ends with a stop bit. Transmission of data is called SYNCHRONOUS if the exact sending or receiving of each bit is determined before it is transmitted or received. It is called ASYNCHRONOUS if the timing of the transmission is not determined by the timing of a previous character.

ASYNCHRONOUS is used in lower speed transmission and by less expensive computer transmission systems. Large systems and computer networks typically use more sophisticated methods of transmission, such as SYNCHRONOUS or BISYNCHRONOUS, because of the large overhead penalty of 20% in ASYNCHRONOUS transmission. This is caused by adding one start bit and one stop bit to an eight bit word — thus 2 bits out of ten.

The second problem with large transfers is error checking. The user sitting in front of his own screen checks his ASYNCHRONOUS transmission by looking at the screen and re-typing his mistakes. This is impractical for transferring long files at high speed if there is not a person in attendance.

In SYNCHRONOUS transmission start and stop bits are not used. According to the book Understanding Data Communications, characters are sent in groups called blocks with special synchronization characters placed at the beginning of the block and within it to ensure that enough 0 to 1 or 1 to 0 transitions occur for the receiver clock to remain accurate. Error checking is done automatically on the entire block. If any errors occur, then the entire block is retransmitted. This technique also carries an overhead penalty (nothing is free), but the overhead is far less than 20% for blocks or more than a few dozen characters.

*ASYNCHRONOUS TERMINAL*

A terminal which utilizes asynchronous transmissions.

*ASYNCHRONOUS TRANSFER MODE (ATM)*

ATM is the technology selected by the Consultative Committee on International Telephone & Telegraph (CCITT) International standards organization in 1988 (now called the ITU-T) to realize a Broadband Integrated Services Digital Network (B-ISDN). It is a fast, cell-switched technology based on a fixed-length 53-byte cell. All broadband transmissions (whether audio, data, imaging or video) are divided into a series of cells and routed across an ATM network consisting of links connected by ATM switches. Each ATM link comprises a constant stream of ATM cell slots into which transmissions are placed or left idle, if unused. The most significant benefit of ATM is its uniform handling of services, allowing one network to meet the needs of many broadband services. ATM accomplishes this because its cell-switching technology combines the best advantages of both circuit-switching (for constant bit rate services such as voice and image) and packet-switching (for variable bit rate services such as data and full motion video) technologies. The result is the bandwidth guarantee of circuit switching combined with the high efficiency of packet switching.

*AUTOMATIC ADDRESS DISCOVERY*

This refers to the process by which a network device can poll other network devices to discover the network addresses that each device supports. Automatic address discovery makes the set up and on-going maintenance of complex internetworks much simpler than if all address updates were performed manually.

*AUTOMATIC NETWORK RESTORAL*

Automatic network restoral is a term which reflects the ability of a network to restore service rapidly and automatically following a catastrophic failure, such as a network cable cut. The result is higher network availability and reliability.

*AUTOMATIC REROUTING*

This refers to the process by which an intelligent voice or data network can automatically route a call or virtual circuit around a network failure. With frame relay, PVCs represent a fixed path through the network. However, in the event of a network failure along the primary path over which the PVC is routed, the PVC will be automatically routed to a secondary network path until the primary path is physically restored.

*BANDWIDTH*

The range of electrical frequencies a device can handle. The amount of bandwidth a channel is capable of carrying tells you what kinds of communications can be carried on it. A wide band circuit, for example, can carry a TV channel. A wide band circuit capable of providing one video channel can also provide 1,200 voice telephone channels.

***Bc (Committed Burst Rate)***

In the frame relay standards, this is the ratio between time and throughput over an individual virtual connection. Bc is equated with the committed information rate, or the rate at which traffic can be transmitted over the network without being eligible for discard.

***Be (Excess Burst)***

Traffic in excess of Bc is Be traffic. Traffic which is transmitted in excess of the CIR, often called burst traffic, is typically termed Be and is eligible for discard in the event of network congestion.

*BECN (Backward Explicit Congestion Notification)*

This bit notifies the user that congestion-avoidance procedures should be initiated for traffic in the opposite direction of the received frame. It indicates that the frames that the user transmits on this logical connection may encounter congested resources. In other words, slow down, you move too fast. Your bits may not get through or get delayed.

*BGP (Border Gateway Protocol)*

An interdomain routing protocol that is an alternative to EGP (Exterior Gateway Protocol). BGP is defined by RFC 1105.

*BISYNC*

(pron. Bye-sink). BISYNChronous Transmission. A half-duplex, character-oriented, synchronous data communications transmission method originated by IBM in 1964. See SYNCHRONOUS.

*BIT*

Bit is a contraction of the term BInary digiT. It is the smallest unit of information (data) a computer can process, representing either high or low, yes or no, or 1 or O. It is the basic unit in data communications. A bit can have a value of zero (a mark) or one (a space).

*BIT ROBBING*

The use of the least significant bit per channel in every sixth frame for signaling. See BIT STUFFING and ROBBED BIT SIGNALING.

*BIT STUFFING*

Process in some data communications protocols where a string of "one" bits is broken by an inserted "zero." This inserted zero is added by the sender and stripped by the receiver. The idea of inserting the zero is to avoid confusing the receiver into thinking the series of one bits mean something else, like a flag control character. See ZERO STUFFING.

*BIT-ORIENTED SYNCHRONOUS PROTOCOLS (BOP)*

A data link control protocol that uses specific bit patterns to transfer controlling information. Examples are IBM's Synchronous Data Link Control (SDLC) and the ITU-T High-Level Data Link Control (HDLC). Bit-oriented protocols are normally used for synchronous transmission only. Bit-oriented protocols are code transparent (meaning they work regardless of the character encoding method used), since no encoded characters are used in the control sequence.

*BRIDGE*

1. Verb: To connect one circuit or component to another in parallel. Imagine a phone line. It winds from your central office directly to your phone. Now imagine you want to connect another phone to that line. A phone works on two wires, tip and ring (positive and negative). You simply clamp each one of the phone's wires to the cable coming in. That's called bridging. You can do it with analog circuits. Because bridging often causes a loss in volume on the phone circuit and occasionally introduces spurious "noise" on the line, most of today's phone systems insist that the cabling from the central switching cabinet to the phone not be bridged — but be a direct run from the phone to the cabinet. You cannot bridge digital circuits, which require a direct, unbridged, link. That prohibition against bridging digital circuits applies to both digital telecommunications circuits and digital local area networks. 2. When two phones share the same number — line or trunk — they are considered bridged. Sometimes a bridge has associated components — e.g., amplifiers — to compensate for losses. 3. Noun: A device that connects two or more networks and forwards packets between them. The bridge may use similar or dissimilar media and signaling systems such as Ethernet, Token-Ring, and X.25. It operates at the data-link layer of the OSI model. Bridges sometimes work within a PC and sometimes within a special purpose computer. Bridges read and filter data packets and frames. A bridge is also called a data link relay or level 2 relay." When used for connecting LANs, a bridge connects LANs at the Medium Access Control (MAC) sub-layer of the OSI model's Data Link Layer. Bridges forward packets destined for another LAN. Bridges can be classified as source routing bridges, which are used in IBM environments, or transparent bridges, which operate primarily in non-IBM environments. A third bridging method, Source Routing Transparent (SRT), enables a bridge to act as both a transparent and a source routing bridge.

In voice and videoconferencing, a bridge connects three or more telecommunications channels so that they can all communicate together. In video conferencing, bridges are often called MCUs — Multipoint Conferencing Units. One feature of some video bridges is their ability to figure who's speaking and turn the camera onto that person and have that person be on everyone's screen. See INTERNETWORKING, ROUTERS, SOURCE ROUTING, and TRANSPARENT ROUTING.

*BROUTING*

Concatenation of "bridge" and "router." Used to refer to devices which perform both bridging and routing functions. In local area networking, a brouter is a device that combines the dynamic routing capability of an internetwork router with the ability of a bridge connect dissimilar local area networks (LANs). It has the ability to route one or more protocols, such as TCP/IP and XNS, and bridge all other traffic.

*BURSTING*

In data communication, a sequence of signals, noise, or interface counted as a unit in accordance with some specific criterion or measure.

*BYTE*

A popular microcomputer magazine, which derives its name from the true meaning of BYTE, which is eight bits of information composed of zeros or ones, one of which may include a parity bit. Most character sets, e.g. ASCII or EBCDIC, use one byte per character of information such as a letter, a number or digit, a punctuation mark or a symbol, such as $. A byte is to a bit what a word is to a character. In some circles a byte is called an octet. See BYTE COUNT.

*BYTE COUNT*

The number of 8-bit bytes in a message. Since ASCII characters typically have 8-bits, the byte count is also called the character count.

*CCITT (ITU-TSS)*

Comite Consultatif Internationale de Telegraphique et Telephonique, which, in English, means the Consultative Committee on International Telegraphy and Telephony. The CCITT is one of the four permanent parts of the International Telecommunications Union, the ITU, based in Geneva Switzerland. The scope of its work is now much broader than just telegraphy and telephony. It now also includes telematics, data, new services, systems and networks (like ISDN). The ITU is a United Nations Agency and all UN members may also belong to the ITU (at present 182), represented by their governments. In most cases the governments give their rights on their national telecom standards to their telecommunications administrations (PITs). But other national bodies (in the US, for example, the State Department) may additionally authorize Recognized Private Operating Agencies (RPOAs) to participate in the work of the CCITT. After approval from their relevant national governmental body, manufacturers and scientific organizations may also be admitted, as well as other international organizations. This means, says the ITU, that participants are drawn from the broad arena. The activities of the CCITT divide into three areas:

Study Groups (at present 15) to set up standard ("recommendations") for telecommunications equipment, systems, networks and services.

Plan Committees (World Plan Committee and Regional Plan Committee) for developing general plans for a harmonized evolution of networks and services.

Specialized Autonomous Groups (GAS, at present three) to produce handbooks, strategies and case studies for support mainly of developing countries.

Each of the 15 Study Groups draws up standards for a certain area — for example, Study Group XVIII specializes in digital networks, including ISDN. Members of Study Groups are experts from administrations, RPOAs, manufacturing companies, scientific or other international organizations — at times there are as many as 500 to 600 delegates per Study Group. They develop standards which have to be agreed upon by consensus. This, says the ITU, can sometimes be rather time-consuming, yet it is a democratic process, permitting active participation from all CCITT member organizations.

The long-standing term for such standards is "CCITT recommendations." As the name implies, recommendations have a non-binding status and they are not treaty obligations. Therefore, everyone is free to use CCITT recommendations without being forced to do so. However, there is increasing awareness of the fact that using such recommendations facilitates interconnection and interoperability in the interest of network providers, manufacturers and customers. This is the reason why CCITT recommendations are now being increasingly applied — not by force, but because the advantages of standardized equipment are obvious. ISDN is a good example of this.

CCITT has no power of enforcement, except moral persuasion. Sometimes, manufacturers adopt the CCITT specs. Sometimes they don't. Mostly they do. The CCITT standardization process runs in a four-year cycle ending in a Plenary Session. Every four years a series of standards known as Recommendations are published in the form of books. These books are color-coded to represent different four cycles. In 1980 the CCITT published the Orange Books, in 1984 the Red Books and, in 1988, the Blue Books.

The CCITT has now been incorporated into its parent organization, the International Telecommunication Union (ITU). Telecommunication standards are now covered under Telecommunications Standards Sector (TSS). ITU-T replaces CCITT. For example, the Bell 212A standard for 1200 bps communication in North America was referred to as CCITT V.22. It is now referred to as ITU-T V.22.

*CELL RELAY*

A form of packet switching using fixed length packets which results in lower processing and higher speeds. Cell relay is a generic term for a protocol based on small fixed packet sizes capable of supporting voice video and data at very high speeds. Information is handled in fixed length cells of 53 octets (bytes). A cell has 48 bytes of information and 5 bytes of address. The objective of cell relay is to develop a single high-speed network based on a switching and multiplexing scheme that works for all data types. Small cells (like 53 bytes) favor low-delay, a requirement of isochronous service. The downside to small cells is that the address information is almost 10 percent of the total packet. That's a high overhead. See ATM.

*CENTRALIZED ENVIRONMENT*

Refers to a network environment, or topology, in which decision making , file storage and other network functions are performed at a single, or centralized, location instead instead of being distributed through the network. This type of environment is typical hierarchical architectures, such as IBM's System Network Architecture and with mainframe-based applications.

*CHANNEL*

1. Typically what you rent from the telephone company. A voice-grade transmission facility with defined frequency response, gain and bandwidth. Also, a path of communication, either electrical or electromagnetic, between two or more points. Also called a circuit, facility, line, link or path. 2. An SCSA term. A transmission path on the SCbus or SCxbus Data Bus that transmits data between two end points. 3. A channel of a GPS (Global Positioning System) receiver consists of the circuitry necessary to tune the signal from a single GPS satellite.

*CHANNEL BANK*

A multiplexer. A device which puts many slow speed voice or data conversations onto one high-speed link and controls the flow of those "conversations." Typically the device that sits between a digital circuit — say a T-1 — and a couple of dozen voice grade lines coming out of a PBX. One side of the channel bank will be connections for terminating two pairs of wires or a coaxial cable — those bringing the T-1 carrier in. On the other side are connections for terminating multiple tip and ring single line analog phone lines or several digital data streams. Sometimes you need channel banks. Sometimes, you don't. For example, if you're shipping a bundle of voice conversations from one digital PBX to another across town in a T-1 format — and both PBXs recognize the signal — then you will probably not need a channel bank. You'll need a Channel Service Unit (CSU). If one, or both, of the PBXs is analog, then you will need a channel bank at the end of the transmission path whose PBX won't take a digital signal. See CHANNEL SERVICE UNIT and T-1.

*CHANNEL SERVICE UNIT (CSU)*

A device used to connect a digital phone line (T-1 or Switched 56 line) coming in from the phone company to either a multiplexer, channel bank or directly to another device producing a digital signal, e.g., a digital PBX, a PC, or data communications device. A CSU performs certain line-conditioning, and equalization functions, and responds to loopback commands sent from the central office. A CSU regenerates digital signals. It monitors them for problems. And it provides a way of testing your digital circuit. You can buy your own CSU or rent one from your local or long distance phone company.

*CHANNELIZED*

Subdividing a wideband channel into many smaller channels so it may carry many different streams of information.

*CIR (Committed Information Rate)*

A performance measurement of minimum "guaranteed" throughput on a user's PVC circuit for Frame Relay Service.

*CIRCUIT SWITCHED*

The process of setting up and keeping a circuit open between two or more users, such that the users have exclusive and full use of the circuit until the connection is released. There are basically three types of switching:

> CIRCUIT SWITCHING is like circuit switching in that you can also switch information between people or devices, but in packet switching (as in circuit switching), no circuit is left open on a dedicated basis. Circuit switching is like having your own railroad track for your conversation to travel on that's yours as long as you keep the connection open. Once you hang up, the next caller gets to use that track.
>
> PACKET SWITCHING is a data switching technique only. In packet switching, the addresses on your packets are read by the switches as they approach, and are switched down the tracks.

The next packet is read to throw the switches to send THAT packet where it needs to go. The data conversation is sent in packets. Each packet can be sent along different tracks as they are open. The packets are assembled at the other end — typically in the last switching office before the packets reach the distant computer or distant user.

MESSAGE SWITCHING sends a message from one end to the other. But it's not interactive, as in packet or circuit switching. In message switching, the message is typically received in one block, stored in one central place, then retrieved or sent in one clump to the other end.

*CLEAR CHANNEL*

1. Characteristic of a transmission path where the full bandwidth is available to the user. Primarily of digital circuits that do not require some part of the channel to be reserved for carrier framing or control bits, i.e., signaling. For example, a 56K bps circuit is typically a 64K bps digital circuit with 8K bps used for signaling. Sometimes called Switched 56, DDS or ADN. Each of the carriers have their own name for this service. The phone companies are obsoleting this service in favor of the more modern ISDN BRI, which has two 64K bps circuits and one 16K bps packet service, part of which is used for signaling on the 64K bps channels. 2. An SCSA term. A channel which is used exclusively for data transmission, with no bandwidth required for administrative messages such as signaling or synchronization. All SCbus data channels are clear.

*CLIENT-SERVER*

A computer on a local area network that you can request information or applications from. The idea is that you — the user — are the client and it — the slave — is the server. That was the original meaning of the term. Over time, client server began to refer to a computing system that splits the workload between PCs and one or more larger computers on a network. A good analogy, according to Peter Lewis of the New York Times is to think of client-server as a restaurant where the waiter takes your order for a hamburger, goes to the kitchen and comes back with some raw meat and a bun. You get to cook the burger at your table and add your favorite condiments. In computerese, this is distributed computing, where some processing work is done by the customer at his or her table, instead of entirely in the kitchen (centralized computing in the old mainframe days).

It sounds like more work, but it has many advantages. The service is faster. The food is cooked exactly to your liking, and the giant, expensive stove in the kitchen can be replaced by lots of cheap little grills. See DOWNSIZING, REENGINEERING and SERVER.

*CLUSTER CONTROLLER*

A device that can control input/output operations of more than one device connected to it (e.g., a terminal). An interface between several bisynchronous devices and a PAD, NC or communication facility. The cluster controller handles remote communications processing for its attached devices. Most common types are IBM 327X.

*CONCENTRATOR*

1. This telecommunications device allows a number of circuits (typically slow speed ones) to be connected to a smaller number of lines for transmission under the assumption that not all of the larger group of lines will be used at the same time. The concentrator allows a shared transmission medium to accommodate more data sources than there are channels currently available within the transmission medium. A concentrator's job is to save money on transmission. 2. Some LANs use concentrators, or access units, that allow network devices to be interconnected through a central point. The wiring is star, also called home run. Attaching devices through a central concentrator typically simplifies the maintenance of the LAN. A concentrator is used when connecting a LAN over the "normal" twisted wires in a building which were put there originally to carry voice and which now have to be used because — for one reason or another — it's not possible to connect the LAN using its normal bus coaxial cable connection.

*CONFIGURATION MANAGEMENT*

One of five categories of network management defined by the ISO (International Standards Organization), configuration management is the process of adding, deleting and modifying connections, addresses and topologies within a network.

*CONFIGURATION MANAGER*

1. A SCSA system service which manages configuration information and controls system startup. 2. An Intel Plug'n Play term. A driver, such as the ISA Configuration Utility, that configures devices and informs other device drivers of the resource requirements of all devices installed in a computer system.

*CONGESTION MANAGEMENT*

The ability of a network to effectively deal with heavy traffic volumes; solutions include traffic scheduling and enabling output ports to control the traffic flow.

*CONNECTIVITY*

Property of a network that allows remote network sites to communicate with each other.

*CONTIGUOUS SLOTTING*

This term refers to the process of selecting individual DS-0 circuits, within a DS-1 circuit or DS-3 circuit, which are adjacent to one another. Due to the timing difference that can result when non-adjacent channels are selected, contiguously slotted channels are preferable when the end equipment is designed to multiplex the individual low-speed channels into a single, higher speed connection.

***CPE (Customer Provided Equipment or Customer Premise Equipment)***

Originally it referred to equipment on the customer's premises which had been bought from a vendor who was not the local phone company. Now it simply refers to telephone equipment — routers, CSUs, key systems, PBXs, answering machines, etc. — which reside on the customer's premises. "Premises" might be anything from an office to a factory to a home.

***CPU (Central Processing Unit)***

The computing part of a computer. The "brain" of the computer. It manipulates data and processes instructions coming from software or a human operator.

*CSU*

1. Channel Service Unit. Also called a Channel Service Unit/Data Service Unit or CSU/DSU because it contains a built in DSU device. A device to terminate a digital channel on a customer's premises. It performs certain line coding, line-conditioning and equalization functions, and responds to loopback commands sent from the central office. A CSU sits between the digital line coming in from the central office and devices such as channel banks or data communications devices. A Channel Service Unit is found on every digital link and allows the transfer of data at a range greater than 56K bps. A 56K bps circuit would need a 56K bps DSU on both ends to transfer data from one end to the other. A CSU looks like a basic "modem," except it

can pass data at rates much greater and does not permit dial-up functions (unless it has an async dial-backup feature). 2. Channel Sharing Unit. Line bridging devices that allow several inputs to share one output. CSUs exist to handle any input/output combination of sync or async terminals, computer ports, or modems and thus these units are variously called modem sharing units, digital bridges, port sharing units, digital sharing devices, modem contention units, multiple access units, control signal activated electronic switches or data-activated electronic switches.

*D CHANNEL*

In an ISDN interface, the "D" channel (the Data channel) is used to carry control signals and customer call data in a packet switched mode. In the BRI (Basic Rate Interface, i.e., the lowest ISDN service), the "D" channel operates at 16,000 bits per second, part of which will carry setup, teardown, ANI and other characteristics of the call. 9,600 bps will be free for a separate conversation by the user. In the PRI (Primary Rate Interface, i.e. ISDN equivalent of T-1), the "D" channel runs at 64,000 bits per second. The "D" channel provides the signaling information for each of the 23 voice channels (referred to as "B channels"). The actual data which travels on the "D" channel is much like that of a common serial port.

Bytes are loaded from the network and shifted out to the customer site in a serial bit stream. The customer site, of course, responds with its serial bit stream, too. An example of a data packet sent from the network to indicate a new call has the following components:

Customer Site ID

Type of Channel Required (Usually a "B" channel)

Call Handle (Not unlike a file handle)

ANI and DNIS information

Channel Number Requested

A Request for a Response

This packet is responded to by the customer site with a format similar to:

Network ID

Channel Type is OK

Call Handle

The packets change as the state of the call changes, and finally ends with one side or the other sending a disconnect notice. The important concept here is the fact the information on the "D" channel could actually store anything

— any kind of serial data. It could just as well be sports scores! So with that in mind, consider the Channel Number Requested packet above. This is the networks' selected channel for the customer site to use.

Normally, this number is between 1 and 23, but could be a higher number if needed. This is what NFAS is all about. NFAS (Non Facility Associated signaling, pronounced N-FAST without the T) allows a "D" channel to carry call information regarding channels which may not even exist in the same PBX or PC system. See also ISDN and DS-0.

*DATA*

This is AT&T Bell Labs' definition: "A representation of facts, concepts or instructions in a formalized manner, suitable for communication, interpretation or processing." Typically anything other than voice.

*DATA LINK*

A term used to describe the communications link used for data transmission from a source to a destination. In short, a phone line for data transmission. Or, a fiber optic transmitter, cable, and receiver that transmits digital data between two points.

*DATA LINK CONNECTION IDENTIFIER (DLCI)*

The frame relay virtual circuit number corresponding to a particular destination which is part of the frame relay header and is usually ten bits long. The DLCI is typically associated with a particular PVC on the network.

*DCS or DACS (Digital Cross-Connection System)*

A specialized type of high-speed data channel switch. It differs from a normal voice switch, which switches transmission paths in response to dialing instructions. In a digital cross-connect system, you give it separate and specific instructions to connect this line to that. These instructions are given independently of any calls that might flow over the system. This contrasts with a normal voice switching in which switching instructions and conversations go together. Commands to a digital cross-connect system can be given by an operator at a console or can be programmed to switch at certain times. For example, you might want to change the T-1 24-voice conversation circuit to Chicago at 11 A.M. each day to allow for the president's 30 minute video conference call.

*DDS*

1. Dataphone Digital Service, also called Digital Data System. DDS is private line digital service, typically with data rates at 2,400, 4,800, 9,600 and 56,000 bits per second. DDS is offered on an inter-LATA basis by AT&T and on an intra-LATA basis by the Bell operating companies. AT&T has now incorporated it into their Accunet family of offerings. But, by the time you read this, they may have a new name for the service, like Accunet. 2. Digital Data Storage. A DAT format for storing data. It is sequential — all data that is recorded to the tape falls after the previous block of data.

*DE (Discard Eligible)*

The frame relay standard specifies that data sent across a virtual connect in excess of that connection's committed information rate (CIR) will be marked by the network as being eligible for discard in the event of network congestion. DE data is the first to be discarded by the network when congestion occurs, thus providing protection for data sent within the parameters of the CIR. It is the responsibility of the intelligent end equipment and/or protocol to recognize the discard and respond by resending the information.

*DEC (Digital Equipment Corporation)*

A leading manufacturer of minicomputers. The Unix operating system, developed at Bell Labs, runs on DEC computers. DEC, with its headquarters in Massachusetts and having sold so many computers to Western Electric for inclusion in central office switches and toll switches, is sometimes referred to as "Eastern Electric." Kenneth H. Olsen founded DEC in 1957 with three employees in 8,500 square feet of leased space in a corner of an old woolen mill.

*DEC LAT*

A proprietary data communications protocol developed by DEC.

*DECnet*

DEC's proprietary Ethernet LAN that works across all of the company's machines, endowed with a peer-to-peer methodology. See DEC.

*DIGITAL SUBSCRIBER LINE*

A fancy name for an ISDN BRI channel. Here's AT&T's definition: "A three-channel digital line that links the ISDN customer's terminal to the telephone company switch with four ordinary copper telephone wires. Operated at the Basic Rate Interface (with two 64-kilobit per second circuit switched channels and one 16-kilobit packet switched channel), the DSL can carry both voice and data signals at the same time, in both directions, as well as the signaling date used for call information and customer data. With the introduction of the AT&T 5E5 generic, up to eight different users can be served by a single DSL." See also ISDN.

*DISTANCE VECTOR*

An approach, or algorithm, used by network equipment in selecting the best available network path by calculating the total distance over which a packet would travel on each alternative route. The shortest distance is usually the most preferred. However, it is possible to consider other factors in the decision as well.

*DISTRIBUTED ENVIRONMENT*

Refers to a network environment, or topology, in which decision making, file storage and other network functions are not centralized but, instead, are found through the network. This type of environment is typical for client-server applications and peer-to-peer architectures.

*DISTRIBUTION FRAME*

Cables coming in from thousands of subscribers need to connect to the correct ports on a central office. Similarly, cables coming in from many PBX extensions need to connect to the PBX. The cables could be directly wired to the CO or to the PBX. This would be inflexible. It would make future moves and changes a nightmare. So the solution is something called a Distribution Frame. Basically it's a giant wire connecting devices made of metal. There are no electronics in it. On one side we punch down the wires coming in from the outside world. On the other side, we punch down the wires coming in from the CO or PBX. Both sides are connected with wire that's called "jumper" wire. By pulling off one end of the jumper wire and moving it to another location we can quickly change phone numbers, add or subtract cabling (one, two or three pairs for normal or electronic phones, etc.). In big central offices, distribution frames can span whole city blocks and the "jumper" wires can be several hundred yards long. Designing distribution frames and their layout in advance is critical. Otherwise, it becomes a mess and tracing where jumper wires go becomes an enormously time consuming job.

*DLCI (Data Link Connection Identifier)*

The frame relay virtual circuit number corresponding to a particular destination which is part of the frame relay header and is usually ten bits long.

*DLSw (Data Link Switching)*

IBM's method for carrying SNA and NetBIOS over TCP/IP operating at the Data Link layer. DLSw, now an open Internet spec, can be used with OSPF or PPP.

*DOS (Disk Operating System)*

As in MS-DOS, which stands for MicroSoft Disk Operating System. DOS is the software that organizes how a computer reads, writes and reacts with its disks — floppy or hard — and talks to its various input/output devices, including keyboards, screens, serial and parallel ports, printers, modems, etc. The most popular operating system for PCs is MS-DOS from Microsoft, Bellevue, WA.

*DOWNSIZING*

Downsizing is what happens when companies move from large computer systems to smaller systems. There are four major reasons companies downsize from mainframe-based computer to local area network-based computing:

1. They save money. There are several reasons: a. Mainframe computers cost lots each month in maintenance. They require costly maintenance agreements with the supplier, e.g. IBM. Servers are usually bought without maintenance agreements. When they break, the managers or the workers simply replace the broken parts themselves. b. Mainframe computers cost lots to program. There are comparatively few programs available for mainframes, compared to the plethora of off-the-shelf programs available for workstations. c. Servers require far less costly homes to live. You don't need air-conditioning, special buildings with raised floors, etc.

2. Servers today have the power of mainframes from 10 years ago. In fact, servers are now beginning to acquire more power than the mainframes of ten years ago. And, as servers increasingly acquire several processors, they will leap in power beyond what mainframes have.

3. Servers are typically manufactured from off-the-shelf, standard components that are usually available from several manufacturers. As a result, there is constant competition and constant improvement in quality and features.

4. Servers are much more flexible tools to design networks. You can start with one baby network containing one server and several workstations (a.k.a. clients) and confined to one floor of one small building and grow to a huge, complex network containing thousands of workstations, dozens of servers and spanning the globe.

To most people, downsizing is not only swapping out the "big iron" (the mainframe) and bringing in servers and local area networks. It's also a new way of thinking about the way corporations are organized. Downsizing is often accompanied by re-engineering, which is basically re-organizing for a greater focus on the customer — a focus which means responding faster to customer needs. See SERVERS.

*DS-0 (Digital Service, level 0)*

It is 64,000 bps, the worldwide standard speed for digitizing one voice conversation using pulse code modulation (PCM). There are 24 DS channels in a DS-1.

*DS-1 (Digital Service, level 1)*

It is 1.544 M bps in North America, 2.048 M bps elsewhere. Why there's no consistency is one of those wonderful, unanswered, questions. The 1.544 standard is an old Bell System standard. The 2.048 standard is a ITU-T standard. Standard for 1.544 M bps is 24 voice conversations each encoded at 64K bps. Standard for 2.048 megabits is 30 conversations.

*DS-3 (Digital Service, level 3)*

Equivalent to 28 T-1 channels, and it operates at 44.736 M bps. Also called T-3.

*DSU (Data Service Unit)*

Device designed to connect a DTE (Data Terminal Equipment like a PC or a LAN) to a digital phone line to allow fully-digital communications. A DSU is sort of the digital equivalent of a modem. In more technical terms, a DSU is a type of short haul, synchronous data line driver, normally installed at a user location that connects a user's synchronous equipment over a 4-wire circuit to a serving dial-central-office. This service can be for a point-to-point or multipoint operation in a digital data network. DSUs are typically used for low-speed leased lines. For switched digital services or high-speed private lines of speeds greater than 56K bps, you need a CSU/DSU also called a DSU/CSU. See CSU/DSU and DSU/CSU.

### *DTMF (Dual Tone Multi-Frequency)*

A fancy term describing push button or Touchtone dialing. (Touchtone is a not registered trademark of AT&T, through until 1984 it was.) In DTMF, when you touch a button on a push button pad, it makes a tone, actually a combination of two tones, one high frequency and one low frequency. Thus the name Dual Tone Multi Frequency. In U.S. telephony, there are actually two types of "tone" signaling, one used on normal business or home push button/touchtone phones, and one used for signaling within the telephone network itself. When you go into a central office, look for the test board. There you'll see what looks like a standard touchtone pad. Next to the pad there'll be a small toggle switch that allows you to choose the sounds the touchtone pad will make — either normal touchtone dialing (DTMF) or the network version (MF). The eight possible tones that comprise the DTMF signaling system were specially selected to easily pass through the telephone network without attenuation and with minimum interaction with each other. Since these tones fall within the frequency range of the human voice, additional considerations were added to prevent the human voice from inadvertently imitating or "falsing" DTMF signaling digits. One way this was done to break the tones into two groups, a high frequency group and a low frequency group. A valid DTMF tone has only one tone in each group. Here is a table of the DTMF digits with their respective frequencies. One Hertz (abbreviated Hz.) is one cycle per second of frequency.

| | Low frequency | High frequency |
|---|---|---|
| 1 | 697 Hz. | 1209 Hz. |
| 2 | 697 | 1336 |
| 3 | 697 | 1477 |
| 4 | 770 | 1209 |
| 5 | 770 | 1336 |
| 6 | 770 | 1477 |
| 7 | 852 | 1209 |
| 8 | 852 | 1336 |
| 9 | 852 | 1477 |
| 10 | 941 | 1336 |
| 11 | 941 | 1209 |
| 12 | 941 | 1477 |

There are four other digits defined in the DTMF system and usable for specialized applications that cannot be generated by standard telephones. They are:

| | | |
|---|---|---|
| A | 697 Hz. | 1633 Hz. |
| B | 770 | 1633 |
| C | 852 | 1633 |
| D | 941 | 1633 |

Normal telephones (yours and mine) have 12 buttons, thus 12 combinations. Government Autovon (Automatic Voice Network) telephones have 16 combinations, the extra four (those above) being used for "precedence," which in Federal government parlance is a designation assigned to a phone call by the caller to indicate to communications personnel the relative urgency (therefore the order of handling) of the call and to the called person the order in which the message is to be noted.

***DUAL (Distributed Update Algorithm)***

A routing algorithm that provides fast rerouting (convergence) with minimal consumption of resources.

*DUAL HOMING*

1. The process of using two geographically diverse frame relay port connections, each with its own set of virtual circuits, to support a network location running critical business applications which cannot afford network down time.

2. A method of cabling FDDI concentrators and stations that permits a alternative path to the dual ring. Can be used in a tree or dual ring of trees topology.

*DUMB TERMINAL*

A computer terminal with no processing or no programming capabilities. Hence, it derives all its power from the computer it is attached to — typically over a local hardwire or a phone line. A dumb terminal does not employ a data transmission protocol and only sends or receives data one character at a time, sequentially. There are many reasons for "dumb" terminals. They're cheap. They're foolproof. Operators don't have to mess with floppy disks, etc. The require minimal training. Dumb terminals are typically used for simple data entry and data retrieval tasks. Their disadvantage is that everything must come from the central computer — not only the information (data record) but also the form in which to put it. This has led to the creation of "intelligent" terminals, which have a modicum of capabilities — such as an inbuilt (with software) form, some smart function keys and perhaps, a modicum of processing power, etc.

*EA (Extended Addressing)*

In many bit-oriented protocols, extended addressing is a facility allowing larger addresses than normal to be used. In IBM's SNA, it is the addition of two high-order bits to the basic addressing scheme. The frame relay standard also includes extended addressing bits.

*EDGE SITE*

A remote network site. A site at the edge of the network.

*EGRESS*

The exit point. This typically refers to information being sent out of, as opposed to being sent into, a frame relay port connection or other network element.

*EIGRP (Enhanced Interior Gateway Routing Protocol)*

Cisco System's newest version of its proprietary routing algorithm, IGRP.

*E-MAIL*

A colloquial term for electronic mail. See E-MAIL address.

*E-MAIL ADDRESS*

The UUCP or domain-based address by which a user is referred to.

*EMULATE*

To duplicate one system with another. To imitate a computer or computer system by a combination of hardware and software that allows programs written for one computer or terminal to run on another. The most common data terminal is a DEC VT-100. Our communications program, Crosstalk, allows us to "emulate" a DEC-VT100 on our IBM PCs and PC clones.

*EMULATION*

What happens one gadget emulates another. See EMULATE.

*EN (End Node)*

A node such as a PC that can only send and receive information for its own use. It cannot route and forward information to another node.

### *ENCAPSULATION*

1. Encasing a splice or closure in a protective material to make it watertight. 2. In object-oriented programming, the grouping of data and the code that manipulates it into a single entity or object. Encapsulation refers to the hiding of most of the details of the object. Both the attributes (data structure) and the methods (procedures) are hidden. Associated with the object is a set of operations that it can perform. These are not hidden. They constitute a well-defined interface — that aspect of the object that is externally visible. The point of encapsulation is to isolate the internal workings of the object so that, if they must be modified, those changes will also be isolated and not affect any part of the program.

### *ERLANG*

A measurement of telephone traffic. One Erlang is equal to one full hour of use (e.g. conversation), or 60 x 60 = 3,600 seconds of phone conversation. You convert CCS (hundred call seconds) into Erlangs by multiplying by 100 and then dividing by 3,600 (i.e. dividing by 36). Numerically, traffic on a trunk group, when measured in erlangs, is equal to the average number of trunks in use during the hour in question. Thus, if a group of trunks carries 12.35 erlangs during an hour, a little more than 12 trunks were busy, on the average.

Erlang gets its name from the father of queuing theory, A. K. Erlang, a Danish telephone engineer, who, in 1908, began to study congestion in the telephone service of the Copenhagen Telephone Company. A few years later he arrived at a mathematical approach to assist in designing the size of telephone switches. Central to queuing theory are basic facts of queuing life. First, traffic varies widely. Second, anyone who designs a telephone switch to completely handle all peak traffic will find the switch idle for most of the time. He was also to find that he had built a very expensive switch. Third, it is possible, with varying degrees of certainty to predict upcoming "busy" periods. See also ERLANG, A.K., ERLANG B, ERLANG C and POISSON.

### *ERLANG B*

A probability distribution developed by A.K. Erlang to estimate the number of telephone trunks needed to carry a given amount of traffic. Erlang B assumes that, when a call arriving at random finds all trunks busy, it vanishes (the blocked calls cleared condition). Erlang B is also known as "Lost Calls Cleared." Erlang B is used when traffic is random and there is no queuing. Calls which cannot get through, go away and do not return. This is the primary assumption behind Erlang B. Erlang B is easier to program than Poisson or Erlang C. This convenience is one of its main recommendations. Using Erlang B will produce a phone network with fewer trunks than one using Poisson formulae. See also ERLANG, ERLANG A. K., ERLANG C, and TRAFFIC ENGINEERING.

*ERLANG C*

A formula for designing telephone traffic handling for PBXs and networks. Used when traffic is random and there is queuing. It assumes that all callers will wait indefinitely to get through. Therefore offered traffic (see ERLANG) cannot be bigger than the number of trunks available (if it is, more traffic will come in than goes out, and queue delay will become infinite). Erlang C is not a perfect traffic engineering formula. There are none.

*ERLANG, A. K.*

In 1918, A. K. Erlang, a Danish telephone engineer, published his work on blocking in The Post Office Electrical Engineers' Journal, a British publication. Like E.C. Molina, an AT&T engineer, Erlang assumed a Poisson distribution of calls arriving in a given time. Molina had assumed a constant holding time for all calls, whereas Erlang assumed an exponential distribution for holding times. That means that longer calls occur less frequently than shorter calls. Erlang assumed that blocked calls are immediately cleared and lost and do not return. A formula that Erlang worked out based on these assumptions (Erlang B) is still in use in telephone engineering. See ERLANG, ERLANG B, ERLANG C and POISSON.

*ERLANG (Formula)*

A mathematical way of making predictions about randomly arriving work-load (such as telephone calls) based on known information (such as average call duration). Although traditionally used in telephone traffic engineering (to determine the required number of trunks), Erlang formulas have application in call center staffing as well. See ERLANG.

*ERROR CHECKING AND CORRECTION*

Error checking is the process of checking a "packet" being transmitted over a network to determine if the package, or the data content within the package, has been damaged. Damaged packets are discarded. Error correction in the process of correcting the damage by resending a copy of the original packet. In public frame relay services, the network performs the function of error checking, but not error correction. That function is left to the intelligent end equipment.

*ESF (Extended Superframe Format)*

A new T1 framing standard used in Wide Area Networks (WANs). With this format 24 frames — instead of 12 — are grouped together. In this grouping, the 8,000 bps frame is redefined as follows:

> 2,000 bps for framing and signaling to provide the functions generally defined in the D-4 format.
>
> 2,000 bps are CRC-6 (Cyclic Redundancy Check-code 6) to detect logic errors caused by line equipment, noise, lightning and other interference. Performance checking is done by both the carrier and the customer without causing any interference with the T-1 traffic.
>
> 4,000 bps are used as a data link. This link is to perform functions such as enhanced end-to-end diagnostics, networking reporting and control, channel or equipment switching, and/or optional functions or services.

*ETHERNET*

A local area network used for connecting computers, printers, workstations, terminals, etc., within the same building. Ethernet operates over twisted wire and over coaxial cable at speeds up to 10M bps. For LAN interconnection, Ethernet is a physical link and data link protocol reflecting the two lowest layers of the DNA/OSI model. The theoretical limit of Ethernet, measured in 64 byte packets, is 14,800 packets per second (PPS). By comparison, Token Ring is 30,000 and FDDI is 170,000.

Ethernet specifies a CSMA/CD (Carrier Sense Multiple Access with Collision Detection). CSMA/CD is a technique of sharing a common medium (wire, coaxial cable) among several devices. As Byte Magazine explained in its January, 1991 issue, Ethernet is based on the same etiquette that makes for a polite conversation: "Listen before talking." Of course, even when people are trying not to interrupt each other, there are those embarrassing moments when two people accidentally start talking at the same time. This is essentially what happens in Ethernet networks, where such a situation is called a collision. If a node on the network detects a collision, it alerts the other nodes by jamming the network. Then, after a random pause, the sending nodes try again. The messages are called frames:

1. Preamble - 8 bytes
2. Destination address - 6 bytes
3. Source address - 6 bytes

4. Type - 2 bytes
5. Data - up to 1500 bytes
6. Frame check sequence - 4 bytes (contains CRC check)

The first personal computer Ethernet LAN adapter was shipped by 3Com on September 29, 1982 using the first Ethernet silicon from SEEQ Technology. Bob Metcalfe created the original Ethernet specification at Xerox PARC and later went on to found 3Com. This Ethernet cable and Ethernet cards dropped from about $5,000 to $750 and 3Com went off like a rocket ship. Now you can buy an Ethernet card to connect your PC to an Ethernet LAN for under $100. Ethernet PC cards now come in a couple of basic varieties — for connecting to an Ethernet LAN via coaxial cable or via two twisted pairs of phone wires, called 10Base-T.

*EXTENDED ADDRESSING*

In many bit-oriented protocols, extended addressing is a facility allowing larger addresses than normal to be used. In IBM's SNA, it is the addition of two high-order bits to the basic addressing scheme.

*FAST PACKET MULTIPLEXING*

Multiplexing is putting more than one "conversation" onto one circuit. You can do this in either of two ways — by splitting the channels sideways into subchannels of narrower frequency. This is called Frequency Division Multiplexing. Or you could split it by time, like a railroad train. The first car carries "Conversation 1." The second carries "Conversation 2." And split them apart at the other end.

*FAULT ISOLATION*

The process of determining where a network problem, or fault, is located.

*FAULT MANAGEMENT*

Detects, isolates and corrects network faults. It is also one of five categories of network management defined by the ISO (International Standards Organization).

*FECN (Forward Congestion Notification Bits)*

This bit notifies the user that congestion-avoidance procedures should be initiated where applicable for traffic in the same direction as the received frame. It indicates that this frame, on this logical connection, has encountered congested resources.

### *FIBER OPTIC*

A technology in which light is used to transport information from one point to another. More specifically, fiber optics are thin filaments of glass through which light beams are transmitted over long distances carrying enormous amounts of data. Modulating light on thin strands of glass produces major benefits in high bandwidth, relatively low cost, low power consumption, small space needs, total insensitivity to electromagnetic interference and great insensitivity to being bugged. All of these benefits have great attraction to anyone who needs vast, clean transmission capacity, to the military and to anyone who runs a factory with lots of electronic machinery.

The first field trial of an AT&T lightwave system took place in Chicago in 1977. There has been a rapid improvement in cost effectiveness of fiber systems, expressed as cost per bit per kilometer. A one hundredfold decrease in cost in one five year period — from about 1980 to 1985! Some versions of fiber optics new carry two billion pulses of light a second to carry more than 30,000 times the information of electronic signals over copper wire. See LEDs.

### *FILTERING TRAFFIC*

This is the process of selecting which traffic will be allowed into a certain portion of a network, such as the wide area network. It is also the process of determining which traffic is transmitted first, then next, and so on. The traffic is compared to a filter, or a set of specifications, to determine if it can pass through or not.

### *FLAG*

1. A variable in a program to inform the program later on that a condition has been met. 2. In synchronous transmission, a flag is a pattern of six consecutive "1" bits used to mark the beginning and end of a "Frame" (IBM jargon for a packet). The character representation of the six consecutive "1" bits is 01111110. See ZERO STUFFING.

### *FLOW CONTROL*

1. The hardware, software and procedure for controlling the transfer of messages or characters between two points in a data network — such as between a protocol converter and a printer — to prevent loss of data when the receiving device's buffer begins to reach its capacity. 2. The process of protecting network service by denying access to additional traffic that would further add to congestion. See FLOW CONTROL PROCEDURE.

*FLOW CONTROL PROCEDURE*

The procedure for controlling the rate of transfer of data among elements of a network, e.g., between a DTE and a data switching exchange network, to prevent overload.

*FOUR-WIRE CIRCUIT*

A path in which four wires are presented to the terminal equipment (phone or data), thus allowing for simultaneous transmission and reception. Two wires are used for transmission in one direction and two in the other direction.

*FRACTIONAL T-1*

Fractional T-1 refers to any data transmission rate between 56 kbps (DSO rate) and 1.544 megabits per second (M bps), which is a full T-1. Fractional T-1 is simply a digital line that's not as fast as a T-1. Fractional T-1 is popular because it's typically provided by a phone company (local or long distance) at less money than a full T-1. FT-1 is typically used for LAN interconnection, video conferencing, high-speed mainframe connection and computer imaging. Fractional T-1 is typically provided on four-wire (two-pair) copper circuits. See also ASDS.

*FRADs (Frame Relay Assembler/Disassembler)*

Frame relay access devices.

*FRAME*

1. Generally, a group of data bits in a specific format with a flag at each end to indicate the beginning and end of the frame. The defined format enables network equipment to recognize the meaning and purpose of specific bits. The group of bits are sent serially (one after another). Generally a frame is a logical transmission unit. A frame usually contains its own control information for addressing and error checking. A frame is the basic data transmission unit employed in bit-oriented protocols. In this way, a frame is similar to a block. 2. In TV video, a frame is a single, complete picture in video or film recording. A video frame consists of two interlaced fields of either 525 lines (NTSC) or 625 lines (PAL/SEACAM), running at 30 frames per second (NTSC) or 25 frames per second (PAL/SEACAM). 24 frames are sent in moving picture films and a variable number, typically between 8 and 30, sent in videoconferencing systems, depending on the transmission bandwidth available. Up to about 12 frames a second looks "jerky." 3. One complete cycle of events in time division multiplexing. The frame usually includes a

sequence of time slots for the various sub-channels as well as extra bits for control, calibration, etc. 4. A distribution frame. A rectangular steel bar framework having "verticals and horizontals" which is used to place semi-permanent wire cross connections to permanent equipment. Found in telephone rooms and central offices. See DISTRIBUTION FRAME.

*FRAME ALIGNMENT*

The extent to which the frame of the receiving equipment is correctly phased (synchronized) with respect to that of the received signal.

*FRAME CHECK SEQUENCE*

Bits added to the end of a frame for error detection. Similar to a block check character (BCC). In bit-oriented protocols, a frame check sequence is a 16-bit field added to the end of a frame that contains transmission error-checking information. In a token ring LAN, the FCS is a 32-bit field which follows the data field in every token ring packet. This field contains a value which is calculated by the source computer. The receiving computer performs the same calculation. If the receiving computer's calculation does not match the result sent by the source computer, the packet is judged corrupt and discarded. An FCS calculation is made for each packet. This calculation is done by plugging the numbers (1's and 0's) from three fields in the packet (destination address, source address, and data) into a polynomial equation. The result is a 32-bit number (again 1's and 0's) that can be checked at the destination computer. This corruption detection method is accurate to one packet in 4 billion.

*FRAME MULTIPLEXING*

The process of handling traffic from multiple simultaneous inputs by sending the frames out one at a time in accordance with a specific set of rules. Instead of multiplexing traffic from a lower-speed connection into a higher speed connection based on a specific time duration for each low-speed channel, frame multiplexing using the length of a given frame as the measurement.

*FRAME RELAY*

Frame relay switching is a form of packet switching, but uses smaller packets and requires less error checking than traditional forms of packet switching. Frame Relay is very good at efficiently handling high-speed, bursty data over wide area networks. It offers lower costs and higher performance for those applications in contrast to the traditional point-to-point services. With frame relay, a pool of bandwidth is made instantly available to any of the concurrent data sessions sharing the circuit whenever a burst of data occurs. An addressed frame is sent into the network, which in turn interprets the address and sends the information to its destination at up to 2.048M bps.

Like traditional X.25 packet networks, frame relay networks use bandwidth only when there is traffic to send. Frame relay is often provided to the end user at three speeds — 56/64 kilobits per second, 256 kbps and 1,024M bps. Frame relay does not support voice, because voice traffic is highly sensitive to variations in the transmission delay introduced by the packet networks, while such small variations are usually not as critical to data traffic. For voice to be supported satisfactorily in a packet network, each packet must have a time stamp which is monitored by the network. Frame relay lacks such a mechanism. The American National Standards Institute (ANSI) describes frame relay service in the following documents:

ANSI T1.602 — Telecommunications - ISDN — Data Link Layer Signaling Specification for Application at the User Network Interface.

ANSI T1.606 — Frame Relaying Bearer Service — Architectural Framework and Service Description.

ANSI T1S1/90 - 175 - Addendum to T1.606 - Frame Relaying Bearer Service — Architectural Framework and Service Description.

ANSI T1S1/90-214 - DSS1 - Core Aspects of Frame Protocol for Use with Frame Relay Bearer Service.

ANSI T1S1/90-213 - DSS1 — Signaling Specific for Frame Relay Bearer Service.

### *FRAME RELAY FORUM*

Organization of frame relay equipment vendors and service providers, working to speed the development and deployment of frame relay products and interfaces with other broadband technologies, such as ATM.

### *FRND (Frame Relay Network Device)*

A frame relay access device or frame relay network switch.

### *FRONT END PROCESSOR (FEP)*

A FEP is a computer under the control of another, larger computer (typically a mainframe) in a network. The FEP does simple, basic "housekeeping" operations on the data streams as they arrive to be processed by the bigger computer. The FEP acts as a sort of intelligent traffic cop. It relieves the bigger, host computer of some of its telecommunications Input/Output burden, so that the host computer can concentrate on handling the processing burden. Depending on its sophistication, the front end processor might also perform serial to parallel conversion, protocol conversion, block or message assembly, etc. Here's a more technical definition: A dedicated communications system that intercepts and handles activity for the host. Can perform line control, message handling, code conversion, error control, and such applications functions as control and operation of special-purpose terminals. Designed to offload from the host computer all or most of its data communications functions. IBM 3705, 3725 and 3745 are Front End Processors. Front end processors are not used in client/server networks.

*FULL-DUPLEX*

Transmission in two directions simultaneously, or, more technically, bidirectional, simultaneous two-way communications. The best two-way phone conversations take place on four-wire circuits, two for transmission in one direction and two for transmission in the other. All long distance circuits are four wire. Most local lines are two wire, which means they're a compromise. Most speakerphones are half-duplex, meaning they only transmit in one direction at one time. The speakerphone flips its direction based on who's talking, or, more precisely, who's talking the loudest. Full duplex speakerphones are the best, but they're expensive. See SPEAKERPHONES and FOUR-WIRE CIRCUITS.

*GROUPWARE*

A term for software which runs on a local area network and which allows people on the network (typically a team) to participate in a joint (often complex) project. According to Fortune Magazine, March 23, 1992, using groupware, "Boeing has cut the time needed to complete a wide range of team projects by an average of 91%, or to one-tenth of what similar work took in the past." Groupware can be used in a meeting, with everyone sitting around a conference table and typing their ideas into the PC in front of them. Groupware can also be used off-line, with members of the "team" in different cities adding their comments. The "bellwether" of groupware software is Lotus' program called notes.

*HDLC (High level Data Link Control)*

A standard bit-oriented protocol developed by the International Standards Organization (ISO). In HDLC, control information is always placed in the same position. And specific bit patterns used for control differ dramatically from those used in representing data, so that errors are less likely to occur. SDLC and ADCCP are similar protocols.

*HISTOGRAM*

An imaging term. A display plotting the density of the various colors and/or values in an image.

*HOST*

An intelligent device attached to a network.

*HP OPENVIEW*

Hewlett-Packard's Openview network management products allow network administrators to monitor and control network devices from an MS-DOS PC or UNIX workstation.

*HPR (High Performance Routing)*

A local area networking term. HPR is the next-generation APPN — referred to in the past as APPN+ — that adds IP-like dynamic networking — e.g., dynamic alternate routing in the event of path failure — features to APPN, and uses a routing mechanism that works at Layer 2 using a RIF concept similar to that found in SRB.

*HUB*

The point on a network where a bunch of circuits are connected. Also, a switching node. In Local Area Networks, a hub is the core of a star as in ARCNET, StarLAN, Ethernet, and Token Ring. Hub hardware can be either active or passive. Wiring hubs are useful for their centralized management capabilities and for their ability to isolate nodes from disruption.

*HUB SITE*

The location(s) on a network where many circuits are brought together to be multiplexed into a single higher speed connection.

*HYBRID NETWORK*

1. A communications network which has some links capable of sending and receiving only analog signals and other links capable of handling only digital signals. The current public switched telephone network is Hybrid. Or a network with a combination of dissimilar network services, such as frame relay, private lines and/or X.25. 2. An amalgam of public and private network transmission facilities.

*IBM*

International Business Machines, the major computer manufacturer. IBM is powerful in many parts of the computer industry. This is why many of the IBM terms in this book are described as how IBM defines them.

*IBM TOKEN RING*

A local area network using star wiring architecture of two pair cabling to each drop location — one pair from the hub to the workstation and one pair from the workstation back to the hub to continue the ring. The IBM 8228 Multiple Access Unit (MAU) will support communications for eight PCs (workstations). Up to 33 IBM 8228 MAUs may be connected together into a single ring, supporting up to 260 data devices. MAU to MAU connection is accomplished with data connectors equipped with Type 1 cables from a MAU's RO (Ring Out) connection to the next MAU's RI (Ring In). The final MAU's RO connects back to the initial MAU's RI to complete the ring. See also TOKEN PASSING and TOKEN RING.

*INGRESS*

The incoming traffic, or incoming direction into a network device.

*INTEGRATED ACCESS*

An AT&T term for the provision of access for multiple services such as voice and data through a single system built on common principles and providing similar service features for the different classes of services.

*INTELLIGENT HUBS*

A hub that functions both as a bridge and multiprotocol router.

*INTELLIGENT PREMISES EQUIPMENT*

This refers to modern equipment, such as routers and intelligent switches. These devices are often capable of taking on roles traditionally performed by the network service, such as error correction.

*INTERFACE*

1. A mechanical or electrical link connecting two or more pieces of equipment together. 2. A shared boundary. A physical point of demarcation between two devices where the electrical signals, connectors, timing and handshaking are defined. The procedures, codes and protocols that enable two entities to interact for a meaningful exchange of information. 3. To bring two things or people together to allow them to talk.

*INTERFACE DEVICE*

A device which meets a standard electrical interface on one side and meets some other nonstandard interface on the other. The purpose of the device is to allow a device with a nonstandard interface to connect to a device with a standard interface. See also INTERFACE.

*InterLATA*

Telecommunications services that originate in one and terminate in another Local Access and Transport Area (LATA). Under provisions of Divestiture, the Bell operating companies cannot provide Inter-LATA service, but can provide Intra-LATA service. Some LATAs are very large. So some "local" phone companies provide the equivalent of long distance service. And some of these phone companies have different pricing packages. Some of these packages are cheap, but not highly-publicized. See also LATA.

*INTERNET*

Internet is a computer network which joins many government and university and some private computers together over phone lines (mostly T-1s). Internet traces its origins to a network set up in 1969 by the Defense Department. In 1991 it was running off $20 million a year in federal subsidies and managed by the National Science Foundation. An IBM/MCI venture known as Advanced Network and Services manages a network called NSFnet, which connects hundreds of research centers and universities. NSFnet also manages links to dozens of other countries. All these networks are collectively known as Internet. NSFnet was founded by the National Science Foundation, a Federal Government agency and is composed of leased telephone lines that link special computers called routers, which transmit packages of data to three million users in 33 countries.

*INTERNET MIB SUBTREE*

A tree-shaped data structure in which network devices on a local area network and their attributes can be identified within the confines of a network management scheme. The name of an object or attribute is derived from its location on this tree.

For example, an object in MIB-I might be named 1.2.1.1.1.0. the first 1 indicates the object is on the Internet. The 2 denotes that it falls within the Management category. The second 1 shows the object is part of the first fully defined MIB, known as MIB-I. The third 1 indicates which of the eight object groups is being referenced. And the fourth 1 is a textual description of the network component. The O indicates there is only one object instance. An object instance links a particular object to a specific node on the network. The numbering system is infinitely extendible to accommodate additions to this base identification scheme. This common naming structure permits equipment from a variety of vendors to be managed by a single management station that uses SNMP. The four main categories of the tree are Directory, Management, Experimental and Private/Enterprises.

*INTERNETWORKING*

Communication between two networks or two types of networks or end equipment. This may or may not involve a difference in signaling or protocol elements supported. And, in the narrower sense — to join local area networks together. This way users can get access to other files, databases and applications. Bridges and routers are the devices which typically accomplish the task of joining LANs. Internetworking may be done with cables — joining LANs together in the same building, for example. Or it may be done with telecommunications circuits — joining LANs together across the globe.

*INTEROPERABILITY*

The ability to operate software and exchange information in a heterogeneous network, i.e. one large network made up of several different local area networks.

*INTERWORKING*

The ability to seamlessly communicate between devices supporting dissimilar protocols, such as frame relay and ATM, by translating between the protocols, not through encapsulation. Many carriers are planning to implement the necessary equipment and conversion algorithms to allow the network itself to transparently convert from frame relay to ATM, and vice versa.

***IntraLATA***

Telecommunications services that originate and end in the same Local Access and Transport Area.

*IP*

1. Internal Protocol. 2. Internetwork Protocol in ISO or in ARPA. A standard describing software that keeps track of the Internetwork address for different nodes, routes outgoing messages, and recognizes incoming messages. 3. Intelligent Peripheral. A device in an IN (Intelligent Network) that provides capabilities such as voice announcements and help guidance. 4. The Internet Protocol; the most important of the protocols on which the

Internet is based. It allows a packet to traverse multiple networks on the way to its final destination. See INTERNET.

*IPX (Internet Packet eXchange)*

Novell NetWare's native LAN communications protocol, used to move data between server and/or workstation programs running on different network nodes. IPX packets are encapsulated and carried by the packets used in Ethernet and the similar frames used in Token Ring networks.

*IS-IS (Intermediate System to Intermediate System)*

OSI link-state hierarchical routing protocol, based on DECnet Phase V routing, whereby intermediate systems (routers) exchange routing information based on a single metric to determine network topology.

*ISDN (Integrated Services Digital Network)*

A totally new concept of what the world's telephone system should be. According to AT&T, today's public switched phone network has the following limitations:

1. Each voice line is only 4 kHz, which is very narrow.

2. Most signaling is in-band signaling, which is very consuming of bandwidth (i.e. it's expensive and inefficient).

3. The little out-of-band signaling that exists today runs on lines separate to the network. (This includes signaling for PBX attendants, hotel/motel, Centrex and PBX calling information.)

4. Most users have separate voice and data networks (which is inefficient, expensive and limiting).

5. Premises telephone and data equipment must be separately administered from the network it runs on.

6. There is a wide and growing variety of voice, data and digital interface standards, many of which are incompatible.

*ISO*

1. The Greek prefix which means equal. 2. The International Standards Organization in Paris, devoted to figuring standards for international and national data communications. The U.S. representative to the ISO is ANSI. 3. The initials also stand for Independent Service Organizations or Independent Sales Organizations in the computer sales community.

*IXC*

IntereXchange Channel, or IntereXchange Carrier — as contrasted to the LEC — the Local Exchange Carrier, a new word for a local phone company.

InterExchange Carriers used to be called "Other Common Carriers," except that didn't include AT&T. Now, AT&T, MCI, Sprint and all the long distance carriers are called InterExchange Carriers.

*K bps (KiloBits Per Second)*

One thousand bits per second.

*LAN (Local Area Network)*

A short distance data communications network (typically within a building or campus) used to link together computers and peripheral devices (such as printers) under some form of standard control.

*LAP-D Link (Access Procedure-D)*

Also called Link Access Protocol for the D channel. Link-level protocol devised for ISDN connections, differing from LAPB (LAP-Balanced) in its framing sequence. Likely to be used as basis for LAPM, the proposed ITU-T modem error-control standard.

*LATA (Local Access and Transport Area)*

One of 161 local geographical areas in the US within which a local telephone company may offer telecommunications services — local or long distance. AT&T is expressly prohibited from offering intraLATA calls by the terms of the Divestiture. Other competitors, such as MCI and Sprint, are not, though rules vary by state, according to state regulation.

*LEASED LINES*

Same as a LEASED or DEDICATED CIRCUIT, PRIVATE LINE, LEASED CHANNEL.

*LED (Light Emitting Diode)*

A semiconductor diode which emits light when a current is passed through it. In lightwave transmission systems, light emitting diodes or lasers are used as sources of light. These devices are fabricated from multi-layered structures of compound semiconductors epitaxially grown on a single-crystal substrate. LEDs are used as sources for optical data link applications in which the data rates are less than about 500 megabits per second and the transmission distances do not exceed a few kilometers. LEDs are also used in alphanumeric displays on calculators and computer devices. LEDs use less power than normal incandescent light bulbs, but more power than LCDs (Liquid Crystal Displays).

*LEN (Low-End Node)*

An IBM term for a specific category of network devices. Also see EN (End Node)

*LINK STATE*

A type of routing protocol in which updates to routing tables are exchanged when modifications are made to the table, but are not exchanged on a highly regular and predetermined basis. Link State protocols consume less networking resources and reduce network congestion by only providing updates when needed, and only sending the changes. Periodically, the entire route table will be sent as a precautionary procedure.

*LLC (Logical Link Control)*

A protocol developed by the IEEE 802.2 committee for data-link-level transmission control. It is the upper sublayer of the IEEE Layer 2 (OSI) protocol that complements the MAC protocol. IEEE standard 802.2 includes end-system addressing and error checking. It also provides a common access control standard and governs the assembly of data packets and their exchange between data stations independent of how the packets are transmitted on the LAN.

*LMI (Local Management Interface)*

A specification for the use of frame-relay products that define a method of exchanging status information between devices such as routers.

*LOCAL LOOP*

The physical wires that run from the subscriber's telephone set, or PBX or key telephone system, to the telephone company central office. Increasingly, the local loop now goes from the main distribution frame in the basement to the phone company. And the subscriber is responsible for getting his/her wires from the box in the basement to his/her phone, PBX or key system.

*LU*

1. Line Unit. 2. Logical Unit, access port for users in SNA. In a bisync network, a port through which the user gains access to the network services. A LU can support sessions with the host-based System ServicesControl Point (SSCP) and other LUs. 3. Local Use flag. Occasionally used to initialized

approval for local cellular calls. The Cellular carrier insures that local users are registered with a local system.

*M BPS (MegaBits Per Second)*

Million bits per second.

*MAC*

1. Moves, Adds and Changes. 2. Media Access Control. A media-specific access control protocol within IEEE 802 specifications. Currently includes variations for the token ring, token bus and CSMA/CD. The lower sublayer of the IEEE's link layer (OSI) which complements the Logical Link Control (LLC).

*MAINFRAME*

A powerful computer, almost always linked to a large set of peripheral devices (disk storage, printers, and so forth), and used in a multipurpose environment at the corporate or major divisional level. The term — main frame — derives from the racks that typically hold a large computer and its memory.

*MAU*

1. Math Acceleration Unit. 2. Multistation Access Unit. A MAU is a wiring concentrator used in Local Area Networks. In token ring networks it's called a Multi-station Access Unit. In Ethernet networks it's called a Medium Attachment Unit. Basically a MAU is a device that allows terminals, PCs, printers, and other devices to be connected in a star-based configuration to Token Ring or Ethernet LANs. MAU hardware can be either active or passive.

*METROPOLITAN FIBER RINGS*

A metropolitan fiber ring is an advanced, high-speed local network that can also be used to connect businesses and residences directly to a long distance carrier's network, and provide alternatives to the local telecommunications services they have today. This definition, courtesy MCI.

*MIB (Management Information Database)*

A directory listing the logical names of all information resources residing in a network and pertinent to the network's management. Within the Internet MIB employed for SNMP (Simple Network Management Protocol)-based management, ASN.1 (Abstract Syntax Notation One) is used to describe network management variables. These variables, which include such information as error counts or on/off status of a device, are assigned a place on a tree data structure. MIB is used in X.400 electronic mail. See INTERNET MIB TREE

*MODEM*

Acronym for MOdulator/DEModulator. Equipment which converts digital signals to analog signals and vice-versa. Modems are used to send data signals (digital) over the telephone network, which usually is analog. The Modem modulates the "1's" and "0's" into tones which can be carried by the phone network. At the other end, the demodulator part of the modem converts the tones back into digital 1's and 0's.

*MULTI-POINT CIRCUIT*

A circuit connecting three or more locations. It is often called a multidrop circuit. See also MULTI-POINT and MULTI-DROP LINE.

*MULTI-POINT LINE*

A single communications link for two or more devices shared by one computer and or more computers or terminals. Use of this line requires a polling mechanism. It is also called a multidrop line.

*MULTIMEDIA*

Multimedia is the combination of multiple forms of media in the communication of information. Multimedia enables people to communicate using integrated media: audio, video, text, graphics, fax, and telephony. The benefit is more powerful communication. The combination of several media often provides richer, more effective communication of information or ideas than a single media such as traditional text-based communication can accomplish. Multimedia communication formats vary, but they usually include voice communications (vocoding, speech recognition, speaker verification and text-to-speech), audio processing (music synthesis, CD-ROMs), data communications, image processing and telecommunications using LANs, MANs and WANs in ISDN and POTS networks. Multimedia technology will ultimately take the disparate technologies of the computer, the telephone, the fax machine, the CD player, and the video camera and combine them into one powerful communication center. Technologies that were once analog — video, audio, telephony — are now digital. The power of multimedia is the integration of these digital technologies. To many people, "multimedia" (as defined above) is a disparate collection of technologies in search of a purpose. And it's true: most of the merger of media (as above) is taking place in business communications in the moving around of compound documents. Meantime, multimedia has moved into training and in the home for education and entertainment.

*MULTIPLEXER*

Electronic equipment which allows two or more signals to pass over one communications circuit. That "circuit' may be a phone line, a microwave circuit, a through-the-air TV signal. That circuit may be analog or digital. There are many multiplexing techniques to accommodate both.

*MULTIPLEXiING EFFICIENCY*

Figure of merit for multiplexers. The ratio of the aggregate channel input data rate to the composite output data rate. Many statistical multiplexers achieve a multiplexing efficiency of 8 or more.

*MULTIPOINT CIRCUITS*

A circuit connecting three or more locations. It is often called a multidrop circuit. See also MULTI-POINT and MULTI-DROP LINE.

*MULTI-POINT*

A configuration or topology, designed to transmit data between a central site and a number of remote terminals on the same circuit. Individual terminals will generally be able to transmit to the central site but not to each other.

*NCP*

1. In AT&T language, Network Control Point. A routing, billing, and call control data base system for DSDC which uses the AT&T 3B2OD computer as the feature processor. 2. In IBM language, Network Control Program, which is a program that controls the operations of the communication controllers, 3704 and 3705 in an IBM SNA network. 3. In Northern Telecom language, it means Network Configuration Process. 4. In Novell language, it means NetWare Core Protocol. It is NetWare's format for requesting and replying to requests for file and print services.

*NetBIOS (Network Basic Input/Output System)*

A layer of software originally developed by IBM and Sytek to link a network operating system with specific hardware. Originally designed as the network controller for IBM's PC Network LAN, NetBIOS has now been extended to allow programs written using the NetBIOS interface to operate on the IBM Token ring. NetBIOS has been adopted as something of an industry standard and now it's common to refer to NetBIOS-compatible LANs. It offers LAN applications, a variety of "hooks" to carry out inter-application communications and data transfer. Essentially, NetBIOS is a way for application programs to talk to the network. Other applications interfaces are also being used these days, such as IBM's APPC. To run an application that works with NetBIOS, a non-IBM network operating system or network interface card must offer a NetBIOS emulator. More and more hardware and software vendors offer these emulators. They aren't always perfectly compatible, though. Today, many vendors either provide a version of NetBIOS to interface with their hardware or emulate its transport layer communications services in their network products.

*NETVIEW*

An IBM product for management of heterogeneous networks that integrates the functions of three formerly separate Communications Network Management (CNM) software programs: 1. NCCF. Network Communication Control Facility. 2. NLDM. Network Logical Data Manager, which uses functions from NCCF and helps pinpoint problems along the logical connection/path of an SNA session. 3. NPDA. Network Problem Determination Application, which displays various alerts using IBM equipment located at strategic points in the network and allows diagnostic information to be displayed. Also, NetView incorporates some of the functions from two other programs: VNCA (Virtual Telecommunications Access Method/Node Control Application) which monitors the status and current activity of all resources in a domain, and NMPF (Network Management Productivity Facility) which helps the network operator to install, learn and use many network management products.

*NETWARE LOADABLE MODULE (NLM)*

An driver that runs in a server on a local area network under Novell's NetWare operating system and can be loaded or unloaded on the fly as it's needed. In other networks, such applications could require dedicated PCs. A telephony NLM might allow a workstation on a LAN to control a PBX attached to a NetWare file server. It might also allow the workstation to control one or more voice processing cards sitting on in a NetWare server. In early 1993, AT&T became the first PBX maker to ink a deal with Novell, the creator of NetWare, to put telephony onto Novell LANs. AT&T created a PC-card resident in a Novell File server. The card connects to the ASAI (Adjunct Switch Applications Interface) BRI port on the AT&T Definity PBX. Anyone with a PC on the Novell network and an AT&T phone on their desk can use telephone features, such as auto-dialing, conference calling and message management (a new term for integrating voice, fax and e-mail on your desktop PC via your LAN). The Novell/AT&T deal intends to create open Application Programming Interfaces (APIs) that third party developers can work with. A Novell/AT&T example of what could be developed: A user could select names from a directory on his PC. He could tell the Definity PBX through the PC over the LAN to place a conference call to those names. At the same time, a program running under NetWare would automatically send an e-mail to the people, alerting them to the conference call and giving them the agenda. All participants would have access to both the document and the conference call simultaneously. See TELEPHONY SERVICES.

*NETWORK*

Networks are common in our lives. Think about trains and phones. A networks ties things together. Computer networks connect all types of computers and computer related things — terminals, printers, modems, door entry sensors, temperature monitors, etc. The networks we're most familiar with are long distance ones, like phones and trains. But there are also Local Area Networks (LANs) which exist within a limited geographic area — like the few hundred feet of a small office, an entire building or even a "campus," such as a university or industrial park. There are also Metropolitan Area Networks (MANs). See also LAN and MAN.

*NETWORK MANAGEMENT*

A set of procedures, software, equipment and operations designed to keep a network operating near maximum efficiency. Network management generally falls into five areas:

1. CONFIGURATION MANAGEMENT deals with installing, initializing, "boot" loading, modifying and tracking the configuration parameters of network hardware and software.

2. FAULT LOCATION and REPAIR MANAGEMENT tools let you find out what's going wrong with what equipment or lines and give you the ability to fix those resources — by re-routing traffic on different lines or reporting problems to the carrier, or suggesting to whoever that certain equipments should be replaced. Fault location and management tools have strong error and alarm characteristics.

3. SECURITY MANAGEMENT tools allow the network manager to restrict access to various resources in the network. There are devices such as password protection schemes, giving users different levels of access to different network resources.

4. PERFORMANCE MANAGEMENT tools provide real-time and historical statistical information about the network's operation. Such tools show, for example, how many packets are being transmitted at any given moment, the number of users logged into a specific server and use of network lines.

5. ACCOUNTING MANAGEMENT applications help users allocate the costs of the various network resources — from lines to PBXs, from access to a mainframe to time used on printers.

*NETWORK REDUNDANCY*

Network redundancy means that the network topology has been constructed so that a failure of a network component can be automatically and/or rapidly recovered by using identical components engineered into the network for recovery purposes. For example, IXC network redundancy may take the form of spare network capacity on geographically diverse IXC circuits so that applications can be recovered to an alternative network path in the event of a failure on the primary path.

*NIC*

1. Near Instantaneous Companding. This describes the very fast, essentially real-time, process of quantizing an analog signal into digital symbols. 2. Network Interface Card. The attachment that connects a device to a network. The NIC, usually a PC expansion board, executes the code needed by the connected device to share a cable or some other media with other stations. 3. Network Information Center. Any organization that's responsible for supplying information about any network. 4. The InterNIC, which plays an important role in overall Internet coordination.

*NLM (Network Loadable Modules)*

Applications and drivers that run in a server on a local area network under Novell's NetWare operating system and can be loaded or unloaded on the fly. In other networks, such applications could require dedicated PCs. See NETWARE LOADABLE MODULE for a larger explanation.

*NN (Network Node)*

In frame relay, a network node is typically the frame relay service port connection and its associated virtual circuits.

*NNI (Network to Network Interface)*

There are two types of network interfaces specified by the frame relay standards. The first is a user-to-network (UNI) interface and the second is a network-to-network interface (NNI). The NNI describes the connection between two public frame relay services, and includes elements such as bidirectional polling, to assist the network services providers with gaining information on the status of the public networks being interconnected.

*NODAL ARCHITECTURES*

Also called Hub architectures. Nodal network architectures means that network traffic from many locations are connected into a single network site for consolidation and aggregation to higher speed circuits. The traffic is then transmitted from this hub site to a central network site, or to other hub sites. Nodal architectures save money, but also increase the risk of a single network failure affecting multiple network locations.

*NODES*

A point of connection into a network. In multipoint networks, it means it's a unit that's polled. In LANs, it's a device on the ring. In packet switched networks, it's one of the many packet switches which form the network's backbone.

***NOVELL IPX***

See IPX.

***NOVELL NLSP (NetWare Link Services Protocol)***

See NLSP ·

***NOVELL SAP (Service Advertisement Protocol)***

See SAP

*OCTETS*

An eight-bit byte.

***OS/2 (Operating System/2)***

An operating system originally developed by IBM and Microsoft for use with Intel's microprocessors and for use with IBM personal system/2 personal computers. Now OS/2 is the prime responsibility of IBM and it will run on many PCs, including those using the Intel family of PC microprocessors. OS/2 is a multitasking operating system. This means many programs can run at the same time. See OS/2 EXTENDED EDITION.

***OSI (Open System Interconnect)***

An ISO publication that defines seven independent layers of communication protocols. Each layer enhances the communication services of the layer just below it and shields the layer above it from the implementation details of the lower layer. In theory, this allows communication systems to be built from independently developed layers.

*OSI MODEL (include layers 1-7)*

The only internationally accepted framework of standards for communication between different systems made by different vendors. ISO's major goal is to create an open systems networking environment where any vendor's computer system, connected to any network, can freely share data with any other computer system on that network or a linked network. OSI was developed by the International Standards Organization. Most of the dominant communications protocols used today have a structure based on the OSI model. Although OSI is a model and not an actively used protocol, and there are still very few pure OSI-based products on the market today, it is still important to understand its structure. The OSI model organizes the communications process into seven different categories and places these categories in a layered sequence based on their relation to the user. Layers 7 through 4 deal with end to end communications between the message source and the message destination, while layers 3 through 1 deal with network access.

Layer 1 — The Physical layer deals with the physical means of sending data over lines (i.e., the electrical, mechanical and functional control of data circuits).

Layer 2 — The Data Link layer is concerned with procedures and protocols for operating the communications lines. It also has a way of detecting and correcting message errors.

Layer 3 — The Network layer determines how data is transferred between computers. It also addresses routing within and between individual networks.

Layer 4 — The Transport layer defines the rules for information exchange and manages end-to-end delivery of information within and between networks, including error recovery and flow control.

Layer 5 — The Session layer is concerned with dialog management. It controls the use of the basic communications facility provided by the Transport layer.

Layer 6 — The Presentation layer provides transparent communications services by masking the differences of varying data formats (character codes, for example) between dissimilar systems.

Layer 7 — The Applications layer contains functions for particular applications services, such as file transfer, remote file access and virtual terminals.

*OSPF (Open Shortest Path First)*

Link state, hierarchical Interior Gateway Protocol (IGP) routing algorithm proposed as a successor to RIP.

*OUT-OF-BAND NETWORK MANAGEMENT*

A method of managing LAN bridges and routers that uses telephone lines for communications between the network management station and the managed devices. This type of management is normally in addition to the conventional method which uses the LANs and WANs that are being connected by these devices. The principal advantage is that in the event of a system failure (which may take a LAN or a WAN down), a network supervisor can bypass the failed system and use a telephone link to reach a bridge/router to diagnose a network problem. Bridges and routers must have built-in telephone modems for this to work.

*OUT-OF-BAND SIGNALING*

Signaling that is separated from the channel carrying the information — the voice, data, video, etc. Typically the separation is accomplished by a filter. The signaling includes dialing and other supervisory signals.

*OVERSUBSCRIPTION*

In frame relay, this refers to a port connection state where the sum total of the committed information rates for the permanent virtual circuits supported by that port is greater than the port connections speed. While the port connection cannot simultaneously support transmissions at greater than its connection speed, its ability to dynamically allocate traffic makes oversubscription a cost-effective way to gain a high level of direct network interconnectivity.

*P-BURST (Packet Burst Mode)*

A protocol built on top of IPX that speeds the transfer of NCP data between a workstation and a NetWare server by eliminating the need to sequence and acknowledge each packet. With packet burst, the server sends a whole set (or burst) of packets before it requires an acknowledgement.

*PACKET*

A bundle of data, usually in binary form, organized in a specific way for transmission. Three principal elements are included in the packet: 1. Control information — destination, origin, length of packet, etc., 2. the data to be transmitted and, 3. error detection and correction bits.

*PACKET INTERLEAVING*

Refers to the process of multiplexing multiple incoming packets from multiple channels on to a single outgoing channel by sampling one or more packets from the first channel, then the next, and so on.

*PACKET-SWITCHING*

Sending data in packets through a network to some remote location. The data to be sent is subdivided into individual packets of data, each packet having a unique identification and each packet carrying its own destination address. This way each packet can go by a different route. The packets may also arrive in a different order than how they were shipped. The packet ID lets the data be reassembled in proper sequence. Packet switching is a very efficient method of moving digital data around. It is not useful for voice, yet, though experiments are underway.

*PAD (Packet Assembler/Disassembler)*

A hardware/software combination that forms the interface between an X.25 network such as PDN and an asynchronous device such as a PC. The PAD generates call request, call clear, and other information packets in addition to the ones that contain user data.

*PARALLEL NETWORKS*

Parallel networks, or segregated networks, exist when a single network location supports more than one physical wide area network connection for the purpose of supporting one or more applications.

*PARTIAL MESHED NETWORK*

A type of wide area network topology in which every remote location is not connected directly to every other remote location, but instead is connected directly to a small subset of locations. It is a topology with more direct connectivity than a star configuration, but less direct connectivity than a fully meshed configuration.

*PC*

1. Personal Computer. 2. Peg Count. 3. Printed Circuit. 4. Product Committee.

*PEAK-TO-AVERAGE TRANSMISSION RATIO (P/AR)*

An analog test that provides a measure of data circuit quality by sending a pulse into one end of a circuit and measuring its envelope at the distant end of the circuit.

*PERFORMANCE MANAGEMENT*

Measures and records resource utilization. It is one of the categories of network management defined by the ISO (International Standards Organization).

*PILOT*

In networking this refers to a trial network in which a small subset of locations are interconnected for the purpose of testing network, protocol and application performance.

*PLATFORM*

Measures and records resource utilization. It is one of the categories of network management defined by the ISO (International Standards Organization).

*POISSON*

See POISSON DISTRIBUTION.

*POISSON DISTRIBUTION*

A mathematical formula named after the French mathematician S. D. Poisson, which indicates the probability of certain events occurring. It is used in traffic engineering to design telephone networks. It is one method of figuring how many trunks you will need in the future based on measurements of past calls. Poisson distribution describes how calls react when they encounter blockage (see QUEUING THEORY for a detailed explanation of blockage). There are two main formulas used today in traffic engineering: Erlang B and Poisson. The Erlang B formula assumes all blocked calls are cleared. This means they disappear, never to reappear. The Poisson formula assumes no blocked calls disappear. The user simply redials and redials. If you use the Poisson method of prediction, you will buy more trunks than if you use Erlang B. Poisson typically overestimates the number of trunks you will need, while Erlang B typically underestimates the number of trunks you will need. There are other more complex but more accurate ways of figuring trunks — Erlang C (blocked calls delayed or queued) and computer simulation. Poisson has been used extensively by AT&T to recommend to its customers the number of trunks they needed. Since AT&T was selling the circuits and preferred its customers to have excellent service, it made sense to use the Poisson formula. As competition in long distance has heated up, as circuits have become more costly and as companies have become more economically-minded (more aware of their rising phone bills), Poisson has become widely ignored.

After I wrote the above definition, Lee Goeller, a noted traffic engineering expert contributed the following definition of Poisson Distribution: A probability distribution developed by E.C. Molina of AT&T in the early 1900s for use in solving problems in telephone traffic (see TRAFFIC ENGINEERING), although it has many other uses and is widely applied in many fields. When made aware of Poisson's prior effort (circa 1820), Molina gave him full credit and even taught himself French so he could read Poisson in the original. The Poisson distribution assumes a call is in the system for one holding time, whether it is served or not (blocked calls held); the first form of the distribution estimates the probability that exactly X calls will be in the system, while the second estimates the probability that X or more calls will be present. If there are only X trunks to serve the calls, the second form gives the probability of blocking. Although limited tabulations of the Poisson distribution had been made earlier, Molina published an extensive set of tables in 1942. The Poisson distribution slightly overstates the number of trunks needed when compared to the Erlang B distribution (see ERLANG B).

*POLLING*

Connecting to another system to check for things like mail or news. A form of data or fax network arrangement whereby a central computer or fax machine asks each remote location in turn (and very quickly) whether they want to send some information. The purpose is to give each user or each remote data terminal an opportunity to transmit and receive information on a circuit or using facilities which are being shared. Polling is typically used on a multipoint or multidrop line. Polling is done to save money on telephone lines.

*POP (Point of Presence)*

Physical place within a LATA where a long distance carrier interfaces with the network of the local exchange carrier (LEC), also called the local telephone company. The point at which the local telephone company terminates subscribers circuits for long-distance dial-up or leased-line communications.

*PORT*

1. An entrance to or exit from a network. 2. The physical or electrical interface through which one gains access. 3. The interface between a process or program and a communications or transmission facility. 4. A point in the computer or telephone system where data may be accessed. Peripherals — like call accounting devices — are connected to ports. The two most common ports are the parallel and serial ports. 5. To move a process, program or subroutine from one processor to controller to another ("port it over").

*PORT CONNECTION*

The point of entry into a public frame relay network service.

*PORT SHARING*

1. A system which connects multiple lines to a single port by means of a manual or automatic line selection method. 2. In frame relay, where multiple virtual connections share the same port connection.

*PRIORITIZATION PARAMETERS*

The hierarchical rules which a network device, such as a router, applies to incoming traffic to determine which traffic should be handled first, next, and so on.

*PRIVATE LINE*

A direct channel specifically dedicated to a customer's use between specified points. A line leased from a carrier, local or long distance. A non-switched circuit. One end of the line is directly connected to the other end. Here's the AT&T definition of a private line. "A dedicated, nonswitchable link from one or more customer-specified locations to one or more customer-specified locations..."

*PRIVATE NETWORK*

A series of offices connected together by leased and non-leased phone lines with switching facilities and transmission equipment owned and operated by the user or by the carrier and leased to the user. This is a broad definition. But these days with SDN and other virtual private networks, it's hard to see the difference between using a private network and using the public network except that you hope your private network will be cheaper, better quality and perhaps offer a little more flexibility in the types of traffic — voice, video, data and fax — you carry on it. See PRIVATE VOICEBAND NETWORK.

*PRIVATE VOICEBAND NETWORK*

A network that is made up of voice band circuits, and sometimes switching arrangements, for the exclusive use of one customer. These networks can be nationwide in scope and typically serve large corporations or government agencies.

*PROTOCOL*

A procedure for adding order to the exchange of data. A protocol is a specific set of rules, procedures or conventions relating to format and timing of data transmission between two devices. A standard procedure that two data devices must accept and use to be able to understand each other. Sort of like us both speaking English so we can communicate. The protocols for data communications cover such things as framing, error handling, transparency and line control. There are three basic types of protocol: character-oriented, byte-oriented and bit-oriented.

Protocols break a file into equal parts called blocks or packets. These packets are sent and the receiving computer checks the arriving packet and sends an acknowledgement (ACK) back to the sending computer. Because modems use phone lines to transfer data, noise or interference on the line will often mess up the block. When a block is damaged in transit, an error occurs. The purpose of a protocol is to set up a mathematical way of measuring if the block came through accurately. And if it didn't, ask the distant end to retransmit the block until it gets it right. See PROTOCOLS for a list of the more common prototypes.

*PROTOCOL ANALYZER*

A specialized computer and/or program that hooks into a LAN and analyzes its traffic. Good protocol analyzers can record and display data on all levels of traffic on a LAN cable, from the lowest media access control packets to NetBIOS commands and application data. They are excellent for diagnosing network problems, but they require some expertise, as their data output can be obscure.

*PROTOCOL CONVERSION*

A data communications procedure which permits computers operating with different protocols to communicate with each other. See PROTOCOL and PROTOCOL CONVERTER.

### *PROTOCOL CONVERTER*

A device which does protocol conversion. It's your classic "black box." Glasgal Communications defines a protocol converter as any device which translates a binary data stream from one format to another according to a fixed algorithm. Compare with bridge and gateway, which are different animals and may contain protocol converters...and more.

### *PROTOCOL STACK*

A group of drivers that work together to span the layers in the network protocol hierarchy.

### *PROTOCOLS*

For an explanation of protocols, see PROTOCOL. Here are the more common PC protocol types:

MODULATION PROTOCOLS: Bell 103: Low Speed (300 baud), Bell 212: Low Speed (1200bps), ITU-T V.22bis: Medium (2400bps), ITU-T V.32 High Speed (9600bps), ITU-T V.32bis: High Speed (14400bps)

ERROR CONTROL PROTOCOLS: Microcom Network Protocol (MNP), ITU-T V.42 (Includes LAP-M & MNP)

DATA COMPRESSION PROTOCOLS: MNP/5, ITU-T V.42bis, All data compression requires an underlying error control protocol.

FILE TRANSFER PROTOCOLS: Kermit: 7-bit data path, quotes control characters. XMODEM: 8 bit data path, ACK/NAK protocol. YMODEM: 8-bit data path, batch capability. ZMODEM: 8-bit data path, quotes some control characters.

### *PUBLIC NETWORK*

A network operated by common carriers or telecommunications administrations for the provision of circuit switched, packet switched and leased-line circuits to the public. Compare with private network.

### *PVC (Permanent Virtual Circuits)*

A virtual circuit that provides the equivalent of a dedicated private line service over a packet switching network between two DTEs. The path between users is fixed. A PVC uses a fixed logical channel to maintain a permanent association between the FTEs. Once a PVC is defined, it requires no setup operation before data is sent and no disconnect operation after data is sent. A new connection between the same users may be routed along a different path. See also VIRTUAL CIRCUIT and SDN for another type of virtual network.

*QUEUE*

A stream of tasks waiting to be executed. A series of calls or messages waiting for connection to a line. See QUEUING.

*QUEUE SERVICE INTERVAL*

The maximum length of time a queue will go unsampled.

*QUEUING*

The act of "stacking" or holding calls to be handled by a specific person, trunk or trunk group. There are two reasons to queue telephone calls:

1. Because you simply don't have enough trunks.
2. Because you want to save money.

You can queue calls mechanically using your telephone switch or manually using a human operator or attendant. There are two ways you can queue calls — hold-on or call-back. In "hold-on" queuing, you dial, you get some queuing tone (or the operator tells you you're being queued), then you wait on-line until a line becomes free and you're connected. In "call-back" queuing, you tell the operator or the machine you want to dial a call. And you hang up. When the line becomes free you are called back and connected. There are advantages and disadvantages to both systems. In "hold-on" queuing, you waste your time but save on phone time. In call-back queuing, you waste less of your time, but more phone line time. In call-back queuing, the operator or the phone system has to grab the line you want and simultaneously call you. By then, you may have left your desk. The call may be wasted, etc. The line given to you could have been used by someone else, etc. Queuing calls as a method to save money on long distance calling makes sense ONLY:

1. IF you are out of trunks because of a temporary surge in telephone traffic — perhaps at your peak, peak busy time and it's very expensive to buy sufficient "cheap long distance" trunks to handle every conceivable peak, and

2. IF you never plan on having a queue longer than 20 seconds for a hold-on queue and 60 seconds for a call-back queue and

3. IF you are queuing calls into an expensive fixed-cost line. For example a tie line between New York and London. If you queue calls into a variable cost line, like an interstate WATS line, you will save money over throwing the call onto DDD, but the pennies you save usually won't be worth it — considering the aggravation you're going to cause your people. Queuing is a very

sensitive subject in corporate telecommunications departments. People don't like to wait for telephone lines. They consider that insulting to them personally, damaging to their "productivity" and to heck with the cost. Queues do, however, make enormous sense. Even a queue as short as ten seconds can save big amounts of money. Queues of a maximum length of ten seconds are rarely noticed. These days some of the more modern PBXs will allow you to offer "selective" queuing, or levels of queuing. Upper management doesn't have to queue for the cheap long distance lines before it's bounced to the expensive ones. While lower management has to wait up to 30 seconds. And the worker bees (non-management) have to wait even longer. Queuing is also used on incoming trunks. See QUEUING THEORY.

*QUEUING THEORY*

The study of the behavior of a system that uses queuing, such as a telephone system. Much of queuing theory derives from the science of Operations Research (OR). Dr. Leonard Kleinrock has written the authoritative books on the subject. He is probably a genius. His books are very difficult to understand for laymen. Here is an explanation of Queuing Theory from James Henry Green's Dow Jones-Irwin Handbook of Telecommunications (you can get a copy from Telecom Library at 1-800- LIBRARY or 1-212-691-8215.):

"The most common (telephone) network design method involves modeling the (phone) network according to principles of queuing theory, which describes how customers or users behave in a queue. Three variables are considered in network design. The first is the arrival or input process that describes the way users array themselves as they arrive to request service...The second variable is the service process, which describes the way users are handled when they are taken from queue and admitted into the service providing mechanism. The third method is the queue discipline, which describes the way users behave when they encounter blockage in the network...Three reactions to blockage are possible:

Blocked calls held (BCH). When users encounter blockage, they immediately redial and reenter the queue. Blocked calls cleared (BCC). When users encounter blockage, they wait for some time before redialing. Blocked calls delayed (BCD). When users encounter blockage, they are placed in a holding circuit until capacity to serve them is available. (See QUEUE.)

"Traffic engineers have different formulas or tables to apply, corresponding to the assumption about how users behave when they encounter blockage." See POISSON.

After I wrote the above definition, Lee Goeller, a noted traffic engineering expert contributed the following definition:

The study of systems in which customers wait in line for servers to become available, the "blocked calls delayed" condition in telephony (see TRAFFIC ENGINEERING). Although seldom used in designing voice networks (other techniques are usually more cost-effective), queuing is very important in the design of packet networks where speed of transmission more than offsets the delay of waiting for a transmission facility to become available, and in staffing Automatic Call Distributors.

*RBOC (Regional Bell Operating Company)*

One of the seven Bell operating companies set up after Divestiture, each of which own two or more BOCs (Bell Operating Companies). The RBOCs were carved out of the old AT&T/Bell System by Judge Harold Greene when he signed off on the divestiture of the Bell operating companies from AT&T at the end of 1984. There is nothing magical about seven — nor the grouping of Bell Operating Companies (BOCs) into RBOCs — except the Judge wanted to keep them all roughly the same size. The seven RBOCs are Ameritech, Bell Atlantic, Bell South, NYNEX, Pacific Telesis, Southwestern Bell and US West. In early October, 1994, Southwestern Bell changed its name to SBC Communications Inc. But its telephone companies, it said, would still operate under the Southwestern name.

*RE-ENGINEERING*

A term probably invented by Michael Hammer in the July-August, 1990 issue of Harvard Business Review. In that issue, he wrote, "It is time to stop paving the cowpaths. Instead of embedding outdated processes in silicon and software, we should obliterate them and start over. We should 're engineer' our business: use the power of modern information technology to radically redesign our business processes in order to achieve dramatic improvements in their performance." The term re-engineering now seems to me to mean taking tasks presently running on mainframes and making them run on file servers running on LANs — Local Area Networks. The idea is to save money on hardware and make the information more freely available to more people. More intelligent companies also redesign their organization to use the now, more-freely available information. Also called VALUE DRIVEN RE-ENGINEERING.

*RFC (Request For Comment)*

An Internet term. The contents of an RFC may range from an official standardized protocol specification to research results or proposals. A set of papers in which the Internet's standards, proposed standards and generally agreed-upon ideas are documented and published.

*RFC 1144*

This RFC will provide overhead compression for the TCP/IP protocol down to 5 octets. It does this by anticipating that the next packet in a file transfer sequence that will have the same address as the previous and will have the same sequence number plus one. This compression technique will be useful where SDLC encapsulation, or other bridging protocol encapsulation, is being utilized with low-speed PVCs. In these cases, the slight increase in processing power to perform the compression is more than balanced by the increase in application performance and throughput.

*RFC 1294*

This is Inverse ARP, which allows the automatic discovery of the addresses on the router at each end of another router's DLCIs. Right now, the RFC only applies to IP, but some equipment vendors have already expanded the protocol support to include Novell, AppleTalk, Vines, and DECnet. The benefit of the RFC is to simplify network configuration.

*RFC 1315*

This is the frame relay MIB (management information database), which standardizes what management information is made available on frame relay devices and where/how that information is accessed. This simplifies the process of integrating frame relay devices into your network monitoring and management process and programs. More information on frame relay network management is covered in the chapter on this topic.

*RFC 1490*

RFC 1294, now renumbered RFC 1490, is for multiprotocol encapsulation. The bottom line benefits are to increase interoperability between frame relay devices from different vendors. This means that you can use one vendor's routers (or other equipment type) at some locations, and a different vendor's equipment at other locations. This ability to mix and match allows you to pick the best and most cost-effective tool for the job.

*RFP (Request for Proposal)*

A detailed document prepared by a buyer defining his requirements for service and equipment sent to one or several vendors. A vendor's response to an RFP will typically be binding on the vendor, i.e. he will be obliged to deliver what he says in his RFP at the prices and following the conditions explained in that RFP. See RFQ for a detailed explanation.

*RING*

1. As in Tip and Ring. One of the two wires (the two are Tip and Ring) needed to set up a telephone connection. 2. Also a reference to the ringing of the telephone set. 3. The design of a Local Area Network (LAN) in which the wiring loops from one workstation to another, forming a circle (thus, the term "ring"). In a ring LAN, data is sent from workstation to workstation around the loop in the same direction. Each workstation (which is usually a PC) acts as a repeater by re-sending messages to the next PC in the ring. The more PCs, the slower the LAN. Network control is distributed in a ring network. Since the message passes through each PC, loss of one PC may disable the entire network. However, most ring LANs recover very quickly should one PC die or be turned off. If it dies, you can remove it physically from the network. If it's off, the network senses that and the token ignores that machine. In some token LANs, the LAN will close around a dead workstation and join the two workstations on either side together. If you lose the PC doing the control functions, another PC will jump in and take over. This is how the IBM Token-Passing Ring works. See TOPOLOGY and TOKEN RING.

*RING NETWORK CONFIGURATION*

A network that links PBXs, computers, terminals, printers and other devices in a circular communications link. See RING.

*RIP (Routing Information Protocol)*

RIP is based on distance-vector algorithms that measure the shortest path between two points on a network in terms of the number of "hop" between those points.

*ROUTER*

1. A system level function that directs a call to an application. 2. An interface between two networks. While routers are like bridges, they work differently. Routers provide more functionality than bridges. For example, they can find the best route between any two networks, even if there are several different networks in between. Routers provide network management capabilities such as load balancing, partitioning of the network, use statistics, communication priority, and trouble shooting tools that allow network managers to detect and correct problems even in a complex network of networks. Given these capabilities, routers are often used in building wide area or enterprise wide networks.

There are two types of routers, protocol dependent and protocol independent. Protocol dependent routers rely on the end stations (computers on a LAN) for routing information. Computers tell the routers where (on which network) the destination computer is located and the routers find the best way to get there. This means that routers must understand the language (LAN protocol) the computers are talking, this makes them protocol dependent. Protocol independent routers discover the location of the destination device on their own and without any assistance from the communicating computers. They therefore, do not need to understand the language the computers are using which makes them protocol independent.

Protocol independent routers are easier to install and use. Most importantly, they can route non routable protocols, like those used by IBM networks. See also INTERNETWORKING and BRIDGES.

*ROUTE XPANDER CARD*

A board manufactured by IBM for insertion into a PC which provide the PC with a wide area interface to a frame relay network, including handling all of the necessary protocol encapsulation.

*SCREEN RESPONSE TIME*

The time it takes to refresh a terminal screen.

*SDLC (Synchronous Data Link Control)*

A bit-oriented synchronous communications protocol developed by IBM where the message may contain any collection or sequence of bits without being mistaken for a control character. SDLC is used in IBM's SNA — System Network Architecture. See HDLC and IBM.

*SDN (Software Defined Network)*

Generically, a software defined network refers to a virtual private network. Specifically, it refers to AT&T's Software Defined Network Service, which was introduced in 1985 for AT&T's largest customers and provided only dedicated access services. In 1989, AT&T extended its SDN Network to switched access. Currently, SDN is the most commonly resold of all long distance services. The AT&T Software Defined Network Service Description of July 1986 describes SDN as a service developed for multi-location businesses which allows network managers to tailor their network to their own specific communications needs. Call processing information is stored in a database that is accessed during a call. Calls are transferred over AT&T facilities to either a location that is a dedicated part of the network (for "on-net calling") or to non-dedicated facilities that are part of the network ("on-net" calling). Any company location can become part of a network through SDN dedicated access lines to an AT&T SDN serving office. Here is further explanation of SDN by Siemens Information Systems, whose Saturn PBX has the capability to interface to and mesh neatly with an AT&T SDN network. Here is Siemens' explanation (it's good): When a company establishes an SDN, each phone on the network has a unique seven digit number. This number may or may not be the same as the Listed Directory Number (LDN). When a call is placed at one PBX, it is sent over a dedicated access line to the long distance network. The call is received by the SDN Serving Office and digits are sent via a CCIS (Common Channel Interoffice Signaling) link to the Network Control Point (NCP) for analysis and routing. There is one NCP per SDN network. The NCP contains the unique database for the company using the SDN. The NCP analyzes the digits received against the database, determines whether it is an on-net or off-net call, and sets up the path over which the call will be rerouted on the long distance network. If it is an on-net call, the NCP translates the unique seven digit locator code to one that will be recognized by the AT&T network, sends the call over the network to another SDN Serving Office, and completes the call over dedicated lines to the PBX being called. There is a discount for any call which remains on-net throughout. If the call is off-net, the digits dialed are sent over the long distance network to a Central Office that is not part of the SDN. The call is then completed to the corporate PBX over DID (Direct Inward Dial) lines. Since the introduction of route selection features in PBXs, the caller now has the ability to dial the 10-digit LDN (Long Distance Number) and have the PBX make the decisions on the route and make the decisions on any digit translation or deletion that is necessary to route the call. The CCIS network which carries SDN call signaling is a packet switching network operating at 4,800 bits per second. It will eventually be replaced by CCITT 7 Signaling, a more powerful internationally-accepted signaling system. See SIGNALING SYSTEM 7.

*SECURITY MANAGEMENT*

Protects a network from invalid accesses. It is one of the management categories defined by the ISO (International Standards Organization).

*SERIALIZATION*

To change from parallel-by-byte to serial-by-bit.

*SERVER*

A server is a shared computer on the local area network that can be as simple as a regular PC set aside to handle print requests to a single printer. Or, more usually, it is the fastest and brawniest PC around. It may be used as a repository and distributor of oodles of data. It may also be the gatekeeper controlling access to voice mail, electronic-mail, facsimile services. At one stage, a local area network had only one server. These days networks have multiple servers. Servers these days have multiple brains, large arrays of big disk drives (often in redundant arrays) and other powerful features. New powerful servers are called superservers. A $35,000 superserver today can match the performance of a $2 million mainframe of ten years ago. Then again, according to Peter Lewis of the New York Times, the lowliest client today has more computing power than was available to the entire Allied Army in World War II. See DOWNSIZING for some of the benefits of running servers as against mainframes.

*SF (Superframe)*

The superframe transmission structure consists of 12 DS1 frames (2316 bits). The DS1 frame comprises 193 bit positions, the first of which is the frame overhead-bit position. Frame overhead bit positions are used for the frame and signaling phase alignment only.

*SIGNALING SYSTEM (SS7)*

All phone systems need signaling. According to James Henry Green, author of the Dow Jones-Irwin Handbook of Telecommunications, signals have three basic functions:

1. SUPERVISING. Monitoring the status of a line or circuit to see if it is busy, idle or requesting service. Supervision is a term derived from the job telephone operators perform in manually monitoring circuits on a switchboard. On switchboards, supervisory signals are shown by a lit lamp indicating a request for service on an incoming line or an on-hook condition of a switchboard cord circuit. In the network (i.e. the automated part of the network), supervisory signals are indicated by the voltage level on signaling leads, or the on-hook/off-hook status of signaling tones or bits.

2. ALERTING. Indicates the arrival of an incoming call. Alerting signals are bells, buzzers, woofers, tones, strobes and lights.

3. ADDRESSING. Transmitting routing and destination signals over the network. Addressing signals are in the form of dial pulses, tone pulses or data pulses over loops, trunks and signaling networks.

Most signaling today is MF (multi-frequency) and SF (single frequency) and is inband. This means that it goes along and occupies the same circuits as those which carry voice conversations. There are two problems with this. First, about 35% of all toll calls are not completed because the phone doesn't answer or is busy, or there are equipment problems along the way. The circuit time used in signaling is substantial, expensive and wasteful. Second, inband signaling is vulnerable to fraud. So the idea of out-of-band signaling came about. It got the name of Common Channel Interoffice Signaling (CCIS) because it used a communications network totally separate from the switched voice network. In North America, CCIS started out as an AT&T packet switched network operating at 4800 bits per second. Each of the packet switches in this network (they are no longer exclusively AT&T's) are called Signal Transfer Points — STPs. CCIS has the following advantages over SF/MF signaling:

Fraud is reduced. "Talk-off" is reduced. (Talk-off occurs when your voice contains enough 2600 Hz energy to activate the tone-detecting circuits in the central office.) Signaling is faster allowing circuits and conversations to be set up and torn down (i.e. disconnected) faster. Signals can be sent in both directions simultaneously and during voice conversation if necessary. Network management information is routed over the CCIS network. For example, when trunks fail, switching systems can be told with CCIS data messages to reroute traffic around problem areas.

The older CCIS signaling is being replaced with a newer out-of-band signaling system called CCITT Signaling System 7. According to an AT&T technical paper delivered at the International Switching Symposium in Spring, 1987, CCITT Signaling System 7 is being required by telecommunications administrations worldwide (i.e., all the local country-owned telephone companies) for their networks. AT&T continued with the introduction of digital switches and transmission equipment with 56K bps and 64K bps transmission rates, the International Telegraph and Telephone Consultative Committee (CCITT in French) in 1980 approved the CCITT 7 recommendations optimized for digital networks. This new protocol uses destination routing, octet oriented fields, variable length messages and a maximum message length allowing for 256 bytes of data. Addition of flow control, connectionless services and Integrated Services Digital Network (ISDN) capabilities were approved by CCITT in 1984. A major characteristic of CCITT #7 is its layered functional structure. Its transport functions are divided into four levels, three of which constitute the Message Transfer Part (MTP). The fourth consists of a common Signaling Connection Control Part (SCCP).

The SS7 protocol consists of four basic sub-protocols:

Message Transfer Part (MTP), which provides functions for basic routing of signaling messages between signaling points. Signaling Connection Control Part (SCCP), which provides additional routing and management functions for transfer of messages other than call setup between signaling points. Integrated Services Digital Network User Part (ISUP), which provides for transfer of call setup signaling information between signaling points. Transaction Capabilities Application Part (TCAP), which provides for transfer of non-circuit related information between signaling points.

Signaling System 7 provides two major capabilities:

1. Fast call setup, via high-speed circuit-switched connections.

2. Transaction capabilities which deal with remote data base interactions. What this means in its simplest terms and in one simple application is that Signaling System 7 information can tell the called party who's calling and, more important, tell the called party's computer. A scenario: when you call a direct mail order business, Signaling System 7 will send a signal as to which phone is calling. The agent's CRT screen will pop the caller's name and perhaps the caller's most recent buying information. The agent may answer the phone "Good morning, Mr. Newton. Did you enjoy the three khaki pants we sent you last week?..." Signaling System 7 will be an integral part of ISDN. It will enable us to extend full PBX and Centrex-based services like call forwarding, call waiting, call screening, call transfer, etc. outside the switch to the full international network. In effect, with Signaling System 7, the entire network will acquire the "smarts" of today's smartest electronic digital PBX.

*SIMPLEX*

1. Operating a channel in one direction only with no ability to operate in the other direction. For example one side of a telephone conversation is all that could be carried by a Simplex line. 2. One-sided printing.

*SLIP (Serial Line IP)*

A protocol that allows a computer to use the Internet protocols (and become a full-fledged Internet member) with a standard telephone line and a high-speed modem. SLIP is being superseded by PPP, but is still in common use.

*SMDS (Switched Multimegabit Services)*

A 1.544M bps public data service with an IEEE 802.6 standard user interface. It can support Ethernet, Token Ring and FDDI (OC-3c) LAN-to-LAN connections.

*SNA (System Network Architecture)*

An IBM product. The most successful computer network architecture in the world. See IBM and SYSTEMS NETWORK ARCHITECTURE.

*SNMP (Simple Network Management Protocol)*

In 1988, the Department of Defense and commercial TCP/IP implementors designed a network management architecture for the needs of the average Internet (a collection of disparate networks joined together with bridges or routers). Although SNMP was designed as the TCP's stack network management protocol, it can now manage virtually any network type and has been extended to include non-TCP devices such as 802.1 Ethernet bridges. SNMP is widely deployed in TCP/IP (Transmission Control Protocol/Internet Protocol) networks, but actual transport independence means it is not limited to TCP/IP. SNMP has been implemented over Ethernet as well as OSI transports. SNMP became a TCP/IP standard protocol in May 1990. SNMP operates on top of the Internet Protocol, and is similar in concept to IBM's NetView and ISO's CMIP. In 1991, Microsoft started referring to SNMP as SubNetwork Access Protocol. In November of 1993 Cisco Systems announced that its internetwork routers will support version 2 of the Simple Network Management Protocol (SMNP)and it has licensed SNMP v2 developed by SNMP Research, Inc. of Knoxville, TN.

*SOCKETS*

1. A synonym for a port. 2. The socket in a PC which is responsible for accepting a PCMCIA Card and mapping the host's internal bus signals to the PCMCIA interface signals. 3. A paring of an IP address and a port number.

*SONET (Synchronous Optical Network)*

A family of fiber-optic transmission rates from 51.84M bps to 13.22 Gbps, created to provide the flexibility needed to transport many digital signals with different capacities, and to provide a standard for manufacturers to design from. Sonet is an optical interface standard that allows interworking of transmission products from multiple vendors (i.e. mid-span meets). It defines a physical interface, optical line rates known as Optical Carrier (OC) signals, frame format and an OAM&P protocol (Operations, Administration, Maintenance, And Provisioning). The OC signals have electrical called Synchronous Transport Signals (STSs). The base rate is 51.84M bps (OC-1/STS-1) and higher rates are direct multiples of the base rate.

SONET was created by the Exchange Carriers Standards Association for the American National Standards Institute (ANSI). The standard is being defined in phases — Phase 1, adopted in March of 1988 by ANSI, and Phase 2, planned or completion by February of 1990. SONET has also been adopted by the Consultive Committee for International Telephone and Telegraph (CCITT).

SONET was initiated by Bellcore on behalf of the Regional Bell Operating Companies to attain these goals: Multi-vendor interworking, to be cost effective for existing services on an end-to-end basis, to create an infrastructure to support new broadband services and for enhanced operations, administration, maintenance and provisioning (OAM&P).

SONET, according to Northern Telecom, offers many advantages over asynchronous transport including: Opportunity for back-to-back multiplexing, digital cross-connect panels; Easy evolution to broadband transport; Compatibility with evolving operations standards; Enhanced performance monitoring and Extension of OAM&P capabilities to end users.

SONET transmission equipment interweaves STSs in simple integer multiples to form a synchronous high speed signal. This permits easy access to low speed signals (e.g. DS-O, DS-1, etc.) without multi-stage multiplexing and demultiplexing. The low speed signals are mapped into sub-STS-1 signals called Virtual Tributaries (VTs).

SONET uses a 51.84M bps STS-1 signal as the basic building block. Higher rate signals are multiples of STS-1 (e.g. the STS-12/OC-12 signal has a rate of 12 x 51.84M bps or 622.080M bps). The frame format consists of 90 x 9 bytes. The SONET frame format is divided into two main areas: Synchronous Payload Envelope (SPE) and Transport Overhead (TOH). The SPE contains the information being transported by the frame. The TOH supports the OAM&P functions of SONET, and includes a data communication channel that provides an OAM&P communication path between multiple interconnected SONET network elements.

The SPE can handle payloads in any of three ways:

1. As a continuous 50.1M bps envelope for carrying asynchronous DS-3, and other payloads requiring up to 50.11M bps capacity in asynchronous (byte invisible) or byte visible format;

2. In a VT structured envelope to accommodate DS-1, DS-1C, DS-2, European CEPT1, or future VT based services (see chart below). These signals can have either an asynchronous or byte visible format; and

3. As concatenated payloads to accommodate services requiring more than 50.11M bps capacity. For example, three STS-1 SPEs may be concatenated (combined) to transport a broadband ISDN signal of 135M bps.

According to AT&T, the main Sonet characteristics are a family of rates at N x 51.84M bps; Optical interconnect allowing mid-span meet; Intra office mixed vendor interconnects; Overhead channels for OAM & P functions and Synchronous networking.

SONET RATES ARE

| OC Level | Line Rates | Capacity |
|---|---|---|
| OC-1 | 52M bps | 28 DS1s or 1 DS3 |
| OC-3 | 155M bps | 84 DS1s or 3 DS3s |
| OC-9 | 466M bps | 252 DS1s or 9 DS3s |
| OC-12 | 622M bps | 336 DS1s or 12 DS3s |
| OC-18 | 933M bps | 504 DS1s or 18 DS3s |
| OC-24 | 1.2G bps | 672 DS1s or 24 DS3s |
| OC-36 | 1.9G bps | 1008 DS1s or 36 DS3s |
| OC-48 | 2.5G bps | 1344 DS1s or 48 DS3s |

*SOURCE ROUTE BRIDGING*

IBM method of bridging, popular in Token Ring networks. See SOURCE ROUTING.

*SOURCE ROUTING*

A method used by a bridge for moving data between two networks. Originally developed by IBM's token ring network, it relies on information contained within the token to route the packet between the two networks. Since the information in the token is supplied by the computer that sent the data packet, that computer must know on which network the destination computer is located. IBM developed a special protocol that lets computers discover that information. For source routing to work, every computer and every bridge on all networks must support this protocol. If some computers do not use this protocol, they will not receive packets from bridges that use source routing. See BRIDGE. Compare to TRANSPARENT ROUTING.

In IBM's method of routing local area network data across bridges, IBM's bridges can be configured as either single-route broadcast or all-routes broadcast. The default is single-route broadcast. Single-route broadcasting means that only one designated single-route bridge will pass the packet and only one copy of the packet will arrive at its destination. Single-route broadcast bridges can transmit both single-route and all-routes packets. All-routes broadcasting sends the packet across every possible route in the network, resulting in as many copies of the frame at the destination as there are all-routes broadcasting bridges in the network. All-routes broadcast bridges only pass all-routes broadcast packets.

### *SPEAKERPHONE*

A telephone which has a speaker and microphone for hands free, two-way conversation.

### *SPLIT HORIZON*

The view a router has of a wide area network interface in a partial mesh environment where an incoming packet may need to be sent out of the same interface, over which it is received, in order to reach its ultimate destination. Split horizon is normally disabled to ensure that this cannot occur and that routing loops are not created. This posed a problem with frame relay because packets should be sent back out the same physical interface over which they have been received, but not the same logical interface. Router vendors have now solved this problem, enabling routers to support partially meshed frame relay networks.

### *SPOOFING*

1. In COMSEC applications, the interception, alteration, and retransmission of a cipher signal or data in such a way as to mislead the receiver. 2. In automated-information-systems applications, an attempt to gain access to an automated information system by posing as an authorized user.

### *STAR CONFIGURATION*

1. A topology in which all phones or workstations are wired directly to a central service unit or workstation that establishes, maintains and breaks connections between the workstations. Virtually all phone systems are stars configurations. ISDN BRI bus will be the first phone system to operate on a bus. In datacom language, the center of a star is called the hub. The advantage of a star is that it is easy to isolate a problem node. However, if the central node fails, the entire network fails. The star network we're all most familiar with is our local telephone exchange. At the center (the hub) rests the central office. Spanning out in a star are the lines going to the individual workstations (telephones) in peoples' houses and offices. 2. Advanced telecommunications for the industrially less advanced regions of the European Community.

### *STATISTICAL MULTIPLEXING*

A multiplexing technique that differs from simple multiplexing in that the share of the available transmission bandwidth allocated to a given user varies dynamically. In other words, in statistical multiplexing, a channel is only assigned to communicating devices (voice, modem, etc.) when they actually have data to send or receive. This makes statistical multiplexing more powerful than normal FDM or TDM multiplexing. In other words, statistical multiplexing typically allows you to cram more information down a pipe than you can with FDM or TDM multiplexing. See also FAST PACKET MULTIPLEXING.

*SVC (Switched Virtual Circuit)*

A connection across a network. It is established on an as-needed basis and can provide connection to any other user in the network. The connection lasts only for the duration of the transfer. It is the datacom equivalent of a dialed phone call.

*SWITCH*

A mechanical, electrical or electronic device which opens or closes circuits, completes or breaks an electrical path, or selects paths or circuits.

*SYNCHRONOUS*

1. The condition that occurs when two events happen in a specific time relationship with each other and both are under control of a master clock. 2. Synchronous transmission means there is a constant time between successive bits, characters or events. The timing is achieved by the sharing of a single clock. Each end of the transmission synchronizes itself with the use of clocks and information sent along with the transmitted data. Synchronous is the most popular communications method to and from mainframes. In synchronous transmission, characters are spaced by time, not by start and stop bits. Because you don't have to add these bits, synchronous transmission of a message will take fewer bits (and therefore less time) than an asynchronous transmission. But because precise clocks and careful timing are needed in synchronous transmission, it's usually more expensive to set up synchronous transmission.

*SYSTEMS NETWORK ARCHITECTURE (SNA)*

IBM's successful computer network architecture. At one stage the most successful computer network architecture in the world. In the days of mainframe computers, it was as successful in the computer networking world as AT&T's telephone network design was in telecommunications. The best explanation we've ever read of SNA is in James Henry Green's Dow Jones-Irwin Handbook of Telecommunications. (You can get a copy of this great book by calling the Telecom Library at 1-800-LIBRARY.) Here is an excerpt:

"SNA is a tree-structured architecture, with a mainframe host computer acting as the network control center. The boundaries described by the host computer, front-end processors, cluster controllers and terminals are referred to as the network's domain. Unlike the switched telephone network that establishes physical paths between terminals for the duration of a session, SNA establishes a logical path between network nodes, and it routes each message with addressing information contained in the protocol. The network is therefore incompatible with any but approved protocols. SNA uses the SDLC data link protocol exclusively. Devices using asynchronous or binary synchronous can access SNA only through protocol converters...SNA works in seven layers roughly analogous to ISO's seven level OSI model. Unlike OSI, however, SNA is fully defined at each level. SNA was first announced in 1974 and is the basis for much of the OSI model, but it differs from OSI in several significant respects." For more on these differences, see page 96 in Green's Handbook.

The following is a description we received from IBM's PR department: "What is SNA?" In general, SNA is the description of the rules that enable IBM's customers to transmit and receive information through their computer networks. SNA may also be viewed as three distinct but related entities: a specification, a plan for structuring a network and a set of products. First, SNA is a specification governing the design of IBM products that are to communicate with one another in a network. It is called an architecture because it specifies the operating relationships of those products as part of system. Second, SNA provides a coherent structure that enables users to establish and manage their networks and, in response to new requirements and technologies, to change or expand them. Third, SNA may be viewed as a set of products: combinations of hardware and programming designed in accordance with the specification of SNA. In addition to a large number of computer terminals for both specific industries and general applications, IBM's SNA product line includes host processors, communication controllers, and adapters, modems and data encryption units. The SNA product line also includes a variety of programs and programming subsystems. Telecommunications access methods, network management programs, distributed applications programming and the network control program are examples.

***T-1***

A digital transmission link with a capacity of 1.544M bps (1,544,000 bits per second). T-1 uses two pairs of normal twisted wires, the same as you'd find in your house. T-1 normally can handle 24 voice conversations, each one digitized at 64K bps. But, with more advanced digital voice encoding techniques, it can handle more voice channels. T-1 is a standard for digital transmission in the United States, Canada, Hong Kong and Japan. (For the complete T Carrier hierarchy see the definition for T Carrier above.)

T-1 lines are used for connecting networks across remote distances. Bridges and routers are used to connect LANs over T-1 networks. There are faster services available. T-1 links can often be connected directly to new PBXs and many new forms of short haul transmission, such as short haul microwave systems. It is not compatible with T-1 outside the United States and Canada. In Europe T-1 is called E-1 or E1.

Outside of the United States and Canada, the "T-1" line bit rate is usually 2,048,000 bits per second. France and West Germany impose slight variations that make their formats unique. Only one element remains constant — the DS-0. The 64 kilobit per channel is universal. Most often it represents a PCM voice signal sampled at 8,000 times per second. However, the form of PCM encoding differs between T-1 (mu-law) and E-1 (A-law companding). According to Bill Flanagan's book, the differences are not so great that a multiplexer cannot convert between them. Conversion of E-1 to T-1 involves both the compression law and the signaling format.

At the higher rate of 2,048,000, 32 time slots are defined at the CEPT interface, but two are used for signaling and other housekeeping chores. Typically 30 channels are left for user information — voice, video, data, etc. CEPT is the Conference of European Postal and Telecommunications administrations. standards-setting body whose membership includes European Post, Telephone, and Telegraphy Authorities (PTTs).

For a full explanation of T-1 see Bill Flanagan's book The Guide to T-1 Networking. (Call 1-800-LIBRARY or 212-691-8215 for your copy.)

*TANDEM ARCHITECTURES*

A physical network topology where connectivity between locations is achieved by linking several locations together in a chain using private line circuits. In a tandem architecture, a packet may have to pass through several intermediate locations before reaching its final destination. A single network failure can affect connectivity between several locations, a primary weakness of the topology. See TANDEMING.

*TANDEM POINTS*

An intermediate location in a tandem architecture.

*TANDEMING*

The connection of networks or circuits in series. That is, the connection of the output of one circuit to the input of another. See TANDEM SWITCH.

*TCP/IP (Transmission Control Protocol/Internet Program)*

A set of protocols developed by the Department of Defense to link dissimilar computers across many kinds of networks, including unreliable ones and connected to dissimilar LANs. Developed in the 1970s by the U.S. Department of Defense's Advanced Research Projects Agency (DARPA) as a military standard protocol, its assurance of multi vendor connectivity has made it popular among commercial users as well, who have adopted TCP/IP as an interim step while awaiting the availability of OSI products. Consequently, TCP/IP now is supported by many manufacturers of minicomputers, personal computers, mainframes, technical workstations and data communications equipment. It is also the protocol commonly used over Ethernet (as well as X.25) networks. It has been implemented on everything from PC LANs to minis and mainframes. Although committed to an eventual migration to an OSI architecture, TCP/IP currently divides networking functionality into only four layers:

A Network Interface Layer that corresponds to the OSI Physical and Data Link Layers. This layer manages the exchange of data between a device and the network to which it is attached and routes data between devices on the same network.

An Internet Layer which corresponds to the OSI network layer. The Internet Protocol (IP) subset of the TCP/IP suite runs at this layer. IP provides the addressing needed to allow routers to forward packets across a multiple LAN internetwork. In IEEE terms, it provides connectionless datagram service, which means it attempts to deliver every packet, but has no provision for retransmitting lost or damaged packets. IP leaves such error correction, if required, to higher level protocols, such as TCP.

IP addresses are 32 bits in length and have two parts: the Network Identifier (Net ID) and the Host Identifier (Host ID). Assigned by a central authority, the Net ID specifies the address, unique across the Internet, for each network or related group of networks. Assigned by the local network administrator, the Host ID specifies a particular host, station or node within a given network and need only be unique within that network.

A Transport Layer, which corresponds to the OSI Transport Layer. The Transmission Control Protocol (TCP) subset runs at this layer. TCP provides end-to-end connectivity between data source and destination with detection of, and recovery from, lost, duplicated, or corrupted packets — thus offering the error control lacking in lower level IP routing. In TCP, message blocks from applications are divided into smaller segments, each with a sequence number that indicates the order of the segment within the block. The destination device examines the message segments and, when a complete sequence of segments is received, sends an acknowledgement (ACK) to the source, containing the number of the next byte expected at the destination.

An Application Layer, which corresponds to the session, presentation and application layers of the OSI model. This layer manages the function required by the user programs and includes protocols for remote log-in (Telnet), file transfer (FTP), and electronic mail (SMTP). See OSI.

*TELEPHONY SERVICES*

Telephony Services's real name is Telephony Services for NetWare. NetWare is the name of the best-selling local area network software supplied and sold by Novell, Orem, Utah. Telephony Services for NetWare basically consists of an addition to the NetWare operating system, called Telephony Server NLM. That addition handles communications between a NetWare file server (a PC loaded with NetWare) and an attached telephone switch, e.g., a PBX or ACD (automatic call distributor). The concept is very simple. Picture your department's LAN. You're sitting in front of your PC which is on your department's LAN. You have a telephone which is an extension off your company's or department's PBX. You click on an icon that says "Phone." Bingo, a screen comes up with icons and pull down menus. You can now look up Joe, click on his name. Your PC sends a command to your NetWare file server, which in turn sends a command to your PBX which tells it to dial Joe from your phone. Once it's completed dialing, it might turn on your phone's speakerphone or your telephone headset. You'll then hear Joe say "Hello." Telephony Services for NetWare is basically the software in the NetWare file server which takes care of interpreting your PC commands into commands your switch can understand and respond to.

Telephony Services requires a link to your switch. Each telecom switch manufacturer has been implementing that link in a different way technically. That's fine, because Telephony Services for NetWare insulates the user and the developer. This means that computer telephony applications written for Telephony Services for NetWare will work on any switch conforming to the Telephony Services standard. As of this writing, virtually every switch manufactured in North America and many made in Japan and Europe is conforming to Novell's Telephony Services.

According to a White Paper issued by Novell in March 1994 and called NetWare Telephony Services, "The three main components of Telephony Services are call control, voice processing, and speech synthesis. Call control provides the core service for PBX-to-NetWare communication and an Application Programming Interface (API) for developing client server applications. With call control, users can enjoy features such as making calls, transfers, or conference calling. Voice processing functions include voice mail and interactive voice response. Speech synthesis will be a key area for integrating multiple media types. Through speech/text conversion, users can access voice mail, e-mail, and fax documents through audio or text media types. The initial products Novell is delivering include:

Client/Server API

Telephony Server NetWare Loadable Module (NLM)

PBX Driver

"The Telephony Server NLM is the mechanism for passing information between the PBX and the NetWare server. As part of the NLM, an open PBX Driver Interface allows PBX manufacturers to write drivers that communicate with their respective PBXs. The client/server API provides support across multiple desktop operating systems and allows call control at either the client or the server."

Client server computer telephony (which is what all this is called) delivers ten benefits:

1. Synchronized data screen and phone call pop. Your phone rings. The call comes with the calling number attached (via Caller ID or ANI). Your PBX or ACD passes that number (via Telephony Services) to your server, which does a quick database look up to see if it can find a name and database entry. Bingo, it finds an entry. It passes the call and the database entry simultaneously to whoever is going to answer the phone: The attendant. The boss. The sales agent. The customer service desk. The help desk. All this saves asking a lot of questions. Makes customers happier.

2. Integrated messaging. Also called Unified Messaging. Voice, fax, electronic mail, image and video. All on the one screen. Here's the scenario. You arrive in the morning. Turn on your PC. Your PC logs onto your LAN and its various servers. In seconds, it gives you a screen listing all your messages — voice mail, electronic mail, fax mail, reports, compound documents - Anything and everything that came in for you. Each is one line. Each line tells you who it's from. What it is. How big it is. How urgent. Skip down. Click. Your PC loads up the application. Your LAN hunts down the message. Bingo, it's on screen. If it contains voice — maybe it's a voice mail or compound document with voice in it — it rings your phone (or your headset) and plays the voice to you. Or, if you have a sound card in your PC, it can play the voice through your own PC. If it's an image, it will hunt down (also called launch) imaging software which can open the image you have received, letting you see it. Ditto, if it's a video message.

Messages are deluging us. To stop them is to stop progress. But to run your eye down the list, one line per entry. Pick the key ones. Junk the junk ones. Postpone the others. That's what integrated messaging is all about. Putting some order back into your life.

3. Database transactions. Customer look ups. There are bank account balances, ticket buys, airline reservations, catalog requests, movie times, etc. Doing business over the phone is exploding. Today, the caller inputs his request by touchtone or by recognized speech. The system responds with speech and/or fax. Today's systems are limited in size and flexibility. The voice processing application and the database typically share the same processor, often a PC. Split them. Spread the processing and database access burden. Join them on a LAN (for the data) and on new, broader voice processing "LANs," like SCSA or MVIP. You've suddenly got a computer telephony system that knows no growth constraints. You could also get the system to front-end an operator or an agent. Once the caller has punched in all his information, then the call and the screen can be simultaneously passed to the agent.

4. Telephony work groups. Sales groups. Collections groups. Help desks. R&D. We work in groups. But traditional telephony doesn't. Telephony today is BIG. Telephony today is one giant phone system for the building, for the campus. Everyone shares the same automated attendant, the same voice mail, the same ubiquitous, universal, generic telephone features. But they shouldn't. The sellers need phones that grab the caller's phone number, do a look-up on what the customer bought last and quickly route the call to the appropriate (or available) salesperson. The one who sold the customer last time. The company's help desk needs a front end voice response system that asks for the customer's serial number, some indication of the problem and tries to solve the problem by instantly sending a fax or encouraging the caller to punch his way to one of many canned solutions. "The 10 biggest problems our customers have." When all else fails, the caller can be transferred to a live human, expert at diagnosing and solving his pressing problem. A development group might need e-mails and faxes of meeting agendas sent, meeting reminder notices phoned and scheduled video conferences set up. All automatically. The accounts receivable department needs a predictive dialer to dial all our deadbeats. The telemarketing department also needs a predictor dialer, but different programming.

5. Desktop telephony. There are two important aspects. Call control and media processing services. Call control (also called call processing) is a fancy name for using your PC to get to all your phone system's features — especially those you have difficulty getting to with the forgettable commands phone makers foist on us. *39 to transfer? Or it is *79? With attractive PC

screens, you point and click to easy conferencing, transferring, listening to voice mail messages, forwarding, etc. There are enormous personal productivity benefits to running your office phone from your PC: You can dial by name, not by number you can't remember. You can set up conference calls by clicking on names and have your PC call the participants and call you only when they're all on the phone. You can transfer easily. You can work your voice mail more easily on screen, instead of having to remember "Dial 3 for rewind," "Dial 2 to save," and other obscure commands. Here's a wonderful quote from Marshall R. Goldberg, Developer Relations Group at Microsoft. He says, "Voice mail systems that could benefit through integration with the personal computer largely remain isolated, difficult to use, and inflexible. Browsing, storing messages in hierarchical folders, and integration of address books — functions just about everyone could use — are either unavailable or unusable."

The second benefit is media control. Media control is a fancy name for affecting the content of the call. You may wish to record the phone call you're on. You may wish to have all or part of your phone call clipped and sent to someone else — as you often today with voice mail messages. You may wish to simply file your conversations away in appropriate folders. You may wish to be able to call your PC and get it to read you back any e-mails or faxes you received in the last day or so.

6. Applying intelligence. A PC is programmable. The typical office phone isn't. A PC can be programmed to act as your personal secretary, handling different calls differently. It can be programmed to include commands, such as "If Joe calls, break into my conversation and tell me." "If Robert calls, send him to voice mail." etc.

7. The Compound Document. The typed document lacks life. But add voice, image and video clips to it and it gets life. The LAN makes the compound document easier to achieve. The Compound Document gets attention.

8. Management of phone networks. Today, phone networks are very difficult to manage. Often the PBX is managed separately from the voice mail, which is managed separately from the call accounting, etc. It's a rare day in any corporate life when the whole system is up to date, with extensions, bills and voice mail mailboxes reflecting the reality of what's actually happening. The latest generations of LAN software — NetWare 4.1 and Windows NT — have solid enterprise-wide directories and far easier management tools. Integrate these LAN management tools with telecommunications management, and potentially all you need is to make one entry (for a new employee, a change, etc.) and the whole system — telecom and computing — could update itself automatically, including issuing change orders to the MIS and telecom departments and vendors.

9. No dedicated hardware in the PC. With only one link — from the switch to the LAN — there's no need to open the desktop PC and place specialized telephony hardware in each PC that wants to take advantage of the new LAN-based telephony features.

10. Switch elimination. The ultimate potential advantage of LAN-based telephony is to eliminate the connection to the switch (PBX or ACD) by simply populating the LAN server (now called a telephony server) with specialized computer telephony cards and run the company's or department's phones off the telephony server directly.

*TDM (Time Division Multiplexing)*

A technique for transmitting a number of separate data, voice and/or video signals simultaneously over one communications medium by quickly interleaving a piece of each signal one after another. Here's our problem. We have to transport the freight of five manufacturers from Chicago to New York. Each manufacturer's freight will fit into 20 rail boxcars. We have three basic solutions. First, build five separate railway lines from Chicago to New York. Second, rent five engines and schlepp five complete trains to New York on one railway track. Or, third, join all the boxcars together into one train of 100 boxcars and run them on one track. The train might look like this: Engine, Boxcar from Producer A, Box Car from Producer B, Producer C, Producer D, Producer E, and then the order begins again...Boxcar from Producer A, Producer B...Moving one large train of 100 boxcars is likely to be cheaper and more efficient than moving five smaller trains each of 20 boxcars on five separate railway tracks. Time Division Multiplexing, thus, represents substantial savings over having five separate networks (five separate tracks) and sending five separate transmissions (five separate trains).

This is what Time Division Multiplexing is all about. And the analogy is perfect. Take one large train (fast communications channel) and interleave pieces (boxcars) from each conversation one after another. If you do this fast enough, you'll never notice you've broken the conversations apart, moved them separately, and then put them back together at the distant end.

In TDM, you "sample" each voice conversation, interleave the samples, send them on their way, then reconstruct the several conversations at the other end. There are several ways to do the sampling. You can sample eight bits (one byte) of each conversation or you can sample one bit. The former is called word interleaving; the latter bit interleaving. The basic goal of multiplexing — whether it be time division multiplexing, or any other form — is to save money, to cram more conversations (voice, data, video or facsimile) onto fewer phone lines. To substitute electronics for copper. See MULTIPLEXING.

*TELNET*

The process by which a person using one computer can sign on to a computer in another city, state or country. Terminal-remote host protocol developed for ARPAnet. Using Telnet, you can work from your PC as if it were a terminal attached to another machine by a hard-wired line. The TCP/IP protocol governing the exchange of character-oriented terminal data.

*TERMINAL*

1. The point at which a telephone line ends, or is connected to other circuits of a network. 2. An input/output device for communicating with computers. Typically has a keyboard and a CRT (TV screen) display. See TERMINALS.

*TERMINAL SERVER*

A small, specialized, networked computer that connects many terminals to a LAN through one network connection. Any user on the network can then connect to various network hosts. A terminal server has a single network interface and several ports for terminal connections. The advantage of a terminal server is it allows many terminals to be connected to a host via a single existing LAN cable, rather than a variety of point-to-point cables. Digital Equipment's DECnet makes heavy use of terminal servers.

*THROUGHPUT*

The actual amount of useful and non-redundant information which is transmitted or processed. Throughput is the end result of a data call. It may only be a small part of what was pumped in at the other end. The relationship of what went in one end and what came out the other is a measure of the efficiency of that communications link — a function of cleanliness, speed, etc.

*TOKEN PASSING*

A method whereby each device on a local area network receives and passes the right to use the single channel on the LAN. The key to remember is that a token passing, or token ring LAN has only one channel. It's a high-speed channel. It can move a lot of data. But it can only move one "conversation" at a time. The Token acts like a traffic cop. It confers the privilege to send a transmission. Tokens are special bit patterns or packets, usually several bits in length, which circulate from node to node when there is no message traffic. Possession of the token gives exclusive access to the network for transmission of a message. The token is generated by one device on the network. If that device is turned off or fails, another device will assume the token creation task. When the package of token and message reaches its destination, the computer copies the message. The package is then put back on the network where it continues to circulate until it returns to the source computer. The source computer then releases the token for the next computer in the sequence.

With token passing it is possible to give some computers more access to the token than others. Usually one device on the network is designated the token manager. It generates the token. If that device is turned off or fails, another device will assume management of the token. There is a complicated sequence of events that result in the generation of a token and that deal with the eventuality of token loss or destruction. The logic for this process is built into token ring cards that fit inside computers. In some manufacturers' products, the logic is slightly different and can cause incompatibilities.

*TOKEN RING*

A ring type of local area network (LAN) in which a supervisory frame, or token, must be received by an attached terminal or workstation before that terminal or workstation can start transmitting. The workstation with the token then transmits and uses the entire bandwidth of whatever communications media the token ring network is using. A token ring is a baseband network. Token ring is the technique used by IBM, Arcnet, and others. A token ring LAN can be wired as a circle or a star, with all workstations wired to a central wiring center, or to multiple wiring centers. The most common wiring scheme is called a star-wired ring. In this configuration, each computer is wired directly to a device called a Multi-station Access Unit (MAU). These are usually grouped together in a wiring closet for convenience. The MAU is wired in such a way as to create a ring between the computers. If one of the computers is turned off or breaks or its cable to the MAU is broken, the MAU automatically recreates the ring without that computer. This gives token ring networks great flexibility, reliability, and ease of configuration and maintenance.

Despite the wiring, a token ring LAN always works logically as a circle, with the token passing around the circle from one workstation to another. The advantage of token ring LANs is that media faults (broken cable) can be fixed easily. It's easy to isolate them. Token rings are typically installed in centralized closets, with loops snaking to served workstations. Some other LANs require your going up in the ceiling or into walls and finding coax taps. All the work on a token ring can be done on one or several panels. These panels allow you to isolate workstations, and thus isolate faults.

Token Ring LANs can operate at transmission rates of either 4M bits per second or 16M bits per second. The number of computers that can be connected to a single Token Ring LAN is limited to 256. The typical installation is usually less than 100. Large installations connect multiple token ring LANS with bridges. The theoretical limit of Ethernet, measured in 64 byte packets, is 14,800 packets per second (PPS). By comparison, Token Ring is 30,000 and FDDI is 170,000. See FDDI-II and FDDI TERMS. Help on this definition courtesy Tad Witkowicz of Crosscomm, Marlboro, MA, Tim Becker, Lanquest Group, Santa Clara, CA and Elaine Jones, VP Marketing, Coral Network Corporation, Marlborough, MA. See also BRIDGE. IBM TOKEN RING, MAU, TOKEN PASSING, TOKEN RING, TOKEN RING CARD and TOKEN RING PACKET.

*TOKEN RING CARD*

Name given to the circuit board inserted into a computer device for connection to a token ring LAN. This board provides the physical connection to the LAN. It also participates in the collective management of the token by sending various messages to other token ring cards. Usually, one token ring card on the network is designated the token manager. It automatically generates a token as soon as it discovers one is missing, often with the help of other token ring cards. The sending of messages between token ring cards can be used to gather information about what is taking place on the network. Statistics may be collected. These may indicate that the network should be altered in some way to improve performance. This management capability is a distinct advantage of token ring LANs. One possible drawback is that various manufacturers' token ring cards may differ slightly in how they implement token management, thereby making them incompatible in certain management features. Virtually all token ring cards will work together in basic token passing.

*TOKEN RING PACKET*

Packets on a token ring network are made up of nine fields: starting delimiter, access control, frame control, destination address, source address, routing information, the data, frame check sequence, and ending delimiter.

Starting Delimiter (SD): This is an 8-bit binary (1s and 0s) sequence which marks the beginning of a data packet.

Access Control (AC) and Frame Control (AC): These are two 8-bit sequences that are used by the computers for maintenance purposes.

Destination Address (DA): This is a 48-bit sequence that uniquely identifies the physical name of the computer to which the data packet is being transmitted. Each computer on a ring examines this field to determine if the packet is for it.

Source Address (SA): This is a 48-bit sequence that uniquely identifies the physical name of the computer that send the data packet. This is used by the receiving computer to formulate its acknowledgement.

Routing Information (RI): This is a variable-length sequence used if the data packet is being sent to a computer located on another token ring LAN. (This information can make it impossible for some bridges to route some packets. See BRIDGE.)

Data: This is a variable-length sequence (up to 17,800 bytes) that is the actual data being sent from source to destination.

Frame Check Sequence (FCS): This 32-bit sequence is used to protect the contents of the packet from being corrupted during transmission. See FRAME CHECK SEQUENCE.

Ending Delimiter (ED): This is an 8-bit sequence that signals the end of a packet.

### *TOPOLOGY*

Network Topology. The geometric physical or electrical configuration describing a local communication network — the shape or arrangement of the system. The most common distribution system topologies are the bus, ring, and star.

### *TRAFFIC ENGINEERING*

The science of figuring how many trunks, how much switching equipment, how many phones, how much communications equipment you'll need to handle the telephone, voice, data, image and video traffic you're estimating. Traffic engineering suffers from several problems:

1. You are basing your future needs on past traffic.

2. Most traffic engineering is based on one or more mathematical formulas, all of which approach but never quite match the real world situation of an actual operating phone system. Computer simulation is the best method of predicting one's needs, but it's expensive in both computer and people time.

3. Many people in the telecommunications industry do not understand traffic engineering, have not worked with it sufficiently and make dumb and costly mistakes.

4. Since there are now several hundred long distance companies in the United States and several thousand differently-priced ways of dialing between major cities (most at different prices), traffic engineering has become very complex.

After I wrote the above definition, Lee Goeller, disagreed with me and contributed this definition.

Traffic Engineering: The application of probability theory to estimating the number of servers required to meet the needs of an anticipated number of customers. In telephone work, the servers are often trunks, and the customers are telephone calls, assumed to arrive at random (see POISSON PROCESS). When arriving calls, upon finding all trunks busy, vanish, a "blocked call cleared" situation obtains (see ERLANG B). When a call stays in the system for a given length of time, whether it gets a trunk or not, "blocked calls held" applies (see POISSON DISTRIBUTION). If a call simply waits around until a trunk becomes available and then uses the trunk for a full holding time, the correct term is "blocked calls delayed" (See ERLANG C and QUEUING THEORY). Like any form of predicting the future on the basis of past behavior, traffic engineering has its limitations; however, when used by those who have taken the trouble to learn how it works, its track record is surprisingly good, and vastly better than most forms of simulation.

### *TRANSLATION*

The interpretation by a switching system of all or part of a destination code to determine the routing of a call. See TRANSLATIONS.

### *TRANSLATIONS*

Translations are changes made by the network to dialed telephone numbers to allow the call to progress through the network. Sometimes the translations are made automatically. Take one series of dialed numbers; convert them to another. Sometimes, translations are done with the help of "look up" tables, also called databases. Here's an example of translations done with the help of a database. TELECONNECT Magazine has a WATS line, 1-800-LIBRARY. If you dial it on the phone, you'll see it is really 1-800-542-7279. But this is not its real number. When someone in California dials 1-800-LIBRARY, AT&T's long distance network recognizes the "1-800" portion of the call and sends it to a special AT&T central office in Utah. When the call arrives, a computer looks up the number 542-7279 in its database and translates that to 1-212-206-6871 and puts the call back into the network. Within seconds, that number in New York, 212-206-6871, which we think is our IN-WATS line, rings.

*TRANSMISSION SYSTEM*

Sending electrical signals carrying information over a line to a destination. Bellcore says that transmission has the following definitions: (a) Designates a field work, such as equipment development, system design, planning, or engineering, in which electrical communication technology is used to create systems to carry information over a distance. (b) Refers to the process of sending information from one point to another. (c) Used with a modifier to describe the quality of a telephone connection: good, fair, or poor transmission. (d) refers to the transfer characteristic of a channel or network in general or, more specifically, to the amplitude transfer characteristic. You may sometimes hear the phrase, "transmission as a function of frequency."

*TRANSPARENT*

When applied to telephone communications, the provision of a feature or service such as Automatic Route Selection in a such a way that the user is unaware of it and it has no affect on the way he uses the telephone. It's "transparent" to him. Translations are transparent to the telephone user.

*TRANSPARENT ROUTING*

A method used by a bridge for moving data between two networks. With this type of routing, the bridge learns which computers are operating on which network. It then uses this information to route packets between networks. It does not rely on the sending computers for its decision-making routine. A special kind of bridge combines the practice of transparent routing with source routing. It is called a source routing transparent (SRT) bridge. It examines each packet that comes by to see if it is using IBM's special source routing protocol. If so, this protocol is used to forward the packet. If not, the transparent method is used. Thus, the SRT bridge will support both IBM and non-IBM network protocols. See also BRIDGE and SRT. Compare with SOURCE ROUTING.

*UNI (User Network Interface)*

The physical and electrical demarcation point between the user and the public network service provider.

*UNIX*

An immensely powerful and complex operating system for computers for running data processing and for running telephone systems. UNIX provides multi-tasking, multi-user capabilities that allow both multiple programs to be run simultaneously and multiple users to use a single computer. On a single-user system, such as MS-DOS, only one person at a time, on an individual task basis, can use a computer's files. programs, and other resources. UNIX works on many different computers. This means you can often take applications software which runs on UNIX and move it — with little changing — to a bigger, different computer, or to a smaller, computer. This process of moving programs to other computers is known as "porting." Today, the UNIX operating system is available on a wide range of hardware, from small personal computers to the most powerful mainframes, from a multitude of hardware and software vendors. UNIX was developed in 1969 by Ken Thompson of AT&T Bell Laboratories.

*V.35*

ITU-T standard for trunk interface between a network access device and a packet network that defines signaling for data rates greater than 19.2K bps. V.35 was a definition of a GROUP band modem (meaning, one that used the bandwidth of several telephone circuits). V.36 and V.37 are other group band modems. V.35 just happened to describe, in an appendix, electrical characteristics for a high speed interface. IBM decided to use this for other things, but it was never standardized for those purposes. The ITU-T, in the 1988 Blue Book, says "It is the opinion of the ITU-T that the information contained in Recommendation V.35 is out of date. Therefore it is not recommended to use the techniques described in this Recommendation for new designs. Alternative techniques are described in Recommendations V.36 and V.37. It should be noted that other Recommendations make reference to the electrical characteristics described in Appendix II to this Recommendation [V.35]. As these characteristics are expected to allow interworking with V.11 characteristics, use of V.11 circuits is recommended in those cases." V.35 is no longer published by the ITU-T.

*VIRTUAL CONNECTIONS*

A logical connection that is made to a virtual circuit.

*VIRTUAL CIRCUIT*

A communications link — voice or data — that appears to the user to be a dedicated point-to-point circuit. Virtual circuits are generally set up on a per-call basis and disconnected when the call is ended. The concept of a virtual circuit was first used in data communications with packet switching. A packetized data call may send packets over different physical paths through a network to its destination, but is considered to have a single virtual circuit. Virtual circuits have become more common in ultra-high speed applications, like frame relay or SMDS. There the connection might be permanently connected like a LAN. When the user wants to transmit he simply transmits. There's no dialing in the conventional sense, just the addition of an address field on the information being transmitted. A virtual circuit is referred to as a logical, rather than physical path for a call. A virtual voice circuit is anything from as simple as a phone with an auto dialer in it to a high-speed link in which voice calls are digitized and send on the equivalent of a ultra high-speed, wide-area equivalent of a local area network. There are two basic reasons people buy virtual circuits. They're cheaper and faster.

*VOICE COMPRESSION*

Refers to the process of electronically modifying a 64K bps PCM voice channel to obtain a channel of 32K bps or less for the purpose of increased efficiency in transmission.

*VTAM (Virtual Telecommunications Access Method)*

Pronounced "Vee-Tam." A program component in an IBM computer which handles some of the communications processing tasks for an application program. VTAM also provides resource sharing, a technique for efficiently using a network to reduce transmission costs.

*WAN (Wide Area Network)*

Uses common carrier-provided lines that cover an extended geographical area. Contrast with LAN. This network uses links provided by local telephone companies and usually connects disperse sites.

*WINDOW SIZE*

The minimum number of data packets that can be transmitted without additional authorization from the receiver.

*WINDOWS*

1. A band of wavelengths at which an optical fiber is sufficiently transparent for practical use in communications applications. 2. A flow-control mechanism in data communications, the size of which is equal to the number of frames, packets or messages that can be sent from a transmitter to a receiver before any reverse acknowledgment is required. It's called a pacing group in IBM's SNA. 3. A box on the CRT (cathode ray tube) of your personal computer or terminal. A software program is running inside the box. It's possible with new "windows" software to run several programs simultaneously, each accessible and visible through the "window" on your CRT. 4. A technique of displaying information on a screen in which the viewer sees what appears to be several sheets of paper much as they would appear on a

desktop. The viewer can shift and shuffle the sheets on the screen. Windowing can show two files simultaneously. For example, in one window you might have a letter you're writing to someone and in another window, you might have a boilerplate letter from which you can take a paragraph or two and drop it in your present letter. Being able to see the two letters on the screen makes writing the new letter easier.

*WORKSTATION*

In the telecom industry, a workstation is a computer and a telephone on a desk and both attached to a telecom outlet on the wall. The computer industry tends to refer to workstations as high-speed personal computers, such as Sun workstations, which are used for high-powered processing tasks like CAD/CAM, engineering, etc. A common PC — like the one you find on my desk — is not usually considered a workstation. The term workstation is vague.

*X.25*

From its beginning as an international standards recommendation from ITU-T, the term X.25 has come to represent a common reference point by which mainframe computers, word processors, mini-computers, VDUs, microcomputers and a wide variety of specialized terminal equipment from many manufacturers can be made to work together over a type of data communications network called a packet switched network. On a packet switched data network (private or public), the data to be transmitted is cut up into blocks. Each block has a header with the network address of the sender and that of the destination. As the block enters the network, the number of bits in the block are put through some mathematical functions (an algorithm) to produce a check sum.

The check sum is attached as a "trailer" to the packet as it enters the network. Packets may travel different routes through the network. But, ultimately, the packets are routed by the network to the node where the destination computer or terminal is located. At the destination, the packet is disassembled. The bits are put through the same algorithm, and if the digits computed are the same as the ones attached to the trailer, there are no detected errors. An ACK, or acknowledgement, is then sent to the transmitting end. If the check sum does not match, a NAK, or Negative Acknowledgement is sent back, and the packet is retransmitted. In this manner, high speed, low error rate information can be transmitted around the country using shared telecommunications circuits on public or private data networks.

X.25 is the protocol providing devices with direct connection to a packet switched network. These devices are typically larger computers, mainframes, minicomputers, etc. Word processors, personal computers, workstations, dumb terminals, etc., do not support the X.25 packet switching protocols unless they are connected to the network via PADs — Packet Assembler/ Disassemblers. A PAD converts between the protocol used by the smaller device and the X.25 protocol. This conversion is performed on both outgoing (from the network) and incoming data (to the network), so the transmission looks transparent to the terminal. (See TRANSPARENT.) There's a very good book on X.25 called X.25 Explained, Protocols for Packet Switching Networks by R. J. Deasington of IBM. It is available from Telecom Library on 1-800-LIBRARY, or 1-212-691-8215.

*ZERO STUFFING*

Synchronous data transmission is done by sending what IBM and AT&T call Frames, and what everyone else calls Packets. A frame starts off by sending a bit pattern of 01111110 (notice the six 1's in a row). Synchronous transmission is for sending a bit stream, which means that the bits may (but probably do not) have any relation to the transmission of characters. This is especially true when sending digitized voice. As the bits pass to the receiver, they go through a shift register. When the flag signifying the end of a frame goes by, the last 16 bits in the shift register are the check digits.

The receiver computes the check digits based on the data bits that have gone by. As the sender sent the data, it computed the check digit, sent it after the end of the frame, and then sent the flag. If the receiver computes the same check digit that the sender sent, then one can be reasonably assured the data came through without error. But that's not what I came to talk to you about. I came to talk about Zero Stuffing. The problem is that somewhere in the bit stream, there is the possibility of there being six 1 bits in a row. To the receiving computer, six 1's means a flag. Therefore the sending computer, if it "sees" six 1 bits, will send five 1 bits, and stuff a zero in the bit stream.

In fact, if it sees even five 1 bits, it will stuff a zero anyway, so there will be no ambiguity. The rule is, "If there are five ones in a row and it is NOT the end of a frame, stuff a zero into the bit stream." This way the receiver will know that this is in no way the end of the frame yet. Now if the receiver sees six 1's in a row, it knows without a doubt that it IS at the end of a frame, and should proceed with the error checking.

APPENDIX A:

# FRAME RELAY APTITUDE TEST AND IMPLEMENTATION CHECK LISTS

Implementing a new network infrastructure requires that you think through nearly every element of your existing and future environment. The frame relay aptitude test will help you to evaluate whether or not frame relay makes good business sense for your business.

Following this test, there are two additional sets of questions for your consideration. The first group will assist you in narrowing your alternatives for frame relay carriers. The second group provides a list of questions you should attempt to answer to help your carrier design an optimal frame relay network configuration.

## Frame Relay Aptitude Test

When you are finished, you can add up all of your "yes" answers and get a general idea of whether or not frame relay is worth pursuing further. Keep in mind that this exercise is only an estimation of your "frame relay aptitude." Every network situation is unique, and just one compelling reason may be enough to justify this migration for your company. At the other extreme, you may answer to yes to every question and still not find a compelling enough price/performance advantage to justify the move. These questions simply provide a guideline within which to evaluate your potential benefits from frame relay.

## Consider your current equipment platform(s)

❐Yes ❐No 1. Do you already have routers or bridges already in place for your LANs?

❐Yes ❐No 2a. Do you have a fairly small, or a fully amortized, investment in private network multiplexing equipment?

❐Yes ❐No 2b. Can your existing private networking equipment be redeployed and used elsewhere in the network, or be used as part of a hybrid public/private network solution?

❐Yes ❐No 2c. Does your private network/multiplexing equipment offer standards-based frame relay interface cards and/or trunk cards?

❐Yes ❐No 2d. Do you have sites where more than one wide area equi❐ ment port and CSU/DSU are used to support more than one wide area data network connection?

❐Yes ❐No 3. Do you have remote front end processors that could be replaced with LANs and routers?

## Consider your staff

❐Yes ❐No 1a. Are you downsizing staff size and/or networking resources already stretched too thin?

❐Yes ❐No 1b. If frame relay helped you to reduce the number of network administration and operations personnel needed, would this change be positively received?

❐Yes ❐No 2a. If you plan to manage and operate your own frame relay network, is your staff knowledgeable about router-based environments, TCP/IP, addressing, and/or SNMP?

❐Yes ❐No 2b. If your staff is not knowledgeable, will you consider using a carrier to help manage the day-to-day operation of the data network?

## Consider your current network topology

❐Yes ❐No 1a. Do you currently tandem traffic through one, or a few, hub locations?

❐Yes ❐No 1b. Does this cause network congestion that affects network performance for all users?

❑Yes ❑No 2. Do you currently purchase extra dedicated circuits to achieve geographical diversity and increase network

❑Yes ❑No 3. Is your network designed to handle peak traffic loads, as opposed to average traffic loads?

❑Yes ❑No 4. Are small field offices in the existing configuration vulner - able to network outages from cable cuts, and could this be improved upon with frame relay?

## Consider your budget

❑Yes ❑No 1a. If you will need to purchase frame relay equipment, do you already have the budget?

❑Yes ❑No 1b. If you don't have the budget but need equipment, will you consider leasing the equipment from your carrier?

❑Yes ❑No 2a. If you reduce the monthly recurring network costs, are you rewarded?

❑Yes ❑No 2b. Are you rewarded if you reduce capital expenditures?

❑Yes ❑No 3. If you plan to operate your own frame relay network, do you already have the necessary hardware, software and testing tools to manage it?

❑Yes ❑No 4. Are you trying to reduce your current budget for on-going network maintenance and operation?

❑Yes ❑No 5. Will you be able to decrease or eliminate any software licensing (i.e., SNA) or equipment rental fees by implementing frame relay?

## Consider future trends and requirements

❑Yes ❑No 1a. Do your wide area network requirements change frequently and/or is the network growing rapidly?

❑Yes ❑No 1b. Could the logical connectivity offered by frame relay hel❑ you better keep pace with these changes?

❑Yes ❑No 1c. Does your company tend towards acquisitions, and does this consistently require changes to the network topology?

❑Yes ❑No 1d. Would frame relay make it easier to integrate new sites into the backbone?

❑Yes ❑No 2a. Are you seeing a growing number of WAN applications that are bandwidth intensive?

❐Yes ❐No 2b. If so, will your current solution run short of capacity or prove too expensive to cost-justify the new applications?

❐Yes ❐No 2c. Could frame relay offer a lower price for supporting emerging business applications?

❐Yes ❐No 3a. Is your company moving towards client-server applications and architectures?

❐Yes ❐No 3b. Is more power being distributed to remote desktops?

## Consider your management

❐Yes ❐No 1. Is change encouraged and accepted by your management?

❐Yes ❐No 2. Does the organization view the current network as outdated, too slow, outgrown or too expensive?

❐Yes ❐No 3. Are there strategic business advantages the company can gain through implementation of a frame relay network that executive management would find of value?

## Your Frame Relay Aptitude

For each of the questions to which you answered "Yes" above, give yourself one point. Add up all of your points, and then apply your score to the following matrix:

| Total Points | Frame Relay Aptitude |
|---|---|
| 0 - 8 | Questionable: You could still be a frame relay candidate, but it is difficult to discern from this evaluation If you answered yes to question 2d. in the equipment section, questions 1b. and/or 2 in the network topology section, question 4 in the budget sec tion, questions 1a. and/or 2a. in the future trends section and/ or question 3 in the management section, you are still a very viable frame relay candidate. |
| 9- 15 | Good: You should certainly take the opportunity to evaluate the network price/performance improvement you might gain through frame relay in comparison with your current solution. |
| 15+ | Great: You have a very high likelihood of benefiting from a move to frame relay. |

## Evaluating Carriers

If you decide to pursue further evaluation of frame relay, here are some questions to consider in determining from which carriers you should initially entertain proposals.

### *Consider Your Network Needs*

1. Which carriers can provide frame relay service to all of your locations?
   a. How many of these locations have a local switch versus how many will require backhauled facilities to reach a frame relay switch?
   b. If some connections are backhauled, does the carrier have a DCS or SONET network recovery system in place for that portion of the network?

2. Do you want your carrier to be responsible for end-to-end performance of the frame relay network, including access and equipment?
   a. Which carriers offer the equipment solution you are already using or are most comfortable with using?

3. Do you want or need the carrier to actually operate the network, including keeping the router tables updated, optimizing the configurations, reporting on network performance and availability, and handling all problems?

4. Do you, or will you, need to connect with international locations?
   a. If so, you want to extend your frame relay network internationally?
   b. Do you already have international private lines or X.25 in place, and do you prefer to keep these or replace them?

5. Do you require any special service options?
   a. Do you want to evaluate network management services?
   b. Is interoperability with X.25 or ATM critical now or in the future?
   c. Do you need access to the Internet?
   d. Do have have sales people or telecommuters that need dial-up capability?

e. What maintenance schedules do you require for each site if the carrier is providing equipment? (four-hour response times? Next day?)

f. Do you need a technology obsolescence clause at one or more sites that might need to migrate to a different networking solution during the term of the contract?

### *Network Design*

In preparing to begin the network design process, a map of your current network configuration and answers to the following questions will help to expedite the process and provide an optimal network design.

1. What are your current network applications?

    a. Who uses the network, when and why?

    b. Which applications are distributed and which are centralized?

2. What is the current network topology and traffic pattern?

    a. What does the current network look like?

    b. How is the current network performing?

    c. By application, what are your estimates for average size and frequency of transactions?

    d. What is the traffic pattern to/from each location on the network. Estimate by K bps requirements where possible.

    e. Are there currently times, or places, of network congestion?

    f. What is your current estimated average utilization, by circuit?

3. Do you have any critical network sites and availability requirements at those sites?

    a. Specify your site recovery/disaster recovery requirements, including location of hot or cold sites .

4. Are there near term business conditions that could impact network design?

    a. Are you planning to remove network locations as part of a consolidation or downsizing effort?

    b. Are you planning to add new network locations and/or acquire a new company?

c. Do you expect high growth rates (or sharp declines) in the number of network users?

d. Do you expect any new network applications to be implemented that will affect network capacity needs?

## Implementation Checklist

To implement a frame relay network, follow this yellow brick road.

- ❐ 1. Develop an initial topology and site inventory.
- ❐ 2. Develop an initial frame relay network design based on the applications and protocols being supported.
- ❐ 3. Write and distribute an RFP.
- ❐ 4. Evaluate RFP responses and choose a short list of vendors and carriers who will receive further consideration.
- ❐ 5. Choose a carrier (and one or more equipment vendors) if the carrier is not providing the equipment needed). Determine who will be responsible for initially configuring the equipment.
- ❐ 6. Get the service ordered for each location. This includes the equipment, loops and frame relay network.
- ❐ 7. Decide on the network management solution and begin any necessary preparations for integration into the existing management system.
- ❐ 8. Do a site survey and make sure that each site is ready, or is made ready, for the equipment and network installation.
- ❐ 9. Coordinate planned installation dates for each site. Depending upon whether one or many vendors are involved, you may want the equipment delivered a few days before the network installation. (If a carrier is providing a complete solution, that carrier will have a process for coordinating this; if not, it is your job to make sure the equipment arrives before the network is installed..
- ❐ 10. Make up an implementation schedule that shows the turn-up date of each site.
- ❐ 11. Prior to turn-up at each site, upgrade any of the protocols, equipment, software releases, etc., as needed.
- ❐ 12. Track issues for each site that might jeopardize the implementation date and have contingency plans for missing the date. Issues can include equipment that is not delivered or does not function, access that is not available, and local cabling not in place.

- ❐ 13. Turn each location up and expect a few problems initially with integrating the protocols and addressing over the WAN and achieving remote connectivity. Rely on the experience of your carrier and equipment vendor to get these resolved. Once stable, the frame relay network will typically require a much lower level of ongoing maintenance than a private line network.
- ❐ 14. Review utilization and performance information on the network within three to six months after implementation and fine-tune the network for improved price/performance.

## APPENDIX B:

# THE FRAME RELAY FORUM MEMBERS AND PRODUCTS LISTING

The following is a list of companies that have developed and offer frame relay equipment and services.

### *Access Equipment*

3Com
ACC
Advanced Compression Technology
Alcatel Data Networks
Andrew Corporation
ascom Timeplex
AT&T GIS
AT&T Paradyne
BBN Communications
Cascade Communications
Cisco Systems
CrossComm Corporation
Dynatech Communications
Digital Link Corporation
FastComm Communications
Fujitsu
Gandalf Data Ltd.
General DataComm, Inc.
GTE Telephone
Hughes Network Systems
Hypercom, Inc.
IBM
Kastin Chase Applied Research
Loral Data Systems
MCI Communications
Memotec Communications, Inc.

Motorola Codex
NETLINK, Inc.
Netrix Corporation
Network Equipment Technologies
Network Systems Corporation
Newbridge Networks, Inc.
Nokia Telecommunications
NTT
OST
Premisys Communications
Primary Rate
Proteon
RAD Data Communications
Siemens Stromberg-Carlson
SITA
Sprint
Sync Research
Telco Systems
Telematics International
Toshiba America, Inc.
Wellfleet Communications

### *Service Provider*

Ameritech Services
AT&T Data Comm. Services
Bell Atlantic
BellSouth Telecommunications
Cable & Wireless Communications
CBIS
CompuServe
Concert
Deutsche Bundespost Telekom
GTE Telephone
Helsinki Telephone
Infonet
LCI International
MCI Communications
NTT Corporation

- NYNEX
- Pacific Bell
- Sprint
- Stentor Resource Center
- Swiss Telecom PTT
- Tele Denmark
- Transpac
- Unitel Communications
- US WEST
- WilTel

### *Switch Equipment*

- Advanced Compression Technology
- Alcatel Data Networks
- ascom Timeplex
- BBN Communications
- Cascade Communications
- Digital Link Corporation
- DSC Communications
- Dynatech Communications
- Ericsson Business Networks
- Fujitsu
- Gandalf Data Ltd.
- GTE Telephone
- Hughes Network Systems
- IBM
- LightStream Corporation
- Memotec Communications, Inc.
- Motorola Codex
- Netrix Corporation
- Network Equipment Technologies
- Network Systems Corporation
- Newbridge Networks, Inc.
- Nokia Telecommunications
- Northern Telecom, Inc.
- NTT
- OST
- RAD Data Communications

Siemens Stromberg-Carlson
SITA
Sprint
StrataCom, Inc.
Telematics International
Toshiba America, Inc.

### *Test Equipment*

Digitech Industries, Inc.
Hewlett-Packard/IDACOM
RAD Data Communications
Tekelec
Telenex Corporation
TTC
Wandel & Goltermann

### *Other Offerings*

Bellcore
CSELT
EICON Technology
FastComm Communications
GTE Laboratories
Indiana University
ITV
KDD America
Northern Telecom
Novell
OKI America, Inc.
Unitel Communications

For contact names and addresses, contact the Frame Relay Forum at (415) 578-6900.

## APPENDIX C:

# REGIONAL AND LEC PRODUCT COMPARISON, PRICING, AND COLLATERAL

*Regional/LEC CIR Comparison*

| *COMPANY* | *ELI* | *GTE* | *ICI* | *MFS* | *PacBell* | *US WEST* |
|---|---|---|---|---|---|---|
| CIR Increments: | | | | | | |
| 0K | | X | X | X | | |
| 4K | | X | X | ICB | X | |
| 16K | X | X | X | ICB | X | X |
| 32K | X | X | X | ICB | X | X |
| 48K | X | X | X | ICB | X | X |
| 56/64K | X | X | X | X | X | X |
| Nx64K | X | X | X | X | X | X |
| Other | see E2 | | | | | |

*Regional/LEC Equipment Comparison*

| *COMPANY* | *ELI* | *GTE* | *ICI* | *MFS* | *PacBell* | *US WEST* |
|---|---|---|---|---|---|---|
| Simplex PVCs | | X | X | | | |
| Equipment Packages: | | | | | | |
| Wellfleet routers | | X | X | X | | |
| Cisco routers | planned | X | | | X | X |
| 3Com routers | planned | X | | | | |
| SynOptics smart hub | | | | | X | |
| Cabletron smart hub | | | | | | |
| CSU/DSU | X | X | X | X | X | |
| Cascade concentrator | | | ICB | | | |
| Other | | | see note I1 | | | see note U2 |

### Regional/LEC Financing Comparison

| COMPANY | ELI | GTE | ICI | MFS | PacBell | US WEST |
|---|---|---|---|---|---|---|
| Financing: | | | | | | |
| Lease | X | X | | | X | |
| Purchase | X | X | | | X | X |
| Rental | X | X | | X | X | |

### Regional/LEC Network Management Comparison

| COMPANY | ELI | GTE | ICI | MFS | PacBell | US WEST |
|---|---|---|---|---|---|---|
| Network Management: | | | | | | |
| HP OpenView | X | X | | | X | X |
| SunNet Manager | X | | | | | X |
| IBM NetView | | | | | | |
| IBM NetView6000 | | | | | | X |
| Proprietary | | X | | | | X |
| SNMP | X | X | | planned | X | X |
| Other | | | | | | |

### Regional/LEC Port Speed Comparison

| COMPANY | ELI | GTE | ICI | MFS | PacBell | US WEST |
|---|---|---|---|---|---|---|
| Port Speeds Offered: | | | | | | |
| 56/64K | X | X | X | X | X | X |
| 128K | X | X | X | X | X | |
| 256K | X | X | X | X | | |
| 384K | X | X | X | ICB | X | |
| 512K | X | X | | X | | |
| 768K | X | X | | ICB | | |
| 1.024M | X | X | | ICB | | |
| 1.536M | X | X | X | X | X | X |
| Other | see note E1 | ICB | | see note M1 | | |

*Regional/LEC Value Added Comparison*

| COMPANY | ELI | GTE | ICI | MFS | PacBell | US WEST |
|---|---|---|---|---|---|---|
| **Value-Added Services:** | | | | | | |
| Equip. maintenance | X | X | | X | X | X |
| Configuration management | X | X | | X | X | X |
| Complete outsourcing | X | | | X | X | X |
| Other | | | | | | |

*Regional/LEC Backbone Comparison*

| COMPANY | ELI | GTE | ICI | MFS | PacBell | US WEST |
|---|---|---|---|---|---|---|
| **Backbone:** | | | | | | |
| Cell backbone | | planned | | X | | |
| Frame backbone | X | X | | | X | X |
| Other | | | | | | |

*Reional/LEC Service Availability Comparison*

| COMPANY | ELI | GTE | ICI | MFS | PacBell | US WEST |
|---|---|---|---|---|---|---|
| **Service Availability:** | | | | | | |
| Domestic LATAs (#) | | 19 | | 34 cities | CA | 14 states |
| International | ICB | | | X | | |
| No. of international countries | | | | 3 | | |

*Regional/LEC Additional Services Comparison*

| COMPANY | ELI | GTE | ICI | MFS | PacBell | US WEST |
|---|---|---|---|---|---|---|
| **Additional Services:** | | | | | | |
| Internet connection | X | | | | | planned |
| X.25 interworking | planned | | | | | X |
| Dial-up access | planned | 4Q94 | | planned | | |
| TCP/IP interworking | planned | | | | | |
| ATM interworking | planned | 1Q95 | | planned | | planned |
| Other | see note E3 | | | | | |

## *Notes*

*E1. - Any 64K increment*
*M1. - 1.9M, 3M, 4.5M, and 6M bps*
*U1. - 9.6K, 24K*
*E2. - Any 16K increment*
*I1. - ACC routers also provided*
*U2. - ACC routers*
*E3. - Interworking with native LAN Services*

# GTE COLLATERAL

# GTE Frame Relay Service

## Pricing Structure

GTE Frame Relay pricing varies somewhat by state and jurisdiction (i.e. local tariff vs. FCC tariff). However, in general, the service is offered in a "bundled" package and an "unbundled" package. The bundled package includes the access line, the port on the frame relay switch, and the first PVC. The unbundled package includes only the port on the frame relay switch and the first PVC. In this case, the access line would be purchased out of a separate tariff. Where additional PVC's are required, they are available individually at an extra cost.

The service is offered on a non-mileage sensitive and non-usage sensitive basis (i.e. a flat rate). PVC's are associated with a specific port and are full duplex. That is, a two node network would require two PVC's - one associated with each port. There are no separate charges for specific CIR's. Settings are available up to the speed of the access line. Access lines are available at 56 K/bps, FT1 and T1 rates.

Customers may select an Optional Payment Plan (OPP). OPP's offer lower rates in exchange for signing a longer term contract. OPP's are available for 1, 3 and 5 years. Month-to-month rates are also available. All services are available on an OPP with the exception of PVC's, which have no term commitment.

Frame Relay is available out of the local tariff, the state access tariff and the FCC tariff. The local tariff is for Intra-LATA service while the state access and FCC tariffs are for Inter-LATA service. GTE will work with the customer's long distance carrier of choice to provide the most economical end-to-end Inter-LATA solution.

## Pricing Rates

As noted above, rates vary by state and jurisdiction. Therefore, the following rates are typical of the bundled GTE offering, however, individual states may be higher or lower.

| *Access* | *MM* | *1 Yr OPP* | *3 Yr OPP* | *5 Yr OPP* |
|---|---|---|---|---|
| 56 K/bps | $95 | $90 | $85 | $75 |
| 128 K/bps | $175 | $165 | $150 | $135 |
| 256 K/bps | $275 | $265 | $250 | $235 |
| 384 K/bps | $375 | $365 | $350 | $330 |
| 1.5 M/bps | $500 | $465 | $430 | $400 |

Additional PVC's are available for $6 - $10, depending on state, quantity purchased and jurisdiction.

## Ancillary Services

GTE is in the process of evaluating Customer Network Management and switched access to Frame Relay Service, however, pricing is not available at this time.

# ICI COLLATERAL

| *COMPANY* | *ICI Pricing* |
|---|---|
| **Port Speeds Offered:** | |
| 56/64K | $115/month |
| 128K | $220/month |
| 256K | $340/month |
| 384K | $460/month |
| 1.536M | $600/month |
| **CIR Increments:** | |
| 0K | 1.25/Kb |
| 4K | 1.25/Kb |
| 16K | 1.25/Kb |
| **32K** | 1.25/Kb |
| 48K | 1.25/Kb |
| 56/64K | 1.25/Kb |
| Nx64K | 1.25/Kb |
| WellFleet routers | ICB |
| Cisco routers | ACC routers - $80/month |
| CSU/DSU | $25/month |
| Cascade concentrator | ICB |
| Equip. maintenance | ICB |
| Configuration management | ICB |
| Complete outsourcing | ICB |
| Internet Connection | $1000/month |
| X.25 interworking | $95/month |

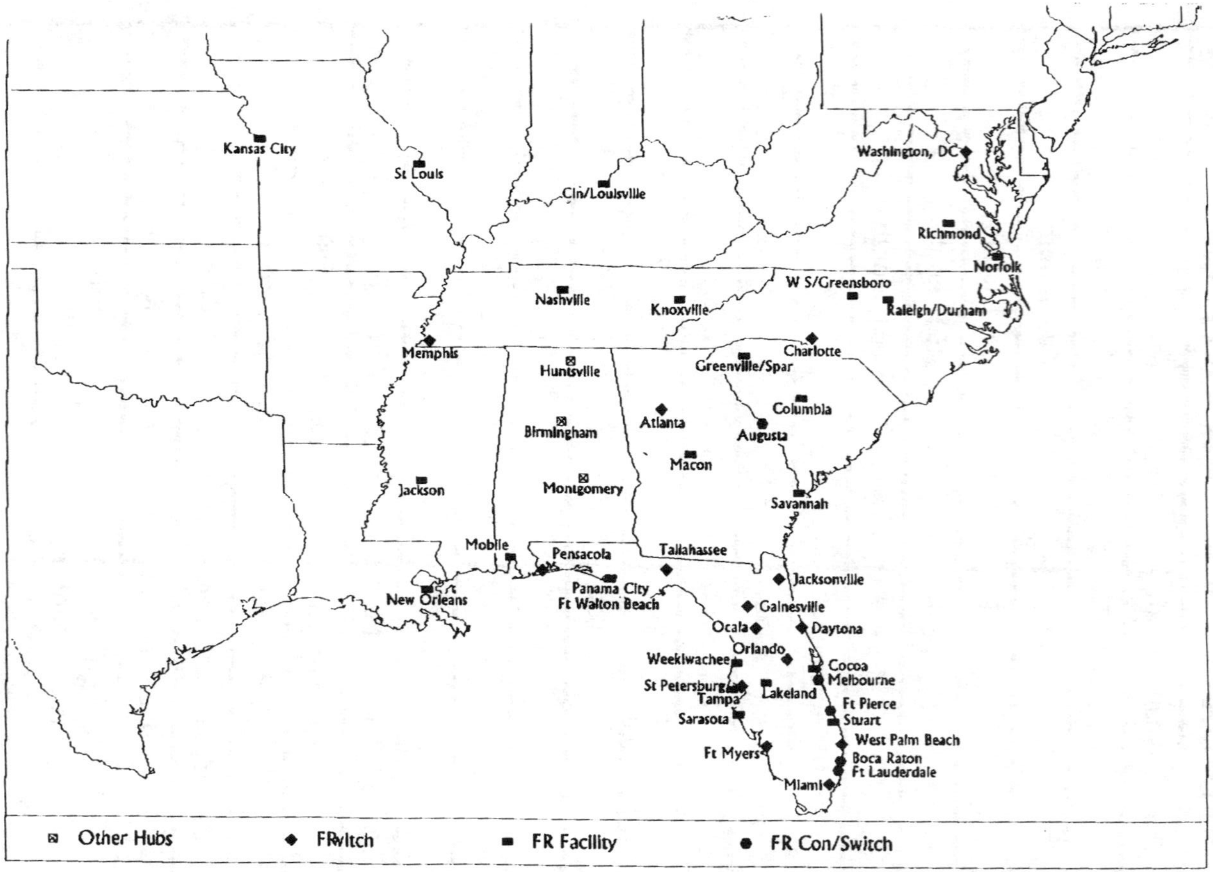


ICI ETS Hubs and Facilities

# MFS COLLATERAL

## Legal Services Customer

## Case Study -- No. 1

**Who:** A large New York-based *corporate and banking law firm* whose main clients are large financial institutions.

**What:** Three offices (Los Angeles, Washington DC, and New York) needed to be interconnected. The firm was planning to purchase LANs and routers in both Los Angeles and Washington DC, and had previously installed a LAN and router in New York. Initially, *LAN-to-LAN connectivity* between the cities was the main objective, but there was also the need for a migration path to higher speeds along with the fear of technological obsolescence if they built a private network. In addition, a resource barrier existed regarding the purchasing and management of data equipment, a local loop carrier, and a long distance carrier.

**Why MFS:** *Ethernet High-speed LAN Interconnect (HLI)* service at a fractional LAN speed of 56 Kbps fit their networking needs. With HLI, the firm achieved LAN connectivity *without capital equipment* purchase, provided for a *scalable* path for future speeds up to full 10 Mbps, and were able to *utilize the equipment* and technology already in place in New York.

**Hidden Benefits:** MFS Datanet's HLI Service released the firm from managing, maintaining, and running a communication network which allowed the lawyers, clerks, and staff to *focus* on corporate and banking law -- their *core business*. The cost of a recurring monthly service, instead of a capital investment, enabled the law firm to purchase LAN interconnect services in the same way that it operates financially.

**Legal Services Customer**
**Case Study -- No. 2**

**Who:** An *international law firm* specializing in Corporate Law is innovative in using a communication network which gives them a competitive advantage in the legal industry.

**What:** Headquartered in Los Angeles with 6 branch offices, the firm needed *LAN interconnection* via Ethernet in the following cities: Los Angeles, Atlanta, Washington DC, New York, and Stamford, CT. The number of employees ranged from 15 to 250 per site with a file server in each location. For their current applications of *e-mail* and distributed *accounting*, 56 Kbps leased lines did not supply adequate bandwidth.

**Why MFS:** *Ethernet High-speed LAN Interconnect (HLI)* service at a fractional LAN speed of 1.5 Mbps provided the turnkey solution which offered features superior to leased lines at a more economical price. The firm was especially excited about two significant values of the service: Network *management* and maintenance across three areas (data equipment/local loop/long distance carriers), AND *scalability* of HLI up to the full 10 Mbps Ethernet speed to keep pace with their networking needs as they continue to grow.

**Hidden Benefits:** MFS Datanet's ATM backbone supplied a complete network with all five sites directly connected to each other. If a single site becomes disabled, the other *sites are still able* to communicate with each other. Other networking options, such as a leased line or Frame Relay network, would require custom addressing with additional cost and complexity. The firm has realized overall savings based upon the cost effectiveness and *increased productivity* from Ethernet High-speed LAN Interconnect services.

# CASE STUDY
# No 3.

*Who:* A commercial Internet service provider which offers access from 300 cities.

*What:* The company operates a nationwide segment of the worldwide commercial Internet and connects the LAN environments of 350 domestic customers with the rest of the Global Commercial Internet. Coverage spans 15 major backbone hubs and over 300 smaller access locations.

*Why MFS?* The MFS Datanet ATM-based network service combines high performance (wide area connectivity at 10 Mbps) with attractive pricing and ease of use (standard Ethernet interface hardware). The customer's main backbone routers have been fully mesh-connected at native 10 Mbps rates at a cost impossible to match using traditional point-to-point 1.5 Mbps T1 links. Network connections have been implemented in New York, Chicago, Dallas, Los Angeles and Washington, DC. Connections are planned for seven more major US cities. (Atlanta, Boston, Houston, San Jose, Pittsburgh, Minneapolis, and Newark).

***Hidden Benefits:*** By teaming with MFS, the customer became the first commercial Internet service provider to move to an operational high-speed ATM backbone. By building on the MFS national backbone instead of trying to replicate it, the customer is free to concentrate on their main business of Internetwork engineering and services.

***Customer Quote:*** "There is nothing to be proud of in building a 45 Mbps IP network and then running it 95% idle. by buying ATM connectivity from MFS instead of building it ourselves, we are able to get all the advantages of DS-3 based networking without the large costs. This allows us to pass the savings along to our customers. Further, MFS owns and operates all of the ATM equipment saving us very large capital equipment costs."

"MFS offers an ideal solution for our needs. They deliver an actual Ethernet AUI to our router. There equipment accepts Ethernet MAC level packets an delivers them to the correct destination. Our routers see a single large Ethernet and we don not have to risk using untried and expensive ATM interface on our routers. If our needs exceed 10Mbps in any city, it's a simple matter of replacing the Ethernet interface to MFS with an FDDI (or ATM) interface. Again, this allows us to use proven technology and avoid the risks of technological obsolescence that go with operating a net work at too low a level."

# CASE STUDY

## No 4.

*Who:* An international consulting and training company dedicated to helping organizations become more customer driven. Corporate headquarters is located in Boston. other offices are in New York City. Washington DC. Chicago. Los Angeles. San Francisco. Toronto. London and Hong Kong.

*What:* This is an information intensive business that relies heavily on computers for sales. scheduling and customer service. Local Area Networks link desktop computers in the Boston. New York. Chicago. and London offices. Stand alone computers are installed in the Los Angeles. San Francisco. Toronto and Hong Kong offices. Remote dial-up access was slow. expensive and inefficient. Available options of private lines or frame relay were expensive. usually required significant capital investment. and in the case of frame relay had unclear throughput capabilities.

*Why MFS:* The company was already a customer of MFS Telecom for private voice lines. MFS Datanet's service matched both geographic coverage needs and higher capacity requirements with no capital investment required and at an economical cost. The MFS service connected Ethernet backbones with four Novell servers in Boston and one each in Chicago and New York. serving a total of 185 workstations. All connections were at 1.544 Mbps. full T1 speed.

***Hidden Benefits:*** Several new applications have emerged to take advantage of the new enhanced communication capability provided by the MFS Datanet service. Network support has been simplified. sharing of documentation has improved project management in the company. and e-mail has improved employee productivity and client communications.

***Customer Quote:*** "Our objective was clear -- we needed to create a cost effect environment that enabled our people to produce top quality products and services for our clients...This environment had to allow users in various locations to quickly access and share information. It was also important that it be flexible to grow with out business and the changing marketplace. MFS's ATM network solution was exactly what we needed to to only meet but exceed our customers' needs of today and in the future."

## CASE STUDY
## No 5.

***Who:*** One of the largest banks in the world with Ethernet LANs in three US cities: Chicago, New York, and San Francisco.

***What:*** Performance and reliability were top priorities. Due to expansion plans in New York and limited capacity of current low-speed interconnections, the bank needed a High-speed LAN Interconnect (HLI) solution.

***Why MFS:*** MFS Datanet's HLI service met all of the requirements: increased bandwidth alleviated the network congestion, inherent diversity and redundancy of the MFS network delivered reliability, and the service was implemented easily with no additional expense for equipment or personnel and no need to learn to support a new technology.

***Hidden Benefits:*** Application processing time was reduced from nine (9) hours at night to just 30 minutes during the day. The bank is now looking at how other applications can benefit from MFS Datanet's services.

# PACBELL COLLATERAL

## Pricing Outline

**Carrier Name:** Pacific Bell

**Pricing Structure:**
Our frame relay pricing includes 3 components - an access link, frame relay port and DLCI charges. The access link is purchased out of standard local loop charges. Users need a 56K dedicated digital line for 56Kbps frame relay. For 128K, 384K and DS-1 frame relay, the access line is a T-1 line.

The service is a LATA-wide service. Users only have to purchase the access to their serving central office. Pacific Bell will backhaul the traffic to our frame relay switch. The service is not mileage sensitive, nor is it usage sensitive. Customers pay a flat monthly fee for unlimited LATA-wide switching.

Each location a user needs to communicate with needs a DLCI. DLCIs are price according to a sliding price schedule (see diagram). We do not charge for CIR, so a PVC with 16K CIR cost the same as a PVC with a 32K CIR.

**Pricing Rates:**
See enclosed diagram.

**Ancillary Services:**
LAN management is available for a fee. The cost of the service depends on the number of nodes, the network architecture and the customer premises equipment involved.

## Pacific Bell frame relay pricing

| | 56K | 128K | 384K | 1.54M |
|---|---|---|---|---|
| **Port charges** | | | | |
| Onetime | $375 | $375 | $375 | $375 |
| Monthly | $75 | $150 | $400 | $500 |
| **Access charges** | $50 | $163 | $163 | $163 |
| **DLCI charges** (monthly per port) | | | | |
| 1 DLCI | $0 | $0 | $0 | $0 |
| 2 DLCI | $15 | $15 | $15 | $15 |
| 3 DLCI | $30 | $30 | $30 | $30 |
| 4 DLCI | $45 | $45 | $45 | $45 |
| 5 DLCI | $60 | $60 | $60 | $60 |
| 6 DLCI | $75 | $75 | $75 | $75 |
| 7-11 (per DLCI) | $10 | $10 | $10 | $10 |
| 12 or more (per DLCI) | $5 | $5 | $5 | $5 |

Each site must pay for a port charge, an access charge and any DLCI charges.

If a user has 4 locations to communicate with and needs 4 PVCs, the user pays for 3 DLCIs since the first one is free.

# Pacific Bell Frame Relay Pricing

**Local Access (Service Purchased from existing Local Loop Tariff):**

| | Recurring | Non-Recurring |
|---|---|---|
| 56 Kbps (DS-0) | $50.05 | $620.00 |
| 1.536 Mbps (DS-1) | $162.59 | $1324.00 |

**Network Port Connections (Frame Relay Tariff):**

| | Recurring | Non-Recurring |
|---|---|---|
| 56 Kbps | $75.00 | $375.00 |
| 128 Kbps | $150.00 | $375.00 |
| 384 Kbps | $400.00 | $375.00 |
| 1.536 Mbps | $500.00 | $375.00 |

**Data Link Connection Identifiers (Frame Relay Tariff):**

| | Recurring |
|---|---|
| 1 | No Charge |
| 2-6 | $15.00 ea |
| 7-11 | $10.00 ea |
| 12 + | $5.00 ea |

# Frame Relay Pricing Example

**Example:** A customer with three locations wants 1.536 Mbps Frame Relay Service and all locations need to exchange data. The customer will purchase the following:

| | LOCATION 1 | LOCATION 2 | LOCATION 3 |
|---|---|---|---|
| 1) Local Loop Access | A-1 @ $163.00 | A-2 @ $163.00 | A-3 @ $163.00 |
| 2) Frame Relay Port | A-1 @ $500.00 | A-2 @ $500.00 | A-3 @ $600.00 |
| 3) DLCI (address) | DLCI 1-2 @ $0.00 | DLCI 2-1 @ $0.00 | DLCI 3-1 @ $0.00 |
| | DLCI 1-3 @ $15.00 | DLCI 2-3 @ $15.00 | DLCI 3-2 @ $15.00 |
| Total Monthly By Location | $678.00 | $678.00 | $678.00 |

Total Monthly Cost = $2034.00

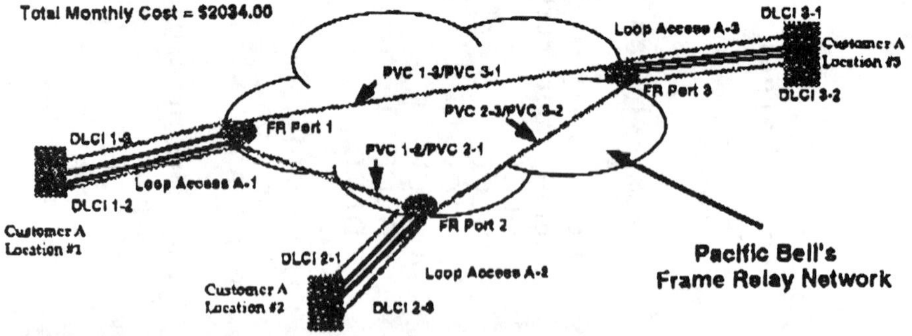

## Customers Will Be Billed For Three Rate Elements: An Access Line To Their Serving Wire Center, A Frame Relay Port Charge And DLCIs

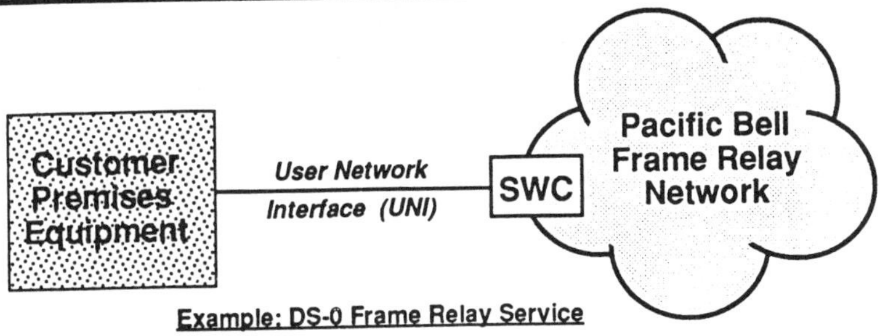


Example: DS-0 Frame Relay Service

- **UNI is a single channel termination out of B5 Tariff (Ex. DS-0 is $50/mo. and $620 IC)**
- **Frame Relay Port Charge is usage insensitive (Rates are $75/mo. and $375 IC under A18 Tariff)**
- **DLCIs are based on tiered pricing on a per port basis (i. e. $15/mo. ea. for the 2nd-6th DLCI at each port)**

## Pacific Bell Frame Relay Service is Priced to Be An Attractive Alternative for Today's Customers

**Local Access (Service Purchased from existing Local Loop Channel Terminations in B tariff):**

| | Recurring | Non-Recurring |
|---|---|---|
| 56 Kbps (ADN) | $50.05 | $620.00 |
| 1.536 Mbps (T-1) | $162.59 | $1324.00 |

**Network Port Connections (A Tariff Components):**

| | Recurring | Non-Recurring |
|---|---|---|
| 56 Kbps | $75.00 | $375.00 |
| 128 Kbps | $150.00 | $375.00 |
| 384 Kbps | $400.00 | $375.00 |
| 1.536 Mbps | $500.00 | $375.00 |

**Data Link Connection Identifiers (A Tariff Components):**

| | Recurring |
|---|---|
| 1 | No Charge |
| 2-6 | $15.00 ea |
| 7-11 | $10.00 ea |
| 12 + | $5.00 ea |

# US WEST COLLATERAL

**FRAME RELAY**

# TECHNICAL SUMMARY

**(Per Technical Publication 77372)**

!NTERPRISE
NETWORKING SERVICES FROM U S WEST

| FRS Access Line Speed | FRS Access Link Usable Bandwidth | Available CIR Options | Max # of PVC's per UNI FRS Access Link | Max # of PVC's per NNI FRS Access Link |
|---|---|---|---|---|
| 56 kb/s | 56 kb/s | 9.6, 16, 24, 32, 48 (kb/s) | 30 | 5 |
| 64 kb/s | 64 kb/s | 9.6, 16, 24, 32, 48 (kb/s) | 30 | 6 |
| 1.54 Mb/s (Nx56 kb/s) | 1.34 Mb/s | 9.6, 16, 24, 32, 48 (kb/s) 56-1008 kb/s (Nx56 kb/s) | 125 | 125 |
| 1.536 Mb/s (Nx56 kb/s) | 1.536 Mb/s | 9.6, 16, 24, 32, 48 (kb/s) 56-1008 kb/s (Nx56 kb/s) | 125 | 125 |

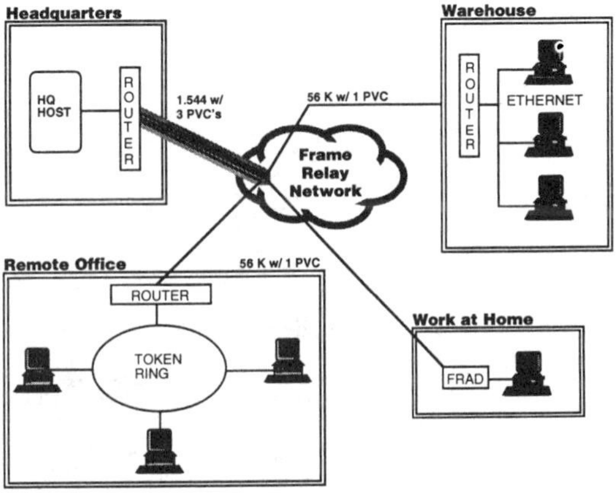


| FLAG |
|---|
| 0 1 1 1 1 1 1 0 |
| Address Field (First octet) <High Order DLCI > C/R EA |
| Address Field (Second octet) <Low Order DLCI > FECN BECN DE EA |
| Frame Relay Info Field (1-4069 octets) |
| Frame Check Sequence (first octet) |
| Frame Check Sequence (second octet) |
| FLAG 0 1 1 1 1 1 1 0 |

U S WEST Frame Relay Service is a connection oriented "fast packet" service. Several Permanent Virtual Circuits (PVCs) can be established over either a 56 kbit/s, 64 kbit/s or 1.544 Mbits/s Access Link. Frame Relay utilizes a variable packet size capability which is beneficial for particularly bursty traffic. As a result of improved efficiencies in the U S WEST transport facilities, less overhead is required for error detection which lends itself to less transit delay and increased throughput.

**U S WEST Sales Office Locations**

8900 N. 22nd Ave., Suite 300
Phoenix, AZ 85021
(602) 371-3000

333 E. Wetmore Rd., #240
Tucson, AZ 85705
(602) 292-5002

1801 California St., Suite 1700
Denver, CO 80202
(303) 391-8300

900 Keo, 1st Floor South
Des Moines, IA 50309
(515) 241-0900

999 Main St., 8th Floor
Boise, ID 83702
(208) 364-3960

100 S. 5th St., Suite 500
Minneapolis, MN 55402
(612) 376-3700

560 N. Park Ave., Room 411
Helena, MT 59601
(406) 441-7446

105 N. 5th St., 3rd Floor
Fargo, ND 58102
(701) 232-3626

1299 Farnam St., 11th Floor
Omaha, NE 68102
(402) 422-6900

201 3rd St. N.W., Suite 600
Albuquerque, NM 87102
(505) 245-5500

1900 S.W. 4th Ave., Room 150
Portland, OR 97201
(503) 425-5200

127 W. 9th St.
Sioux Falls, SD 57194
(605) 339-5451

2567 E. 200 South Suite 200
Salt Lake City, UT 84111
(801) 575-1000

335 W. 1st Street
Casper, WY 82601
(307) 235-3802

1420 5th Ave., Suite 1600
Seattle, WA 98101
(206) 623-8800

**FRAME RELAY**

!INTER**PRISE**
NETWORKING SERVICES FROM U S WEST

# TECHNICAL SUMMARY

**(Per Technical Publication 77372)**

---

## U S WEST CIR Parameters

CIR = Committed Information Rate
Defines the minimum committed throughput of an individual PVC over a period of one second. CIR is expressed in bit/second.

Be = Excess Burst Size
Defines how many bits will be transmitted in time interval (T) marked as discard eligible.

Bc = Committed Burst Size
Defines how many bits will be transmitted in time interval (T) without the DE (Discard Eligible) bit set. Expressed in BITS.

DE = Discard Eligible
May be discarded by the network in event of congestion

T = Time interval expressed in seconds over which measurement occurs.

**Example:** CIR = Bc/T
Bc = CIR/T (ie: If CIR = 32 kbps, Bc = 32kbps/1second = 32 kb)
T = 1 second
Be = (Port Speed/T)-Bc (ie: If port speed = 64 kbps and Bc = 32 kbps, then
Be = (64kbps/1 second)-32 kb = kb Excess Burst size)

Port Speed = 64 kbps

CIR = 32 kbps    Bc = 32 kb    Be = 32 kb

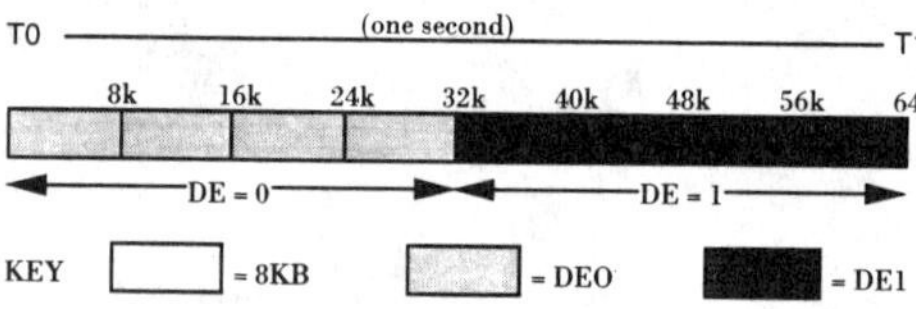


## Other Characteristics:

- Support both symmetrical and asymmetrical CIR ie: 32 kb PVC in one direction, 9.6 kb in other)
- Support LMI and ANNEX D based PVC Management Procedures
- NNI (Network to Network Interface) available
- Support FECN (Forward Explicit Congestion Notification) and BECN (Backward Explicit Congestion Notification)
- CNM (Customer Network Management) available to customer provided management Sun Work Station with either SunNet Manager or HP Openview
- Paper utilization reports available per customer request
- Customer may "oversubscribe" and assign aggregate CIRs in excess of line rate
- MTU (Maximum Transmission Unit)" Largest Packed Size of 4096; consistent with FDDI and Token Ring
- Access Link Options/Alternatives:
  - SHARP Provisioned Access Link
  - Access to Command-a-Link

Physical Connector @ Network Interface (Customer Provided)
(RJ48S, RJ48T, RJ48C, RJ48H, RJ48M or equivalent)

CPE Termination Options:
CSU/DSU
FRAD (Frame Relay Access Device)
PC Expansion Card

U S WEST Network Management: Starkeeper

**FRAME RELAY**

# RATE SHEET

**Arizona, Colorado, Minnesota, Nebraska, Oregon, Utah, Washington**

**!NTERPRISE**
NETWORKING SERVICES FROM U S WEST

## FRAME RELAY RATE AND TARIFF TABLE

| | FRS Port Speed 56 kb/s | FRS Port Speed 1.5 Mb/s | INTERSTATE 56 kb/s | INTERSTATE 1.5 Mb/s |
|---|---|---|---|---|
| **Monthly Recurring Charges** | | | | |
| Access Link | $28.32 | $150.00 | $17.48 | $115.77 |
| C.O. Connecting Channel | $1.00 | $1.00 | $0.65 | $0.65 |
| PVC, Port Connection & Switching | | | | |
| 1 PVC | $71.15 | $196.98 | $52.93 | $192.91 |
| 2 PVCs | $137.90 | $273.61 | $85.52 | $269.17 |
| 3 PVCs | $173.19 | $350.24 | $89.87 | $345.43 |
| 4 PVCs | $201.65 | $426.87 | $94.21 | $421.69 |
| 5 PVCs | $226.70 | $503.50 | $98.16 | $497.95 |
| Ea add'l PVC 6-14 | $6.26 | $26.09 | $1.32 | $27.25 |
| Ea add'l PVC 15-24 | $3.13 | $7.09 | $1.32 | $27.25 |
| Ea add'l PVC 25+ | $1.57 | $3.55 | $1.32 | $27.25 |
| **Nonrecurring Charges** | | | | |
| Access Link Installation | $400.00 | $600.00 | $350.00 | $550.00 |
| PVC Installation Charge(per PVC) | $15.50 | $15.50 | $15.00 | $15.00 |
| C.O. Connecting Channel | $25.00 | $25.00 | $25.00 | $25.00 |
| Subsequent PVC Order | $75.00 | $75.00 | $75.00 | $75.00 |

| Extended Term Discounts (excluding COCC) | | FRS | Interstate |
|---|---|---|---|
| | 1 Year | 5.00% | 5.00% |
| | 2 Year | 6.25% | 5.00% |
| | 3 Year | 7.50% | 7.50% |
| | 4 Year | 8.75% | 7.50% |
| | 5 Year | 10.00% | 10.00% |

**U S WEST has tariffed Frame Relay in all 14 of its states, and deployment to over 68 cities. Please call your nearest U S WEST Sales Office or authorized agent for details on availability or additional pricing/design information.**

## INTRASTATE PRICING EXAMPLE

**Monthly Recurring Charges:**

| | | |
|---|---|---|
| Access Link: | 1.544 @ $150 x 1 = | $150.00 |
| | 56k @ $28.32 x 3 = | $ 84.96 |
| PVC: | 1 @ 56 Kb/s x 3 = | $213.45 |
| | 3 @ 1.544 rate x 1 = | $350.24 |
| | Total Recurring = | $798.65 |

**Non Recurring Charges:**

| | | |
|---|---|---|
| Access Link: | 1.544 @ $600 x 1 = | $600.00 |
| | 56 Kb/s @ $400 x 3 = | $1200.00 |
| PVC Installation: | $15.50 x 6 = | $93.00 |
| | Total Non Recurring = | $1893.00 |

**As compared to Private Line, Frame Relay typically saves 5-40% on sites and PVC's**

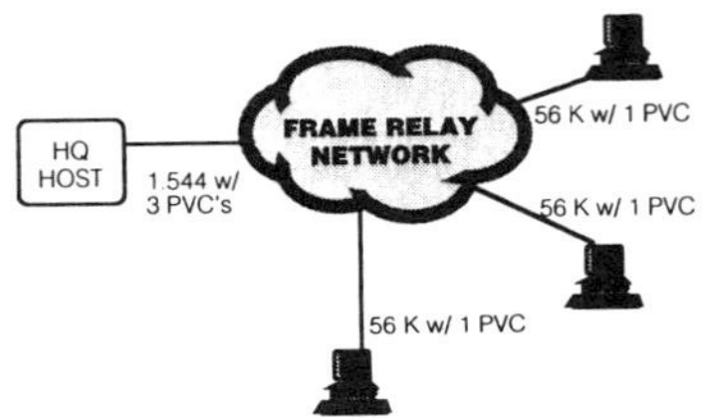

# FRAME RELAY — RATE SHEET

**Iowa**

!INTERPRISE
NETWORKING SERVICES FROM U S WEST

## FRAME RELAY RATE AND TARIFF TABLE

| | FRS Port Speed 56 kb/s | FRS Port Speed 1.5 Mb/s | INTERSTATE 56 kb/s | INTERSTATE 1.5 Mb/s |
|---|---|---|---|---|
| **Monthly Recurring Charges** | | | | |
| Access Link | $28.32 | $150.00 | $17.48 | $115.77 |
| C.O. Connecting Channel | $1.00 | $1.00 | $0.65 | $0.65 |
| PVC, Port Connection & Switching | | | | |
| 1 PVC | $71.15 | $196.98 | $52.93 | $192.91 |
| 2 PVCs | $137.90 | $273.61 | $85.52 | $269.17 |
| 3 PVCs | $173.19 | $350.24 | $89.87 | $345.43 |
| 4 PVCs | $201.65 | $426.87 | $94.21 | $421.69 |
| 5 PVCs | $226.25 | $503.50 | $98.16 | $497.95 |
| Ea add'l PVC 6-14 | $6.26 | $26.09 | $1.32 | $27.25 |
| Ea add'l PVC 15-24 | $3.13 | $7.09 | $1.32 | $27.25 |
| Ea add'l PVC 25+ | $1.57 | $3.55 | $1.32 | $27.25 |
| **Nonrecurring Charges** | | | | |
| Access Link Installation | $400.00 | $600.00 | $350.00 | $550.00 |
| PVC Installation Charge(per PVC) | $15.50 | $15.50 | $15.00 | $15.00 |
| C.O. Connecting Channel | $25.00 | $25.00 | $25.00 | $25.00 |
| Subsequent PVC Order | $75.00 | $75.00 | $75.00 | $75.00 |

| Extended Term Discounts (excluding COCC) | | FRS | Interstate |
|---|---|---|---|
| | 1 Year | 5.00% | 5.00% |
| | 2 Year | 6.25% | 5.00% |
| | 3 Year | 7.50% | 7.50% |
| | 4 Year | 8.75% | 7.50% |
| | 5 Year | 10.00% | 10.00% |

**U S WEST has tariffed Frame Relay in all 14 of its states, and deployment to over 68 cities. Please call your nearest U S WEST Sales Office or authorized agent for details on availability or additional pricing/design information.**

## INTRASTATE PRICING EXAMPLE

**Monthly Recurring Charges:**

| | | |
|---|---|---|
| Access Link: | 1.544 @ $150 x 1 = | $150.00 |
| | 56k @ $28.32 x 3 = | $ 84.96 |
| PVC: | 1 @ 56 Kb/s x 3 = | $213.45 |
| | 3 @ 1.544 rate x 1 = | $350.24 |
| | Total Recurring = | $798.65 |

**Non Recurring Charges:**

| | | |
|---|---|---|
| Access Link: | 1.544 @ $600 x 1 = | $600.00 |
| | 56 Kb/s @ $400 x 3 = | $1200.00 |
| PVC Installation: | $15.50 x 6 = | $93.00 |
| | Total Non Recurring = | $1893.00 |

**As compared to Private Line, Frame Relay typically saves 5-40% on sites and PVC's**

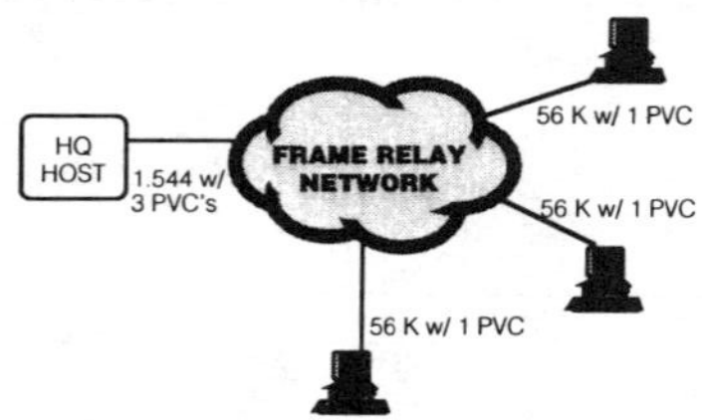

# FRAME RELAY RATE SHEET

Idaho

!NTERPRISE
NETWORKING SERVICES FROM U S WEST

## FRAME RELAY RATE AND TARIFF TABLE

| | FRS Port Speed 56 kb/s | FRS Port Speed 1.5 Mb/s | INTERSTATE 56 kb/s | INTERSTATE 1.5 Mb/s |
|---|---|---|---|---|
| **Monthly Recurring Charges** | | | | |
| Access Link | $28.32 | $150.00 | $17.48 | $115.77 |
| C.O. Connecting Channel | $1.00 | $1.00 | $0.65 | $0.65 |
| PVC, Port Connection & Switching | | | | |
| 1 PVC | $66.91 | $233.13 | $52.93 | $192.91 |
| 2 PVCs | $130.67 | $355.37 | $85.52 | $269.17 |
| 3 PVCs | $165.96 | $477.62 | $89.87 | $345.43 |
| 4 PVCs | $194.42 | $599.87 | $94.21 | $421.69 |
| 5 PVCs | $219.47 | $722.12 | $98.16 | $497.95 |
| Ea add'l PVC 6-14 | $6.25 | $41.63 | $1.32 | $27.25 |
| Ea add'l PVC 15-24 | $3.13 | $9.12 | $1.32 | $27.25 |
| Ea add'l PVC 25+ | $1.57 | $3.55 | $1.32 | $27.25 |
| **Nonrecurring Charges** | | | | |
| Access Link Installation | $400.00 | $600.00 | $350.00 | $550.00 |
| PVC Installation Charge(per PVC) | $15.50 | $15.50 | $15.00 | $15.00 |
| C.O. Connecting Channel | $25.00 | $25.00 | $25.00 | $25.00 |
| Subsequent PVC Order | $75.00 | $75.00 | $75.00 | $75.00 |

| Extended Term Discounts (excluding COCC) | | FRS | Interstate |
|---|---|---|---|
| | 1 Year | 5.00% | 5.00% |
| | 2 Year | 6.25% | 5.00% |
| | 3 Year | 7.50% | 7.50% |
| | 4 Year | 8.75% | 7.50% |
| | 5 Year | 10.00% | 10.00% |

**U S WEST has tariffed Frame Relay in all 14 of its states, and deployment to over 68 cities. Please call your nearest U S WEST Sales Office or authorized agent for details on availability or additional pricing/design information.**

## INTRASTATE PRICING EXAMPLE

**Monthly Recurring Charges:**

| | | |
|---|---|---|
| Access Link: | 1.544 @ $150 x 1 = | $150.00 |
| | 56k @ $28.32 x 3 = | $ 84.96 |
| PVC: | 1 @ 56 Kb/s x 3 = | $200.73 |
| | 3 @ 1.544 rate x 1 = | $477.62 |
| | Total Recurring = | $913.31 |

**Non Recurring Charges:**

| | | |
|---|---|---|
| Access Link: | 1.544 @ $600 x 1 = | $600.00 |
| | 56 Kb/s @ $400 x 3 = | $1200.00 |
| PVC Installation: | $15.50 x 6 = | $93.00 |
| | Total Non Recurring = | $1893.00 |

**As compared to Private Line, Frame Relay typically saves 5-40% on sites and PVC's**

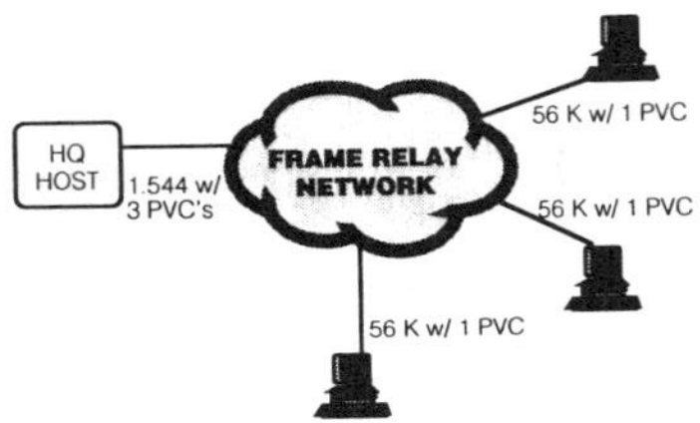

**FRAME RELAY** **RATE SHEET**

**New Mexico**

*!NTERPRISE* NETWORKING SERVICES FROM U S WEST

## FRAME RELAY RATE AND TARIFF TABLE

| | FRS Port Speed 56 kb/s | FRS Port Speed 1.5 Mb/s | INTERSTATE 56 kb/s | INTERSTATE 1.5 Mb/s |
|---|---|---|---|---|
| **Monthly Recurring Charges** | | | | |
| Access Link | $28.32 | $150.00 | $17.48 | $115.77 |
| C.O. Connecting Channel | $1.00 | $1.00 | $0.65 | $0.65 |
| PVC, Port Connection & Switching | | | | |
| 1 PVC | $66.91 | $196.98 | $52.93 | $192.91 |
| 2 PVCs | $130.67 | $273.61 | $85.52 | $269.17 |
| 3 PVCs | $165.96 | $350.24 | $89.87 | $345.43 |
| 4 PVCs | $194.42 | $426.87 | $94.21 | $421.69 |
| 5 PVCs | $219.47 | $503.50 | $98.16 | $497.95 |
| Ea add'l PVC 6-14 | $6.26 | $26.09 | $1.32 | $27.25 |
| Ea add'l PVC 15-24 | $3.13 | $7.09 | $1.32 | $27.25 |
| Ea add'l PVC 25+ | $1.57 | $3.55 | $1.32 | $27.25 |
| **Nonrecurring Charges** | | | | |
| Access Link Installation | $400.00 | $600.00 | $350.00 | $550.00 |
| PVC Installation Charge(per PVC) | $15.50 | $15.50 | $15.00 | $15.00 |
| C.O. Connecting Channel | $25.00 | $25.00 | $25.00 | $25.00 |
| Subsequent PVC Order | $75.00 | $75.00 | $75.00 | $75.00 |

| Extended Term Discounts (excluding COCC) | | FRS Port Speed | INTERSTATE |
|---|---|---|---|
| | 1 Year | 5.00% | 5.00% |
| | 2 Year | 6.25% | 5.00% |
| | 3 Year | 7.50% | 7.50% |
| | 4 Year | 8.75% | 7.50% |
| | 5 Year | 10.00% | 10.00% |

**U S WEST has tariffed Frame Relay in all 14 of its states, and deployment to over 68 cities. Please call your nearest U S WEST Sales Office or authorized agent for details on availability or additional pricing/design information.**

## INTRASTATE PRICING EXAMPLE

**Monthly Recurring Charges:**

| | | |
|---|---|---|
| Access Link: | 1.544 @ $150 x 1 = | $150.00 |
| | 56k @ $28.32 x 3 = | $ 84.96 |
| PVC: | 1 @ 56 Kb/s x 3 = | $200.73 |
| | 3 @ 1.544 rate x 1 = | $350.24 |
| | Total Recurring = | $785.93 |

**Non Recurring Charges:**

| | | |
|---|---|---|
| Access Link: | 1.544 @ $600 x 1 = | $600.00 |
| | 56 Kb/s @ $400 x 3 = | $1200.00 |
| PVC Installation: | $15.50 x 6 = | $93.00 |
| | Total Non Recurring = | $1893.00 |

**As compared to Private Line, Frame Relay typically saves 5-40% on sites and PVC's**

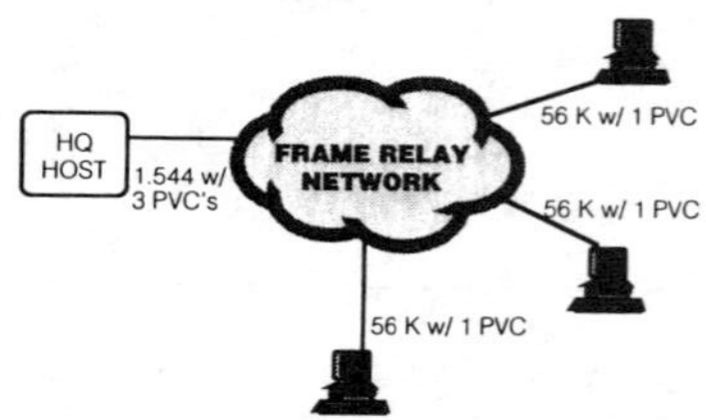

# APPENDIX D: IXC PRODUCT COMPARISON, PRICING, AND COLLATERAL

*IXC CIR Comparison*

| *COMPANY* | *AT&T* | *MCI* | *Sprint* | *WilTel* |
|---|---|---|---|---|
| CIR Increments: | | | | |
| 0K | ICB | X | X | |
| 4K | X | | | |
| 16K | X | X | | X |
| 32K | X | X | | X |
| 48K | X | X | | X |
| 56/64K | X | X | X | X |
| Nx64K | X | X | X | X |
| Other | | | see note S2 | |

*IXC Equipment Comparison*

| *COMPANY* | *AT&T* | *MCI* | *Sprint* | *WilTel* |
|---|---|---|---|---|
| Simplex PVCs | X | X | | X |
| Equipment Packages: | | | | |
| Wellfleet routers | | X | X | X |
| Cisco routers | X | X | X | X |
| 3Com routers | | | | X |
| SynOptics smart hub | | | | X |
| Cabletron smart hub | | | | |
| CSU/DSU | X | X | X | X |
| Cascade concentrator | | | | X |
| Other | | | | |

### IXC Financing Comparison

| COMPANY | AT&T | MCI | Sprint | WilTel |
|---|---|---|---|---|
| Financing: | | | | |
| Lease | X | X | X | X |
| Purchase | X | X | X | X |
| Rental | X | X | X | X |

### IXC Network Management Comparison

| COMPANY | AT&T | MCI | Sprint | WilTel |
|---|---|---|---|---|
| Network Management: | | | | |
| HP OpenView | X | X | X | X |
| SunNet Manager | X | X | X | X |
| IBM NetView | | | | |
| IBM NetView6000 | | X | X | |
| Proprietary | | | | |
| SNMP | X | X | X | X |
| Other | | | | |

### IXC Port Speed Comparison

| COMPANY | AT&T | MCI | Sprint | WilTel |
|---|---|---|---|---|
| Port Speeds Offered: | | | | |
| 56/64K | X | X | X | X |
| 128K | X | X | X | X |
| 256K | X | X | X | X |
| 384K | X | X | X | X |
| 512K | X | X | X | X |
| 768K | X | X | X | X |
| 1.024M | X | X | X | X |
| 1.536M | X | X | X | X |
| Other | see note A1 | | see note S1 | see note W1 |

*IXC Value Added Comparison*

| COMPANY | AT&T | MCI | Sprint | WilTel |
|---|---|---|---|---|
| **Value-Added Services:** | | | | |
| Equip. maintenance | X | X | X | X |
| Configuration management | X | X | X | X |
| Complete outsourcing | X | X | X | X |
| Other | | | | |

*IXC Backbone Comparison*

| COMPANY | AT&T | MCI | Sprint | WilTel |
|---|---|---|---|---|
| **Backbone:** | | | | |
| Cell backbone | X | X | X | X |
| Frame backbone | | X | | |
| Other | | | | |

*IXC Service Availability Comparison*

| COMPANY | AT&T | MCI | Sprint | WilTel |
|---|---|---|---|---|
| **Service Availability:** | | | | |
| Domestic LATAs (#) | all | all | all | all |
| International | X | X | X | X |
| No. of international countries | 22 | 16 | 19 | 7 |

*IXC Additional Services Comparison*

| COMPANY | AT&T | MCI | Sprint | WilTel |
|---|---|---|---|---|
| **Additional Services:** | | | | |
| Internet connection | X | 4Q94 | X | X |
| X.25 interworking | | 4Q94 | | |
| Dial-up access | X | 4Q94 | | |
| TCP/IP interworking | | | X | |
| ATM interworking | planned | | | X |
| Other | | | | |

## *Notes*

*S1. - 192K, 320K, 448K, 576K, 640K, 704K, 896K, 1280K*
*W1. - 1984K*
*A1. - 2.048 in Europe*
*S2. - 19.2K, 38.4K*

# AT&T Collateral

## Case Study

### Company Overview

The subject company NIKE, is the leader in the sports and fitness apparel industry, with a strategic goal of being number one in the world. The company attained that goal with a jump from $1 billion in sales in 1989 to $4 billion in 1993. NIKE focused on U.S. and international growth as a primary method to attaining that goal. Near term expansion is underway in Europe, Latin America and Asia with plans for other global reaches in the long term.

### Network Overview

Although Nike has predominently a private line data network, the company installed a frame relay network to interconnect 18 regional agencies scattered throughout the U.S. Prior to the frame relay network deployment these agencies were not connected. Nike has a two person staff to support data network engineering.

The requirements of the group using frame relay are non-interactive, LAN traffic including extensive e-mail and file transfers. The primary application for the group is market/inventory projections, critical for optimization of inventory management to meet sales requirements.

### Frame Relay Motivation

Alternative methods of interconnecting the agencies were "cost prohibitive", according to the Network Engineering Manager. In his opinion the need to interconnect the agencies was a tailor made application for frame relay. Nike has a need to add and move locations to quickly respond to market conditions. These locations are now connected to critical host databases.

The company is very interested in exploring leading edge ATM applications for the future. AT&T InterSpan Frame Relay Service is designed to be fully interoperable with AT&T's ATM service. Nike indicates that the current work with frame relay is giving them a good foundation to understand and move toward more complex applications enabled by ATM.

Nike networking managers were frustrated by the lack of accurate frame relay information in the marketplace a year ago. "AT&T gave us the straight scoop. We've learned a lot and are looking at how frame may be appropriate for other areas of our business, particularly in the international arena" said Tom Beane.

### Frame Relay Network

18 locations across the country
See map for details on Port and PVC specs

### Frame Relay Benefits

Nike focusses on brand image, product innovation Because Nike's primary focus is customer service, they see a valuable impact in the ability to have what a customer wants in stock. Anticipating that customer demand is a formidable challenge when you have an extensive product line. One of the key requirements to forcasting sales demand and inventory requirements is the accurate and rapid flow of information from the sales agencies.

The communication process to provide the forcasting was previously done manually, with an extensive mail/paper/fax flow. With the new network information is more accurate, timely and has improved inventory management.

The flexibility associated with frame relay is a big benefit for Nike as well. As market conditions change and new markets are identified, Nike relies on the ability to open new locations, combine and reconfigure existing locations including fluctuating bandwidth requirements.

# Nike, Inc.

## U.S. Frame Relay Network

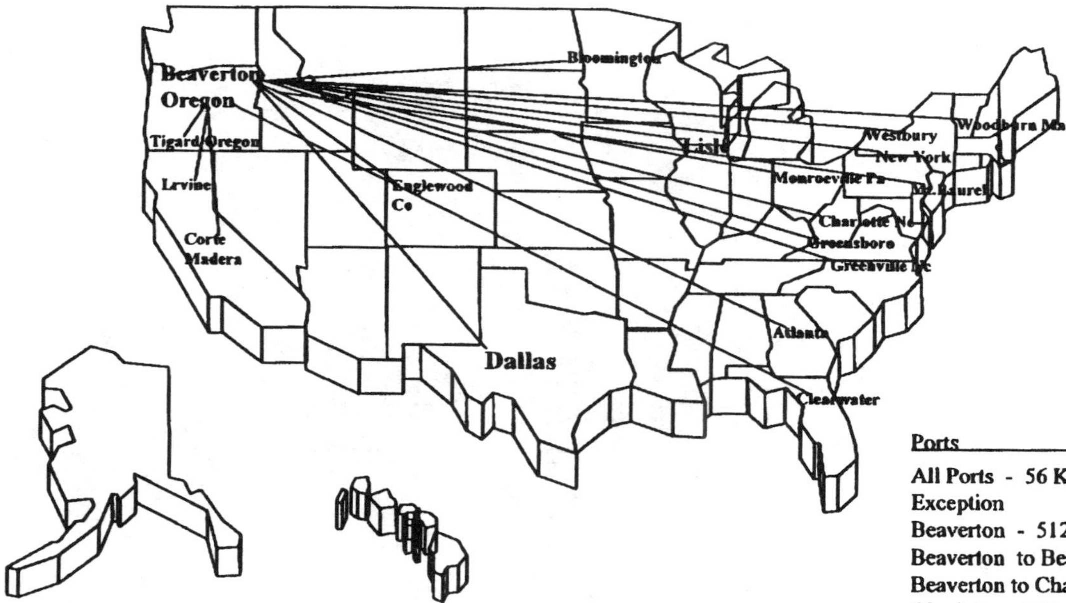


Ports

All Ports - 56 KBPS
Exception
Beaverton - 512
Beaverton to Beaverton - 56
Beaverton to Charlotte NC - 128
Charlotte - 128

All PVCS 56KBPS CIR
Exception
Beaverton to Charlotte NC - 128

# MCI COLLATERAL

VPDS®
VIRTUAL PRIVATE DATA SERVICES

# *HyperStream Frame Relay Service*

MCI DATA SERVICES

## Pricing Overview

HyperStream℠ Frame Relay Service provides the most flexible pricing options of any frame relay service. The HyperStream Frame Relay rate structure enables customers to receive private line equivalent performance, while realizing virtual networking economies, regardless of network geography or applications.

The HyperStream Frame Relay pricing structure is comprised of three basic elements: access, ports and permanent virtual circuits (PVC).

***Access***

| | |
|---|---|
| Local Loop | Standard Tariff |
| Access Coordination | Standard Tariff |

***Ports***

Port charges are based upon the selected bandwidth needed to connect to the HyperStream Frame Relay Network.

***Permanent Virtual Circuit (PVC)***

MCI® offers three types of PVC rate options: Fixed Committed Information Rate (CIR), Usage CIR and Zero CIR. Fixed CIR PVCs are priced on a flat monthly rate based on mileage bands and bandwidth requirements with unlimited use. An industry first, Usage CIR PVCs are similar to Fixed CIR PVCs in performance characteristics, but are priced based upon the amount of data transmitted. Zero CIR PVCs are charged on a usage basis. All PVC rates are mileage sensitive.

Non-Recurring PVC Charges:

| | |
|---|---|
| PVC Installation Charge: | $15 |
| PVC Reconfiguration Charge: | $15 |

| Port Speeds Supported | Rate/Month |
|---|---|
| 56/64 Kbps | $180 |
| 112/128 Kbps | $330 |
| 224/256 Kbps | $400 |
| 336/384 Kbps | $600 |
| 448/512 Kbps | $750 |
| 672/768 Kbps | $950 |
| 896/1024 Kbps | $1,200 |
| 1344/1536 Kbps | $1,600 |
| Port Installation Charge: | $300 |
| Port Reconfiguration Charge: | $300 |

### *Fixed CIR PVC Rates*

| Bandwidth PVC/CIR* | Mileage 0-249 | 250-499 | 500-749 | 750-999 | 1000-1999 | 2000+ |
|---|---|---|---|---|---|---|
| 16 Kbps | $46 | $57 | $67 | $78 | $105 | $132 |
| 32 Kbps | $54 | $66 | $79 | $91 | $116 | $141 |
| 48 Kbps | $73 | $89 | $105 | $122 | $154 | $187 |
| 64 Kbps | $84 | $103 | $122 | $141 | $179 | $217 |
| 128 Kbps | $141 | $173 | $205 | $237 | $301 | $365 |
| 192 Kbps | $210 | $258 | $306 | $354 | $450 | $546 |
| 256 Kbps | $280 | $343 | $407 | $470 | $597 | $724 |
| 320 Kbps | $348 | $427 | $506 | $585 | $743 | $901 |
| 384 Kbps | $419 | $514 | $609 | $705 | $895 | $1,085 |
| 448 Kbps | $489 | $601 | $713 | $825 | $1,048 | $1,272 |
| 512 Kbps | $552 | $680 | $808 | $935 | $1,191 | $1.446 |
| 576 Kbps | $622 | $766 | $909 | $1,053 | $1,341 | $1,629 |
| 640 Kbps | $691 | $851 | $1,010 | $1,170 | $1,489 | $1,809 |
| 704 Kbps | $761 | $939 | $1,116 | $1,294 | $1,648 | $2,003 |
| 768 Kbps | $833 | $1,030 | $1,227 | $1,423 | $1,817 | $2,210 |
| 832 Kbps | $902 | $1,119 | $1,336 | $1,553 | $1,987 | $2,420 |
| 896 Kbps | $970 | $1,207 | $1,445 | $1,682 | $2,157 | $2,631 |
| 960 Kbps | $1.042 | $1,301 | $1,560 | $1,819 | $2,337 | $2,855 |
| 1,024 Kbps | $1.099 | $1,377 | $1,655 | $1,933 | $2,489 | $3,044 |

* Each Simplex PVC is priced separately with unlimited usage.

### *Usage CIR PVC Rates*

| | Mileage 0-249 | 250-499 | 500-749 | 750-999 | 1000-1999 | 2000+ |
|---|---|---|---|---|---|---|
| CIR Usage* | $.0169 | $.0208 | $.0248 | $.0350 | $.0444 | $.0600 |
| DE Usage | $.0017 | $.0021 | $.0025 | $.0035 | $.0045 | $.0060 |

* Each Simplex PVC is priced separately and different rates apply to CIR usage and DE usage.

### *Usage CIR PVC Monthly Minimum*

Monthly minimums are set at 30% of the corresponding Fixed CIR rate and vary according to mileage and bandwidth. All usage charges contribute towards satisfaction of the monthly usage minimum. Minimums are set and assessed on a Simplex PVC basis.

### *Usage CIR PVC Cost Capping*

Usage charges are capped at 120% of the corresponding Fixed CIR rate and vary according to mileage and bandwidth. All usage charges apply to the cap on a Simplex PVC basis.

### *Zero CIR PVC Usage Rates*

| Zero CIR Monthly | Mileage 0-249 | 250-499 | 500-749 | 750-999 | 1000-1999 | 2000+ |
|---|---|---|---|---|---|---|
| Usage* | $.0084 | $.0104 | $.0124 | $.0175 | $.0222 | $.0300 |
| Minimum** | $5.00 | $6.00 | $7.00 | $10.00 | $13.00 | $17.00 |

* Each Simplex PVC is priced according to usage. All frames are marked DE, and all usage is priced at the same rate. Zero CIR usage charges are not capped.

** Monthly minimums vary with mileage and are assessed on a Simplex PVC basis.

MCI®


Control Number C21564 6/93

# SPRINT COLLATERAL

# Business Exchange

## BENEFITS

- Improve interconnectivity among distributed inventory and production systems at remote sites on a real-time basis, increasing the company's ability to respond efficiently to fluctuations of customer demand.
- Manage costs efficiently. Sprint Frame Relay Service lets the company pay only for the bandwidth used; and there is a price cap to keep costs within budget.
- Adapt an implementation schedule to match a company's unique needs. Sprint Frame Relay Service simplifies migration from a centralized to a distributed network environment. A customizable implementation prevents potential changeover difficulties.
- Preserve the technology investments already made by the company; Sprint Frame Relay handles multiple protocols seamlessly.

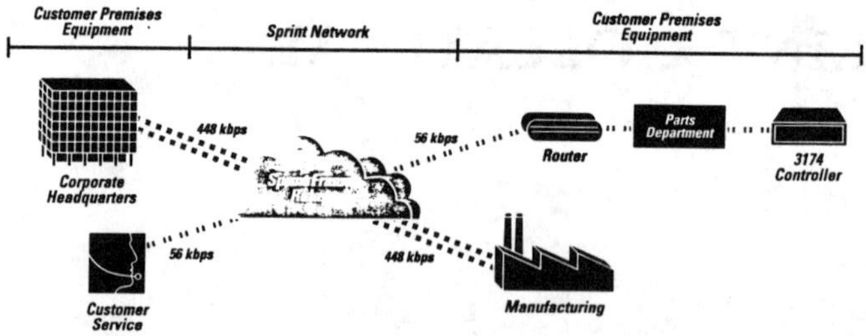


## DESIGN CONSIDERATIONS

- Frame relay allows the integration of various systems with incompatible protocols into a common, protocol-insensitive network.
- Single-line access to frame relay is more cost-effective, and simpler to manage and maintain than the multiple connections associated with traditional leased-line configurations.
- Sprint Frame Relay Service provides global connectivity, allowing easy expansion to international locations.

Sprint.



4601-1

Business Exchange

MANUFACTURING SOLUTION

**INDUSTRY:**
- Manufacturing

**SEGMENT:**
- Computer Equipment

**CHALLENGE** **Manufacturers in competitive markets utilize just-in-time (JIT) inventory control processes to increase their yield and provide better service to their customers. By closely monitoring their inventories these manufacturers can place an order to buy raw materials, or produce and deliver goods only when they are needed. This JIT process requires a dynamic, intelligent system capable of processing information from all phases of the business on a real-time basis.**

**A leading maker of portable tele-transaction computers implemented a mainframe-based Materials Resource Planning (MRP) application to help manage its complex inventory processes. The system provided the company with better JIT inventory control and turnover rates, and helped avoid parts shortages, machine and labor overloads, and other resource-related problems.**

**However, the MRP application lacked flexibility and making changes was cumbersome. Furthermore, the protocols used by the central system were incompatible with the variety of smaller systems distributed throughout the many company sites. In order to keep pace with customer demand, the company needed to improve information flow among its disparate local systems.**

**APPLICATIONS:**
- Inventory Management
- Information Systems Internetworking

**SPRINT® PRODUCT:**
- Sprint Frame Relay Service

**A SPRINT SOLUTION** Sprint proposed that its Frame Relay Service, rather than traditional point-to-point lines, offered the ideal technology through which to develop an effective and powerful distributed environment.

Analysis of T1 and fractional T1 point-to-point leased line solutions showed that the manufacturer's need for meshed connectivity within its distributed network would have meant installing and paying for a large number of point-to-point lines. However, with frame relay, the company required only one T1 access line between any endpoint and the network, even for reciprocal traffic or multiple connections. This reduced line charges upfront by dramatically decreasing the number of lines required.

Most importantly, frame relay provided the ability to combine incompatible workstation protocols; thereby protecting this high-tech firm's previous investment in systems equipment and training.

Sprint's frame relay solution was also well-suited for the company's pragmatic implementation scheme. Company programmers first used the frame relay network as their development environment, allowing them to become familiar with frame relay, with its new router and switching technologies, without bottlenecking the primary production environment during this transitional phase. Developers also began integrating frame relay and distributed environment capabilities into their application programs.

Today, a nationwide frame relay backbone connects manufacturing, engineering and customer service sites with the larger sales offices and crucial parts depots. Eventually, this backbone may be extended to include international offices.

Sprint.

***Sale By: Evan Parke, Account Manager, Cleveland Sales Office***

# FRAME RELAY CASE STUDY

## THE CHALLENGE

Like many rapidly expanding companies, a large privately-held financial services company with 21,000 employees had implemented distributed data applications among its 8 regional headquarters and remote locations.

The local area networks (LANs) at the company's 120 geographically dispersed nationwide offices were not interconnected. Work groups at different locations found it difficult to share files as quickly as they needed, or to pass on proposal and approval information in a timely manner.

A network that would interconnect all locations, be flexible enough to increase capacity as traffic increased without requiring a complete network redesign, and do it economically with a one-stop telecommunications provider, became a core business requirement of the firm

SPRINT showed the financial services firm how a frame relay network was the perfect match for its combination of needs - a better solution than either traditional X.25 or various private line options.

Initially, the company had considered installing an X.25 link to the public data network. However, the intensely bursty nature of the huge files the company needed to transfer among different LANs on a regular basis were not well-suited for an X.25 environment. They also considered private lines as a solution, but given the nature of the company's traffic - heavy traffic during peak hours, little or no traffic at other times - the cost of installing and maintaining private lines between locations could not be justified.

Sprint's frame relay network was recommended as the solution because it offered speed, flexibility and economy not available from other, traditional options. Frame relay provides high-speed data transmission that is protocol-insensitive and cost-efficient for bursty traffic.

## BENEFITS

•Obtain just the amount of bandwidth required for specific voice and data applications and pay only for the bandwidth used.

•Boost productivity downloading information to any network location immediately, eliminating duplicate efforts and saving valuable transaction time.

•Streamline overall company operations. Simplify daily transactions, management reports, proposal boilerplates and approval processes by sharing information in distributed databases. Sprint Frame Relay Service handles a variety of protocols simultaneously.

DESIGN CONSIDERATIONS

•With frame relay, a single access line between an endpoint and the network, supports fully-meshed traffic among multiple locations. It also provides alternative routing possibilities, with a choice of company network management or Sprint network oversight.

•Frame relay can be installed using current lines and equipment. Installation is easy and economical and no additional equipment or lines need to be purchased. It also provides a smooth migration path to future ATM environments.

•Sprint Frame Relay Service, based on the Alcatel 1100TPX intelligent switching platform, ensures high performance.

Sprint.

# Clearline Star Backbone

**8 Regional Nodes with T-1 Lines**
**(2 Hop Limitation)**

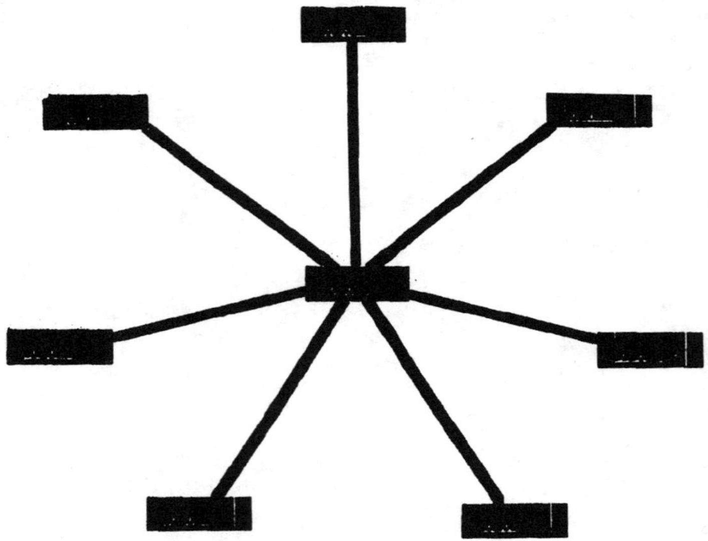

Sprint.

# Partially Meshed Clearline Backbone

**8 Regional Nodes with T-1 Lines**
**(2 Hop Limitation)**

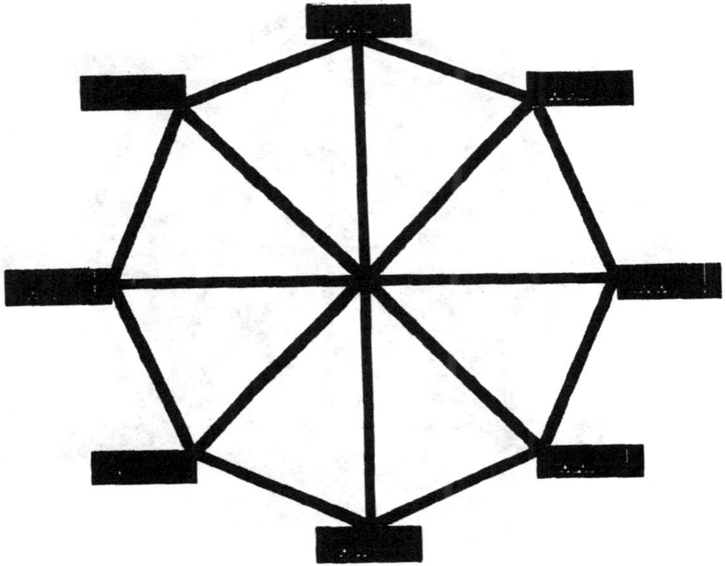

Sprint.

# Fully Meshed Clearline Backbone

**8 Regional Nodes with T-1 Lines**
**(1 Hop - 28 Private Lines)**

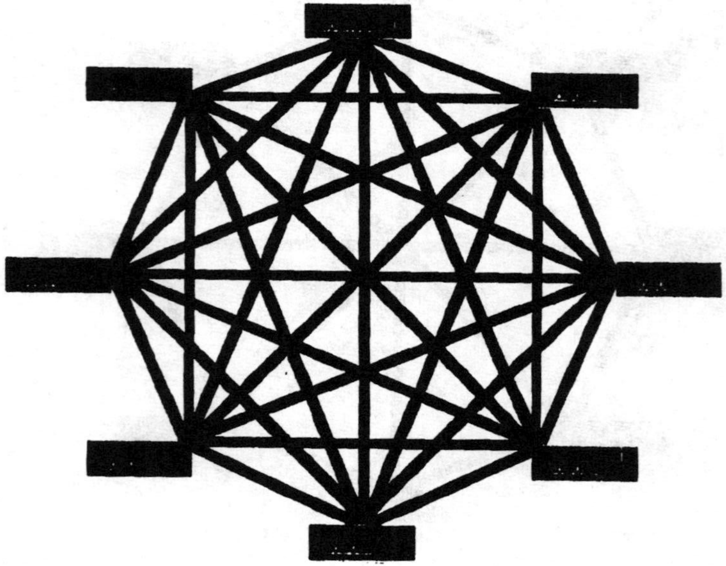

Sprint.

# Frame Relay Backbone

**Fully Meshed PVCs (28 Total)**
**One Hop Across Backbone**

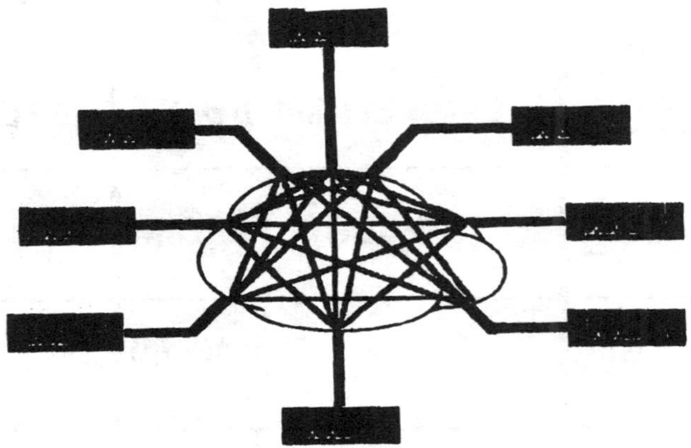

Sprint

# Backbone Design Analysis

| | Frame Relay | Clearline (Partial Mesh) |
|---|---|---|
| Cost | Cost Effective | 2 X Frame Relay |
| Hop Count | Max = 1 | Max = 2 |
| Resilience | Highly Resilient | Resilient |
| Bandwidth per site | 1.544 Mbps | 4.632 Mbps (57% of Traffic - 2 Links) |
| Router Ports per site | 1 | 3 |
| Links per site | 7 - PVCs | 3 - Clearline |

Sprint

# Backbone Designs - Cost Comparison

| | | INSTALL | MONTHLY |
|---|---|---|---|
| CLEARLINE | Star | $24,920 | $ 32,119 |
| | Partial Mesh | $42,720 | $ 56,162 |
| | Full Mesh | $99,380 | $127,209 |
| FRAME RELAY | Full Mesh | $16,940 | $ 25,423 |

Sprint

12490 Sunrise Valley
Reston, VA 22096-0001

# PRICING

## DOMESTIC FRAME RELAY PRICING

~~~~~~~~~~~~~~~~~~~~~~~~~~~~~~

There are three components to be considered when pricing out a domestic frame relay service solution -- LEC access, access channel (port) and PVCs.

o LEC (telco) access

The physical LEC access line (the actual telco local loop) is priced using Sprint's normal access pricing (formerly Tariff 8). All associated charges, such as central office connection (COC), access coordination fee (ACF) and B8ZS, do apply. 56 kbps pricing uses the same access pricing as CLEARLINE(R) DDS.

o Access channel

The access channel (port) speed is selected to accommodate the various PVCs that will use that particular access channel. The access channel must be large enough such that the cumulative egress PVC committed information rate (CIR) does not exceed 100% of the access channel bandwidth (egress in terms of bandwidth exiting the network to the customer premise).

The chart below indicates available access channel speeds. The customer may select channel speeds based on N x 56K or N x 64K, depending on the LEC availability of alternate mark inversion (AMI) or B8ZS encoding respectively.

| ACCESS CHANNEL (N x 64) | (N x 56) |
|---|---|
| 64K | 56K |
| 128 | 112 |
| 192 | 168 |
| 256 | 224 |
| 320 | 280 |
~~~~~~~~~~~~~~~~~~~~~~~~~~~~~~

| | |
|---|---|
| 384 | 336 |
| 448 | 392 |
| 512 | 448 |
| 576 | 504 |
| 640 | 560 |
| 704 | 616 |
| 768 | 672 |
| 896 | 784 |
| 1.024 | 896 |
| 1.280 | 1.120 |
| 1.536 | 1.344 |

INSTALLATION CHARGE: Per access channel, regardless of speed.

o PVC charges

Sprint offers PVCs with a variety of CIRs. A PVC with an assigned CIR is ensured a minimum level of throughput across the frame relay network. PVCs may submit data to the Frame Relay network in excess of their CIR (a "burst"), and the Frame Relay network will make a best effort to deliver that "burst" data. A PVC with an assigned CIR (non-zero) is charged a flat monthly fee; there is no extra charge for bursting above the CIR. PVCs with a Zero-CIR are priced on a usage basis with a monthly cap.

INSTALLATION CHARGE: Per PVC, regardless of CIR.

- CIR-based PVCs

  CIR-based PVCs are charged a flat rate that is based on the CIR rate. There is no extra charge for "bursting" above the CIR.

- Zero-CIR PVCs

  Zero-CIR PVCs are priced on a usage basis with a monthly cap. The usage pricing is determined by the amount of data that gets transferred through the network. An important feature of this service is that it has a monthly cap, allowing the customer to budget for the maximum monthly charges a particular PVC. The actual charges are calculated based on the number of kilocells that are successfully transferred through the Frame Relay network.

Sprint

*12490 Sunrise Valley*
*Reston, VA 22096-0001*

## ANCILLARY SERVICES

o SNMP MANAGEMENT CAPABILITIES. Intended for the SNMP-savvy customer who wishes to take on the responsibility of monitoring the health and performance of their frame relay network.

o HYBRID INTERCONNECTIVITY. Allows Sprint to design and implement comprehensive hybrid solutions that may require multiple protocols for different applications. The end user enjoys the benefits of a seemingly seamless architecture, with the ability of data using different access methods to originate and terminate wherever the application requires.

o ONE-STOP SHOPPING. Design comprehensive and complex networks, provide network management and supply hardware, such as CSU/DSUs, routers, multiplexors and integrated access controllers, with all of the functionality of top-of-the-line PBXs.

o CONSULTING AND DESIGN SERVICES. Sprint can provide consulting and design expertise for extremely complex, integrated service opportunities.

o FULL NETWORK MANAGEMENT SUPPORT. Minimize internal costs for data network management. Full-service frame relay network management support is available 24 hours a day, including monitoring, maintenance and installation.

o NETWORK PERFORMANCE REPORTS. Provides the ability to monitor company data traffic more accurately. Monthly reports provide a snapshot of all data traffic in a variety of formats.

o CPE CERTIFICATION PROGRAM. Sprint's CPE certification program increases the likelihood of CPE compatibility. CPE certification provides a rigorous testbed for vendors to test products and verify service compatibility.

o STANDARDS-COMPLIANCE. Sprint's Frame Relay service is standards-compliant with the International Communications Union (ITU) and American National Standards Institute (ANSI) to ensure interoperability with a wide range of equipment.

Sprint

12490 Sunrise Valley
Reston, VA 22096-0001

o DISASTER RECOVERY CAPABILITIES. Frame Relay can provide built-in redundancy in four key areas: local exchange carrier (LEC) backup, back-up access channel, access switch backup and host disaster recovery. These redundant systems maintain the availability of Sprint's frame relay network and extend from the network side of the customer router to the frame relay access switch.

o FLEXIBLE GATEWAY ACCESS. Expanding data communications worldwide by integrating different products and protocols. Frame Relay provides customers access to the Internet and SprintLink IP Networks.

Sprint

12490 Sunrise Valley
Reston, VA 22096-0001

## PRICING RATES

Sprint's Frame Relay service pricing is considered proprietary and company confidential. Access channels and PVC charges increase commensurately depending upon the access channel speed and CIR of the PVC. For example, a 64k access channel with a 19.2k CIR will be priced around $300. monthly, plus telco access charges. The same 64k access channel with non-CIR pricing would cap at less than $250. monthly, plus telco charges.

A 256k access channel with a CIR of 128k would be near the $850. monthly mark, and dropping to near $650. monthly for a CIR of 64k.

For a location utilizing a 384k access channel, with three PVCs, each with a CIR of 64k, the monthly charges would total less than $1300.00, plus telco charges.

Please keep in mind that a PVC is charged only in one direction, from the origination to the termination. Let's say we have a 4-node network, a central site and three remotes. In the previous example, The 384k access channel and three 64k CIR PVC's would be charged at the central site, assuming the central site is originating the virtual connection. The three remotes would not be charged for the virtual connection, they would be charged for the access channel only, plus telco charges.

# WILTEL COLLATERAL

## Complementary Services

### *Internetworking Equipment*

Several equipment package options are available with WilPak, as are flexible lease and purchase arrangements. Equipment packages include:

| Routers | Concentrators | Smarthubs | CSU/DSUs |
|---|---|---|---|
| Cisco | Cascade | Synoptics | Racal |
| Wellfleet | | | General Datacom |
| 3Com | | | Cray Communications |

Maintenance package options include 5x8, 7x24, and 7x24 with 4 hour response.

WilTel will pre-configure and stage, install, test, and maintain this equipment, providing a single point of contact for all service related issues. Routers purchased from WilTel include configuration of the frame relay connection, loading of pre-defined router tables, mapping for any-to-any connectivity, and activation of the required protocols.

### *Configuration Assistance*

WilTel will configure approved routers for WilPak clients purchasing equipment directly from the router vendor. Included in the service is the configuration of the frame relay connection, loading of pre-defined route tables, mapping for any-to-any connectivity and activation of the required protocols. Configuration Assistance is available for a one-time fee of $480 per site.

### *Full-Service Internetworking*

WilTel provides Full-Service Internetworking as a comprehensive LAN interconnection solution which includes the planning, implementation, operation, and optimization of a corporate or enterprise internet. This complete turn-key service includes all associated internetworking equipment, on-going configuration management of the network, proactive network surveillance and trouble resolution, and monthly performance reporting and optimization.

Full-Service Internetworking can be used as a short term solution when internal resources are limited or unfamiliar with internetworking or frame relay technology. It can also be used as a long term strategy to free up resources to concentrate on core business applications.

### *WilNet Bandwidth-on-Command*

Site recovery can be achieved by combining WilPak service with WilNet Bandwidth-on-Command service and utilizing the reservation-based network capacity to re-route traffic to a network recovery site should a primary data processing center become incapacitated.

### *WilPak Network Management*

WilPak network management options are available through WilView, WilTel's standards-based network management family of products.

WilView can operate on PC, Macintosh, Sun, HP, or DEC platforms. It can be accessed as a stand-alone application or through other network management systems, such as SunNet Manager, HP OpenView, or NetView.

The two WilView products that work in conjunction with WilPak are WilVew/X and WilView/SNMP.

**WilView/X** WilView/X provides WilPak users with access to order tracking, trouble ticket tracking, and trouble ticket entry services. It also provides access to on-line performance reporting for WilPak service. These graphical utilization reports can be requested on-line, and can be received either on-line or via FAX.

### *WilView/SNMP*

WilView/SNMP provides access to WilPak service information via the Simple Network Management Protocol (SNMP). Available information includes WilPak Port and PVC configuration information, Port and PVC utilization and performance data, and near-real-time alarm notification for ports and PVCs.

---

***Note***: WilView/SNMP is scheduled to be available during the third quarter of 1994.

---

### *Service Satisfaction Warranty*

WilTel's commitment to customer satisfaction is evidenced by the following promise:

*WilPak customers have 120 days to evaluate the service. At any time within this period, if a customer is not completely satisfied with WilPak service, WilTel will, upon written notification, pay the charges to switch the customer back to its original network provider and configuration.*

### *Load Balancing and Network Recovery*

Network protection from a local loop or POP failure can be achieved by using two Port Connections within the same or different POPs and load-balancing the traffic between these ports. Two local loops are required, and two Port Connections are required, each with its own set of PVCs. The Port speed and the PVC CIRs should be less than what would be required if only one Port and PVC were being used (i.e., 50%). The associated router must be able to load balance for this solution.

Standard pricing for each node will apply.

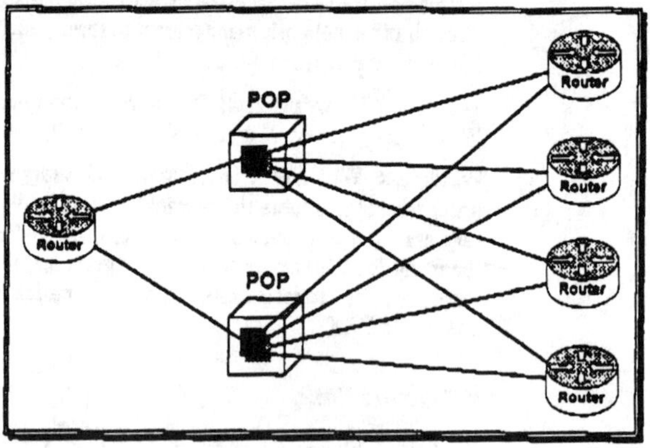


## Pricing

### *Recurring Charges*

WilPak pricing is neither usage nor mileage sensitive. A flat monthly fee per node is assessed based on the Port Connection speed and the percentage of Port subscription. The subscription level is determined by summing the Committed Information Rates for all PVCs *out of* the Port Connection. A

WILPAK NETWORK

| CITY | PORT CONNECTION | TOTAL CIR | BASE PORT MONTHLY | NET 2YR PORT MONTHLY | PORT INSTALL | # OF PVC'S | PVC INSTALL |
|---|---|---|---|---|---|---|---|
| NEW YORK | 768KB | 928KB | $2,904.00 | $2,381.28 | $500.00 | 11 | $275.00 |
| DALLAS | 64KB | 160KB | $521.00 | $427.22 | $250.00 | 4 | $100.00 |
| PORTLAND | 64KB | 160KB | $521.00 | $427.22 | $250.00 | 4 | $100.00 |
| BOSTON #1 | 64KB | 160KB | $521.00 | $427.22 | $250.00 | 4 | $100.00 |
| CHICAGO | 256KB | 416KB | $1,219.00 | $999.58 | $250.00 | 4 | $100.00 |
| SAN FRANCISCO | 256KB | 288KB | $994.00 | $815.08 | $250.00 | 3 | $75.00 |
| ATLANTA | 256KB | 416KB | $1,219.00 | $999.58 | $250.00 | 4 | $100.00 |
| WASHINGTON, DC | 64KB | 64KB | $353.00 | $289.46 | $250.00 | 2 | $50.00 |
| MIAMI | 64KB | 64KB | $353.00 | $289.46 | $250.00 | 2 | $50.00 |
| MINNEAPOLIS | 64KB | 64KB | $353.00 | $289.46 | $250.00 | 2 | $50.00 |
| SEATTLE | 64KB | 64KB | $353.00 | $289.46 | $250.00 | 2 | $50.00 |
| HOUSTON | 64KB | 64KB | $353.00 | $289.46 | $250.00 | 2 | $50.00 |
| KANSAS CITY | 64KB | 64KB | $353.00 | $289.46 | $250.00 | 2 | $50.00 |
| COLORADO SPRINGS | 64KB | 64KB | $353.00 | $289.46 | $250.00 | 2 | $50.00 |
| DENVER | 64KB | 64KB | $353.00 | $289.46 | $250.00 | 2 | $50.00 |
| SAN DIEGO | 64KB | 64KB | $353.00 | $289.46 | $250.00 | 2 | $50.00 |
| BOSTON #2 | 64KB | 64KB | $353.00 | $289.46 | $250.00 | 2 | $50.00 |
| LOS ANGELES | 64KB | 64KB | $353.00 | $289.46 | $250.00 | 2 | $50.00 |
| TOTALS | | | $11,782.00 | $9,661.24 | $4,750.00 | 56 | $1,400.00 |

PRICING IS BUDGETARY
IXC CONNECTING LEG IN COLORADO SPRINGS IS $140.60 MONTHLY AND $0 INSTALL

| CITY A | CITYZ | SERVICE | V&H MILES | BASE MONTHLY | 2YR MONTHLY | INSTALL |
|---|---|---|---|---|---|---|
| PTLDOR | SNFCCA | DS-0 | 540 | $356.20 | $313.46 | $150.00 |
| STTLWA | SNFCCA | DS-0 | 685 | $396.80 | $349.18 | $150.00 |
| STTLWA | SNFCCA | DS-0 | 685 | $396.80 | $349.18 | $150.00 |
| SNFCCA | LSANCA | DS-0 | 350 | $303.00 | $266.64 | $150.00 |
| SNFCCA | LSANCA | DS-0 | 350 | $303.00 | $266.64 | $150.00 |
| SNFCCA | SNDGCA | DS-0 | 461 | $334.08 | $293.99 | $150.00 |
| SNFCCA | CHCGIL | DS-0 | 1852 | $723.56 | $636.73 | $150.00 |
| SNFCCA | ATLNGA | DS-0 | 2134 | $802.52 | $706.22 | $150.00 |
| HSTNTX | ATLNGA | DS-0 | 703 | $401.84 | $353.62 | $150.00 |
| HSTNTX | ATLNGA | DS-0 | 703 | $401.84 | $353.62 | $150.00 |
| DNVRCO | CHCGIL | DS-0 | 918 | $462.04 | $406.60 | $150.00 |
| DNVRCO | CHCGIL | DS-0 | 918 | $462.04 | $406.60 | $150.00 |
| CLSPCO | CHCGIL | DS-0 | 926 | $464.28 | $408.57 | $150.00 |
| DLLSTX | CHCGIL | DS-0 | 799 | $428.72 | $377.27 | $150.00 |
| KSCYMO | CHCGIL | DS-0 | 411 | $320.08 | $281.67 | $150.00 |
| KSCYMO | CHCGIL | DS-0 | 411 | $320.08 | $281.67 | $150.00 |
| MIAMFL | CHCGIL | DS-0 | 600 | $373.00 | $328.24 | $150.00 |
| MIAMFL | ATLNGA | DS-0 | 600 | $373.00 | $328.24 | $150.00 |
| ATLNGA | WASHDC | DS-0 | 542 | $356.76 | $313.95 | $150.00 |
| ATLNGA | WASHDC | DS-0 | 542 | $356.76 | $313.95 | $150.00 |
| BSTNMA | NYCMNY | DS-0 | 189 | $257.92 | $226.97 | $150.00 |
| BSTNMA | NYCMNY | DS-0 | 189 | $257.92 | $226.97 | $150.00 |
| BSTNMA | NYCMNY | DS-0 | 189 | $257.92 | $226.97 | $150.00 |
| CHCGIL | ATLNGA | DS-0 | 585 | $368.80 | $324.54 | $150.00 |
| CHCGIL | MPLSMN | DS-0 | 355 | $304.40 | $267.87 | $150.00 |
| SNFCCA | NYCMNY | FT-1(3) | 2562 | $2,559.54 | $2,047.63 | $150.00 |
| CHCGIL | NYCMNY | FT-1(5) | 710 | $1,716.15 | $1,372.92 | $150.00 |
| ATLNGA | NYCMNY | FT-1(3) | 745 | $1,147.74 | $918.19 | $150.00 |
| TOTALS | | | | $15,206.79 | $12,948.10 | $4,200.00 |

PRICING IS BUDGETARY.
FRACTIONAL PRICING IS TOTAL, NOT PER DS-0.